Stochastic Frontier Analysis

Modern textbook presentations of production economics typically treat producers as successful optimizers. Conventional econometric practice has generally followed this paradigm, and least squares–based regression techniques have been used to estimate production, cost, profit, and other functions. In such a framework deviations from maximum output, from minimum cost and cost-minimizing input demands, and from maximum profit and profit-maximizing output supplies and input demands are attributed exclusively to random statistical noise. However, casual empiricism and the business press both make persuasive cases for the argument that, although producers may indeed attempt to optimize, they do not always succeed. This book develops econometric techniques for the estimation of production, cost and profit frontiers, and for the estimation of the technical and economic efficiency with which producers approach these frontiers. Because these frontiers envelop rather than intersect the data, and because the authors continue to maintain the traditional econometric belief in the presence of external forces contributing to random statistical noise, the work is titled *Stochastic Frontier Analysis*.

Subal C. Kumbhakar is Associate Professor of Economics at the University of Texas, Austin, where he has taught for the past 12 years. He received his Ph.D. from the University of Southern California. Professor Kumbhakar has written more than 60 articles in refereed journals and holds an honorary doctorate from Gothenburg University, Sweden. He is a member of the editorial board of *Technological Forecasting and Social Change: An International Journal* and *The Journal of Productivity Analysis*, and is Associate Editor of the *American Journal of Agricultural Economics*.

C. A. Knox Lovell holds the C. Herman and Mary Virginia Terry Chair in the Department of Economics in the Terry College of Business, University of Georgia, and is Professor in the School of Economics at the University of New South Wales, where he serves as Director of the Centre for Applied Economic Research. He previously taught at the University of North Carolina, Chapel Hill, for 25 years. Professor Lovell is coordinator of the Georgia Productivity Workshop, Editor-in-Chief of *The Journal of Productivity Analysis,* and Associate Editor of *Operations Research.* He has written more than 100 academic papers and authored or edited 6 books, including *Production Frontiers* (with Rolf Färe and Shawna Grosskopf, Cambridge University Press, 1994) and *The Measurement of Productive Efficiency* (with Harold Fried and Shelton Schmidt).

"The authors nicely balance their treatment of econometrics with other issues related to economic theory. Overall, the book is carefully organized and very well written from cover to cover. The book should also be very attractive for use in graduate courses on applied or theoretical production economics. Instructors may wish to supplement the text with added readings or real-data exercises to build a specialized production course around this valuable book."
– Douglas J. Miller, *American Journal of Agricultural Economics*

"*Stochastic Frontier Analysis* is a complete textbook on stochastic frontier models. It deals with stochastic frontier production, cost and profit functions. Models for cross-sectional and panel data are presented and discussed. The analysis of technical change and inefficiency change with panel data is also discussed in detail. The authors are highly qualified to produce such a comprehensive book on stochastic frontiers. Lovell was one of the authors of the seminal paper on the stochastic frontier production function model. He has been undertaking research on many aspects of parametric and non-parametric frontier modelling and efficiency measurement for over twenty-five years. He is a 'pioneer' in this important research area. Kumbhakar has written outstanding papers on stochastic frontier models, both of a theoretical and applied nature, over the last 12 or more years. It will surely be a helpful and widely-cited book for researchers in the field."
– George E. Battese, *University of New England, Australia*

"It is fascinating to see what has been accomplished in the field of stochastic frontier analysis since its beginning in 1977. The authors provide a lucidly written review of all the developments that have taken place in the past quarter of a century. Although hardly any publication has escaped their attention, Kumbhakar and Lovell succeed in keeping the reader focused on the grand lines of research. Well-rooted in recent history, this book will stimulate further research into measurement and explanation of efficiency and productivity (change). I expect this book to be at hand for a long time."
– Bert M. Balk, *Statistics Netherlands*

Stochastic Frontier Analysis

SUBAL C. KUMBHAKAR
University of Texas, Austin

C. A. KNOX LOVELL
University of Georgia
University of New South Wales

PUBLISHED BY THE PRESS SYNDICATE OF THE UNIVERSITY OF CAMBRIDGE
The Pitt Building, Trumpington Street, Cambridge, United Kingdom

CAMBRIDGE UNIVERSITY PRESS
The Edinburgh Building, Cambridge CB2 2RU, UK
40 West 20th Street, New York, NY 10011-4211, USA
10 Stamford Road, Oakleigh, Melbourne 3166, Australia
Ruiz de Alarcón 13, 28014 Madrid, Spain
Dock House, The Waterfront, Cape Town 8001, South Africa

http://www.cambridge.org

First published 2000
First paperback edition 2003

Typeface Times Roman 10.5/13 pt.   *System* QuarkXPress™ [BTS]

A catalog record for this book is available from the British Library

Library of Congress Cataloging in Publication data is available

ISBN 0 521 48184 8 hardback
ISBN 0 521 66663 5 paperback

Transferred to digital printing 2004

Contents

Preface

Modern textbook presentations of production economics, from Samuelson's innovative *Foundations of Economic Analysis* to the present day, treat producers as successful optimizers. They produce maximum outputs allowable by the technology in place and the resources at their disposal. They minimize the cost of producing whatever outputs they choose to produce, given the technology in place and the input prices they face. Cost-minimizing input demands are derived from the resulting minimum cost function by means of Shephard's lemma. They also maximize profit, given the technology in place and the output and input prices they face. Profit-maximizing output supplies and input demands are derived from the resulting profit function by means of Hotelling's lemma.

Conventional econometric practice, beginning with the pioneering work of Cobb and Douglas, has generally followed this theoretical paradigm. Thus least squares–based regression techniques are used to estimate the parameters of production, cost, and profit functions. In such a framework departures from maximum output, from minimum cost and cost-minimizing input demands, and from maximum profit and profit-maximizing output supplies and input demands, are attributed exclusively to random statistical noise.

However casual empiricism and the business press both make persuasive cases for the argument that, although producers may indeed *attempt* to optimize, they do not always succeed. It is desirable, therefore, to develop a theory of producer behavior in which the motivations are unchanged, but in which success is not guaranteed. It is similarly desirable to modify conventional econometric techniques for the estimation of production, cost, and profit relationships that allow for failure in efforts to optimize. Finally it is desirable for the modified econometric approach to allow some producers to be relatively more successful than others, so as to provide the basis for a subsequent investigation into the determinants of variation in the efficiency with which producers pursue their objectives.

This book is concerned with the development of a modified econometric approach to the estimation of productive efficiency. We call it *Stochastic Frontier Analysis* because we are concerned with the estimation of frontiers, which envelop data, rather than with functions, which intersect data. We associate proximity to estimated frontiers with the degree of efficiency with which producers pursue their objectives. Their objectives can be purely technological or economic in nature, and so we are concerned with the estimation of production frontiers and also with the estimation of cost and profit frontiers. Finally, the frontiers we estimate are stochastic, because we continue to maintain the traditional econometric belief in the presence of external forces contributing to random statistical noise.

Portions of this book owe a debt of gratitude to the innovators whose ideas we have borrowed and extended. Without generating a list, which could be very lengthy, we want to mention, in roughly chronological order, Harold Hotelling, Ronald Shephard, and Erwin Diewert for their work on duality theory; Tjalling Koopmans and Michael Farrell for their original work on efficiency measurement; Harvey Leibenstein for his insistence in the face of considerable academic skepticism that X-inefficiency really does Xist in the real world; and Sydney Afriat, Dennis Aigner, Peter Schmidt, and Bill Greene for their early and influential contributions to the stochastic approach to efficiency analysis. Although our book is based on the work of these innovators, it also contains much original material which hopefully extends their work in useful ways.

We wish to express our gratitude to Tim Coelli, whose comments were most helpful in revising Chapters 3 and 4; to Julie Millington, who created all the figures in the text, compiled the indexes, and simply took command during the final stages of the preparation of the manuscript; and to Scott Parris, our patient and understanding editor at Cambridge University Press.

1 Introduction

1.1 THE OBJECTIVES OF THE BOOK

A recent article in the *Economist* notes that most large European banks spend about two-thirds of their revenues on rent and employee expense. Credit Suisse and Deutsche Bank have expense ratios in excess of 70%. But Sweden's Svenska Handelsbanken has an expense ratio of barely 45%, despite relatively high wage rates. The article then proceeds to describe how, ever since a near-fatal financial crisis in the late 1960s, managements at Svenska Handelsbanken have striven to cut costs while, at the same time, increasing revenues. The impression one is left with is that, far from operating in a more favorable environment, Svenska Handelsbanken is more efficient than other large European banks. This and countless other examples raise the question of how conventional microeconomic theory and conventional econometric analysis deal with variation in productive efficiency.

Typical microeconomics texts develop models of production, cost, and profit in something like the following sequence. They begin with a production function, and producers are assumed to operate on their production functions, maximizing outputs obtainable from the inputs they use. First-order conditions for cost minimization are then introduced, and producers are assumed to satisfy these conditions, allocating inputs efficiently and ending up on their cost functions. Finally, first-order conditions for profit maximization are introduced, and producers are assumed to satisfy these conditions as well,

1

allocating outputs and inputs efficiently and ending up on their profit functions.

For many years econometricians have implemented the textbook paradigm by estimating production, cost, and profit functions, on the assumption that producers actually operate on these functions, apart from randomly distributed statistical noise. Cobb and Douglas (1928), Arrow et al. (1961), Berndt and Christensen (1973), and their followers have estimated increasingly flexible production functions in an effort to learn something about the structure of production. Nerlove (1963) was perhaps the first to exploit duality theory to estimate a cost function for the same purpose. Christensen, Jorgenson, and Lau (1973) were perhaps the first to estimate a flexible profit function. It is notable that each of these studies, and the vast majority of subsequent studies, have used least squares techniques, or variants of least squares techniques, in which error terms were assumed to be symmetrically distributed with zero means. The only source of departure from the estimated function was assumed to be statistical noise.

However the anecdotal evidence cited previously, and much other empirical evidence as well, suggests that not all producers are always so successful in solving their optimization problems. Not all producers succeed in utilizing the minimum inputs required to produce the outputs they choose to produce, given the technology at their disposal. In our jargon, not all producers are technically efficient. Consequently not all producers succeed in minimizing the expenditure required to produce the outputs they choose to produce. In addition, even if they are technically efficient, not all producers succeed in allocating their inputs in a cost-effective manner, given the input prices they face, and this misallocation of inputs contributes further to their failure to minimize the expenditure required to produce the outputs they choose to produce. In our jargon, not all producers are cost efficient. Consequently not all producers succeed in maximizing the profit resulting from their production activities. In addition, even if they are cost efficient, not all producers succeed in allocating their outputs in a revenue-maximizing manner, given the output prices they face, and this misallocation of outputs contributes further to their failure to maximize profit. In our jargon, not all producers are profit efficient.

In light of the evident failure of (at least some) producers to optimize, it is desirable to recast the analysis of production, cost, and profit away from the traditional functions toward frontiers. Thus a *production frontier* characterizes the minimum input bundles required to produce various outputs, or the maximum output producible with various input bundles, and a given technology. Producers operating on their production frontier are labeled technically efficient, and producers operating beneath their production frontier are labeled technically inefficient. A dual *cost frontier* characterizes the minimum expenditure required to produce a given bundle of outputs, given the prices of the inputs used in its production and given the technology in place. Producers operating on their cost frontier are labeled cost efficient, and producers operating above their cost frontier are labeled cost inefficient. Similarly a dual *revenue frontier* characterizes the maximum revenue obtainable from a given bundle of inputs, given the prices of the outputs produced and given the technology in place. Producers operating on their revenue frontier are labeled revenue efficient, and producers operating beneath their revenue frontier are labeled revenue inefficient. Finally a dual *profit frontier* characterizes the maximum profit obtainable from production activity, given the prices of the inputs used and the prices of the outputs produced and given the technology in place. Producers operating on their profit frontier are labeled profit efficient, and producers operating beneath their profit frontier are labeled profit inefficient. In each of these four cases interest naturally centers on the magnitude of each type of inefficiency and on the determinants of each type of inefficiency.

The econometric implication of this proposed reformulation from functions to frontiers is that symmetrically distributed error terms with zero means are no longer appropriate when analyzing producer behavior. The possibility remains that a producer will end up above the deterministic kernel of an estimated production, revenue, or profit frontier (or beneath an estimated cost frontier) due to an unusually favorable operating environment. But it is considerably more likely that a producer will end up beneath an estimated production, revenue, or profit frontier (or above an estimated cost frontier), because two factors work in this direction. First, if environmental effects are random as is typically assumed, then an unfavorable operating environment is just as likely to occur as is a favorable operating environment, and this causes a producer to end up beneath an estimated production, revenue, or profit frontier (or above an estimated cost frontier). Second, failure to optimize in each of the senses discussed previously also causes a producer to end up beneath an estimated production, revenue, or profit frontier (or above an estimated cost frontier).

Consequently error terms associated with frontiers are "composed" error terms, composed of a traditional symmetric random-noise component and a new one-sided inefficiency component. These composed error terms cannot be symmetric and they cannot have zero means. They must be skewed (negatively in the case of production, revenue, and profit frontiers and positively in the case of cost frontiers), and they must have nonzero means (negative in the case of production, revenue, and profit frontiers and positive in the case of cost frontiers).

In this reformulation production, cost, revenue, and profit frontiers are stochastic, due to random variation in the operating environment, and deviations from these stochastic frontiers are one-sided, due to various types of inefficiency. The retention of symmetric error components designed to capture the effects of random variation in the operating environment is in keeping with the older least squares–based approach to the estimation of production, cost, revenue, and profit functions. The introduction of one-sided error components designed to capture the effects of inefficiency is new, and constitutes the econometric contribution to the estimation of production, cost, revenue, and profit frontiers. Consequently we refer to this body of work as *Stochastic Frontier Analysis*, the title of our book.

1.2 A BRIEF HISTORY OF THOUGHT

In this section we recall some of the more influential antecedents, both theoretical and empirical, of stochastic frontier analysis (which we abbreviate SFA). We continue by recalling some of the origins of SFA, the events that led to the original developments in the field. We conclude with a brief summary of what we believe to have been some of the most significant developments in SFA since its inception in 1977. Many of these developments are discussed in detail in the remainder of the book.

1.2.1 Intellectual Antecedents of
Stochastic Frontier Analysis

Many years ago Hicks (1935; 8) observed that "people in monopolistic positions . . . are likely to exploit their advantage much more by not bothering to get very near the position of maximum profit, than by straining themselves to get very close to it. The best of all monopoly profits is a quiet life." Hicks's suggestion that the absence of competitive pressure might allow producers the freedom to not fully optimize conventional textbook objectives, and, by implication, that the presence of competitive pressure might force producers to do so, has been adopted by many writers. Thus Alchian and Kessel (1962; 166) asserted that "[t]he cardinal sin of a monopolist . . . is to be too profitable." In a similar vein Williamson (1964) argued that, given the freedom to do so, managers would seek to maximize a utility function with staff and "emoluments" as arguments in addition to profit.

An argument related to Williamson's, arising from the property rights literature, asserts that public production is inherently less efficient than private production. This argument, due originally to Alchian (1965), asserts that concentration and transferability of private ownership shares creates an incentive for private owners to monitor managerial performance, and that this incentive is diminished for public owners, who are dispersed and whose ownership is not transferable. Consequently public managers have greater freedom to pursue their own objectives at the expense of conventional objectives. Thus Niskanen (1971) argued that public managers are budget maximizers, de Alessi (1974) argued that public managers exhibit a bias toward capital-intensive budgets, and Lindsay (1976) argued that public managers exhibit a bias toward "visible" inputs.

Ownership forms are more variegated than just private or public. Hansmann (1988) identifies investor-owned firms, customer-owned firms, worker-owned firms, and firms without owners (nonprofit enterprises). Each deals differently with problems associated with hierarchy, coordination, incomplete contracts, and monitoring and agency costs. This leads to the expectation that different ownership forms will generate differences in performance. Much of the theoretical literature on which this expectation is based is surveyed by Holmstrom and Tirole (1989).

At a somewhat more micro level, Simon (1955, 1957) analyzed the performance of producers in the presence of bounded rationality and satisficing behavior. Later Leibenstein (1966, 1975, 1976, 1978, 1987, and elsewhere) argued that production is bound to be inefficient as a result of motivation, information, monitoring, and agency problems within the firm. This rather amorphous type of inefficiency, inelegantly dubbed "X-inefficiency," has been criticized by Stigler (1976), de Alessi (1983), and others, on the grounds that it reflects an incompletely specified model rather than a failure to optimize. Unfortunately the difficult problem of model specification – including a complete list of inputs and outputs, and perhaps conditioning variables as well, a list of constraints, technological, and other (e.g., regulatory), and a proper specification of the objective function – has faced us forever, and will continue to do so.

The extent to which the literature just cited actually influenced the development of SFA is not obvious. Suffice it to say that most of us were aware of this literature, but that it did not exert the impact that hindsight suggests that it should have. Most of us were more directly influenced by another literature. Nonetheless, in retrospect this literature does suggest that the development of SFA was a useful idea if it could be used to shed empirical light on the theoretical issues raised.

The literature that did directly influence the development of SFA was the theoretical literature on productive efficiency, which began in the 1950s with the work of Koopmans (1951), Debreu (1951), and Shephard (1953). Koopmans provided a definition of technical efficiency: A producer is technically efficient if, and only if, it is impossible to produce more of any output without producing less of some other output or using more of some input. Debreu and Shephard introduced distance functions as a way of modeling multiple-output technology, but more importantly from our perspective as a way of measuring the radial distance of a producer from a frontier, in either an output-expanding direction (Debreu) or an input-conserving direction (Shephard). The association of distance functions with technical efficiency measures was pivotal in the development of the efficiency measurement literature.

Farrell (1957) was the first to measure productive efficiency empirically. Drawing inspiration from Koopmans and Debreu (but apparently not from Shephard), Farrell showed how to define cost efficiency, and how to decompose cost efficiency into its technical and allocative components. He also provided an empirical application to U.S. agriculture, although he did not use econometric methods. His use of linear programming techniques inspired the unfortunately neglected work of Boles (1966), Bressler (1966), Seitz (1966), and Sitorus (1966) in agricultural economics and eventually influenced the development of data envelopment analysis (DEA) by Charnes, Cooper, and Rhodes (1978). DEA is by now a well-established non-parametric (but in practice largely nonstochastic) efficiency measurement technique widely employed in management science.

Of greater significance in the present context is the influence Farrell's work exerted on Aigner and Chu (1968), Seitz (1971), Timmer (1971), Afriat (1972), and Richmond (1974), for it was the work of these writers that led directly to the development of SFA. Although the contributions of these authors differ in a number of important respects, it is probably fair to say that each "estimated" a deterministic production frontier, either by means of linear programming techniques or by modifications to least squares techniques requiring all residuals to be nonpositive. Afriat (p. 581) went so far as to note that "a production function $f(x)$, together with a probability distribution $\rho_\theta(e)$ of efficiency, is constructed so that the derived efficiencies $e_i = y_i/f(x_i)$ have maximum likelihood." Afriat suggested a beta distribution for $\rho_\theta(e)$ and a gamma distribution for $\rho_\theta[-\ln(e)]$ in log-linear models, an idea that Richmond (1974) explored further. Later Schmidt (1976) showed that the programming estimators of Aigner and Chu were consistent with maximum likelihood "estimation" with one-sided errors distributed as either exponential or half normal. Thus began the association of technical inefficiency with specific one-sided error distributions. However it is worth reiterating that the only source of error in these models was inefficiency; they were purely deterministic frontier models lacking a symmetric random-noise error component. However Aigner and Chu recommended, and Timmer experimented with, variants of chance-constrained programming in an ex post attempt to test the sensitivity of their "estimates" to outlying observations.

Aigner, Amemiya, and Poirier (1976) proposed a model in which errors were allowed to be both positive and negative, but in which positive and negative errors could be assigned different weights. Ordinary least squares emerges as a special case of equal weights, and a deterministic frontier model emerges as another special case (weights of zero and one in the case of production, revenue, and profit frontier models). They considered estimation for the case in which the weights are known, and for the considerably more difficult case in which the weights are unknown and are to be estimated along with the other parameters in the model. They did not actually estimate the model, and to our knowledge no one else has estimated the model. Nonetheless, it is a short step from the Aigner, Amemiya, and Poirier model with larger weights attached to negative errors to a composed error stochastic production frontier model. The step took a year.

1.2.2 The Origins of Stochastic Frontier Analysis

SFA originated with two papers, published nearly simultaneously by two teams on two continents. Meeusen and van den Broeck (MB) (1977) appeared in June, and Aigner, Lovell, and Schmidt (ALS) (1977) appeared a month later. The ALS paper was in fact a merged version of a pair of remarkably similar papers, one by Aigner and the other by Lovell and Schmidt. The ALS and MB papers are themselves very similar. Both papers were three years in the making, and both appeared shortly before a third SFA paper by Battese and Corra (1977), the senior author of which had been a referee of the ALS paper.

These three original SFA models shared the composed error structure mentioned previously, and each was developed in a production frontier context. The model can be expressed as $y = f(x; \beta) \cdot \exp\{v - u\}$, where y is scalar output, x is a vector of inputs, and β is a vector of technology parameters. The first error component $v \sim N(0, \sigma_v^2)$ is intended to capture the effects of statistical noise, and the second error component $u \geq 0$ is intended to capture the effects of technical inefficiency. Thus producers operate on or beneath their stochastic production frontier $[f(x; \beta) \cdot \exp\{v\}]$ according as $u = 0$ or $u > 0$. MB assigned an exponential distribution to u, Battese and Corra assigned a half normal distribution to u, and ALS considered both distributions for u. Parameters to be estimated include β, σ_v^2, and a variance parameter σ_u^2 associated with u. Either distributional assumption on u implies that the composed error $(v - u)$ is negatively skewed, and statistical efficiency requires that the model be estimated by maximum likelihood. After estimation, an estimate of mean technical inefficiency in the sample was provided by $E(-u) = E(v - u) = -(2/\pi)^{1/2}\sigma_u$ in the normal–half normal case and by $E(-u) = E(v - u) = -\sigma_u$ in the normal–exponential case.

1.2.3 Developments in Stochastic Frontier Analysis since 1977

In an early survey of various approaches to frontier analysis and efficiency measurement, Førsund, Lovell, and Schmidt (1980; 14) wrote that "the main weakness of the stochastic frontier model [is that] it is not possible to decompose individual residuals into their two components, and so it is not possible to estimate technical inefficiency by observation. The best that one can do is to obtain an estimate of mean inefficiency over the sample." Smart audiences in Washington and Moscow in the winter of 1980–1981 quickly detected the error in that statement. The result was the Jondrow et al. (1982) (JLMS) paper, in which either the mean or the mode of the conditional distribution $[u_i|v_i - u_i]$ was proposed to provide estimates of the technical inefficiency of each producer in the sample. The possibility of obtaining producer-specific estimates of efficiency has greatly enhanced the appeal of SFA.

The half normal and exponential distributions assigned to the one-sided inefficiency error component are single-parameter distributions, and researchers soon developed more flexible two-parameter distributions for the inefficiency error component. Drawing inspiration from Afriat and Richmond, Greene (1980a, b) proposed a Gamma distribution, and Stevenson (1980) proposed Gamma and truncated normal distributions. Other, even more flexible, distributions followed; Lee (1983) even proposed the four-parameter Pearson family of distributions. Nonetheless the two original single-parameter distributions remain the distributions of choice in the vast majority of empirical work.

It is a simple matter to change the sign of the inefficiency error component u and convert the stochastic production frontier model to a stochastic cost frontier model $E = c(y, w; \beta) \cdot \exp\{v + u\}$, where E is expenditure, $[c(y, w; \beta) \cdot \exp\{v\}]$ is a stochastic cost frontier, and u is intended to capture the cost of technical and allocative inefficiency. The JLMS technique may be used to provide an estimate of overall cost inefficiency, but the difficult remaining problem is to decompose the estimate of u into estimates of the separate costs of technical and allocative inefficiency. Schmidt and Lovell (1979) accomplished the decomposition for the Cobb–Douglas case. In a wonderful example of why researchers attend international conferences, Kopp and Diewert (1982) obtained the decomposition for the more general translog case, although econometric difficulties with their decomposition remain to this day.

Cross-sectional data provide a shapshot of producers and their efficiency. Panel data provide more reliable evidence on their performance, because they enable us to track the performance of each producer through a sequence of time periods. Long ago Hoch (1955, 1962) and Mundlak (1961) utilized panel data to purge agricultural production function parameter estimates of bias attributable to variation in what Hoch called technical efficiency and what Mundlak called management bias. Eventually Pitt and Lee (1981) extended cross-sectional maximum likelihood estimation techniques to panel data, and Schmidt and Sickles (1984) extended the pioneering work of Hoch and Mundlak by applying fixed-effects and random-effects methods to the efficiency measurement problem, where the effects are one-sided. The objective of these latter studies was not so much to eliminate bias from parameter estimates as to obtain producer-specific estimates of technical efficiency, or of the management effect. A significant advantage of (sufficiently long) panels is that they permit consistent estimation of the efficiency of individual producers, whereas the JLMS technique does not generate consistent estimators in a cross-sectional context.

Early panel data models were based on the assumption of time-invariant efficiency. The longer the panel, the less tenable this assumption becomes. Eventually this assumption was relaxed, in a series of papers by Cornwell, Schmidt, and Sickles (1990), Kumbhakar (1990), and Battese and Coelli (1992).

If efficiency varies, across producers or through time, it is natural to seek determinants of efficiency variation. Early studies adopted a two-stage approach, in which efficiencies are estimated in the first stage, and estimated efficiencies are regressed against a vector of explanatory variables in a second stage. More recent studies, including those of Kumbhakar, Ghosh, and McGuckin (1991), Reifschneider and Stevenson (1991), Huang and Liu (1994), and Battese and

Coelli (1995), have adopted a single-stage approach in which explanatory variables are incorporated directly into the inefficiency error component. In this approach either the mean or the variance of the inefficiency error component is hypothesized to be a function of the explanatory variables.

Abramovitz (1956) referred to productivity change, the residual between an index of the rates of growth of outputs and an index of the rates of growth of inputs, as a measure of our ignorance. Early studies of productivity change, such as Solow (1957), associated productivity change with technical change. As we became less ignorant, productivity change was decomposed into the magnitude and biases of technical change, and the effect of scale economies. However if productive efficiency changes through time, then it must also contribute to productivity change. Eventually Bauer (1990a) and others incorporated efficiency change into models of productivity change. Griliches (1996) provides an illuminating survey of research into "the residual," although the research surveyed makes only passing reference to the role of efficiency change.

1.3 THE ORGANIZATION OF THE BOOK

Chapter 2 is devoted to the analytical foundations of producer theory and efficiency measurement. In Section 2.2 we characterize production technology with production frontiers in the single-output case and with distance functions in the multiple-output case. We also characterize technology with dual cost, revenue, and profit frontiers, which provide increasingly exacting standards against which to measure producer performance. In Section 2.3 we define producer performance in terms of technical efficiency, and we measure technical efficiency with distance functions. In Section 2.4 we define producer performance in terms of economic (cost, revenue, and profit) efficiency, and we measure economic efficiency relative to cost, revenue, and profit frontiers. We also show how to decompose each type of economic efficiency into technical and allocative components.

Chapter 3 is concerned with the estimation of technical efficiency. In Section 3.2 we develop and show how to estimate cross-sectional production frontier models, both deterministic and stochastic, although most of our effort is directed toward stochastic production frontiers. In Section 3.3 we develop and show how to estimate panel data production frontier models, in which technical efficiency is initially time invariant and then is allowed to vary through time. In Section 3.4 we discuss the problem of heteroskedasticity in stochastic production frontier models.

Chapter 4 is concerned with the estimation and decomposition of cost efficiency. In Section 4.2 we develop and show how to estimate cross-sectional stochastic cost frontier models, in both single-equation and simultaneous-equation settings. In Section 4.3 we develop and show how to estimate panel data stochastic cost frontier models, again in single-equation and simultaneous-equation settings. In Section 4.4 we discuss a pair of novel approaches to the estimation of cost efficiency.

Chapter 5 is concerned with the estimation and decomposition of profit efficiency. In Section 5.2 we develop and show how to estimate single-output stochastic profit frontier models, using both primal and dual approaches. In Section 5.3 we develop and show how to estimate multiple-output stochastic profit frontier models, again using both primal and dual approaches. We pay little attention to the distinction between cross-sectional and panel data models, since the various estimation techniques developed in Chapters 3 and 4 apply equally well to the estimation of stochastic profit frontiers.

In Chapters 3–5 inefficiency is modeled by introducing additional error components and assigning distributions to them. Inefficiencies are then estimated as functions of the parameters of these distributions. In Chapter 6 we take a very different approach, in which both technical and allocative inefficiencies are modeled parametrically, on the assumption that producers optimize with respect to shadow prices, which are parametrically related to actual prices. In Section 6.2 we develop and show how to estimate and decompose both cost and profit efficiency in a cross-sectional setting. In Section 6.3 we do the same thing in a panel data setting. This parametric approach has some advantages, and some disadvantages, relative to the error component approach developed in Chapters 3–5.

Estimation of efficiency is the first of two tasks. The second task is to explain variation in estimated efficiency. In Chapter 7 we discuss alternative approaches to the explanation of variation in efficiency. In Section 7.2 we discuss some early approaches to explanation, and we find these approaches wanting. In Section 7.3 we discuss a variety of recent approaches to explanation, which we find superior to the early approaches. Essentially these recent approaches achieve explanation by making the one-sided inefficiency error component a function of the explanatory variables.

If efficiency varies, either across producers or through time, its variation constitutes a source of producer performance variation. One measure of performance is productivity change, and so if efficiency changes through time, it makes a contribution to productivity change. Chapter 8 concludes the book by incorporating efficiency change into models of productivity change, which heretofore have tended to neglect the contribution of efficiency change. In Section 8.2 we develop a primal approach, based on a stochastic production frontier, to the estimation and decomposition of productivity change. In Sections 8.3 and 8.4 we develop a pair of dual approaches, based on stochastic cost and profit frontiers, to the estimation and decomposition of productivity change.

At least four topics are missing from the book. First, we do not discuss the estimation and decomposition of revenue efficiency relative to stochastic revenue frontiers. This is because all of the techniques developed in Chapter 4 for the estimation and decomposition of cost efficiency relative to stochastic cost frontiers can readily be applied to the revenue efficiency problem. Variables and regularity conditions change, as discussed in Chapter 2, but nothing else of import changes.

Second, we do not explore the efficiency with which producers pursue nonconventional objectives. One prominent example is provided by Shephard's (1974) indirect production frontier, relative to which it is possible to estimate and decompose both cost-indirect output-oriented technical efficiency and revenue-indirect input-oriented technical efficiency. The former allows the measurement of the performance of producers seeking to maximize output (or revenue) subject to a conventional technology constraint and a budget constraint. The latter allows the measurement of the performance of producers seeking to minimize input use (or cost) subject to a conventional technology constraint and a revenue target. The two indirect models of producer behavior are analyzed in Färe, Grosskopf, and Lovell (1988, 1992) and Färe and Grosskopf (1994), and the estimation techniques developed in Chapters 3 and 4 can be adapted to the estimation of cost-indirect and revenue-indirect efficiency. Another example is provided by the literature on labor-managed firms pioneered by Ward's (1958) "Illyrian" firm and Domar's (1966) Soviet collective farm. The duality properties of a stylized labor-managed firm model have been worked out by Neary (1988) and Kahana (1989), and the econometric techniques discussed in Chapters 3–6 can be modified to estimate primal and dual efficiencies in this framework.

The third and fourth omissions are perhaps more serious. We do not discuss the Bayesian approach to stochastic frontier analysis, and we do not discuss semiparametric approaches to stochastic frontier analysis. Our reason for omitting these two topics is that the two literatures are small and not yet influential. However we refer interested readers to van den Broeck et al. (1994) and Osiewalski and Steel (1998) for good treatments of the Bayesian approach to SFA, and to Park and Simar (1994) and Park, Sickles, and Simar (1998) for good treatments of the semiparametric approach to SFA.

2 Analytical Foundations

2.1 INTRODUCTION

The objective of this chapter is to provide an introduction to the analytical foundations of production economics. Our goal is not to provide a detailed exposition of the foundations; this is available in the references provided at the end of the book. Rather, our objective is to provide an analytical foundation that is sufficient to enable the reader to conduct econometric analyses of various types of productive efficiency, which is the ultimate objective of the book. By productive efficiency we mean the degree of success producers achieve in allocating the inputs at their disposal and the outputs they produce, in an effort to meet some objective. Thus in order to measure productive efficiency it is first necessary to specify producers' objectives and then to quantify their degrees of success. This book is primarily concerned with the development of econometric techniques for estimating their degrees of success.

At an elementary level, the objective of producers can be as simple as seeking to avoid waste, by obtaining maximum outputs from given inputs or by minimizing input use in the production of given outputs. In this case the notion of productive efficiency corresponds to what we call *technical* efficiency, and the waste avoidance objective of producers becomes one of attaining a high degree of technical efficiency. Chapter 3 is concerned with the development of econometric techniques for the estimation of technical efficiency.

At a higher level, the objective of producers might entail the production of given outputs at minimum cost, or the utilization of given inputs to maximize revenue, or the allocation of inputs and outputs to maximize profit. In these cases productive efficiency corresponds to what we call *economic* efficiency, and the objective of producers becomes one of attaining a high degree of economic (cost, revenue, or profit) efficiency. Chapters 4–6 are concerned with the development of econometric techniques for the estimation of cost and profit efficiency. We pay little attention to revenue efficiency, because the econometric techniques used to estimate cost efficiency can be modified easily to estimate revenue efficiency.

We begin this chapter by providing an analytical framework for describing the physical structure of production technology, in which multiple inputs are used to produce multiple outputs. This framework is based solely on information on the quantities of the inputs and the outputs. The structure of production technology is initially described in terms of feasible sets of inputs and outputs. Attention then moves to the boundaries of these sets, since the boundaries represent weakly efficient production activities. Eventually the structure of production technology is described in terms of distance functions, evocatively named since they provide measures of the distance of a production activity to the boundary of production possibilities. Distance functions are thus intimately related to the measurement of technical efficiency. Indeed since price information is not exploited, technical efficiency is the only type of efficiency that can be studied using distance functions.

The tools of duality theory are then used to obtain several related economic representations of the structure of production technology, using information on both the quantities and the prices of the inputs and the outputs, and assuming that producers attempt to solve an economic optimization problem. Economic representations of production technology include cost, revenue, and profit frontiers. These economic frontiers are then used as standards against which to measure cost, revenue, and profit efficiency.

Once these frontier representations of production technology have been introduced, productive efficiency is then defined in terms of distance to a particular frontier. Technical efficiency is defined in terms of distance to a production frontier, and economic efficiency is defined in terms of distance to an economic (cost, revenue, or profit) frontier. Whereas technical efficiency is a purely physical notion that can be measured without recourse to price information and without having to impose a behavioral objective on producers, cost, revenue, and profit efficiency are economic concepts whose measurement requires both price information and the imposition of an appropriate behavioral objective on producers.

The remainder of this chapter is organized as follows.

The subject of Section 2.2 is a description of the general structure of production technology with which multiple inputs are used to produce multiple outputs. This structure is described in Section 2.2.1 in terms of the graph of production technology and the corresponding input sets and output sets. In Section 2.2.2 we temporarily make the simplifying assumption that multiple inputs are used to produce a single output, which enables us to describe the structure of production technology in terms of a production frontier. In Section 2.2.3 we revert to the original assumption that multiple inputs are used to produce multiple outputs, and we describe the structure of production technology in terms of input distance functions and output distance functions. We also describe the relationship between output distance functions and the production frontier in the event that only a single output is produced. In Section 2.2.4 the structure of production technology is defined in terms of dual economic frontiers, namely cost, revenue, and profit frontiers. These economic frontiers apply to both the single-output case and the multiple-output case. In Section 2.2.5 we introduce variable cost frontiers and variable profit frontiers. These frontiers are relevant in the short run, or whenever a subset of inputs is fixed and therefore not freely adjustable by producers.

Section 2.3 is concerned with the measurement of technical efficiency. In Section 2.3.1 it is assumed that multiple inputs are used to produce a single output, and output-oriented technical efficiency is defined relative to a production frontier. In Section 2.3.2 it is assumed that multiple inputs are used to produce multiple outputs, and input distance functions and output distance functions are used to provide input-oriented and output-oriented definitions of technical efficiency.

Section 2.4 is concerned with the measurement and decomposition of economic efficiency. It is assumed that producers use multiple inputs to produce multiple outputs. In Section 2.4.1 cost efficiency is defined relative to a cost frontier. Cost efficiency is then decomposed into its two components, input-oriented technical efficiency and input allocative efficiency. The logic behind the decomposition is that both types of inefficiency (excessive input use and misallocation of inputs) are costly, and it is desirable to be able to identify the sources of cost inefficiency. In Section 2.4.2 revenue efficiency is defined relative to a revenue frontier. Revenue efficiency is then decomposed into output-oriented technical efficiency and output allocative efficiency. Once again, both types of inefficiency (output shortfall and an inappropriate output mix) are costly in terms of forgone revenue, and it is desirable to be able to identify the sources of revenue inefficiency. In Section 2.4.3 profit efficiency is defined relative to a profit frontier. Profit efficiency can be decomposed in two ways, depending on the orientation of its technical efficiency component. In Section 2.4.4 we introduce the notions of variable-cost efficiency and variable-profit efficiency for use in situations in which producers seek to minimize cost or to maximize profit in the presence of fixed inputs.

Section 2.5 provides a guide to the relevant literature.

2.2 PRODUCTION TECHNOLOGY

2.2.1 Representing Technology with Sets

We assume that producers use a nonnegative vector of inputs, denoted $x = (x_1, \ldots, x_N) \in R_+^N$, to produce a nonnegative vector of outputs, denoted $y = (y_1, \ldots, y_M) \in R_+^M$. Although the analytical foundations developed in this chapter readily accommodate zero values for some inputs and some outputs, much of the econometric analysis developed in subsequent chapters is based on logarithmic functional forms that do not easily accommodate nonpositive values of variables, and so in later chapters we will assume that $x \in R_{++}^N$ and $y \in R_{++}^M$. The initial task is to characterize the set of feasible production activities. A primitive characterization is provided in Definition 2.1 and illustrated in Figure 2.1.

> **Definition 2.1:** The *graph* of production technology, $GR = \{(y, x): x \text{ can produce } y\}$, describes the set of feasible input–output vectors.

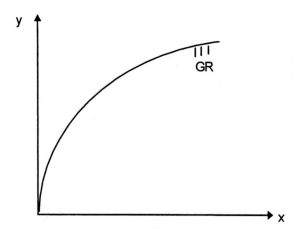

Figure 2.1 The Graph of Production Technology ($M = 1, N = 1$)

Figure 2.1 illustrates the graph of production technology in the single-input, single-output case. The graph, also known as the production possibilities set, is the set of input–output combinations bounded below by the x axis and bounded above by the curve emanating from the origin. Soon the curve that provides the upper boundary of the graph will be given a name.

GR is assumed to satisfy the following properties:

G1: $(0, x) \in GR$ and $(y, 0) \in GR \Rightarrow y = 0$.

unbelievably writes (x,y) as (y,x)!

G2: GR is a closed set.

G3: GR is bounded for each $x \in R_+^N$.

G4: $(y, x) \in GR \Rightarrow (y, \lambda x) \in GR$ for $\lambda \geq 1$.

G5: $(y, x) \in GR \Rightarrow (\lambda y, x) \in GR$ for $0 \leq \lambda \leq 1$.

Property $G1$ states that any nonnegative input vector can produce at least zero output and that there is no free lunch. $G2$ guarantees the existence of technically efficient input and output vectors. $G3$ guarantees that finite input cannot produce infinite output. $G4$ and $G5$ are weak monotonicity properties that guarantee the feasibility of radial expansions of feasible inputs and radial contractions of

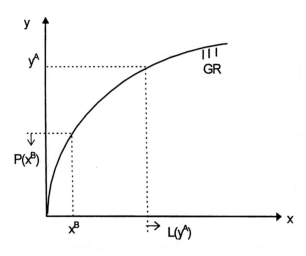

Figure 2.2 The Input Sets and Output Sets of Production Technology ($M = 1, N = 1$)

feasible outputs. These two properties are occasionally replaced with the single stronger monotonicity property

G6: $(y, x) \in GR \Rightarrow (y', x') \in GR \; \forall (y', -x') \le (y, -x)$.

G6 guarantees the feasibility of any increase in feasible inputs, including but not limited to a radial increase, and also guarantees the feasibility of any reduction in feasible outputs, including but not limited to a radial contraction. G4 and G5 are often referred to as weak disposability properties, and G6 as a strong (or free) disposability property.

GR is not generally required to be a convex set. However on occasion this property is required, and so convexity is listed as a final property.

G7: *GR* is a convex set.

A second characterization of the set of feasible production activities is provided in Definition 2.2 and illustrated in Figures 2.2 and 2.3.

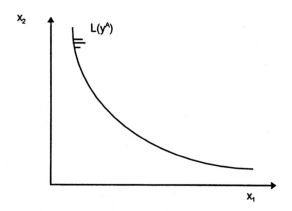

Figure 2.3 The Input Sets of Production Technology ($N = 2$)

Definition 2.2: The *input sets* of production technology, $L(y) = \{x: (y, x) \in GR\}$, describe the sets of input vectors that are feasible for each output vector $y \in R_+^M$.

In Figure 2.2 $L(y^A)$ is the set of inputs on the interval $[x^A, +\infty)$. In Figure 2.3 $L(y^A)$ is the region bounded below by the curve. Soon the curve will be given a name.

Since GR is assumed to satisfy certain properties and since the input sets $L(y)$ are defined in terms of GR, it follows that the input sets $L(y)$ satisfy the following properties:

$L1$: $0 \notin L(y)$ for $y \geq 0$ and $L(0) = R_+^N$.

$L2$: The sets $L(y)$ are closed.

$L3$: x is finite $\Rightarrow x \notin L(y)$ if y is infinite.

$L4$: $x \in L(y) \Rightarrow \lambda x \in L(y)$ for $\lambda \geq 1$.

$L5$: $L(\lambda y) \subseteq L(y)$ for $\lambda \geq 1$.

If the weak monotonicity properties $G4$ and $G5$ are replaced with the strong monotonicity property $G6$, then the weak monotonicity properties $L4$ and $L5$ are replaced with the strong monotonicity property

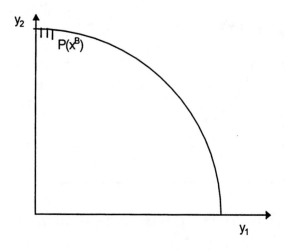

Figure 2.4 The Output Sets of Production Technology ($M = 2$)

L6: $x' \geq x \in L(y) \Rightarrow x' \in L(y)$ and $y' \geq y \Rightarrow L(y') \subseteq L(y)$,

which states that inputs and outputs are strongly, or freely, disposable. Finally, a convexity property is occasionally added to the list of properties satisfied by the input sets $L(y)$:

L7: $L(y)$ is a convex set for $y \in R_+^M$.

It should be noted that *G7* is sufficient, but not necessary, for *L7*.

A third characterization of the set of feasible production activities is provided in Definition 2.3 and illustrated in Figures 2.2 and 2.4.

> **Definition 2.3:** The *output sets* of production technology, $P(x) = \{y: (y, x) \in GR\}$, describe the sets of output vectors that are feasible for each input vector $x \in R_+^N$.

In Figure 2.2 $P(x^B)$ is the set of outputs on the interval $[0, y^B]$. In Figure 2.4 $P(x^B)$ is the region bounded above by the curve. Soon the curve will be given a name.

Since the output sets $P(x)$ are defined in terms of *GR* and since *GR* is assumed to satisfy certain properties, the output sets $P(x)$ satisfy properties corresponding to those satisfied by *GR*. These properties are:

*P*1: $P(0) = \{0\}$.

*P*2: $P(x)$ is a closed set.

*P*3: $P(x)$ is bounded for $x \in R_+^N$.

*P*4: $P(\lambda x) \supseteq P(x)$ for $\lambda \geq 1$.

*P*5: $y \in P(x) \Rightarrow \lambda y \in P(x)$ for $\lambda \in [0, 1]$.

If the weak monotonicity properties *G*4 and *G*5 are replaced with the strong monotonicity property *G*6, then the weak monotonicity properties *P*4 and *P*5 are strengthened to

*P*6: $x' \geq x \Rightarrow P(x') \supseteq P(x)$ and $y \leq y' \in P(x) \Rightarrow y \in P(x)$,

which states that $P(x)$ satisfies strong, or free, disposability of inputs and outputs. Finally, a convexity property

*P*7: $P(x)$ is a convex set for $x \in R_+^N$.

is occasionally required. As in the case of *G*7 and *L*7, *G*7 is sufficient, but not necessary, for *P*7.

We now turn our attention to the boundaries of the sets depicted in Figures 2.1–2.4.

> **Definition 2.4:** The *input isoquants* Isoq $L(y) = \{x : x \in L(y), \lambda x \notin L(y), \lambda < 1\}$ describe the sets of input vectors capable of producing each output vector y but which, when radially contracted, become incapable of producing output vector y.

> **Definition 2.5:** The *input efficient subsets* Eff $L(y) = \{x : x \in L(y), x' \leq x \Rightarrow x' \notin L(y)\}$ describe the sets of input vectors capable of producing each output vector y but which, when contracted in any dimension, become incapable of producing output vector y.

In Figure 2.5 Isoq $L(y)$ is the curve mentioned beneath Definition 2.2 that provides the lower boundary of the input set $L(y)$. Since it is a lower boundary representing one notion of minimal input use, it provides an appealing standard against which to measure the technical efficiency of input use. Eff $L(y)$ is the darkened portion of Isoq $L(y)$, and includes only the downward-sloping portion of Isoq $L(y)$. The upward-sloping portion of Isoq $L(y)$ not contained in Eff $L(y)$ is occasionally described as belonging to the *uneconomic region* of input space. Since Eff $L(y) \subseteq$ Isoq $L(y)$, Eff $L(y)$ provides a more

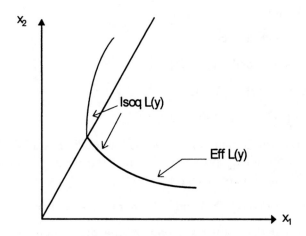

Figure 2.5 The Input Isoquant and the Input Efficient Subset ($N = 2$)

stringent standard against which to measure the technical efficiency of input use.

The weak monotonicity property $L4$ allows Eff $L(y) \subset$ Isoq $L(y)$. Unfortunately the strong monotonicity property given in the first part of $L6$ also allows Eff $L(y) \subset$ Isoq $L(y)$, as in the case of a fixed-proportions Leontief technology. An even stronger version of the first part of $L6$ is required for Eff $L(y) =$ Isoq $L(y)$. Some functional forms employed in the econometric analysis of efficiency, such as Cobb–Douglas, do have the property that Eff $L(y) =$ Isoq $L(y)$, making the distinction irrelevant. Others, such as translog, have the property that Eff $L(y) \subset$ Isoq $L(y)$, making the distinction potentially important. We return to this distinction in Section 2.3.1.

> **Definition 2.6:** The *output isoquants* Isoq $P(x) = \{y: y \in P(x),$ $\lambda y \notin P(x), \lambda > 1\}$ describe the sets of all output vectors that can be produced with each input vector x but which, when radially expanded, cannot be produced with input vector x.

> **Definition 2.7:** The *output efficient subsets* Eff $P(x) = \{y: y \in P(x),$ $y' \geq y \Rightarrow y' \notin P(x)\}$ describe the sets of all output vectors that can be produced with each input vector x but which, when expanded in any dimension, cannot be produced with input vector x.

In Figure 2.6 Isoq $P(x)$ is the curve mentioned beneath Definition 2.3 that provides the upper boundary of the output set $P(x)$. Since it

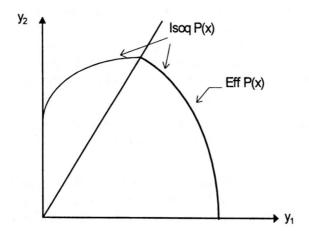

Figure 2.6 The Output Isoquant and the Output Efficient Subset ($M = 2$)

is an upper boundary characterizing one notion of maximum output producible with input vector x, it provides a standard against which to measure the technical efficiency of output production. Eff $P(x)$ is the darkened portion of Isoq $P(x)$, and includes only the downward-sloping portion of Isoq $P(x)$. By analogy with the concept of an uneconomic region in input space, that portion of Isoq $P(x)$ not included in Eff $P(x)$ might be characterized as belonging to the uneconomic region of output space. Since Eff $P(x) \subseteq$ Isoq $P(x)$, Eff $P(x)$ provides a more stringent standard against which to measure the technical efficiency of output production. If the output sets $P(x)$ satisfy the weak monotonicity property $P5$, then Eff $P(x) \subset$ Isoq $P(x)$ is allowed, and again the fixed-proportions Leontief technology shows that even the strong monotonicity property given in the second part of $P6$ allows for Eff $P(x) \subset$ Isoq $P(x)$. As in the case of Eff $L(y)$ and Isoq $L(y)$, the relationship between Eff $P(x)$ and Isoq $P(x)$ depends on the functional form used to characterize the structure of production technology. We return to this distinction in Section 2.3.1.

2.2.2 Production Frontiers

We now provide a functional characterization of the boundary of the graph of production technology. Since the boundary represents the maximum output that can be obtained from any given input vector (or, alternatively, the minimum input usage required to produce any given output vector), it represents another standard against which to measure the technical efficiency of production. We begin with a characterization of the boundary of the graph of production technology in the multiple-input, multiple-output case.

> **Definition 2.8:** A *joint production frontier* is a function $F(y, x) = 0$ having the properties Isoq $L(y) = \{x: F(y, x) = 0\}$ and Isoq $P(x) = \{y: F(y, x) = 0\}$.

A joint production frontier is also referred to as a production possibilities frontier, or a transformation frontier. It is rarely used in empirical analysis, and we will not discuss it further. The notion it characterizes, that of the boundary of the graph of production technology when multiple inputs are used to produce multiple outputs, is more easily characterized by means of input distance functions and output distance functions, to which we turn in Section 2.2.3.

A single-output specification of production activity is valid in two circumstances. It is obviously valid in the rare event that only a single output is produced. It is also valid in the more likely event that multiple outputs are produced, provided that the outputs can be aggregated into a single composite output $y = g(y_1, \ldots, y_M)$. In either case the joint production frontier introduced in Definition 2.8 collapses to a production frontier. Alternatively, Definitions 2.2 and 2.3 can be used to obtain a production frontier, introduced in Definition 2.9 and illustrated in Figure 2.7.

> **Definition 2.9:** A *production frontier* is a function $f(x) = \max\{y: y \in P(x)\} = \max\{y: x \in L(y)\}$.

Since the production frontier is defined in terms of the output sets $P(x)$ and the input sets $L(y)$, both of which satisfy certain properties, so does $f(x)$. These properties are

$f1$: $f(0) = 0$.

$f2$: f is upper semicontinuous on R_+^N.

$f3$: $f(x) > 0 \Rightarrow f(\lambda x) \to +\infty$ as $\lambda \to +\infty$.

$f4$: $f(\lambda x) \geq f(x), \lambda \geq 1$ for $x \in R_+^N$.

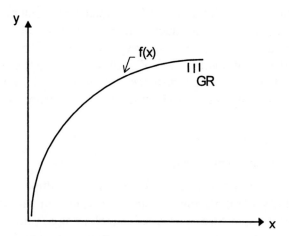

Figure 2.7 A Production Frontier

If the weak monotonicity property *L*4 is replaced by the strong monotonicity property given in the first part of *L*6, the weak monotonicity property *f*4 becomes

   *f*5: $x' \geq x \Rightarrow f(x') \geq f(x)$.

If the convexity property *L*7 is imposed, then

   *f*6: *f* is quasiconcave on R_+^N.

In Figure 2.7 the production frontier $f(x)$ describes the maximum output that can be produced with any given input vector. Remembering that only a single output is being produced, it follows from Definitions 2.4, 2.5, and 2.9 that $L(y) = \{x: f(x) \geq y\}$, Isoq $L(y) = \{x: f(x) = y, f(\lambda x) < y, \lambda < 1\}$, and Eff $L(y) = \{x: f(x) = y, x' \leq x \Rightarrow f(x') < y\}$. That is, the input sets $L(y)$ consist of all input vectors capable of producing at least scalar output *y*. The input isoquants Isoq $L(y)$ consist of all input vectors capable of producing scalar output *y* and which, when radially contracted, are incapable of producing scalar output *y*. The input efficient subsets Eff $L(y)$ consist of all input vectors capable of producing scalar output *y* and which, when contracted in any dimension, are incapable of producing scalar output *y*.

The production frontier provides the upper boundary of production possibilities, and the input–output combination of each producer is located on or beneath the production frontier. The central problem in the measurement of technical efficiency is to measure the distance from the input–output combination of each producer to the production frontier. Two notions of distance are introduced in Section 2.2.3, and used extensively in Section 2.3 to measure technical efficiency.

2.2.3 Distance Functions

When multiple inputs are used to produce multiple outputs, Shephard's (1953, 1970) distance functions provide a functional characterization of the structure of production technology. Input distance functions characterize input sets, and output distance functions characterize output sets. Not only do distance functions characterize the structure of production technology, it turns out that they are intimately related to the measures of technical efficiency that will be introduced in Section 2.3. However the major role distance functions play is in duality theory. Just as under certain conditions a (single-output) production frontier is dual to a (single-output) cost frontier, also under certain conditions an input distance function is dual to a cost frontier and an output distance function is dual to a revenue frontier. Although the main role played by distance functions is in duality theory, they are not without empirical value. They can be estimated econometrically to provide measures of technical efficiency when producers use multiple inputs to produce multiple outputs. However they have rarely been used for this purpose.

The input distance function is introduced in Definition 2.10 and illustrated in Figures 2.8 and 2.9.

> **Definition 2.10:** An *input distance function* is a function $D_I(y, x) = \max\{\lambda: x/\lambda \in L(y)\}$.

An input distance function adopts an input-conserving approach to the measurement of the distance from a producer to the boundary of production possibilities. It gives the maximum amount by which a producer's input vector can be radially contracted and still remain feasible for the output vector it produces. In Figure 2.8 the

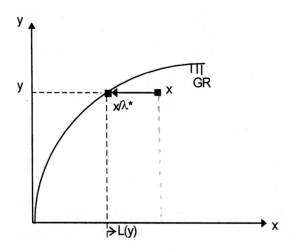

Figure 2.8 An Input Distance Function ($M = 1, N = 1$)

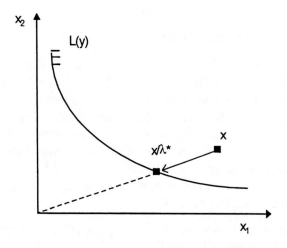

Figure 2.9 An Input Distance Function ($N= 2$)

scalar input x is feasible for output y, but y can be produced with smaller input (x/λ^*), and so $D_I(y, x) = \lambda^* > 1$. In Figure 2.9 the input vector x is feasible for output y, but y can be produced with the radially contracted input vector (x/λ^*), and so $D_I(y, x) = \lambda^* > 1$.

Since the input distance function $D_i(y, x)$ is defined in terms of the input sets $L(y)$, which satisfy certain properties, the input distance function satisfies a corresponding set of properties given by

D_i1: $D_i(0, x) = +\infty$ and $D_i(y, 0) = 0$.

D_i2: $D_i(y, x)$ is an upper-semicontinuous function.

D_i3: $D_i(y, \lambda x) = \lambda D_i(y, x)$ for $\lambda > 0$.

D_i4: $D_i(y, \lambda x) \geq D_i(y, x)$ for $\lambda \geq 1$.

D_i5: $D_i(\lambda y, x) \leq D_i(y, x)$ for $\lambda \geq 1$.

If the weak monotonicity properties $L4$ and $L5$ are replaced with the strong monotonicity property $L6$, then the weak monotonicity properties D_i4 and D_i5 are replaced with

D_i6: $D_i(y, x') \geq D_i(y, x)$ for $x' \geq x$ and $D_i(y', x) \leq D_i(y, x)$ for $y' \geq y$.

If the convexity property $L7$ holds, then

D_i7: $D_i(y, x)$ is a concave function in x.

It should be clear from Definition 2.10 and Figures 2.8 and 2.9 that $L(y) = \{x: D_i(y, x) \geq 1\}$ and that Isoq $L(y) = \{x: D_i(y, x) = 1\}$. Thus the input isoquant, which we have already mentioned as one possible standard against which to measure the technical efficiency of input use, corresponds to the set of input vectors having an input distance function value of unity. All other feasible input vectors have input distance function values greater than unity.

The output distance function is introduced in Definition 2.11 and illustrated in Figures 2.10 and 2.11.

> **Definition 2.11:** An *output distance function* is a function $D_O(x, y) = \min\{\mu: y/\mu \in P(x)\}$.

An output distance function takes an output-expanding approach to the measurement of the distance from a producer to the boundary of production possibilities. It gives the minimum amount by which an output vector can be deflated and still remain producible with a given input vector. In Figure 2.10 scalar output y can be produced with input x, but so can larger output (y/μ^*), and so $D_O(x, y) = \mu^* < 1$. In Figure 2.11 the output vector y is producible with input x, but

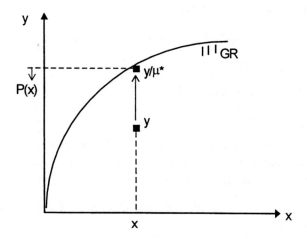

Figure 2.10 An Output Distance Function ($M = 1, N = 1$)

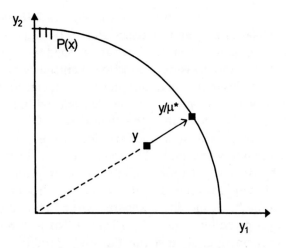

Figure 2.11 An Output Distance Function ($M = 2$)

so is the radially expanded output vector (y/μ^*), and so $D_O(x, y) = \mu^* < 1$.

Since an output distance function $D_O(x, y)$ is defined in terms of the output sets $P(x)$, which satisfy certain properties, the corresponding output distance function satisfies the properties

D_o1: $D_O(x, 0) = 0$ and $D_O(0, y) = +\infty$.

D_o2: $D_O(x, y)$ is a lower-semicontinuous function.

D_o3: $D_O(x, \lambda y) = \lambda D_O(x, y)$ for $\lambda > 0$.

D_o4: $D_O(\lambda x, y) \leq D_O(x, y)$ for $\lambda \geq 1$.

D_o5: $D_O(x, \lambda y) \leq D_O(x, y)$ for $0 \leq \lambda \leq 1$.

If the weak monotonicity properties $P4$ and $P5$ are replaced with the strong monotonicity property $P6$, then D_o4 and D_o5 are replaced with the strong monotonicity property

D_o6: $D_O(x', y) \leq D_O(x, y)$ for $x' \geq x$ and $D_O(x, y') \leq D_O(x, y)$ for $y' \leq y$.

Finally if the convexity property $P7$ holds, then

D_o7: $D_O(x, y)$ is a convex function in y.

It should be clear from Definition 2.11 and Figures 2.10 and 2.11 that $P(x) = \{y: D_O(x, y) \leq 1\}$ and that Isoq $P(x) = \{y: D_O(x, y) = 1\}$. Thus the output isoquant, which we have mentioned as a possible standard against which to measure the technical efficiency of output production, corresponds to the set of output vectors having an output distance function value of unity. All other feasible output vectors have output distance function values less than unity.

Distance functions provide a characterization of the structure of production technology when multiple inputs are used to produce multiple outputs. However if only a single output is produced, an output distance function is related to the production frontier introduced in Definition 2.9. It should be apparent from Figure 2.10 that this relationship is given by $D_O(x, y) = y/f(x) \leq 1$. No such relationship exists between an input distance function and a production frontier. However if a single input is used to produce multiple outputs, then $D_I(y, x) = x/g(y) \geq 1$, where $g(y)$ is an input requirements frontier, or an inverse production frontier.

2.2.4 Cost, Revenue, and Profit Frontiers

Thus far we have employed information on the quantities of inputs and outputs to describe the structure of production technology. We

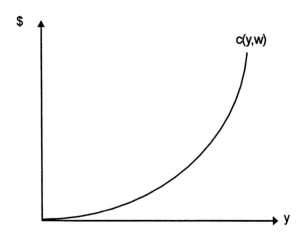

Figure 2.12 A Cost Frontier ($M = 1$)

now add information on the prices of the inputs and the outputs, together with a behavioral assumption, in order to provide additional characterizations of the structure of production technology. These characterizations are provided by the cost, revenue, and profit frontiers. While a joint production frontier describes the best that can be achieved technically, these three frontiers describe the best that can be achieved economically, and so they provide standards against which the economic performance of producers can be measured.

We begin by assuming that producers face a strictly positive vector of input prices given by $w = (w_1, \ldots, w_N) \in R^N_{++}$. We also assume that producers attempt to minimize the cost of producing the output vector y they choose to produce, that cost being $w^T x = \Sigma_n w_n x_n$. Then either the input sets or the input distance function can be used to derive a cost frontier, introduced in Definition 2.12 and illustrated in Figure 2.12.

Definition 2.12: A *cost frontier* is a function $c(y, w) = \min_x\{w^T x: x \in L(y)\} = \min_x\{w^T x: D_I(y, x) \geq 1\}$.

If only a single output is produced, the second equality in Definition 2.12 becomes $c(y, w) = \min_x\{w^T x: y \leq f(x)\}$. In Figure 2.12 the cost frontier $c(y, w)$ shows the minimum expenditure required to produce any scalar output, given input prices. The expenditure of each producer must be on or above $c(y, w)$. Thus the cost frontier provides a standard against which to measure the performance of producers for whom the cost minimization assumption is deemed appropriate.

Since the input sets $L(y)$ and the input distance function $D_I(y, x)$ satisfy certain properties, so does the cost frontier $c(y, w)$, which is obtained from them. These properties are

c1: $c(0, w) = 0$ and $c(y, w) > 0$ for $y \geq 0$.

c2: $c(y, \lambda w) = \lambda c(y, w)$ for $\lambda > 0$.

c3: $c(y, w') \geq c(y, w)$ for $w' \geq w$.

c4: $c(y, w)$ is a concave function in w.

c5: $c(y, w)$ is a continuous function in w.

c6: $c(\lambda y, w) \leq c(y, w)$ for $0 \leq \lambda \leq 1$.

c7: $c(y, w)$ is lower semicontinuous in y.

If the weak monotonicity property $L5 \Leftrightarrow D_I 5$ is replaced with the strong monotonicity property expressed in the second half of $L6 \Leftrightarrow D_I 6$, then the weak monotonicity property c6 is replaced with

c8: $c(y', w) \leq c(y, w)$ for $0 \leq y' \leq y$.

Finally if $G7$ holds, then

c9: If GR is convex, then $c(y, w)$ is a convex function in y.

If $c(y, w) = \min_x \{w^T x : D_I(y, x) \geq 1\}$ satisfies conditions $\{c1-c5, c7, c8\}$, then $c(y, w)$ is *dual* to $D_I(y, x)$ in the sense that $D_I(y, x) = \min_w \{w^T x : c(y, w) \geq 1\}$ satisfies properties $\{D_I 1 - D_I 3, D_I 6, D_I 7\}$. In this case $D_I(y, x)$ and $c(y, w)$ provide equivalent representations of the structure of production technology, under the assumption of cost-minimizing behavior in the presence of exogenously determined input prices. Under these circumstances certain features of the structure of production technology, such as its returns to scale properties, can be inferred from the structure of the cost frontier. Thus, for example, constant returns to scale in production can be characterized as

$$L(\lambda y) = \lambda L(y) \Leftrightarrow D_I(\lambda y, x) = \lambda^{-1} D_I(y, x)$$
$$\Leftrightarrow c(\lambda y, w) = \lambda c(y, w), \qquad \lambda > 0.$$

Although our interest centers on situations in which not all producers succeed in minimizing the cost of producing their chosen output vector, the duality relationship linking a cost frontier with an input distance function remains critical for the measurement and decomposition of cost efficiency. This will become apparent in Section 2.4.1.

If the cost frontier $c(y, w)$ is differentiable with respect to input prices, then Shephard's (1953) lemma states that

$$x(y, w) = \nabla_w c(y, w)$$

Thus the vector of cost-minimizing input demand equations can be obtained as the input price gradient of the cost frontier. For a producer operating on the cost frontier, $w^T x = c(y, w)$ and $x = x(y, w)$. For a producer operating above the cost frontier, $w^T x > c(y, w)$ and $x \neq x(y, w)$. The properties of $x(y, w)$ are inherited from those of $c(y, w)$ from which they are derived. For example, if $c(y, w)$ is concave and twice continuously differentiable in w, then cost-minimizing input demand equations cannot slope upwards with respect to their own prices. The empirical implication of Shephard's lemma is that it allows $x(y, w)$, alone or in conjunction with $c(y, w)$, to be used to infer certain features of the structure of production technology. It will become apparent in later chapters that these cost-minimizing input demand equations play a central role in econometric analyses of cost efficiency.

Next we assume that producers face a strictly positive vector of output prices given by $p = (p_1, \ldots, p_M) \in R_{++}^M$ and that they seek to maximize the revenue $p^T y = \Sigma_m p_m y_m$ obtainable from the input vector x at their disposal. Then either the output sets $P(x)$ or the output distance function $D_O(x, y)$ can be used to derive a revenue frontier, introduced in Definition 2.13 and illustrated in Figure 2.13.

Definition 2.13: A *revenue frontier* is a function $r(x, p) = \max_y \{p^T y : y \in P(x)\} = \max_y \{p^T y : D_O(x, y) \leq 1\}$.

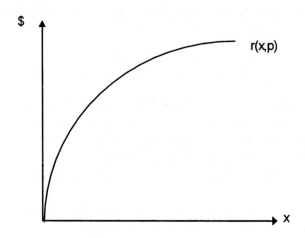

Figure 2.13 A Revenue Frontier ($N = 1$)

If only a single output is produced, the second equality in Definition 2.13 becomes $r(x, p) = \max_y\{py: y \leq f(x)\} = pf(x)$, since $D_O(x, y) = y/f(x)$. In Figure 2.13 $r(x, p)$ shows the maximum revenue obtainable from any scalar input x, given output prices, and so observed revenue must be on or beneath $r(x, p)$. Thus the revenue frontier provides a standard against which to measure the performance of producers for whom the revenue maximization assumption is deemed appropriate.

Since the output sets $P(x)$ and the output distance function $D_O(x, y)$ satisfy certain properties, so does the revenue frontier $r(x, p)$, which is obtained from them. These properties are

r1: $r(0, p) = 0$ and $r(x, p) > 0$ for $x \geq 0$.

r2: $r(x, \lambda p) = \lambda r(x, p)$ for $\lambda > 0$.

r3: $r(x, p') \geq r(x, p)$ for $p' \geq p$.

r4: $r(x, p)$ is a convex function in p.

r5: $r(x, p)$ is a continuous function in p.

r6: $r(\lambda x, p) \geq r(x, p)$ for $\lambda \geq 1$.

r7: $r(x, p)$ is upper semicontinuous in x.

If the weak monotonicity property $P5 \Leftrightarrow D_O5$ is replaced with the strong monotonicity property expressed in the second half of $P6 \Leftrightarrow D_O6$, then the weak monotonicity property $r6$ is replaced with

$r8$: $r(x', p) \geq r(x, p)$ for $x' \geq x$.

Finally, if $G7$ holds, then

$r9$: If GR is convex, then $r(x, p)$ is a concave function in x.

If $r(x, p) = \max_y\{p^T y: D_O(x, y) \leq 1\}$ satisfies conditions $\{r1-r5, r7, r8\}$, then $r(x, p)$ is *dual* to $D_O(x, y)$ in the sense that $D_O(x, y) = \max_p\{p^T y: r(x, p) \leq 1\}$ satisfies conditions $\{D_O1-D_O3, D_O6, D_O7\}$. In this case $D_O(x, y)$ and $r(x, p)$ provide equivalent representations of the structure of production technology, under the assumption of revenue-maximizing behavior in the presence of exogenously determined output prices. Just as in the case of duality between $D_I(y, x)$ and $c(y, w)$, duality between $D_O(x, y)$ and $r(x, p)$ enables certain features of the structure of production technology to be inferred from $r(x, p)$. In addition, this duality relationship plays a central role in the measurement and decomposition of revenue efficiency, which is the subject of Section 2.4.2.

If the revenue frontier $r(x, p)$ is differentiable with respect to output prices, then a derivative property similar to Shephard's lemma yields

$$y(x, p) = \nabla_p r(x, p),$$

so that the vector of revenue-maximizing output supply equations is obtained as the output price gradient of the revenue frontier. For a producer operating on the revenue frontier, $p^T y = r(x, p)$ and $y = y(x, p)$. For a producer operating beneath the revenue frontier, $p^T y < r(x, p)$ and $y \neq y(x, p)$. The properties of $y(x, p)$ are inherited from those of $r(x, p)$ from which they are derived. Thus, for example, if $r(x, p)$ is convex and twice continuously differentiable in p, then revenue-maximizing output supply equations cannot slope downwards with respect to their own prices. Although revenue frontiers are rarely employed in the econometric analysis of productive efficiency, these revenue-maximizing output supply equations would provide a suitable framework for analysis, just as the cost minimizing input demand

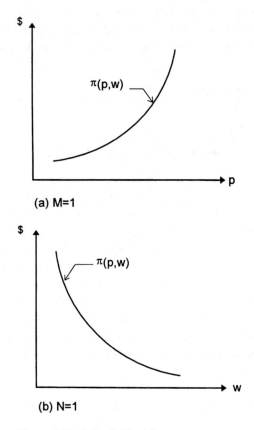

(a) M=1

(b) N=1

Figure 2.14 A Profit Frontier

equations do in the measurement and decomposition of cost efficiency.

We now assume that producers face strictly positive input prices $w \in R_{++}^N$ and strictly positive output prices $p \in R_{++}^M$, and attempt to maximize the profit $\{p^T y - w^T x\}$ they obtain from using $x \in R_+^N$ to produce $y \in R_+^M$. The graph of production technology can be used to obtain a profit frontier, which is introduced in Definition 2.14 and illustrated in Figure 2.14.

> **Definition 2.14:** A *profit frontier* is a function $\pi(p, w) = \max_{y,x}\{p^T y - w^T x: (y, x) \in GR\}$.

If successful cost-minimizing behavior is assumed, then $\pi(p, w) = \max_y\{p^Ty - c(y, w)\}$, since $w^Tx = c(y, w)$. Alternatively, if successful revenue-maximizing behavior is assumed, then $\pi(p, w) = \max_x\{r(x, p) - w^Tx\}$, since $p^Ty = r(x, p)$. In Figure 2.14 $\pi(p, w)$ shows the maximum profit obtainable from a given scalar output price in panel (a) and the maximum profit obtainable from a given scalar input price in panel (b). In each panel observed profit must be on or beneath $\pi(p, w)$, and so $\pi(p, w)$ provides a standard against which to measure the performance of producers for whom the profit maximization objective is deemed appropriate.

Since *GR* satisfies certain properties, so does $\pi(p, w)$. In addition to the properties listed in Section 2.2.1, we assume that *GR* exhibits strict decreasing returns to scale, since constant returns to scale would imply that either $\pi(p, w) = 0$ or $\pi(p, w) = +\infty$. With this in mind, the properties satisfied by $\pi(p, w)$ are

π1: $\pi(p', w) \geq \pi(p, w)$ for $p' \geq p$.

π2: $\pi(p, w') \leq \pi(p, w)$ for $w' \geq w$.

π3: $\pi(\lambda p, \lambda w) = \lambda\pi(p, w)$ for $\lambda > 0$.

π4: $\pi(p, w)$ is a convex function in (p, w).

If $\pi(p, w) = \max_{y,x}\{p^Ty - w^Tx: (y, x) \in GR\}$ satisfies $\{\pi1–\pi4\}$, then $\pi(p, w)$ and *GR* are *dual*, in the sense that $GR = \{(y, x): p^Ty - w^Tx \leq \pi(p, w)\}$ satisfies $\{G1–G3, G6, G7\}$. In this case $\pi(p, w)$ and *GR* provide equivalent representations of the structure of production technology, under the assumption of profit-maximizing behavior in the presence of exogenously determined output prices and input prices.

If $\pi(p, w)$ is differentiable, then Hotelling's (1932) lemma states that

$$y(p,w) = \nabla_p\pi(p,w),$$

$$-x(p,w) = \nabla_w\pi(p,w).$$

Thus the vectors of profit-maximizing output supply and input demand equations can be obtained from the profit frontier as the output price gradient and the negative of the input price gradient, respectively. For a producer operating on the profit frontier, $\{p^Ty - w^Tx\} = \pi(p, w)$ and $y = y(p, w), x = x(p, w)$. For a producer operating beneath the profit frontier, $\{p^Ty - w^Tx\} < \pi(p, w)$ and either $y \neq y(p, w)$ or $x \neq x(p, w)$ or both.

Particularly in the single-output case, it is frequently convenient to work with a normalized profit frontier. Since the profit frontier $\pi(p, w)$ is homogeneous of degree +1 in (p, w), it is possible to divide maximum profit $\pi(p, w)$ by $p > 0$ to obtain

> **Definition 2.15:** Let $M = 1$. A *normalized profit frontier* $\pi^*(w/p)$ $= \pi(p, w)/p = \max_{y,x}\{y - (w/p)^Tx: (y, x) \in GR\}$.

The normalized profit frontier $\pi^*(w/p)$ is nonincreasing, convex, and homogeneous of degree 0 in $(w; p)$. For a normalized profit frontier Hotelling's lemma generates

$$-x\left(\frac{w}{p}\right) = \nabla_{(w/p)}\pi^*\left(\frac{w}{p}\right),$$

$$y\left(\frac{w}{p}\right) = \pi^*\left(\frac{w}{p}\right) - \left(\frac{w}{p}\right)^T \nabla_{(w/p)}\pi^*\left(\frac{w}{p}\right).$$

A normalized profit frontier can also be defined in the multiple-output case, with the normalizing price being any positive output price or any positive input price.

2.2.5 Variable Cost Frontiers and Variable Profit Frontiers

It may not be possible for producers to minimize cost, or to maximize profit, if some inputs are fixed, perhaps by contractual arrangement. In this case the focus shifts from a cost frontier to a variable cost frontier, and from a profit frontier to a variable profit frontier. In this section we briefly discuss the properties of variable cost frontiers and variable profit frontiers. We leave the treatment of variable revenue frontiers to the reader.

We begin by assuming that producers use variable input vector $x \in R_+^N$, available at prices $w \in R_{++}^N$, and fixed input vector $z \in R_+^Q$, to produce output vector $y \in R_+^M$. We assume that producers seek to minimize the variable cost w^Tx required to produce y, given technology and (w, z). A variable cost frontier can be defined as

Definition 2.16: A *variable cost frontier* is a function $vc(y, w, z)$ $= \min_x\{w^Tx: (y, x, z) \in GR\}$.

The variable cost frontier $vc(y, w, z)$ shows the minimum expenditure on variable inputs required to produce output vector y when variable input prices are w and fixed input quantities are z. Consequently $w^Tx \geq vc(y, w, z)$, and $vc(y, w, z)$ becomes the standard against which to measure the performance of producers for whom the variable cost minimization assumption is appropriate.

The properties satisfied by $vc(y, w, z)$ are similar to those satisfied by the cost frontier $c(y, w)$. Thus $vc(y, w, z)$ is a nonnegative function that is homogeneous of degree +1 and concave in w for given (y, z). Under a weak monotonicity property akin to $G6$, $vc(y, w, z)$ is also nondecreasing in w for given (y, z), nondecreasing in y for given (w, z), and nonincreasing in z for given (y, w). Under a convexity property akin to $G7$, $vc(y, w, z)$ is a convex function in (y, z) for given w. If $vc(y, w, z)$ is differentiable in the elements of w, then Shephard's lemma states that variable input demand equations are given by $x(y, w, z) = \nabla_w vc(y, w, z)$. Finally, if $vc(y, w, z)$ is differentiable in the elements of z, then a vector of shadow prices for the fixed inputs is given by $q^s = -\nabla_z vc(y, w, z)$.

We now assume that producers sell their outputs at prices $p \in R_{++}^M$ and attempt to maximize variable profit, the difference between total revenue p^Ty and variable cost w^Tx, given technology and (p, w, z). A variable profit frontier can be defined as

Definition 2.17: A *variable profit frontier* is a function $v\pi(p, w, z) = \max_{y,x}\{p^Ty - w^Tx: (y, x, z) \in GR\}$.

The variable profit frontier $v\pi(p, w, z)$ shows the maximum excess of total revenue over variable cost when output prices are p, variable input prices are w, and fixed input quantities are z. It follows that $(p^Ty - w^Tx) \leq v\pi(p, w, z)$, and $v\pi(p, w, z)$ becomes the standard against which to measure the performance of producers for whom the variable profit maximization assumption is appropriate.

Suppose that GR satisfies properties akin to $\{GR1–GR3, GR6, GR7\}$, extended from (y, x) to (y, x, z). Suppose also that GR is a cone, so that technology satisfies constant returns to scale in (y, x, z). Then the variable profit frontier $v\pi(p, w, z)$ is a nonnegative function that is (i) convex and homogeneous of degree +1 in (p, w) for given

z; (ii) nondecreasing in p and nonincreasing in w for given z; and (iii) nondecreasing, concave, and homogeneous of degree +1 in z for given (p, w). If $v\pi(p, w, z)$ is differentiable in the elements of (p, w), then Hotelling's lemma states that output supply equations are given by $y(p, w, z) = \nabla_p v\pi(p, w, z)$ and variable input demand equations are given by $x(p, w, z) = -\nabla_w v\pi(p, w, z)$. Finally if $v\pi(p, w, z)$ is differentiable in the elements of z, $\nabla_z v\pi(p, w, z) = q^s$, q^s being a vector of shadow prices of the fixed inputs. Note that this notion of shadow prices differs from the notion introduced within the context of a variable cost frontier because the objective of producers is different.

2.3 TECHNICAL EFFICIENCY

In Section 2.2 we introduced various types of frontiers. A production frontier exploits only input and output quantity data, while cost, revenue, and profit frontiers exploit input and/or output quantity data, together with input and/or output price data and a behavioral assumption as well. The next step is to introduce measures of distance to each of these frontiers, with distances providing measures of technical or economic efficiency. In this section we introduce a pair of measures of distance to a production frontier, these distances providing measures of technical efficiency. In Section 2.3.1 we define technical efficiency, and we introduce the two measures of technical efficiency. In Section 2.3.2 we discuss the two measures of technical efficiency under the assumption that producers produce a single output, and in Section 2.3.3 we discuss the two measures of technical efficiency under the assumption that producers produce multiple outputs.

2.3.1 Definitions and Measures of Technical Efficiency

Generally speaking, technical efficiency refers to the ability to minimize input use in the production of a given output vector, or the ability to obtain maximum output from a given input vector. A formal definition of technical efficiency, due to Koopmans (1951), is provided in Definition 2.18. Two special cases of Koopmans' definition, the first being input oriented and the second being output oriented, are provided in Definitions 2.19 and 2.20. Following these definitions of technical efficiency, two measures of technical efficiency, the first being input oriented and the second being output oriented, are provided in Definitions 2.21 and 2.22. These measures were first proposed by Debreu (1951) and Farrell (1957), and so they are often referred to jointly as the Debreu–Farrell measures of technical efficiency.

> **Definition 2.18:** An output–input vector $(y, x) \in GR$ is *technically efficient* if, and only if, $(y', x') \notin GR$ for $(y', -x') \geq (y, -x)$.

> **Definition 2.19:** An input vector $x \in L(y)$ is *technically efficient* if, and only if, $x' \notin L(y)$ for $x' \leq x$ or, equivalently, $x \in$ Eff $L(y)$.

> **Definition 2.20:** An output vector $y \in P(x)$ is *technically efficient* if, and only if, $y' \notin P(x)$ for $y' \geq y$ or, equivalently, $y \in$ Eff $P(x)$.

Definition 2.18 calls a feasible output–input vector technically efficient if, and only if, no increase in *any* output or decrease in *any* input is feasible. Definition 2.19 holds the output vector fixed and calls a feasible input vector technically efficient if, and only if, no reduction in *any* input is feasible (recall Definition 2.5). Definition 2.20 holds the input vector fixed and calls a feasible output vector technically efficient if, and only if, no increase in *any* output is feasible (recall Definition 2.7). Thus technical efficiency is defined in terms of membership in an efficient subset. Definitions 2.19 and 2.20 of technical efficiency should be carefully compared with the following two measures of technical efficiency.

> **Definition 2.21:** An *input-oriented measure of technical efficiency* is a function $TE_I(y, x) = \min\{\theta: \theta x \in L(y)\}$.

> **Definition 2.22:** An *output-oriented measure of technical efficiency* is a function $TE_O(x, y) = [\max\{\phi: \phi y \in P(x)\}]^{-1}$.

Definitions 2.21 and 2.22 measure technical efficiency in terms of equiproportionate contraction of all inputs and equiproportionate expansion of all outputs, respectively. If no equiproportionate contraction of *all* inputs is feasible, that input vector is called technically efficient, whereas if no equiproportionate expansion of *all* outputs is feasible, that output vector is called technically efficient. Recalling Definitions 2.4 and 2.6, the Debreu–Farrell measures of technical efficiency associate technical efficiency with membership in isoquants. Since membership in isoquants is necessary, but not sufficient, for membership in efficient subsets, it follows that technical efficiency on the basis of the Debreu–Farrell measures is necessary, but not sufficient, for technical efficiency on the basis of Koopmans' definitions.

Throughout this book, and also throughout the vast majority of econometric work, technical efficiency is measured radially, using isoquants as standards, following Debreu and Farrell. It is natural to ask why technical efficiency is not measured relative to the more exacting standards provided by efficient subsets, following Koopmans. The answer is that radial measures have nice properties, and using efficient subsets as standards would require nonradial measures. The properties of the two Debreu–Farrell measures of technical efficiency are given in Proposition 2.1.

Proposition 2.1: The input-oriented measure of technical efficiency $TE_I(y, x)$ satisfies the properties:

(i) $TE_I(y, x) \leq 1$.

(ii) $TE_I(y, x) = 1 \Leftrightarrow x \in \text{Isoq } L(y)$.

(iii) $TE_I(y, x)$ is nonincreasing in x.

(iv) $TE_I(y, x)$ is homogeneous of degree -1 in x.

(v) $TE_I(y, x)$ is invariant with respect to the units in which y and x are measured.

The output-oriented measure of technical efficiency $TE_O(x, y)$ satisfies the properties:

(i) $TE_O(x, y) \leq 1$.

(ii) $TE_O(x, y) = 1 \Leftrightarrow y \in \text{Isoq } P(x)$.

(iii) $TE_O(x, y)$ is nondecreasing in y.

(iv) $TE_O(x, y)$ is homogeneous of degree $+1$ in y.

(v) $TE_O(x, y)$ is invariant with respect to the units in which x and y are measured.

All but one of these properties are desirable properties that any measure of technical efficiency should satisfy. Since both $TE_I(y, x)$ and $TE_O(x, y)$ are used to measure technical efficiency throughout the book, it is worthwhile to discuss these properties. The first property is a normalization property, which states that both $TE_I(y, x)$ and $TE_O(x, y)$ are bounded above by unity. [Elsewhere in the literature $TE_O(x, y)$ is frequently defined without the reciprocal operation; for such a definition $TE_O(x, y)$ is bounded below by unity.] The third property is a weak monotonicity property, which states that $TE_I(y, x)$ does not increase when usage of any input increases and that $TE_O(x, y)$ does not decrease when production of any output increases. The fourth property is a homogeneity property, which states that an equiproportionate change in all inputs results in an equivalent change in the opposite direction in $TE_I(y, x)$ and an equiproportionate change in all outputs results in an equivalent change in the same direction in $TE_O(x, y)$. The final property is an invariance property, which states that if the units in which any output or any input is measured are changed (say, from acres to hectares), efficiency scores are unaffected.

The second property is the only undesirable property. It states that $TE_I(y, x)$ and $TE_O(x, y)$ use the relaxed standards Isoq $L(y)$ and Isoq $P(x)$, rather than the more stringent standards Eff $L(y)$ and Eff $P(x)$, to measure technical efficiency. Property (ii) can be strengthened to $TE_I(y, x) = 1 \Leftrightarrow x \in$ Eff $L(y)$ and $TE_O(x, y) = 1 \Leftrightarrow y \in$ Eff $P(x)$, provided production technology satisfies a sufficiently strong monotonicity condition to guarantee that Eff $L(y) =$ Isoq $L(y)$ and Eff $P(x)$ = Isoq $P(x)$. This strong monotonicity condition is satisfied by a Cobb–Douglas production frontier, but it is not necessarily satisfied by a flexible production frontier such as translog, and the translog functional form is widely used in empirical efficiency analysis. Alternatively, technical efficiency can be defined relative to efficient subsets, but this would require replacing the radial Debreu–Farrell measures with nonradial measures that would not satisfy the homogeneity and invariance properties. In the econometric literature the tradeoff between radial efficiency measures satisfying the undesirable property (ii) and nonradial efficiency measures failing to satisfy the desirable properties (iv) and (v) has been resolved in favor of Debreu and Farrell.

In some cases it is appropriate to adopt an input-conserving approach to the measurement of technical efficiency, whereas in other cases it is appropriate to adopt an output-expanding approach. This makes it desirable to know the nature of the relationship between the input oriented measure and the output-oriented measure. The relationship between $TE_I(y, x)$ and $TE_O(x, y)$ is given by

> **Proposition 2.2:** $TE_I(y, x) = TE_O(x, y) \; \forall (y, x) \in GR \Leftrightarrow L(\lambda y) = \lambda L(y) \Leftrightarrow P(\lambda x) = \lambda P(x)$.

Thus $TE_I(y, x)$ and $TE_O(x, y)$ assign the same technical efficiency score to a producer if, and only if, technology is homogeneous of degree +1; that is, technology is characterized by constant returns to scale. This condition is stringent, and is unlikely to be satisfied in empirical work. Consequently it is very likely that a ranking of producers will be sensitive to the orientation of the efficiency measurement. This makes it essential to choose the orientation with care.

2.3.2 Single-Output Production Frontiers and the Measurement of Technical Efficiency

We now consider the case in which producers use multiple inputs to produce a single output. In this case we can use Definition 2.9 to simplify the two Debreu–Farrell measures of technical efficiency. The single-output versions of these technical efficiency measures are given in Definitions 2.23 and 2.24, and illustrated in Figures 2.15–2.17.

> **Definition 2.23:** If only a single output is produced, an *input-oriented measure of technical efficiency* is given by the function $TE_I(y, x) = \min\{\theta: y \leq f(\theta x)\}$.

> **Definition 2.24:** If only a single output is produced, an *output-oriented measure of technical efficiency* is given by the function $TE_O(x, y) = [\max\{\phi: \phi y \leq f(x)\}]^{-1}$.

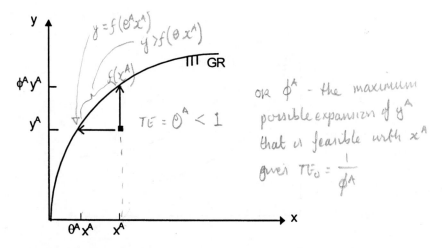

Figure 2.15 Input-Oriented and Output-Oriented Measures of Technical Efficiency ($M = 1, N = 1$)

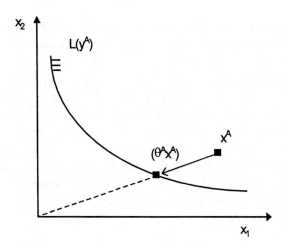

Figure 2.16 An Input-Oriented Measure of Technical Efficiency ($N = 2$)

Figure 2.15 uses the production frontier $f(x)$ to illustrate both measures of technical efficiency. A producer using x^A to produce y^A is technically inefficient, since it operates beneath $f(x)$. $TE_I(y^A, x^A)$ measures the maximum contraction of x^A that enables continued

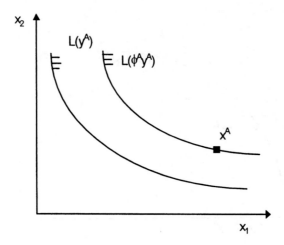

Figure 2.17 An Output-Oriented Measure of Technical Efficiency
($N = 2$)

production of y^A, and $TE_I(y^A, x^A) = \theta^A < 1$, since $y^A = f(\theta^A x^A)$. $TE_O(x^A, y^A)$ measures the reciprocal of the maximum expansion of y^A that is feasible with x^A, and $TE_O(x^A, y^A) = (\phi^A)^{-1} < 1$, since $\phi^A y^A = f(x^A)$. Figure 2.16 uses the input set $L(y)$ and its isoquant Isoq $L(y)$ to illustrate the input-oriented measure of technical efficiency. $TE_I(y^A, x^A)$ measures the maximum radial contraction in x^A that enables continued production of y^A, and $TE_I(x^A, y^A) = \theta^A < 1$, since $\theta^A x^A \in$ Isoq $L(y^A)$. Figure 2.17 uses the input set $L(y)$ and its isoquant Isoq $L(y)$ to illustrate the output-oriented measure of technical efficiency. The reciprocal of $TE_O(x^A, y^A)$ measures the maximum expansion of y^A that is feasible with inputs x^A, and $TE_O(x^A, y^A) = (\phi^A)^{-1} < 1$, since $x^A \in$ Isoq $L(\phi^A y^A)$.

2.3.3 Multiple-Output Distance Functions and the Measurement of Technical Efficiency

We now assume that producers use multiple inputs to produce multiple outputs. The analytical framework is very similar to that of Section 2.3.2; the only difference is that the (single-output) production frontier is replaced with distance functions. Input distance functions are used to define an input-oriented measure of technical

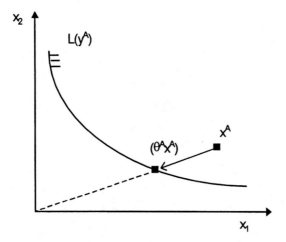

Figure 2.18 An Input-Oriented Measure of Technical Efficiency ($N = 2$)

efficiency, and output distance functions are used to define an output-oriented measure of technical efficiency. The following two definitions are straightforward extensions of Definitions 2.23 and 2.24 to the multiple-output case.

> **Definition 2.25:** If any number of outputs is produced, an *input-oriented measure of technical efficiency* is given by the function $TE_I(y, x) = \min\{\theta: D_I(y, \theta x) \geq 1\}$.

> **Definition 2.26:** If any number of outputs is produced, an *output-oriented measure of technical efficiency* is given by the function $TE_O(x, y) = [\max\{\phi: D_O(x, \phi y) \leq 1\}]^{-1}$.

In Figure 2.18 the input-oriented measure of the technical efficiency of producer (x^A, y^A) is given by $TE_I(y^A, x^A) = \theta^A < 1$, since $\theta^A x^A \in \text{Isoq } L(y^A)$. In Figure 2.19 the output-oriented measure of the technical efficiency of producer (x^A, y^A) is given by $TE_O(x^A, y^A) = (\phi^A)^{-1} < 1$, since $\phi^A y^A \in \text{Isoq } P(x^A)$.

The efficiency measures introduced in Definitions 2.25 and 2.26, and illustrated in Figures 2.18 and 2.19, look very much like the distance functions introduced in Definitions 2.10 and 2.11, and illustrated in Figures 2.9 and 2.11. This should not be surprising, since distance functions provide radial measures of the distance from an

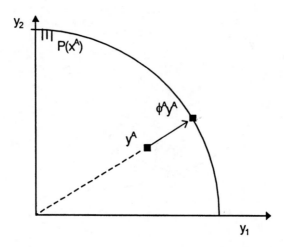

Figure 2.19 An Output-Oriented Measure of Technical Efficiency ($M = 2$)

output–input bundle to the boundary of production technology. The relationships between distance functions and radial efficiency measures are provided in

Proposition 2.3: $TE_I(y, x) = [D_I(y, x)]^{-1}$ and $TE_O(x, y) = D_O(x, y)$.

The input-oriented measure of technical efficiency $TE_I(y, x)$ is the reciprocal of the input distance function $D_I(y, x)$, and the output-oriented measure of technical efficiency $TE_O(x, y)$ coincides with the output distance function $D_O(x, y)$. Thus as we indicated in Section 2.2.3, distance functions are intimately related to the measurement of technical efficiency. This should be clear from a comparison of the properties of $TE_I(y, x)$ and $TE_O(x, y)$ given in Proposition 2.1 with the properties of $D_I(y, x)$ and $D_O(x, y)$ given in Section 2.2.3.

2.4 ECONOMIC EFFICIENCY

In Section 2.3 we introduced a pair of measures of technical efficiency, for both the single-output case and the multiple-output case. The standards against which technical efficiency is measured are provided by the production frontier in the single-output case and by isoquants in both the single-output case and the multiple-output case. These are fairly weak standards, since no behavioral objective is imposed. If a behavioral objective of cost minimization is appropriate, the cost frontier $c(y, w)$ and its associated system of cost-minimizing input demand equations $x(y, w)$ provide a standard against which to measure cost efficiency. This provides a more exacting input-oriented standard against which to measure producer performance. Alternatively, if a behavioral objective of revenue maximization is appropriate, the revenue frontier $r(x, p)$ and its associated system of revenue-maximizing output supply equations provides a standard against which to measure revenue efficiency. This provides a more exacting output-oriented standard against which to measure producer performance. Finally, if a behavioral objective of profit maximization is appropriate, the profit frontier $\pi(p, w)$ and its associated system of profit-maximizing output supply equations $y(p, w)$ and input demand equations $x(p, w)$ provides a still more exacting standard against which to measure producer performance. We consider each of these economic standards in the next three subsections.

2.4.1 Cost Frontiers and Cost Efficiency

We assume that producers face input prices $w \in R_{++}^N$, and seek to minimize the cost $w^T x$ they incur in producing the outputs $y \in R_+^M$ they choose to produce. The standard against which their performance is evaluated shifts from the production frontier to the cost frontier. We will see that the achievement of input-oriented technical efficiency is necessary, but not sufficient, for the achievement of cost efficiency. This is because a technically efficient producer could use an inappropriate input mix, given the input prices it faces. A measure of cost efficiency is introduced in Definition 2.27 and illustrated in Figures 2.20 and 2.21.

> **Definition 2.27:** A measure of *cost efficiency* is a function $CE(y, x, w) = c(y, w)/w^T x$.

The measure of cost efficiency is given by the ratio of minimum cost to observed cost. In Figure 2.20 the cost efficiency of a producer

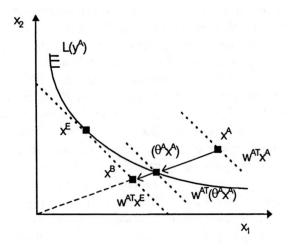

Figure 2.20 The Measurement and Decomposition of Cost Efficiency ($N = 2$)

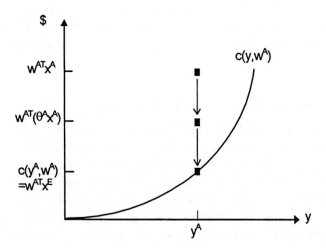

Figure 2.21 The Measurement and Decomposition of Cost Efficiency ($M = 1$)

using inputs x^A, available at prices w^A, to produce output y^A is measured using Isoq $L(y^A)$. The measure of cost efficiency is given by the ratio of minimum cost $c(y^A, w^A) = w^{AT}x^E$ to actual cost $w^{AT}x^A$. The same scenario is depicted in Figure 2.21, using $c(y, w^A)$.

For $x \in L(y)$, the measure of cost efficiency satisfies the following properties:

*CE*1: $0 < CE(y, x, w) \leq 1$, with $CE(y, x, w) = 1 \Leftrightarrow x = x(y, w)$ so that $w^T x = c(y, w)$.

*CE*2: $CE(y, \lambda x, w) = \lambda^{-1} CE(y, x, w)$ for $\lambda > 0$.

*CE*3: $CE(\lambda y, x, w) \geq CE(y, x, w)$ for $\lambda \geq 1$.

*CE*4: $CE(y, x, \lambda w) = CE(y, x, w)$ for $\lambda > 0$.

Thus the measure of cost efficiency is bounded between zero and unity, and achieves its upper bound if, and only if, a producer uses a cost-minimizing input vector. The measure is homogeneous of degree -1 in inputs (e.g., a doubling of all inputs doubles cost and halves cost efficiency), nondecreasing in outputs, and homogeneous of degree 0 in input prices (e.g., a doubling of all input prices has no effect on cost efficiency). Property *CE*4 implies that the measure of cost efficiency depends only on relative input prices.

It is apparent from Figure 2.20 that not all cost inefficiency is necessarily attributable to technical inefficiency. Using Definition 2.20, the input-oriented technical efficiency of the producer being examined is given by $TE_I(y^A, x^A) = \theta^A = w^{AT}(\theta^A x^A)/w^{AT} x^A$. Thus cost efficiency is given by the ratio of expenditure at x^E (which is equal to expenditure at x^B) to expenditure at x^A, whereas input-oriented technical efficiency is given by the ratio of expenditure at $\theta^A x^A$ to expenditure at x^A. The remaining portion of cost inefficiency is given by the ratio of expenditure at x^E to expenditure at $\theta^A x^A$, and is attributable to a misallocation of inputs in light of their relative prices. In Figure 2.20 the input vector $\theta^A x^A$ is technically efficient, but not cost efficient because $(\theta^A x_1^A/\theta^A x_2^A) > x_1^E/x_2^E = x_1(y^A, w^A)/x_2(y^A, w^A)$. The notion of input allocative efficiency is introduced in Definition 2.28 and illustrated in Figures 2.20 and 2.21.

Definition 2.28: A measure of *input allocative efficiency* is a function $AE_I(y, x, w) = CE(y, x, w)/TE_I(y, x)$.

Thus a measure of input allocative efficiency is provided by the ratio of cost efficiency to input-oriented technical efficiency. Since $CE(y^A, w^A) = c(y^A, w^A)/w^{AT} x^A$ and $TE_I(y^A, x^A) = w^{AT}(\theta^A x^A)/w^{AT} x^A$, it follows that $AE_I(y^A, x^A, w^A) = c(y^A, w^A)/w^{AT}(\theta^A x^A)$.

The properties satisfied by $AE_I(y, x, w)$ are

AE_I1: $0 < AE_I(y, x, w) \leq 1$.

AE_I2: $AE_I(y, x, w) = 1 \Leftrightarrow$ there exists a $\lambda \leq 1$ such that $\lambda x = x(y, w)$.

AE_I3: $AE_I(y, \lambda x, w) = AE_I(y, x, w)$ for $\lambda > 0$.

AE_I4: $AE_I(y, x, \lambda w) = AE_I(y, x, w)$ for $\lambda > 0$.

Thus $AE_I(y, x, w)$ is bounded between zero and unity, and attains its upper bound if, and only if, the input vector can be radially contracted to the cost-minimizing input vector. $AE_I(y, x, w)$ is also homogeneous of degree 0 in input quantities and in input prices, being dependent on the input mix and on relative input prices.

The decomposition of cost efficiency into input-oriented technical efficiency and input allocative efficiency illustrated in Figures 2.20 and 2.21 is formalized in Proposition 2.4.

> **Proposition 2.4:** The measure of cost efficiency decomposes as $CE(y, x, w) = TE_I(y, x) \cdot AE_I(y, x, w)$.

Using Proposition 2.4, still another way of expressing the necessary and sufficient condition for cost efficiency is $CE(y, x, w) = 1 \Leftrightarrow TE_I(y, x) = AE_I(y, x, w) = 1$.

2.4.2 Revenue Frontiers and Revenue Efficiency

The structure of this section is essentially the same as the structure of the preceding section; only the orientation changes. We now assume that producers face output prices $p \in R_{++}^M$, and seek to maximize the revenue $p^T y$ they can generate from the input vector $x \in R_+^N$ they employ. The standard against which their performance is evaluated is provided by the revenue frontier. We will see that failure to maximize revenue can be attributed to either or both of two sources: output-oriented technical inefficiency and production of an inappropriate output mix in light of the prevailing output price vector. A measure of revenue efficiency is introduced in Definition 2.29 and illustrated in Figures 2.22 and 2.23.

> **Definition 2.29:** A measure of *revenue efficiency* is a function $RE(x, y, p) = p^T y / r(x, p)$.

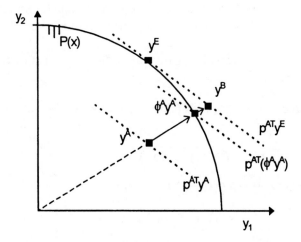

Figure 2.22 The Measurement and Decomposition of Revenue Efficiency ($M = 2$)

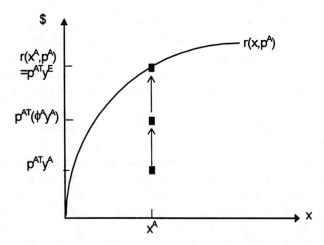

Figure 2.23 The Measurement and Decomposition of Revenue Efficiency ($N = 1$)

The measure of revenue efficiency is given by the ratio of actual revenue to maximum revenue. In Figure 2.22 the revenue efficiency of a producer using inputs x^A to produce outputs y^A for sale at prices p^A is measured using Isoq $P(x^A)$. The measure of revenue efficiency is given by the ratio of observed revenue $p^{AT}y^A$ to maximum revenue $r(x^A, p^A) = p^{AT}y^E$. The same scenario is portrayed in Figure 2.23, using $r(x, p^A)$.

For $y \in P(x)$, the measure of revenue efficiency satisfies the following properties:

*RE*1: $0 < RE(x, y, p) \leq 1$, with $RE(x, y, p) = 1 \Leftrightarrow y = y(x, p)$ so that $p^T y = r(x, p)$.

*RE*2: $RE(x, \lambda y, p) = \lambda RE(x, y, p)$ for $\lambda > 0$.

*RE*3: $RE(\lambda x, y, p) \leq RE(x, y, p)$ for $\lambda \geq 1$.

*RE*4: $RE(x, y, \lambda p) = RE(x, y, p)$ for $\lambda > 0$.

Thus the measure of revenue efficiency is bounded between zero and unity, and achieves its upper bound if, and only if, a producer produces a revenue-maximizing output vector. The measure is homogeneous of degree +1 in outputs (i.e., an equiproportionate change in all outputs generates the same proportionate change in revenue efficiency), nonincreasing in inputs, and homogeneous of degree 0 in output prices (e.g., a doubling of all output prices has no effect on revenue efficiency). Property *RE*4 implies that the measure of revenue efficiency depends only on relative output prices.

It should be clear from Figure 2.22 that not all revenue inefficiency is necessarily due to technical inefficiency. Using Definition 2.22, the output-oriented technical efficiency of the producer being evaluated is given by $TE_O(x^A, y^A) = p^{AT}y^A / p^{AT}(\phi^A y^A) = (\phi^A)^{-1}$. Revenue efficiency is given by the ratio of revenue at y^A to revenue at y^E (which is equal to revenue at y^B), whereas output-oriented technical efficiency is given by the ratio of revenue at y^A to revenue at $\phi^A y^A$. The remaining portion of revenue inefficiency is given by the ratio of revenue at $\phi^A y^A$ to revenue at y^E, and is due to a misallocation of outputs in light of their relative prices. In Figure 2.22 the output vector $\phi^A y^A$ is technically efficient, but not revenue efficient because $(\phi^A y_1^A / \phi^A y_2^A) > y_1^E / y_2^E = y_1(x^A, p^A) / y_2(x^A, p^A)$. The notion of output allocative efficiency is introduced in Definition 2.30 and illustrated in Figures 2.22 and 2.23.

Definition 2.30: A measure of *output allocative efficiency* is a function $AE_O(x, y, p) = RE(x, y, p)/TE_O(x, y)$.

Thus a measure of output allocative efficiency is provided by the ratio of revenue efficiency to output-oriented technical efficiency. Since $RE(x^A, p^A) = p^{AT}y^A/r(x^A, p^A)$ and $TE_O(x^A, y^A) = p^{AT}y^A/p^{AT}(\phi^A y^A)$, it follows that $AE_O(x^A, y^A, p^A) = p^{AT}(\phi^A y^A)/r(x^A, p^A)$.

The properties satisfied by $AE_o(x, y, p)$ are

AE_O1: $0 < AE_O(x, y, p) \leq 1$.

AE_O2: $AE_O(x, y, p) = 1 \Leftrightarrow$ there exists a $\lambda \geq 1$ such that $\lambda y = y(x, p)$.

AE_O3: $AE_O(\lambda y, x, p) = AE_O(x, y, p)$ for $\lambda > 0$.

AE_O4: $AE_O(x, y, \lambda p) = AE_O(x, y, p)$ for $\lambda > 0$.

Thus $AE_O(x, y, p)$ is bounded between zero and unity, and achieves its upper bound if, and only if, the output vector can be radially expanded to the revenue-maximizing output vector. $AE_O(x, y, p)$ is also homogeneous of degree 0 in output quantities and in output prices, being dependent on the output mix and on relative output prices.

The decomposition of revenue efficiency into output-oriented technical efficiency and output allocative efficiency illustrated in Figures 2.22 and 2.23 is formalized in Proposition 2.5.

Proposition 2.5: The measure of revenue efficiency decomposes as $RE(x, y, p) = TE_O(x, y) \cdot AE_O(x, y, p)$.

It follows from Proposition 2.5 that $RE(x, y, p) = 1 \Leftrightarrow TE_O(x, y) = AE_O(x, y, p) = 1$. Thus for a producer to achieve maximum revenue it is necessary and sufficient that the producer be technically efficient and produce the correct mix of outputs. Failure to do either results in less than maximum revenue.

2.4.3 Profit Frontiers and Profit Efficiency

We now assume that producers face output prices $p \in R_{++}^M$ and input prices $w \in R_{++}^N$, and seek to maximize the profit $(p^T y - w^T x)$ they obtain from using $x \in R_+^N$ to produce $y \in R_+^M$. The standard against

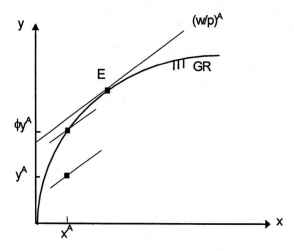

Figure 2.24 The Measurement of Profit Efficiency

which their performance is measured shifts again, from the revenue frontier to the profit frontier. The notion of profit efficiency is introduced in Definition 2.31 and illustrated in Figure 2.24. We will see that several of the previously introduced notions of efficiency are necessary for the achievement of profit efficiency, but that none by itself is sufficient. This is because profit efficiency requires (either input-oriented or output-oriented) technical efficiency and both input allocative efficiency and output allocative efficiency. Moreover, even these efficiencies are not collectively sufficient for profit efficiency, since profit efficiency also requires technical efficiency and both types of allocative efficiency to be achieved at the proper scale. Thus profit efficiency also requires a type of scale efficiency.

Definition 2.31: A measure of *profit efficiency* is a function $\pi E(y, x, p, w) = (p^T y - w^T x)/\pi(p, w)$, provided $\pi(p, w) > 0$.

Thus a measure of profit efficiency is provided by the ratio of actual profit to maximum profit, and obviously $\pi E(y, x, p, w) \leq 1$. In Figure 2.24 a producer facing prices (p^A, w^A) achieves $\pi E(y, x, p, w) = 1$ at output–input combination E, and $\pi E(y, x, p, w) < 1$ for all other feasible output–input combinations.

For $(y, x) \in GR$, the measure of profit efficiency satisfies the following properties:

$\pi E1$: $\pi E(y, x, p, w) \le 1$, with $\pi E(y, x, p, w) = 1 \Leftrightarrow y = y(p, w)$,
$x = x(p, w)$ so that $(p^T y - w^T x) = \pi(p, w)$.

$\pi E2$: $\pi E(\lambda y, x, p, w) \ge \pi E(y, x, p, w), \lambda \ge 1$.

$\pi E3$: $\pi E(y, \lambda x, p, w) \le \pi E(y, x, p, w), \lambda \ge 1$.

$\pi E4$: $\pi E(y, x, \lambda p, \lambda w) = \pi E(y, x, p, w), \lambda > 0$.

Thus the measure of profit efficiency is bounded above by unity, and achieves its upper bound if, and only if, a producer actually adopts a profit-maximizing combination of inputs and outputs. Unlike the measures of cost efficiency and revenue efficiency, however, the measure of profit efficiency is not bounded below by zero, since negative actual profit is possible. The measure is nondecreasing in outputs and nonincreasing in inputs. (If $G4$ and $G5$ are replaced with $G6$, then these monotonicity properties are strengthened by replacing λy with $y' \ge y$ and λx with $x' \ge x$, respectively.) Finally, the measure is homogeneous of degree 0 in output prices and input prices collectively (but it is not generally homogeneous in output prices or input prices separately).

A decomposition of profit efficiency into its constituent parts is somewhat arbitrary, depending on whether an input-oriented or an output-oriented measure of technical efficiency is used. Suppose that an output-oriented measure is used, and consider the producer in Figure 2.24 facing prices (p^A, w^A) and using input vector x^A to produce output y^A. Clearly increasing output-oriented technical efficiency by increasing output radially to ϕy^A will increase profit and profit efficiency. But output allocative inefficiency can remain at ϕy^A, and input vector x^A may exhibit input allocative inefficiency, although neither can be depicted in this two-dimensional figure. Figures 2.20 and 2.22 illustrate the possibilities. Both output allocative inefficiency at ϕy^A and input allocative inefficiency at x^A reduce profit beneath $\pi(p^A, w^A)$, and so both contribute to profit inefficiency. Finally, even after accounting for technical inefficiency and both types of allocative inefficiency, scale inefficiency can remain. In Figure 2.24, $(\phi y^A, x^A)$ occurs at an inefficiently small scale to maximize profit, and so scale inefficiency constitutes the final source of profit inefficiency. A similar line of reasoning based on an input-oriented measure of technical efficiency would lead to the conclusion that technical inefficiency, both types of allocative inefficiency, and scale inefficiency contribute to profit inefficiency, although the magnitudes of each component would differ from their magnitudes when an output-oriented measure of technical efficiency is adopted.

The following decomposition of profit efficiency is based on the output-oriented measure of technical efficiency, and makes use of Definitions 2.27 and 2.28 and Propositions 2.3 and 2.4. We leave it to the reader to develop an analogous decomposition based on the input-oriented measure of technical efficiency.

Proposition 2.6: The measure of profit efficiency decomposes as

$$
\begin{aligned}
\pi E(y,x,p,w) = \{ & TE_o(x,y) \cdot AE_o(x,y,p) \\
& \cdot [r(x,p)/p^T y(p,w)] \cdot p^T y(p,w) \\
& -[AE_I(y,x,w)]^{-1} \cdot [c(y/TE_o(x,y),w)/ \\
& w^T x(p,w)] \cdot w^T x(p,w) \} / \pi(p,w).
\end{aligned}
$$

The first two terms in the numerator are less than or equal to unity, and act as a drag on profit-maximizing revenue $p^T y(p, w)$. The fifth term in the numerator is greater than or equal to unity, and inflates profit-maximizing expenditure $w^T x(p, w)$. The third and sixth terms in the numerator can be greater than, equal to, or less than unity, depending on the relationships between x and $x(p, w)$ and between $y/TE_o(x, y)$ and $y(p, w)$. Three of these terms have already been identified as measures of output-oriented technical efficiency, output allocative efficiency, and input allocative efficiency. The two new terms constitute our measure of scale efficiency. Clearly $\pi E(y, x, p, w) = [p^T y(p, w) - w^T x(p, w)]/\pi(p, w) = 1$ if, and only if, all five terms are unity. Thus the attainment of maximum profit requires technical efficiency, use of the right input mix in light of w, production of the right output mix in light of p, and operation at the right scale in light of (p, w).

2.4.4 Variable Cost Efficiency and Variable Profit Efficiency

In Section 2.2.5 we introduced variable cost frontiers and variable profit frontiers as standards against which to measure producer performance in the presence of fixed inputs. In such a circumstance it would be inappropriate to measure economic efficiency relative to cost and profit frontiers, because producers do not have the flexibility to adjust all inputs. In this section we show how to modify the definitions of cost efficiency and profit efficiency when some inputs are fixed.

Suppose producers use variable inputs $x \in R_+^N$, available at prices $w \in R_{++}^N$, to produce outputs $y \in R_+^M$ in the presence of fixed inputs $z \in R_+^Q$. Suppose also that producers seek to minimize the variable cost $w^T x$ required to produce y, given technology and (w, z). The standard against which their performance is measured is the variable cost frontier $vc(y, w, z)$. A measure of variable cost efficiency is given by

> **Definition 2.32:** A measure of *variable cost efficiency* is a function $VCE(y, x, w, z) = vc(y, w, z)/w^T x$.

For given z, $VCE(y, x, w, z)$ satisfies the same properties as $CE(y, x, w)$ does. In addition, since $vc(y, w, z)$ is nonincreasing in the elements of z, so is $VCE(y, x, w, z)$. Finally, for given z, $VCE(y, x, w, z)$ decomposes into a measure of variable input allocative efficiency and a measure of variable input technical efficiency, exactly as $CE(y, x, w)$ does in Proposition 2.4, and the two components satisfy the same properties as $AE_i(y, x, w)$ and $TE_i(y, x)$ do.

Suppose now that producers face output prices $p \in R_{++}^M$ and seek to maximize variable profit $(p^T y - w^T x)$, given technology and (p, w, z). The standard against which their performance is measured shifts to the variable profit frontier $v\pi(p, w, z)$. A measure of variable profit efficiency is given by

> **Definition 2.33:** A measure of *variable profit efficiency* is a function $V\pi E(y, x, p, w, z) = (p^T y - w^T x)/v\pi(p, w, z)$, provided $v\pi(p, w, z) > 0$.

For given z, $V\pi E(y, x, p, w, z)$ satisfies the same properties as $\pi E(y, x, p, w)$ does. In addition, since $v\pi(p, w, z)$ is nondecreasing in the elements of z, $V\pi E(y, x, p, w, z)$ is nonincreasing in the elements of z. Finally, for given z, $V\pi E(y, x, p, w, z)$ can be decomposed exactly as $v\pi(p, w, z)$ is decomposed in Proposition 2.6.

2.5 A GUIDE TO THE LITERATURE

The first objective of this chapter has been to provide an introduction to the fundamentals of production economics. We make no claim to originality. Our exposition derives ultimately from the pioneering work of Shephard (1953, 1970), who introduced distance functions into the economics profession. We have relied heavily on a more recent treatment of this basic material provided by Färe (1988) and Russell (1998), who provides a comprehensive guide to the role of distance functions in producer and consumer theory. Cost, revenue, and profit frontiers are treated by Debreu (1959), Diewert (1973, 1974, 1982), and McFadden (1978), and Lau (1972, 1976, 1978) provides an extensive analysis of normalized profit frontiers. Diewert (1981a) discusses the properties of variable cost frontiers, and Gorman (1968), Diewert (1973, 1982), Lau (1972, 1976, 1978), and McFadden (1978) discuss the properties of variable profit frontiers. Duality theory is surveyed by Diewert (1982), who also provides an excellent history of thought on the subject, and more recently by Cornes (1992), who provides an exceptionally readable exposition, and by Färe and Primont (1995), who provide a more advanced exposition.

The second objective of this chapter has been to provide an introduction to the fundamentals of efficiency measurement. Here again we make no claim to originality. The measurement of technical and economic efficiency was pioneered by Farrell (1957), who first showed how to measure input-oriented technical efficiency, input allocative efficiency, and cost efficiency. Debreu (1951) introduced a measure of output-oriented technical efficiency, which he called a "coefficient of resource utilization." Detailed analyses of the measurement of all types of efficiency appear in Färe, Grosskopf, and Lovell (1985, 1994), who also provide extensive references to the theoretical and empirical literatures.

3 The Estimation of Technical Efficiency

3.1 INTRODUCTION

In this chapter we begin our econometric analysis of productive efficiency. The chapter is long, but our focus is fairly narrow. Throughout the chapter we explore various econometric models designed to provide estimates of *technical* efficiency, and so we are implementing the theoretical material developed in Section 2.3. Throughout most of the chapter we confine our exploration to the estimation of technical efficiency under the assumption that producers produce only a single output, either because they actually do produce only a single output or because it is possible to aggregate their multiple outputs into a single-output index. Thus we are implementing the theoretical material developed in Section 2.3.2. Production frontiers provide the standards against which producer performance is evaluated, and performance is evaluated by means of an output-oriented measure of technical efficiency. Only in Section 3.2.3 do we relax the single-output assumption. There we implement the theoretical material developed in Section 2.3.3 by exploring the estimation of stochastic distance functions, which do accommodate multiple outputs.

Throughout the chapter we limit our discussion to single-equation models. In these models the parameters describing the structure of a production frontier are estimated, and estimates of the output-oriented technical efficiency of each producer are obtained as a by-product of the exercise. The data underlying the exercise consist of observations on the quantities of inputs employed and the output

63

produced by each producer. No price information is used, and no behavioral objective is imposed on producers.

The estimation techniques employed depend in part on the richness of the quantity data available. In Section 3.2 we discuss alternative estimation techniques under the assumption that cross-sectional data are available on a sample of producers. In Section 3.3 we discuss estimation techniques under the assumption that panel data are available on a sample of producers over a period of time; in this case a wider range of estimation techniques is available. The output of the exercise in both cases consists of estimates of the parameters describing the structure of the production frontier, and estimates of the output-oriented technical efficiency of each producer. The difference between the two cases is that with cross-sectional data we are only able to take a snapshot of the performance of each producer during a period of time (such as a calendar year), whereas with panel data we are able to make a movie of the performance of each producer as it evolves through a longer period of time.

In Section 3.4 we discuss appropriate modifications to the estimation techniques, for both cross-sectional and panel data models, when heteroskedasticity is present. We devote an entire section to this topic because heteroskedasticity causes more serious problems in a stochastic frontier regression model than in a typical least squares regression model.

Section 3.5 concludes with a guide to the relevant literature.

3.2 CROSS-SECTIONAL PRODUCTION FRONTIER MODELS

In this section we assume that cross-sectional data on the quantities of N inputs used to produce a single output are available for each of I producers. A production frontier model can be written as

$$y_i = f(x_i; \beta) \cdot TE_i, \tag{3.2.1}$$

where y_i is the scalar output of producer i, $i = 1, \ldots, I$, x_i is a vector of N inputs used by producer i, $f(x_i; \beta)$ is the production frontier, and β is a vector of technology parameters to be estimated.

In Chapter 2 we expressed the output-oriented technical efficiency of a producer as $TE_o(x, y)$. To reduce notational clutter, we now write

$TE_o(x, y)$ as TE_i, replacing the subscript and the arguments with a producer identifier. Since TE_i is the output-oriented technical efficiency of producer i, we have

$$TE_i = \frac{y_i}{f(x_i; \beta)}, \tag{3.2.2}$$

which defines technical efficiency as the ratio of observed output to maximum feasible output. y_i achieves its maximum feasible value of $f(x_i; \beta)$ if, and only if, $TE_i = 1$. Otherwise $TE_i < 1$ provides a measure of the shortfall of observed output from maximum feasible output.

In equation (3.2.1) the production frontier $f(x_i; \beta)$ is *deterministic*. Consequently in equation (3.2.2) the entire shortfall of observed output y_i from maximum feasible output $f(x_i; \beta)$ is attributed to technical inefficiency. Such a specification ignores the fact that output can be affected by random shocks that are not under the control of a producer. To incorporate producer-specific random shocks into the analysis requires the specification of a *stochastic* production frontier. To do so, we rewrite equation (3.2.1) as

$$y_i = f(x_i; \beta) \cdot \exp\{v_i\} \cdot TE_i, \tag{3.2.3}$$

where $[f(x_i; \beta) \cdot \exp\{v_i\}]$ is the stochastic production frontier. The stochastic production frontier consists of two parts: a deterministic part $f(x_i; \beta)$ common to all producers and a producer-specific part $\exp\{v_i\}$, which captures the effect of random shocks on each producer. If the production frontier is specified as being stochastic, equation (3.2.2) becomes

$$TE_i = \frac{y_i}{f(x_i; \beta) \cdot \exp\{v_i\}}, \tag{3.2.4}$$

which defines technical efficiency as the ratio of observed output to maximum feasible output in an environment characterized by $\exp\{v_i\}$. Now y_i achieves its maximum feasible value of $[f(x_i; \beta) \cdot \exp\{v_i\}]$ if, and only if, $TE_i = 1$. Otherwise $TE_i < 1$ provides a measure of the shortfall of observed output from maximum feasible output in an environment characterized by $\exp\{v_i\}$, which is allowed to vary across producers.

Technical efficiency can be estimated using either the deterministic production frontier model given by equations (3.2.1) and (3.2.2) or the stochastic production frontier model given by equations (3.2.3) and (3.2.4). Since the former model ignores the effect of random shocks on the production process, and the latter model includes their effect, the latter model is preferred. This is because the former model runs the risk of improperly attributing unmodeled environmental variation to variation in technical efficiency. However the deterministic production frontier model was introduced first, and so we consider it first.

3.2.1 Deterministic Production Frontiers

We begin by rewriting equation (3.2.1) as

$$y_i = f(x_i; \beta) \cdot \exp\{-u_i\}, \tag{3.2.5}$$

where $TE_i = \exp\{-u_i\}$. Since we require that $TE_i \leq 1$, we have $u_i \geq 0$. Next, assuming that $f(x_i; \beta)$ takes the log-linear Cobb–Douglas form, the deterministic production frontier model becomes

$$\ln y_i = \beta_o + \sum_n \beta_n \ln x_{ni} - u_i. \tag{3.2.6}$$

where $u_i \geq 0$ guarantees that $y_i \leq f(x_i; \beta)$. Equation (3.2.6) is a linear regression model with a nonpositive disturbance. The objective is to obtain estimates of the parameter vector β, which describes the structure of the production frontier, and also to obtain estimates of the u_i, which can be used to obtain estimates of TE_i for each producer by means of $TE_i = \exp\{-u_i\}$. Whatever estimation strategy is followed, it must somehow incorporate the restriction $u_i \geq 0$. Three methods have been proposed.

Goal Programming Aigner and Chu (1968) showed that the deterministic production frontier model (3.2.6) can be converted to either of a pair of mathematical programming models. The first model is a *linear* programming model, in which the goal is to calculate a parameter vector β for which the sum of the proportionate deviations of the observed output of each producer beneath maximum feasible output is minimized. The resulting deviations are then converted to measures of technical efficiency for each producer. Such a model can be expressed as

$$\min \quad \sum_i u_i,$$

$$\text{subject to} \quad \left[\beta_o + \sum_n \beta_n \ln x_{ni}\right] \geq \ln y_i, \qquad i = 1, \ldots, I. \qquad (3.2.7)$$

The second model is a *quadratic* programming model, in which the goal is to calculate a parameter vector β for which the sum of *squared* proportionate deviations of the observed output of each producer beneath maximum feasible output is minimized. This model can be expressed as

$$\min \quad \sum_i u_i^2,$$

$$\text{subject to} \quad \left[\beta_o + \sum_n \beta_n \ln x_{ni}\right] \geq \ln y_i, \qquad i = 1, \ldots, I. \qquad (3.2.8)$$

Nonnegativity constraints on the parameters $\beta_n, n = 1, \ldots, N$, can be appended to either model (although it would be inappropriate to constrain *all* parameters in a more flexible functional form). Once parameter values are calculated from either model, the technical efficiency of each producer can be calculated from the slacks in the functional constraints in (3.2.7) or (3.2.8). Thus, from equation (3.2.5), $TE_i = \exp\{-u_i\}$, where

$$u_i = \left[\beta_o + \sum_n \beta_n \ln x_{ni}\right] - \ln y_i, \qquad i = 1, \ldots, I. \qquad (3.2.9)$$

A major drawback of the goal programming approach is that the parameters are *calculated* (using mathematical programming techniques) rather than *estimated* (using regression techniques), which complicates statistical inference concerning the calculated parameter values. However Schmidt (1976) pointed out that the goal programming models can be given a statistical interpretation if a distributional assumption is imposed on the u_i. The linear programming "estimates" are maximum likelihood estimates of the parameters of the deterministic production frontier if the $u_i \geq 0$ follow an exponential distribution

$$f(u) = \frac{1}{\sigma_u} \cdot \exp\left\{-\frac{u}{\sigma_u}\right\}, \qquad (3.2.10)$$

in which case the log likelihood function is

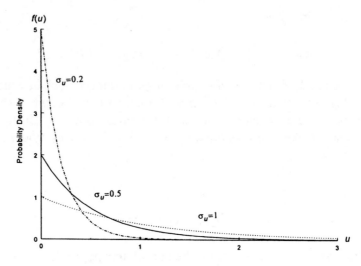

Figure 3.1 Exponential Distributions

$$\ln L = I \ln \sigma_u - \frac{1}{\sigma_u} \sum_i |u_i|. \tag{3.2.11}$$

Since the exponential distribution is a single-parameter distribution, it is easily depicted graphically. Figure 3.1 shows three different exponential distributions corresponding to three values of the standard deviation parameter σ_u.

The quadratic programming "estimates" are maximum likelihood estimates of the parameters of the deterministic production frontier if the $u_i \geq 0$ follow a half normal distribution

$$f(u) = \frac{2}{\sqrt{2\pi}\sigma_u} \cdot \exp\left\{-\frac{u^2}{2\sigma_u^2}\right\}, \tag{3.2.12}$$

in which case the log likelihood function is

$$\ln L = \text{constant} - \frac{1}{2}\ln \sigma_u^2 - \frac{1}{2\sigma_u^2}\sum_i u_i^2. \tag{3.2.13}$$

The half normal distribution is also a single-parameter distribution, and Figure 3.2 shows three different half normal distributions

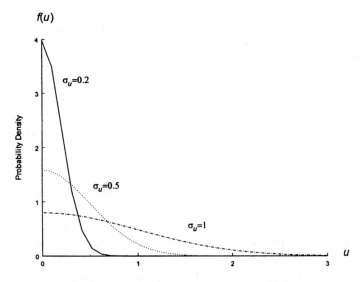

Figure 3.2 Half Normal Distributions

corresponding to three values of the standard deviation parameter σ_u.

Since goal programming techniques calculate rather than estimate the technology parameter vector β, these calculated values do not come with standard errors attached. Thus establishing a linkage between production frontiers calculated by goal programming methods and production frontiers estimated by maximum likelihood methods might seem to endow the former with a statistical foundation. However Schmidt noted that the statistical properties of the maximum likelihood estimators cannot be obtained by traditional methods, since the range of the $\ln y_i$ depends on β, which violates a regularity condition for maximum likelihood estimation (MLE). Later Greene (1980a) showed that the Hessians of the log likelihood functions are singular under both exponential and half normal distributions, making it impossible to estimate the precision of the maximum likelihood estimators using the Hessian as in other models. He also suggested an alternative model in which $u_i \geq 0$ follows a gamma distribution, and which satisfies all regularity conditions for obtaining asymptotic properties of the maximum likelihood estimators. Although this result may be comforting to those who use MLE

to estimate deterministic production frontiers with technical inefficiency distributed as gamma, it is of no apparent value to those who
use goal programming to calculate deterministic production frontiers.
This is because there is no known goal programming problem that
corresponds to a maximum likelihood problem with inefficiency distributed as gamma. Thus the two goal programming problems that
have known MLE counterparts have uncertain statistical properties,
whereas the MLE problem that does have desirable statistical properties has no known goal programming counterpart.

Corrected Ordinary Least Squares (COLS) In his discussion of
Farrell's original paper, Winsten (1957) suggested that the deterministic production frontier model (3.2.6) could be estimated in two
steps. In the first step ordinary least squares (OLS) is used to obtain
consistent and unbiased estimates of the slope parameters and a consistent but biased estimate of the intercept parameter. In the second
step the biased OLS intercept β_o is shifted up ("corrected") to ensure
that the estimated frontier bounds the data from above. The COLS
intercept is estimated consistently by

$$\hat{\beta}_o^* = \hat{\beta}_o + \max_i\{\hat{u}_i\}, \qquad (3.2.14)$$

where the $\hat{u}_i$ are the OLS residuals. The OLS residuals are corrected
in the opposite direction, and so

$$-\hat{u}_i^* = \hat{u}_i - \max_i\{\hat{u}_i\}. \qquad (3.2.15)$$

The COLS residuals $\hat{u}_i^*$ are nonnegative, with at least one being zero,
and can be used to provide consistent estimates of the technical
efficiency of each producer by means of $TE_i = \exp\{-\hat{u}_i^*\}$.

The COLS technique is easy to implement, and generates an estimated production frontier that lies on [for at least one producer, by
virtue of (3.2.15)] or above the data. However this simplicity comes
at a cost: The estimated production frontier is parallel (in natural logarithms of the variables) to the OLS regression, since only the OLS
intercept is corrected. This implies that the structure of "best practice" production technology is the same as the structure of the
"central tendency" production technology. This is an undesirably
restrictive property of the COLS procedure, since the structure of
best practice production technology ought to be permitted to differ

from that of production technology down in the middle of the data, where producers are less efficient than best practice producers. Stated somewhat differently, the COLS frontier does not necessarily bound the data from above as closely as possible, since it is required to be parallel to the OLS regression.

Modified Ordinary Least Squares (MOLS) Afriat (1972) and Richmond (1974) proposed an interesting variation on COLS. They suggested that the deterministic production frontier model (3.2.6) could be estimated by OLS, under the assumption that the disturbances follow an explicit one-sided distribution, such as exponential or half normal. A motivation for such an assumption is that technical efficiency might reasonably be expected to follow one of these distributions, with increasing degrees of technical inefficiency being increasingly less likely. The MOLS procedure is very similar to the two-step COLS procedure. After estimation by OLS, the estimated intercept is shifted up ("modified") by the mean of the assumed one-sided distribution. In this case equations (3.2.14) and (3.2.15) become

$$\hat{\beta}_o^{**} = \hat{\beta}_o + E(\hat{u}_i) \tag{3.2.16}$$

and

$$-\hat{u}_i^{**} = \hat{u}_i - E(\hat{u}_i), \tag{3.2.17}$$

respectively. The OLS residuals can then be used to provide consistent estimates of the technical efficiency of each producer, exactly as in the COLS model.

The MOLS procedure is also easy to implement. However there is no guarantee that the modification of OLS shifts the estimated intercept up by enough to ensure that all producers are bounded from above by the estimated production frontier, since if a producer has a sufficiently large positive OLS residual it is possible that $[\hat{u}_i - E(\hat{u}_i)]$ > 0 for that producer. If this happens, one is left in the uncomfortable position of having to explain a technical efficiency score greater than unity. It is also possible that MOLS shifts the estimated intercept so far up that no producer is technically efficient, although this is a much less uncomfortable outcome to explain. Finally, the MOLS production frontier is parallel to the OLS regression, since only the OLS intercept is modified. We have already commented on this property in the context of the COLS model.

The three techniques just described share the virtue of simplicity. However they also share a serious deficiency: Each of them measures technical efficiency relative to a deterministic production frontier. All variation in output not associated with variation in inputs is attributed to technical inefficiency. None of these techniques makes allowance for the effect of random shocks, which might also contribute (positively or negatively) to variation in output. Thus these three techniques are in a sense polar opposites of conventional OLS estimation of a production function. OLS attributes all variation in output not associated with variation in inputs to random shocks, and makes no allowance for technical inefficiency. Each of these techniques attributes all variation in output not associated with variation in inputs to technical inefficiency, and makes no allowance for random shocks. What is required is a model that attributes variation in output not associated with variation in inputs to some combination of random shocks and technical inefficiency. Such a model is necessarily more complex than either an OLS production function model or a deterministic production frontier model, but it is also more realistic.

3.2.2 Stochastic Production Frontiers

Aigner, Lovell, and Schmidt (ALS) (1977) and Meeusen and van den Broeck (MB) (1977) simultaneously introduced stochastic production frontier models. These models allow for technical inefficiency, but they also acknowledge the fact that random shocks outside the control of producers can affect output. The great virtue of stochastic production frontier models is that the impact on output of shocks due to variation in labor and machinery performance, vagaries of the weather, and just plain luck can at least in principle be separated from the contribution of variation in technical efficiency.

If we again assume that $f(x_i; \beta)$ takes the log-linear Cobb–Douglas form, then the stochastic production frontier model given in equation (3.2.3) can be written as

$$\ln y_i = \beta_o + \sum_n \beta_n \ln x_{ni} + v_i - u_i, \qquad (3.2.18)$$

where v_i is the two-sided "noise" component, and u_i is the nonnegative technical inefficiency component, of the error term. Since the error term in (3.2.18) has two components, the stochastic production frontier model is often referred to as a "composed error" model. The noise component v_i is assumed to be iid and symmetric, distributed independently of u_i. Thus the error term $\varepsilon_i = v_i - u_i$ is asymmetric, since $u_i \geq 0$. Assuming that v_i and u_i are distributed independently of x_i, estimation of (3.2.18) by OLS provides consistent estimates of the β_ns, but not of β_o, since $E(\varepsilon_i) = -E(u_i) \leq 0$. Moreover, OLS does not provide estimates of producer-specific technical efficiency.

OLS does, however, provide a simple test for the presence of technical inefficiency in the data. If $u_i = 0$, then $\varepsilon_i = v_i$, the error term is symmetric, and the data do not support a technical inefficiency story. However if $u_i > 0$, then $\varepsilon_i = v_i - u_i$ is negatively skewed, and there is evidence of technical inefficiency in the data. This suggests that a test for the presence of technical inefficiency can be based directly on the OLS residuals. Schmidt and Lin (1984) proposed the test statistic

$$\left(b_1\right)^{1/2} = \frac{m_3}{\left(m_2\right)^{3/2}},$$

(3.2.19)

where m_2 and m_3 are the second and third sample moments of the OLS residuals. Since the v_i are symmetrically distributed, m_3 is simply the third sample moment of the u_i. Thus $m_3 < 0$ implies that the OLS residuals are negatively skewed, and suggests the presence of technical inefficiency. $m_3 > 0$ implies that the OLS residuals are positively skewed, which makes no sense in this context. Thus positive skewness in the OLS residuals provides an indication that the model is misspecified. However since the distribution of $(b_1)^{1/2}$ is not widely published, Coelli (1995) proposed an alternative test statistic that is asymptotically distributed as $N(0, 1)$. Since negative skewness occurs when $m_3 < 0$, a test of the hypothesis that $m_3 \geq 0$ is appropriate. Under the null hypothesis of zero skewness of the errors in equation (3.2.18), the test statistic $m_3/(6m_2^3/I)^{1/2}$ is asymptotically distributed as $N(0, 1)$.

The advantage of both tests is that they are based on OLS results, which are easy to obtain. The disadvantage of both tests is that they are based on asymptotic theory, and many samples are relatively small. However Coelli reports encouraging Monte Carlo results concerning the power of his OLS-based test. We consider MLE-based tests next.

Henceforth we assume that there is negative skewness in the OLS residuals, so that there is evidence of technical inefficiency in the data, and it does make sense to proceed to the estimation of a stochastic production frontier. Our two objectives are to obtain estimates of the production technology parameters β in $f(x; \beta)$ and to obtain estimates of the technical efficiency of each producer. Meeting the second objective requires that separate estimates of statistical noise v_i and technical inefficiency u_i be extracted from estimates of ε_i for each producer, and this requires distributional assumptions on the two error components. Under the assumption that the u_i are distributed independently of the inputs, OLS provides consistent estimates of all production technology parameters except for the intercept. However additional assumptions, and a different estimation technique, are required to obtain a consistent estimate of the intercept and estimates of the technical efficiency of each producer.

We begin by discussing a maximum likelihood method that can be used to estimate β and the u_i. This is followed by a discussion of a two-step procedure, in which the first step involves the use of OLS to estimate the slope parameters, and the second step involves the use of maximum likelihood to estimate the intercept and the variances of the two error components. Thus distributional assumptions are used in the maximum likelihood method and in the second step of the two-step procedure. Finally, to estimate the technical efficiency of each producer, distributional assumptions are required.

The Normal–Half Normal Model Consider the stochastic production frontier model given in equation (3.2.18). We make the following distributional assumptions:

(i) $v_i \sim$ iid $N(0, \sigma_v^2)$.

(ii) $u_i \sim$ iid $N^+(0, \sigma_u^2)$, that is, as nonnegative half normal.

(iii) v_i and u_i are distributed independently of each other, and of the regressors.

Assumption (i) is conventional, and is maintained throughout. Assumption (ii) is based on the plausible proposition that the modal value of technical inefficiency is zero, with increasing values of technical inefficiency becoming increasingly less likely. It is also based on tractability, since it is relatively easy to derive the distribution of the sum of v and u under distributional assumptions (i) and (ii). The first part of assumption (iii) seems innocuous, but the second part is more problematical, since if producers know something about their technical efficiency, this may influence their choice of inputs. We will reconsider this assumption in Section 3.3.

The density function of $u \geq 0$ is given in equation (3.2.12) and illustrated in Figure 3.2. The density function of v is

$$f(v) = \frac{1}{\sqrt{2\pi}\sigma_v} \cdot \exp\left\{-\frac{v^2}{2\sigma_v^2}\right\}. \tag{3.2.20}$$

Given the independence assumption, the joint density function of u and v is the product of their individual density functions, and so

$$f(u,v) = \frac{2}{2\pi\sigma_u\sigma_v} \cdot \exp\left\{-\frac{u^2}{2\sigma_u^2} - \frac{v^2}{2\sigma_v^2}\right\}. \tag{3.2.21}$$

Since $\varepsilon = v - u$, the joint density function for u and ε is

$$f(u,\varepsilon) = \frac{2}{2\pi\sigma_u\sigma_v} \cdot \exp\left\{-\frac{u^2}{2\sigma_u^2} - \frac{(\varepsilon+u)^2}{2\sigma_v^2}\right\}. \tag{3.2.22}$$

The marginal density function of ε is obtained by integrating u out of $f(u,\varepsilon)$, which yields

$$\begin{aligned} f(\varepsilon) &= \int_0^\infty f(u,\varepsilon)\, du \\ &= \frac{2}{\sqrt{2\pi}\sigma} \cdot \left[1 - \Phi\left(\frac{\varepsilon\lambda}{\sigma}\right)\right] \cdot \exp\left\{-\frac{\varepsilon^2}{2\sigma^2}\right\} \\ &= \frac{2}{\sigma} \cdot \phi\left(\frac{\varepsilon}{\sigma}\right) \cdot \Phi\left(-\frac{\varepsilon\lambda}{\sigma}\right), \end{aligned} \tag{3.2.23}$$

where $\sigma = (\sigma_u^2 + \sigma_v^2)^{1/2}$, $\lambda = \sigma_u/\sigma_v$, and $\Phi(\cdot)$ and $\phi(\cdot)$ are the standard normal cumulative distribution and density functions. The reparameterization from σ_u^2 and σ_v^2 to σ and λ is convenient, since λ provides an indication of the relative contributions of u and v to ε. As $\lambda \to 0$ either $\sigma_v^2 \to +\infty$ or $\sigma_u^2 \to 0$, and the symmetric error component dominates the one-sided error component in the determination of ε. As $\lambda \to +\infty$ either $\sigma_u^2 \to +\infty$ or $\sigma_v^2 \to 0$, and the one-sided error component dominates the symmetric error component in the determination of ε. In the former case we are back to an OLS pro-

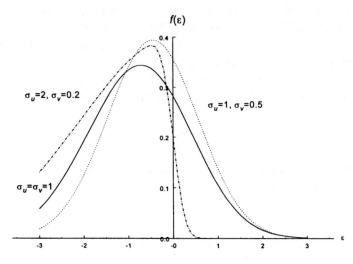

Figure 3.3 Normal–Half Normal Distributions

duction function model with no technical inefficiency, whereas in the latter case we are back to a deterministic production frontier model with no noise.

The normal–half normal distribution contains two parameters, σ_u and σ_v (or σ and λ). Figure 3.3 shows three different normal–half normal distributions corresponding to three combinations of σ_u and σ_v. All three distributions are negatively skewed, with negative modes (and means), since $\sigma_u > 0$ in each case.

The distribution parameters σ and λ are estimated along with the technology parameters β, and it is desirable to conduct a statistical test of the hypothesis that $\lambda = 0$, where the test is based on the maximum likelihood estimate of λ. There is no difficulty in computing a Wald test statistic or conducting a likelihood ratio test, but since the hypothesized value of λ lies on the boundary of the parameter space, it is difficult to interpret the test statistic. However Coelli (1995) has shown that in this case the appropriate one-sided likelihood ratio test statistic is asymptotically distributed as a mixture of χ^2 distributions rather than as a single χ^2 distribution.

The marginal density function $f(\varepsilon)$ is asymmetrically distributed, with mean and variance

$$E(\varepsilon) = -E(u) = -\sigma_u \sqrt{\frac{2}{\pi}},$$

$$V(\varepsilon) = \frac{\pi - 2}{\pi} \sigma_u^2 + \sigma_v^2. \tag{3.2.24}$$

ALS suggested $[1 - E(u)]$ as an estimator of the mean technical efficiency of all producers. However Lee and Tyler (1978) proposed

$$E(\exp\{-u\}) = 2[1 - \Phi(\sigma_u)] \cdot \exp\left\{\frac{\sigma_u^2}{2}\right\}, \tag{3.2.25}$$

which is preferred to $[1 - E(u)]$ since $[1 - u]$ includes only the first term in the power series expansion of $\exp\{-u\}$. Also, unlike $[1 - E(u)]$, $E(\exp\{-u\})$ is consistent with the definition of technical efficiency given in equation (3.2.4).

Using equation (3.2.23), the log likelihood function for a sample of I producers is

$$\ln L = \text{constant} - I \ln \sigma + \sum_i \ln \Phi\left(-\frac{\varepsilon_i \lambda}{\sigma}\right) - \frac{1}{2\sigma^2} \sum_i \varepsilon_i^2. \tag{3.2.26}$$

The log likelihood function in equation (3.2.26) can be maximized with respect to the parameters to obtain maximum likelihood estimates of all parameters. These estimates are consistent as $I \to +\infty$.

The next step is to obtain estimates of the technical efficiency of each producer. We have estimates of $\varepsilon_i = v_i - u_i$, which obviously contain information on u_i. If $\varepsilon_i > 0$, chances are that u_i is not large [since $E(v_i) = 0$], which suggests that this producer is relatively efficient, whereas if $\varepsilon_i < 0$, chances are that u_i is large, which suggests that this producer is relatively inefficient. The problem is to extract the information that ε_i contains on u_i. A solution to the problem is obtained from the conditional distribution of u_i given ε_i, which contains whatever information ε_i contains concerning u_i. Jondrow et al. (JLMS) (1982) showed that if $u_i \sim N^+(0, \sigma_u^2)$, the conditional distribution of u given ε is

$$f(u|\varepsilon) = \frac{f(u, \varepsilon)}{f(\varepsilon)}$$

$$= \frac{1}{\sqrt{2\pi}\sigma_*} \cdot \exp\left\{-\frac{(u - \mu_*)^2}{2\sigma_*^2}\right\} \Big/ \left[1 - \Phi\left(-\frac{\mu_*}{\sigma_*}\right)\right], \tag{3.2.27}$$

where $\mu_* = -\varepsilon\sigma_u^2/\sigma^2$ and $\sigma_*^2 = \sigma_u^2 \sigma_v^2/\sigma^2$. Since $f(u|\varepsilon)$ is distributed as $N^+(\mu_*,\sigma_*^2)$, either the mean or the mode of this distribution can serve as a point estimator for u_i. They are given by

$$E(u_i|\varepsilon_i) = \mu_{*_i} + \sigma_* \left[\frac{\phi(-\mu_{*_i}/\sigma_*)}{1 - \Phi(-\mu_{*_i}/\sigma_*)} \right]$$

$$= \sigma_* \left[\frac{\phi(\varepsilon_i\lambda/\sigma)}{1 - \Phi(\varepsilon_i\lambda/\sigma)} - \left(\frac{\varepsilon_i\lambda}{\sigma} \right) \right] \qquad (3.2.28)$$

and

$$M(u_i|\varepsilon_i) = \begin{cases} -\varepsilon_i\left(\dfrac{\sigma_u^2}{\sigma^2}\right) & \text{if } \varepsilon_i \leq 0, \\ 0 & \text{otherwise,} \end{cases} \qquad (3.2.29)$$

respectively. $E(u_i|\varepsilon_i)$ is used more frequently than $M(u_i|\varepsilon_i)$, despite the fact that $M(u_i|\varepsilon_i)$ has an appealing interpretation as a maximum likelihood estimator. Materov (1981) showed that $M(u_i|\varepsilon_i)$ can be derived by maximizing the joint density of u_i and v_i given in equation (3.2.21) with respect to u_i and v_i, subject to the constraint that $v_i - u_i = \varepsilon_i$.

Once point estimates of u_i are obtained, estimates of the technical efficiency of each producer can be obtained from

$$TE_i = \exp\{-\hat{u}_i\}, \qquad (3.2.30)$$

where $\hat{u}_i$ is either $E(u_i|\varepsilon_i)$ or $M(u_i|\varepsilon_i)$.

Battese and Coelli (1988) proposed the alternative point estimator for TE_i:

$$TE_i = E(\exp\{-u_i\}|\varepsilon_i) = \left[\frac{1 - \Phi(\sigma_* - \mu_{*_i}/\sigma_*)}{1 - \Phi(-\mu_{*_i}/\sigma_*)} \right] \cdot \exp\left\{ -\mu_{*_i} + \frac{1}{2}\sigma_*^2 \right\}. \qquad (3.2.31)$$

The point estimators given in equations (3.2.30) [using $E(u_i|\varepsilon_i)$] and (3.2.31) can give different results, since $\exp\{-E(u_i|\varepsilon_i)\} \neq E[\exp\{-u_i\}|\varepsilon_i]$. The estimator in equation (3.2.31) is preferred, particularly when u_i is not close to zero, for reasons given beneath equation (3.2.25). Regardless of which estimator is used, however, the estimates of technical efficiency are inconsistent because the variation associated with the distribution of $(u_i|\varepsilon_i)$ is independent of i. Unfortunately this appears to be the best that can be achieved with cross-sectional data.

It is possible to obtain confidence intervals for the point estimates of technical efficiency, by exploiting the fact that the density of $(u_i|\varepsilon_i)$ is known to be that of an $N^+(\mu_*, \sigma_*^2)$. Horrace and Schmidt (1995, 1996) have derived upper and lower bounds on $(u_i|\varepsilon_i)$, which imply lower and upper bounds on $(\exp\{-u_i\}|\varepsilon_i)$. A $(1 - \alpha)100\%$ confidence interval (L_i, U_i) for $(\exp\{-u_i\}|\varepsilon_i)$ is provided by

$$L_i = \exp\{-\mu_{*i} - z_L \sigma_*\},$$
$$U_i = \exp\{-\mu_{*i} - z_U \sigma_*\}, \tag{3.2.32}$$

where

$$Pr(Z > z_L) = \frac{\alpha}{2}\left[1 - \Phi\left(-\frac{\mu_{*i}}{\sigma_*}\right)\right],$$

$$Pr(Z > z_U) = \left(1 - \frac{\alpha}{2}\right)\left[1 - \Phi\left(-\frac{\mu_{*i}}{\sigma_*}\right)\right], \tag{3.2.33}$$

and Z is distributed as $N(0, 1)$. Consequently

$$z_L = \Phi^{-1}\left\{\left[1 - \frac{\alpha}{2}\right]\left[1 - \Phi\left(-\frac{\mu_{*i}}{\sigma_*}\right)\right]\right\},$$

$$z_U = \Phi^{-1}\left\{\left[1 - \left(1 - \frac{\alpha}{2}\right)\right]\left[1 - \Phi\left(-\frac{\mu_{*i}}{\sigma_*}\right)\right]\right\}. \tag{3.2.34}$$

Bera and Sharma (1996) and Hjalmarsson, Kumbhakar, and Heshmati (1996) also obtained confidence intervals for the JLMS point estimator $E(u_i|\varepsilon_i)$, and Bera and Sharma obtained confidence intervals for the Battese and Coelli point estimator $E(\exp\{-u_i\}|\varepsilon_i)$. Kumbhakar and Löthgren (1998) conducted a Monte Carlo study of the performance of the JLMS point estimator and the subsequent interval predictors when the true values of the underlying parameters are unknown, and must be replaced by their ML estimates. They found negative bias in the estimated inefficiencies, and a mean empirical coverage accuracy of the confidence intervals to be significantly below the corresponding theoretical confidence levels for all values of λ and for sample sizes less than 200.

Thus far we have based our analysis of stochastic production frontiers on the assumption that $u \sim N^+(0, \sigma_u^2)$. This distributional assumption is both plausible and tractable, and so it is typically employed in empirical work. It can even be tested. Lee (1983) tested the half normal distributional assumption against a Pearson family of distributions, and Bera and Mallick (1998) developed a specification test for the half normal distributional assumption, based on White's (1982) information matrix test. However other distributional assumptions on the one-sided error component u have been proposed, and they have also been employed, albeit less frequently, in empirical work. ALS and MB each suggested the exponential distribution for u, to which we now turn.

The Normal–Exponential Model We return to the stochastic production frontier model given in equation (3.2.18), but we now make the distributional assumptions:

(i) $v_i \sim$ iid $N(0, \sigma_v^2)$.

(ii) $u_i \sim$ iid exponential.

(iii) u_i and v_i are distributed independently of each other, and of the regressors.

The remarks we made concerning the distributional assumptions underlying the normal–half normal model apply with equal force to the normal–exponential model.

The density functions for u_i and v_i are given in equations (3.2.10) and (3.2.20), and various densities for u_i appear in Figure 3.1. As a consequence of the independence assumption, the joint density function of u and v is the product of their individual density functions, and so

$$f(u,v) = \frac{1}{\sqrt{2\pi}\,\sigma_u\sigma_v} \cdot \exp\left\{ -\frac{u}{\sigma_u} - \frac{v^2}{2\sigma_v^2} \right\}. \tag{3.2.35}$$

The joint density function of u and ε is

$$f(u,\varepsilon) = \frac{1}{\sqrt{2\pi}\,\sigma_u\sigma_v} \cdot \exp\left\{ -\frac{u}{\sigma_u} - \frac{1}{2\sigma_v^2}(u+\varepsilon)^2 \right\}. \tag{3.2.36}$$

Thus the marginal density function of ε is

$$f(\varepsilon) = \int_0^\infty f(u,\varepsilon)\, du = \left(\frac{1}{\sigma_u}\right) \cdot \Phi\left(-\frac{\varepsilon}{\sigma_v} - \frac{\sigma_v}{\sigma_u} \right) \cdot \exp\left\{ \frac{\varepsilon}{\sigma_u} + \frac{\sigma_v^2}{2\sigma_u^2} \right\} \tag{3.2.37}$$

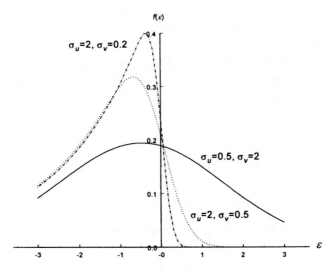

Figure 3.4 Normal–Exponential Distributions

where again $\Phi(\cdot)$ is the standard normal cumulative distribution function. The marginal density function $f(\varepsilon)$ is asymmetrically distributed, with mean and variance

$$E(\varepsilon) = -E(u) = -\sigma_u,$$

$$V(\varepsilon) = \sigma_u^2 + \sigma_v^2. \tag{3.2.38}$$

The shape of the normal–exponential distribution is determined by the standard deviation parameters σ_u and σ_v. Three such distributions are depicted in Figure 3.4. All three are negatively skewed, with negative mode (and mean). As σ_u/σ_v increases, the distribution looks more and more like a negative exponential distribution, whereas as σ_v/σ_u increases, the distribution looks more and more like a normal distribution.

The log likelihood function for a sample of I producers can be written as

$$\ln L = \text{constant} - I \ln \sigma_u + I \left(\frac{\sigma_v^2}{2\sigma_u^2} \right) + \sum_i \ln \Phi(-A) + \sum_i \frac{\varepsilon_i}{\sigma_u}, \tag{3.2.39}$$

where $A = -\tilde{\mu}/\sigma_v$ and $\tilde{\mu} = -\varepsilon - (\sigma_v^2/\sigma_u)$. $\ln L$ can be maximized with respect to the parameters to obtain maximum likelihood estimates of all parameters.

As in the normal–half normal case, point estimates of technical efficiency can be obtained from either the mean or the mode of the conditional distribution of u given ε. The conditional distribution $f(u|\varepsilon)$ is given by

$$f(u|\varepsilon) = \frac{f(u,\varepsilon)}{f(\varepsilon)}$$

$$= \frac{1}{\sqrt{2\pi}\,\sigma_v\,\Phi(-\tilde{\mu}/\sigma_v)} \cdot \exp\left\{-\frac{(u-\tilde{\mu})^2}{2\sigma^2}\right\}. \tag{3.2.40}$$

$f(u|\varepsilon)$ is distributed as $N^+(\tilde{\mu}, \sigma_v^2)$, with mean

$$E(u_i|\varepsilon_i) = \tilde{\mu}_i + \sigma_v\left[\frac{\phi(-\tilde{\mu}_i/\sigma_v)}{\Phi(\tilde{\mu}_i/\sigma_v)}\right]$$

$$= \sigma_v\left[\frac{\phi(A)}{\Phi(-A)} - A\right], \tag{3.2.41}$$

where again $\phi(\cdot)$ and $\Phi(\cdot)$ are the standard normal density and cumulative distribution functions, and mode

$$M(u_i|\varepsilon_i) = \begin{cases} \tilde{\mu}_i & \text{if } \tilde{\mu}_i \geq 0, \\ 0 & \text{otherwise.} \end{cases} \tag{3.2.42}$$

As in the normal–half normal case, either $E(u_i|\varepsilon_i)$ or $M(u_i|\varepsilon_i)$ can be used to provide producer-specific estimates of technical efficiency, by substituting into equation (3.2.30) or equation (3.2.31). These estimates are unbiased, but not consistent. Confidence intervals can be constructed for the point estimates of technical efficiency, just as in the normal–half normal case. The only difference is that $(u_i|\varepsilon_i)$ has a different density in the normal–exponential case than in the normal–half normal case.

The Normal–Truncated Normal Model The normal–half normal model can be generalized by allowing u to follow a truncated normal distribution. The normal–truncated normal formulation was introduced by Stevenson (1980). In this formulation we make the distributional assumptions:

(i) $v_i \sim$ iid $N(0, \sigma_v^2)$.

(ii) $u_i \sim$ iid $N^+(\mu, \sigma_u^2)$.

(iii) u_i and v_i are distributed independently of each other, and of the regressors.

The remarks we made previously concerning distributional assumptions apply here with one exception. The truncated normal distribution assumed for u generalizes the one-parameter half normal distribution, by allowing the normal distribution, which is truncated below at zero, to have a nonzero mode. Thus the truncated normal distribution contains an additional parameter μ to be estimated (its mode), and so provides a somewhat more flexible representation of the pattern of efficiency in the data.

The density function $f(v)$ is given in equation (3.2.20). The truncated normal density function for $u \geq 0$ is given by

$$f(u) = \frac{1}{\sqrt{2\pi}\sigma_u \, \Phi(\mu/\sigma_u)} \cdot \exp\left\{-\frac{(u-\mu)^2}{2\sigma_u^2}\right\}, \tag{3.2.43}$$

where μ is the mode of the normal distribution, which is truncated below at zero, and $\Phi(\cdot)$ is the standard normal cumulative distribution function. Thus $f(u)$ is the density of a normally distributed variable with possibly nonzero mean μ, truncated below at zero. If $\mu = 0$ the density function in equation (3.2.43) collapses to the half normal density function given in equation (3.2.12).

In contrast to the normal distribution, the truncated normal distribution is a two-parameter distribution depending on placement and spread parameters μ and σ_u. Three such distributions are depicted in Figure 3.5, with σ_u set to unity and μ allowed to be negative, zero, and positive.

The joint density function of u and v is the product of their individual density functions, and so

$$f(u,v) = \frac{1}{2\pi\sigma_u\sigma_v\Phi(\mu/\sigma_u)} \cdot \exp\left\{-\frac{(u-\mu)^2}{2\sigma_u^2} - \frac{v^2}{2\sigma_v^2}\right\}. \tag{3.2.44}$$

The joint density of u and ε is

$$f(u,\varepsilon) = \frac{1}{2\pi\sigma_u\sigma_v\Phi(\mu/\sigma_u)} \cdot \exp\left\{-\frac{(u-\mu)^2}{2\sigma_u^2} - \frac{(\varepsilon+u)^2}{2\sigma_v^2}\right\}. \tag{3.2.45}$$

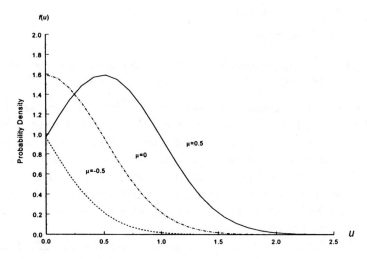

Figure 3.5 Truncated Normal Distributions

The marginal density of ε is

$$f(\varepsilon) = \int_0^\infty f(u, \varepsilon)\, du$$

$$= \frac{1}{\sqrt{2\pi}\,\sigma\Phi(\mu/\sigma_u)} \cdot \Phi\left(\frac{\mu}{\sigma\lambda} - \frac{\varepsilon\lambda}{\sigma}\right) \cdot \exp\left\{-\frac{(\varepsilon + \mu)^2}{2\sigma^2}\right\}$$

$$= \frac{1}{\sigma} \cdot \phi\left(\frac{\varepsilon + \mu}{\sigma}\right) \cdot \Phi\left(\frac{\mu}{\sigma\lambda} - \frac{\varepsilon\lambda}{\sigma}\right) \cdot \left[\Phi\left(\frac{\mu}{\sigma_u}\right)\right]^{-1}, \qquad (3.2.46)$$

where $\sigma = (\sigma_u^2 + \sigma_v^2)^{1/2}$ and $\lambda = \sigma_u/\sigma_v$ as in the normal–half normal model, and $\phi(\cdot)$ is the standard normal density function. If $\mu = 0$ equation (3.2.46) collapses to the half normal marginal density function (3.2.23).

$f(\varepsilon)$ is asymmetrically distributed, with mean and variance

$$E(\varepsilon) = -E(u) = -\frac{\mu a}{2} - \frac{\sigma_u a}{\sqrt{2\pi}} \cdot \exp\left\{-\frac{1}{2}\left(\frac{\mu}{\sigma_u}\right)^2\right\},$$

$$V(\varepsilon) = \mu^2 \frac{a}{2}\left(1 - \frac{a}{2}\right) + \frac{a}{2}\left(\frac{\pi - a}{\pi}\right)\sigma_u^2 + \sigma_v^2, \qquad (3.2.47)$$

respectively, where $a = [\Phi(\mu/\sigma_u)]^{-1}$.

The normal–truncated normal distribution has three parameters, a placement parameter μ and two spread parameters σ_u and σ_v. Three such distributions are depicted in Figure 3.6, in which $\sigma_u = \sigma_v = 1$ and

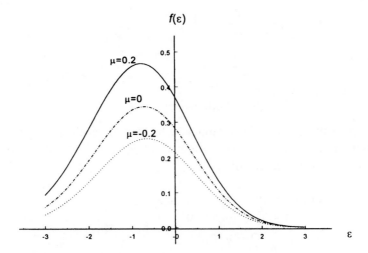

$f(\varepsilon)$

Figure 3.6 Normal–Truncated Normal Distributions

μ is allowed to be negative, zero, and positive. All three distributions are negatively skewed, with negative mode (and mean).

The log likelihood function for a sample of I producers is

$$\ln L = \text{constant} - I \ln\sigma - I \ln\Phi\left(\frac{\mu}{\sigma_u}\right)$$

$$+ \sum_i \ln\Phi\left(\frac{\mu}{\sigma\lambda} - \frac{\varepsilon_i\lambda}{\sigma}\right) - \frac{1}{2}\sum_i \left(\frac{\varepsilon_i + \mu}{\sigma}\right)^2, \qquad (3.2.48)$$

where $\sigma_u = \lambda\sigma/\sqrt{1+\lambda^2}$. The log likelihood function can be maximized with respect to the parameters to obtain maximum likelihood estimates of all of the parameters.

The conditional distribution $f(u|\varepsilon)$ is given by

$$f(u|\varepsilon) = \frac{f(u,\varepsilon)}{f(\varepsilon)}$$

$$= \frac{1}{\sqrt{2\pi}\sigma_* [1 - \Phi(-\tilde{\mu}/\sigma_*)]} \cdot \exp\left\{-\frac{(u-\tilde{\mu})^2}{2\sigma_*^2}\right\}. \qquad (3.2.49)$$

$f(u|\varepsilon)$ is distributed as $N^+(\tilde{\mu}_i, \sigma_*^2)$, where $\tilde{\mu}_i = (-\sigma_u^2\varepsilon_i + \mu\sigma_v^2)/\sigma^2$ and $\sigma_*^2 = \sigma_u^2\sigma_v^2/\sigma^2$. Thus either the mean or the mode of $f(u|\varepsilon)$ can be used to estimate the technical efficiency of each producer, and we have

$$E(u_i|\varepsilon_i) = \sigma_* \left[\frac{\tilde{\mu}_i}{\sigma_*} + \frac{\phi(\tilde{\mu}_i/\sigma_*)}{1 - \Phi(-\tilde{\mu}_i/\sigma_*)} \right] \tag{3.2.50}$$

and

$$M(u_i|\varepsilon_i) = \begin{cases} \tilde{\mu}_i & \text{if } \tilde{\mu}_i \ge 0, \\ 0 & \text{otherwise.} \end{cases} \tag{3.2.51}$$

Point estimates of the technical efficiency of each producer can be obtained by substituting either $E(u_i|\varepsilon_i)$ or $M(u_i|\varepsilon_i)$ into equation (3.2.31), or by means of

$$\begin{aligned} TE_i &= E(\exp\{-u_i\}|\varepsilon_i) \\ &= \frac{1 - \Phi[\sigma_* - (\tilde{\mu}_i/\sigma_*)]}{1 - \Phi(-\tilde{\mu}_i/\sigma_*)} \cdot \exp\left\{ -\tilde{\mu}_i + \frac{1}{2}\sigma_*^2 \right\}, \end{aligned} \tag{3.2.52}$$

which collapses to equation (3.2.31) when $\mu = 0$. The use of either equation (3.2.31) or equation (3.2.52) produces unbiased but inconsistent estimates of technical efficiency. Confidence intervals for any of these point estimates can be obtained by modifying the procedure outlined in equations (3.2.32)–(3.2.34), taking into account the fact that $(u|\varepsilon)$ has a different density in the truncated normal case than in the half normal case.

The Normal–Gamma Model Just as the normal–half normal model can be generalized by assuming that u follows a truncated normal distribution, the normal–exponential model also can be generalized by assuming that u follows a gamma distribution. The normal gamma formulation was introduced by Greene (1980a, b) and Stevenson (1980), and extended by Greene (1990). We now make the distributional assumptions:

    (i) $v_i \sim$ iid $N(0, \sigma_v^2)$.

    (ii) $u_i \sim$ iid gamma.

    (iii) u_i and v_i are distributed independently of each other, and of the regressors.

Previous remarks concerning distributional assumptions apply here as well, with one exception. The gamma distribution assumed for u generalizes the one-parameter exponential distribution by introducing an additional parameter to be estimated, and so provides a more

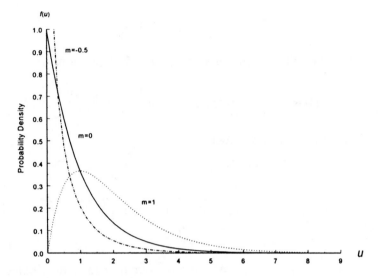

Figure 3.7 Gamma Distributions

flexible representation of the pattern of technical efficiency in the data.

The density function $f(v)$ is given in equation (3.2.20). The gamma density function $f(u)$ for $u \geq 0$ is

$$f(u) = \frac{u^m}{\Gamma(m+1)\sigma_u^{m+1}} \cdot \exp\left\{-\frac{u}{\sigma_u}\right\}, \qquad m > -1. \qquad (3.2.53)$$

When $m = 0$ the gamma density function becomes the density function of the exponential distribution given in equation (3.2.10). For $-1 < m < 0$ the gamma density has the shape of an exponential density, and so the mass of the density remains concentrated near zero. For $m > 0$ the density is concentrated at a point farther away from zero as m increases.

The gamma distribution is a two-parameter distribution, depending on m and σ_u. Three such distributions are depicted in Figure 3.7. Each assumes that $\sigma_u = 1$, and m is allowed to be negative, zero (the exponential special case), and positive.

In light of the independence assumption, the joint density function of u and v is

$$f(u,v) = \frac{u^m}{\Gamma(m+1)\sigma_u^{m+1}\sqrt{2\pi}\sigma_v} \cdot \exp\left\{-\frac{u}{\sigma_u} - \frac{v^2}{2\sigma_v^2}\right\}, \qquad (3.2.54)$$

and so the joint density function of u and $\varepsilon = v - u$ is

$$f(u,\varepsilon) = \frac{u^m}{\Gamma(m+1)\sigma_u^{m+1}\sqrt{2\pi}\sigma_v} \cdot \exp\left\{-\frac{u}{\sigma_u} - \frac{(\varepsilon+u)^2}{2\sigma_v^2}\right\}. \qquad (3.2.55)$$

The marginal density function of ε is

$$f(\varepsilon) = \int_0^\infty f(u,\varepsilon)\,du$$

$$= \frac{\sigma_v^m}{\Gamma(m+1)\sqrt{2\pi}\sigma_u^{m+1}} \cdot \exp\left\{\frac{\varepsilon}{\sigma_u} + \frac{\sigma_v^2}{2\sigma_u^2}\right\} \cdot \int_w^\infty (t-w)^m \exp\left\{-\frac{t^2}{2}\right\} dt,$$

$$(3.2.56)$$

where $w = (\varepsilon/\sigma_v) + (\sigma_v/\sigma_u)$. $f(\varepsilon)$ is asymmetrically distributed, with mean and variance

$$E(\varepsilon) = -E(u) = -(m+1)\sigma_u,$$
$$V(\varepsilon) = \sigma_v^2 + (m+1)\sigma_u^2. \qquad (3.2.57)$$

This marginal density function contains an integral term that poses some problems in estimation. Stevenson showed that equation (3.2.56) collapses to the normal–exponential density given in equation (3.2.37) when $m = 0$, and he also derived closed-form expressions for the normal–gamma density given in equation (3.2.56) for $m = 1$ and $m = 2$. However these integer values of m restrict the gamma distribution to the Erlang form. Beckers and Hammond (1987) obtained a closed-form expression for equation (3.2.56) that does not restrict m to integer values. They showed that $f(\varepsilon)$ can be written as

$$f(\varepsilon) = \frac{1}{\Gamma(m+1)\sqrt{2\pi}\sigma_u^{m+1}\sigma_v} \cdot \exp\left\{-\frac{\varepsilon^2}{2\sigma_v^2}\right\}$$

$$\cdot \int_0^\infty u^m \exp\left\{-\frac{u}{\sigma_u} - \frac{u\varepsilon}{\sigma_v^2} - \frac{u^2}{2\sigma_v^2}\right\} du, \qquad (3.2.58)$$

where the integral

$$\int_0^\infty u^m \exp\left\{-\left(\frac{1}{\sigma_u} + \frac{\varepsilon}{\sigma_v^2}\right)u - \frac{u^2}{2\sigma_v^2}\right\} du = J(m,\sigma_u,\sigma_v,\varepsilon)$$

does have a known closed-form expression. The log likelihood function corresponding to $f(\varepsilon)$ can be written as

$$\ln L = \text{constant} - I \ln \Gamma(m+1) - (m+1)I \ln \sigma_u$$

$$-I \ln \sigma_v - \frac{1}{2\sigma_v^2} \sum_i \varepsilon_i^2 + \sum_i \ln J_i(m, \sigma_u, \sigma_v, \varepsilon)$$

$$= \text{constant} - I \ln \Gamma(m+1) - (m+1)I \ln \sigma_u + I\left(\frac{\sigma_v^2}{2\sigma_u^2}\right)$$

$$+ \sum_i \frac{\varepsilon_i}{\sigma_u} + \sum_i \ln \Phi\left[-\frac{(\varepsilon_i + \sigma_v^2/\sigma_u)}{\sigma_v}\right] + \sum_i \ln h(m, \varepsilon_i),$$

$$(3.2.59)$$

where $h(m, \varepsilon_i) = E[z^m | z > 0, \varepsilon_i]$ and $z \approx N[-(\varepsilon_i + \sigma_v^2/\sigma_u), \sigma_v^2]$. When $m = 0$ the gamma log likelihood function collapses to the exponential log likelihood function given in equation (3.2.39). Greene (1990) provides the derivatives of this function with respect to the parameters, which can be solved to obtain maximum likelihood estimates of all parameters.

In order to obtain estimates of the technical efficiency of each producer, we need the conditional distribution $f(u|\varepsilon)$. This is given by

$$f(u|\varepsilon) = \frac{f(u, \varepsilon)}{f(\varepsilon)}$$

$$= \frac{u^m \cdot \exp\left\{-\frac{u}{\sigma_u} - \frac{\varepsilon u}{\sigma_v^2} - \frac{u^2}{2\sigma_v^2}\right\}}{J(m, \sigma_u, \sigma_v, \varepsilon)}, \qquad (3.2.60)$$

from which it follows that

$$E(u_i | \varepsilon_i) = \frac{h(m+1, \varepsilon_i)}{h(m, \varepsilon_i)}, \qquad (3.2.61)$$

which can be approximated numerically. Greene (1990) discusses approximation techniques and their accuracy.

Ritter and Simar (1997a) paint a fairly pessimistic picture of the empirical value of the normal–gamma specification. They begin by reiterating that in general the log likelihood function must be evaluated numerically and that approximation error can be a serious problem. They also note that there need not exist a maximum of the log likelihood function. Finally, they report that unless the sample size reaches several hundreds of observations the critical shape parameter m of the gamma density is hard to estimate, and this difficulty carries over to estimation of $E(u_i|\varepsilon_i)$. They also argue that this identification problem applies equally to the normal–truncated normal specification with its placement parameter μ. Ritter and Simar (1997b) provide an empirical illustration of the difficulties encountered in attempting to estimate the normal–gamma model.

Do Distributional Assumptions Matter? Sample mean efficiencies are no doubt apt to be sensitive to the distribution assigned to the one-sided error component v. There is plenty of empirical evidence of this sensitivity. What is not so clear is whether a ranking of producers by their individual efficiency scores, or the composition of the top and bottom efficiency score deciles, is sensitive to distributional assumptions. Indeed there is some evidence that neither rankings nor decile compositions are particularly sensitive. We provide one example, based on Greene (1990), who estimated a stochastic cost frontier for a cross section of 123 U.S. electric utilities, using all four of the preceding one-sided densities. He reported sample mean efficiencies of 0.8766 (half normal), 0.9011 (exponential), 0.8961 (truncated normal), and 0.8949 (gamma). We have calculated rank correlation coefficients between pairs of efficiency estimates for all sample observations. The lowest rank correlation coefficient is 0.7467 (somewhat surprisingly between exponential and gamma), and the highest is 0.9803 (half normal and truncated normal). If this strong concordance is generally true, it provides support for Ritter and Simar, who argue for the use of a relatively simple distribution, such as half normal or exponential, rather than a more flexible distribution, such as truncated normal or gamma. It also suggests that the choice between the two one-parameter densities is largely immaterial.

A Method of Moments Approach The estimation strategy developed so far consists of two steps. In the first step the maximum likelihood method is used to estimate all parameters of the model. In the second step, conditional on these maximum likelihood estimates, technical efficiency is estimated for each producer by decomposing the maximum likelihood residual term into a noise component and a technical inefficiency component.

An alternative to the first step would be to break it into two parts. In the first part of the estimation procedure, OLS is used to generate consistent estimates of all parameters describing the structure of the production frontier, apart from the intercept. This part is thus independent of distributional assumptions on either error component. In the second part of the estimation procedure, distributional assumptions are invoked in order to obtain consistent estimates of the intercept and the parameter(s) describing the structure of the two error components. This two-part estimation procedure amounts to the application of MOLS to a stochastic production frontier model. We then repeat the second step, in which the JLMS technique is used to estimate u_i for each producer. This strategy can be applied to each of the four models just discussed. Greene (1993, 1997) discusses the method of moments approach for the normal–exponential and normal–gamma specifications, and Harris (1992) employs a method of moments estimator for the normal–truncated normal model. Here we apply the method of moments approach to the normal–half normal model analyzed by Olson, Schmidt, and Waldman (1980).

We begin by rewriting the stochastic production frontier model given in equation (3.2.4) as

$$\ln y_i = [\beta_o - E(u_i)] + \sum_n \beta_n \ln x_{ni} + v_i - [u_i - E(u_i)]. \tag{3.2.62}$$

We assume that v_i is symmetrically distributed with zero mean and that $u_i \geq 0$. Thus the error term $\{v_i - [u_i - E(u_i)]\}$ has zero mean and constant variance. Consequently in the first part of the estimation procedure OLS can be used to obtain consistent estimates of the β_ns.

The second part of the estimation procedure involves estimation of β_o, σ_u^2, and σ_v^2. Here we need distributional assumptions on the error components v_i and u_i. As usual, we assume that $v_i \sim N(0, \sigma_v^2)$. If u_i follows a half normal distribution, then $E(u_i) = \sqrt{2/\pi}\, \sigma_u$, $V(u_i) = [(\pi - 2)/\pi]\sigma_u^2$, and $E(u_i^3) = -\sqrt{2/\pi}(1 - 4/\pi)\sigma_u^3$. Thus the first two central moments of $\varepsilon_i = v_i - u_i$ are $\mu_2 = \sigma_v^2 + [(\pi - 2)/\pi]\sigma_u^2$ and $\mu_3 = \sqrt{2/\pi}(1 - 4/\pi)\sigma_u^3$. The second and third central moments of $\varepsilon_i = v_i - u_i$ are the same as those of $\varepsilon_i^* = \{v_i - [u_i - E(u_i)]\}$ since $E(u_i)$ is a constant. However it is the second and third central moments m_2 and m_3 of the OLS residuals that are used to estimate σ_u^2 and σ_v^2. These estimates are

$$\hat{\sigma}_u^2 = \left(\frac{m_3}{\sqrt{2/\pi}(1 - 4/\pi)} \right)^{2/3} \tag{3.2.63}$$

and

$$\hat{\sigma}_v^2 = m_2 - \left(1 - \frac{2}{\pi} \right) \hat{\sigma}_u^2, \tag{3.2.64}$$

respectively.

After obtaining an estimate of σ_u^2, we obtain a consistent estimate of β_o from

$$\hat{\beta}_o = [\beta_o - E(\hat{u}_i)] + \sqrt{\frac{2}{\pi}} \, \hat{\sigma}_u$$

$$= \text{OLS intercept} + \sqrt{\frac{2}{\pi}} \, \hat{\sigma}_u. \tag{3.2.65}$$

We now have consistent estimates of all parameters in the model. The final step in the procedure consists of applying the JLMS technique to obtain either $E(u_i|\varepsilon_i)$ or $M(u_i|\varepsilon_i)$. This technique is described previously at equations (3.2.27)–(3.2.31). The confidence interval construction technique described in equations (3.2.32)–(3.2.34) can also be applied to the method of moments approach.

Olson, Schmidt, and Waldman pointed out two potential problems with the method of moments approach. The first is that, although the third central moment μ_3 of the OLS *disturbances* must be negative, it is possible for the third central moment m_3 of the OLS *residuals* to be positive. In this event the implied $\hat{\sigma}_u$ is negative. This provides a useful diagnostic, suggesting that the model is misspecified. If the model is not respecified, for example by changing the functional form or the variables of $f(x; \beta)$, it is natural to set $\hat{\sigma}_u = 0$; this leads to the conclusion that there is no technical inefficiency in the data. The second potential problem arises when m_3 is negative as expected, but sufficiently large to cause $\hat{\sigma}_v^2 < 0$. In this event it is natural to set $\hat{\sigma}_v^2 = 0$, which leads to the conclusion that there is no noise in the data.

The first problem ($\sigma_u < 0$) occurs when the true but unknown $\lambda = \sigma_u/\sigma_v$ is small, whereas the second problem ($\sigma_v^2 < 0$) occurs when λ is large. Based on the results of a Monte Carlo experiment, Olson, Schmidt, and Waldman concluded that the choice of estimator (MLE versus method of moments) depends on the value of λ and the sample size. For sample sizes below 400 and for $\lambda < 3.16$, the method of moments estimator outperforms MLE (in a mean-squared error sense). In a subsequent Monte Carlo study, Coelli (1995) found MLE to outperform method of moments (again in a mean-squared error sense) when λ is large, with the advantage increasing as the sample size increases. We are not aware of similar evidence concerning the relative performance of the method of moments estimator when u is assumed to be distributed as exponential, truncated normal, or gamma.

Although the MOLS procedure generates consistent estimators for all parameters in the model, they are inefficient compared to the maximum likelihood estimators that are based on distributional assumptions, and the procedure is subject to the two problems just mentioned. On the other hand, the MOLS method uses distributional assumptions only in the second step, and so the first-step estimators are robust to distributional assumptions on v_i and u_i.

3.2.3 Stochastic Distance Functions

It is possible to adapt the techniques developed for the estimation of a stochastic production frontier in the single-output case to the estimation of a stochastic output distance function in the multiple-output case. The two main complications are that there is no natural choice for a dependent variable in the multiple-output case, and endogeneity of regressors is apt to pose a problem. Nonetheless a wide range of possibilities exists. Once these issues are resolved, estimation of a stochastic distance function proceeds essentially as described before in the single-output case.

In the single-output case we have written a stochastic production frontier as

$$y_i = f(x_i;\beta)\cdot\exp\{v_i - u_i\}, \tag{3.2.66}$$

which can be rewritten as

$$\frac{y_i}{f(x_i;\beta)} = \exp\{v_i - u_i\}. \tag{3.2.67}$$

We know from Chapter 2 that in the single-output case $y_i/f(x_i; \beta) = D_o(x_i, y_i; \beta)$. Consequently the multiple-output version of equation (3.2.67) is

$$D_o(x_i, y_i; \beta) = \exp\{v_i - u_i\},\qquad(3.2.68)$$

which can be rewritten as a stochastic distance function model

$$1 = D_o(x_i, y_i; \beta)\cdot\exp\{u_i - v_i\},\qquad(3.2.69)$$

since the random-noise error component v_i is distributed symmetrically around zero. Since $D_o(x_i, y_i; \beta) \leq 1$, $\exp\{u_i - v_i\} \geq 1$, and $E(u_i|u_i - v_i) \geq 0$ provides a reciprocal measure of output-oriented technical efficiency.

The next task is to convert equation (3.2.69) into an estimable regression model. This can be accomplished by exploiting property D_o3 of output distance functions, which states that $D_o(x_i, \lambda y_i; \beta) = \lambda D_o(x_i, y_i; \beta)$, $\lambda > 0$. Setting $\lambda = |y_i|^{-1} = (\Sigma_m y_{mi}^2)^{-1/2}$, the reciprocal of the Euclidean norm of the output vector, generates $D_o(x_i, y_i/|y_i|; \beta) = |y_i|^{-1}\cdot D_o(x_i, y_i; \beta)$, which leads to $D_o(x_i, y_i; \beta) = |y_i|\cdot D_o(x_i, y_i/|y_i|; \beta)$. Substituting this last inequality into equation (3.2.69) and dividing both sides by $|y_i|$ generates an estimable composed error regression model

$$|y_i|^{-1} = D_o\left(x_i, \frac{y_i}{|y_i|}; \beta\right)\cdot\exp\{u_i - v_i\}.\qquad(3.2.70)$$

The dependent variable in this regression model is the reciprocal of the norm of the output vector; the regressors are the inputs (as in a single-output production frontier model) and the normalized outputs. The symmetric error component v_i is assumed to capture the effects of random noise; the one-sided error component u_i is nonnegative, and provides the basis for a reciprocal measure of output-oriented technical efficiency. The entire analysis of Section 3.2.2 can be applied to equation (3.2.70), with a simple change of sign from $+u_i$ to $-u_i$, and with an appropriately flexible functional form selected for $D_o(x_i, y_i/|y_i|; \beta)$. [Cobb–Douglas is not appropriate, since it has the wrong curvature in $(y_i/|y_i|)$ space.] It is possible to select alternative normalizing variables; for example, Coelli and Perelman (1996), Fuentes, Grifell-Tatjé, and Perelman (1997), Morrison and Johnston (1997), and Reinhard and Thijssen (1997) all use y_{mi}^{-1}. We have chosen $|y_i|^{-1}$ because it is neutral with respect to outputs.

A potentially serious problem with the estimation of stochastic distance functions is that the outputs appearing as regressors in equation (3.2.69), or the normalized outputs appearing as regressors in equation (3.2.70), may not be exogenous. Hetemaki (1996) argues that although the outputs in equation (3.2.69) may not be exogenous, the normalized outputs $y_i/|y_i|$ in equation (3.2.70) may be assumed to be exogenous. The other authors cited previously claim that not even the normalized outputs $y_i/|y_i|$ are likely to be exogenous, since they are just outputs scaled to the unit simplex. They argue that the alternative normalization y_i/y_{mi} creates an output mix vector that is more likely to be exogenous than either y_i or $y_i/|y_i|$. Atkinson, Färe, and Primont (1998) and Atkinson and Primont (1998) also claim that not all regressors in equation (3.2.69) [and presumably therefore in equation (3.2.70) as well] can be exogenous. They use nonlinear three-stage least squares techniques to estimate a system of equations consisting of equation (3.2.69) and a set of shadow price ratio equations obtained from the distance function. However the endogeneity issue is ultimately resolved, the main point is that it is possible to estimate technical efficiency using stochastic (output or input) distance functions. This should put to rest the claim that the presence of multiple outputs requires that a dual economic stochastic frontier be estimated.

3.3 PANEL DATA PRODUCTION FRONTIER MODELS

A panel (repeated observations on each producer) contains more information than does a single cross section. Consequently it is to be expected that access to panel data will either enable some of the strong distributional assumptions used with cross-sectional data to be relaxed or result in estimates of technical efficiency with more desirable statistical properties. Schmidt and Sickles (1984) noted three difficulties with cross-sectional stochastic production frontier models:

(i) Maximum likelihood estimation of the stochastic production frontier model, and the subsequent separation of technical inefficiency from statistical noise, both require strong distributional assumptions on each error component. The robustness of inferences to these assumptions is not well documented, although we made some observations on robustness in the preceding section.

(ii) Maximum likelihood estimation also requires an assumption that the technical inefficiency error component be independent of the regressors, although it is easy to imagine that technical inefficiency might be correlated with the input vectors producers select.

(iii) While the technical efficiency of producers can be estimated using the JLMS technique, it cannot be estimated consistently, since the variance of the conditional mean or the conditional mode of $(u_i|\varepsilon_i)$ for each individual producer does not go to zero as the size of the cross section increases.

Each of these limitations is avoidable if we have access to panel data. First, having access to panel data enables us to adapt conventional panel data estimation techniques to the technical efficiency measurement problem, and not all of these techniques rest on strong distributional assumptions. Repeated observations on a sample of producers can serve as a substitute for strong distributional assumptions. Second, not all panel data estimation techniques require the assumption of independence of the technical inefficiency error component from the regresssors. Repeated observations on a sample of producers can also serve as a substitute for the independence assumption. Finally, since adding more observations on each producer generates information not provided by adding more producers to a cross section, the technical efficiency of each producer in the sample can be estimated consistently as $T \rightarrow +\infty$, T being the number of observations on each producer. Repeated observations on a sample of producers resolves the inconsistency problem with the JLMS technique. This final benefit of having access to panel data can be overstated, however, since many panels are relatively short.

In Section 3.3.1 we consider panel data production frontier models in which technical efficiency is allowed to vary across producers, but is assumed to be constant through time for each producer. In this framework several conventional panel data models can be adapted to the problem of estimating technical efficiency. However the assumption of time invariance of technical efficiency may be considered tenuous, particularly in long panels. Consequently in Section

3.3.2 we consider panel data production frontier models in which technical efficiency is allowed to vary across producers and through time for each producer. These latter models make relatively little use of the conventional panel data literature, and rely primarily on extending maximum likelihood cross-sectional production frontier models to the panel data context.

In order to avoid unnecessary notational complications, we assume throughout this section that the panel is *balanced*, in the sense that each producer is observed T times. *Unbalanced* panels, in which producer i is observed $T_i \leq T$ times, with not all T_i equal, can be accommodated by each of the panel data models we discuss. Details are available in the cited references.

3.3.1 Time-Invariant Technical Efficiency

We begin by assuming that we have observations on I producers, indexed by $i = 1, \ldots, I$, through T time periods, indexed by $t = 1, \ldots, T$. A Cobb–Douglas production frontier with time-invariant technical efficiency can be written as

$$E\left[\ln y_{it}\right] = \beta_0 + \sum_n \beta_n \ln x_{nit} - E\left[u_i\right]$$

$$\ln y_{it} = \beta_o + \sum_n \beta_n \ln x_{nit} + v_{it} - u_i, \tag{3.3.1}$$

where v_{it} represents random statistical noise and $u_i \geq 0$ represents technical inefficiency. Notice that the structure of production technology is assumed to be constant through time; that is, no allowance is made for technical change. This model is structurally similar to the cross-sectional production frontier model given in equation (3.2.18). The only difference is the addition of time subscripts to the output, to the inputs, and to statistical noise. This model is also very similar to a conventional panel data model with producer effects but without time effects. The only difference is that the producer effects are required to be nonnegative, since they represent technical inefficiency. The parameters of the model can be estimated, and technical efficiency can be estimated, in a number of ways.

The Fixed-Effects Model The simplest panel data model is a fixed-effects model. To adapt such a model to the efficiency measurement context, we modify only one assumption. The modification requires that $u_i \geq 0$, and is embodied in equations (3.3.3) and (3.3.4). We assume that the v_{it} are iid $(0, \sigma_v^2)$ and are uncorrelated with the regressors. We make no distributional assumption on the u_i, and we allow the u_i to be correlated with the regressors or with the v_{it}. Since the u_i are treated as fixed (i.e., nonrandom) effects, they become producer-specific intercept parameters to be estimated along with the β_ns. The model can be estimated by applying OLS to

$$\ln y_{it} = \beta_{oi} + \sum_n \beta_n \ln x_{nit} + v_{it}, \tag{3.3.2}$$

where the $\beta_{oi} = (\beta_o - u_i)$ are producer-specific intercepts. Estimation is accomplished in any of three equivalent ways: (i) by suppressing β_o and estimating I producer-specific intercepts; (ii) by retaining β_o and estimating $(I - 1)$ producer-specific intercepts; or (iii) by applying the within transformation, in which all data are expressed in terms of deviations from producer means and the I intercepts are recovered as means of producer residuals. We refer to each variant as least squares with dummy variables, LSDV for short.

After estimation we employ the normalization

$$\hat{\beta}_o = \max_i \{\hat{\beta}_{oi}\}, \tag{3.3.3}$$

and the u_i are estimated from

$$\hat{u}_i = \hat{\beta}_o - \hat{\beta}_{oi}, \tag{3.3.4}$$

which ensures that all $\hat{u}_i \geq 0$. Producer-specific estimates of technical efficiency are then given by

$$TE_i = \exp\{-\hat{u}_i\}. \tag{3.3.5}$$

Thus in the fixed-effects model at least one producer is assumed to be 100% technically efficient, and the technical efficiencies of other producers are measured relative to the technically efficient producer(s). The similarity of the fixed-effects model to the COLS model based on cross-sectional data should be apparent.

The LSDV estimates of the β_ns are consistent as either $I \to +\infty$ or $T \to +\infty$, and the consistency property does not require that the u_i be uncorrelated with the regressors. The LSDV estimates of the β_{oi} are consistent as $T \to +\infty$, although consistency of the LSDV estimates of u_i requires both $I \to +\infty$ and $T \to +\infty$. Neither consistency property requires the assumption that the v_{it} be normally distributed.

Horrace and Schmidt (1995, 1996) have adapted the "multiple comparisons with the best" technique to construct confidence intervals for the $\hat{u}_i$, which can be transformed to confidence intervals for the $TE_i = \exp\{-\hat{u}_i\}$. The procedure is similar to the procedure we outlined previously to construct confidence intervals for maximum likelihood estimators of technical efficiency in a cross-sectional context. A set of $(1 - \alpha)100\%$ simultaneous confidence intervals for $(\hat{u}_1, \ldots, \hat{u}_I)$ is given by

$$P\{[L_i \le \hat{u}_i \le U_i, \ i=1,\ldots,I] \cap [[I] \in \zeta]\} \ge 1 - \alpha, \tag{3.3.6}$$

where

$$\zeta = \left\{ j\colon \beta_{oj} \ge \max_i \beta_{oi} - d \right\},$$

$$L_i = \max\left\{ \min_{j \in \zeta}[\beta_{oj} - \beta_{oi} - d], 0 \right\}, \qquad i = 1, \ldots, I,$$

$$U_i = \max\left\{ \max_{j \ne i}[\beta_{oj} - \beta_{oi} + d], 0 \right\}. \qquad i = 1, \ldots, I,$$

$$d = |T|_{I-1,v,\rho}^{(\alpha)}\, s \left(\frac{2}{T} \right)^{1/2}$$

and $|T|_{I-1,v,\rho}^{(\alpha)} s(2/T)^{1/2}$ is the solution in t for

$$\int_0^\infty \int_{-\infty}^\infty \left\{ \Phi^{I-1}\left[(z\rho^{1/2} + ts)(1-\rho)^{-1/2} \right] \right.$$
$$\left. - \Phi^{I-1}\left[(z\rho^{1/2} - ts)(1-\rho)^{1/2} \right] \right\} d\Phi(z)\, dQ_v(s) = 1 - \alpha.$$

Here s is the square root of the pooled variance estimator, $\rho = 1/2$, and Q_v is the cumulative distribution function of a $\chi_v v^{-1/2}$ random variable. Horrace and Schmidt cite tabled values of $|T|_{I-1,v,\rho}^{(\alpha)} s(2/T)^{1/2}$ for small values of I, and they discuss simulation strategies for large I. In their empirical analysis of three panel data sets, they found confidence intervals around efficiency estimates based on the fixed-effects model to be quite wide, and they attributed this to a combination of estimation error, uncertainty over the identity of the most efficient observation, and the multiplicity (I) of the probability statements.

The fixed-effects model has the virtue of simplicity, and it has nice consistency properties. In particular, and in contrast to the MLE cross-sectional model, the fixed-effects panel data model provides consistent estimates of producer-specific technical efficiency. However the fixed-effects model has a potentially serious drawback. The fixed effects (the u_i) are intended to capture variation across producers in time-invariant technical efficiency. Unfortunately they also capture the effects of *all* phenomena (such as the regulatory environment, for example) that vary across producers but that are time invariant for each producer. This confounding of variation in technical efficiency with variation in other effects occurs whether or not the other effects are included as regressors in the model. This shortcoming motivates interest in another panel data model, to which we now turn.

The Random-Effects Model In the fixed-effects model we assumed that the u_i were fixed, but we allowed them to be correlated with the regressors. We now consider the opposite situation, in which the u_i are randomly distributed with constant mean and variance, but are assumed to be uncorrelated with the regressors and with the v_{it}. We still do not make any distributional assumption on the u_i, although we continue to require that they be nonnegative. As before, we assume that the v_{it} have zero expectation and constant variance. This modification in the assumptions has the virtue of allowing us to include time-invariant regressors in the model.

We rewrite the model given in equation (3.3.1) as

$$\ln y_{it} = [\beta_o - E(u_i)] + \sum_n \beta_n \ln x_{nit} + v_{it} - [u_i - E(u_i)]$$

$$= \beta_o^* + \sum_n \beta_n \ln x_{nit} + v_{it} - u_i^*, \qquad (3.3.7)$$

where the assumption that the u_i are random rather than fixed allows some of the x_{nit} to be time invariant. This random-effects model fits exactly into the one-way error components model in the panel data literature, and can be estimated by the standard two-step generalized least squares (GLS) method. In the first step OLS is used to obtain estimates of all parameters. The two variance components are estimated by any of several methods. In the second step β_o^* and the β_ns are reestimated using feasible GLS. Notice that β_o^* does not depend on i, since $E(u_i)$ is a positive constant, so there is only one intercept term to be estimated.

Once β_o^* and the β_ns have been estimated using feasible GLS, the u_i^* can be estimated from the residuals by means of

$$\hat{u}_i^* = \frac{1}{T}\sum_t \left(\ln y_{it} - \hat{\beta}_o^* - \sum_n \hat{\beta}_n \ln x_{nit} \right). \tag{3.3.8}$$

Estimates of the u_i are obtained by means of the normalization

$$\hat{u}_i = \max_i\{\hat{u}_i^*\} - \hat{u}_i^*. \tag{3.3.9}$$

These estimates are consistent as both $I \to +\infty$ and $T \to +\infty$. Estimates of producer-specific technical efficiency are then obtained by substituting $\hat{u}_i$ into equation (3.3.5), as in the fixed-effects model. Thus consistent estimates of producer-specific technical efficiency can also be obtained using a random-effects panel data model.

An alternative estimator of u_i^* is the best linear unbiased predictor (BLUP). The BLUP of u_i^* is

$$\tilde{u}_i^* = -\left[\frac{\hat{\sigma}_u^2}{T\hat{\sigma}_u^2 + \hat{\sigma}_v^2}\right] \cdot \sum_t \left(\ln y_{it} - \hat{\beta}_o^* - \sum_n \hat{\beta}_n \ln x_{nit} \right), \tag{3.3.10}$$

and the resulting estimator of u_i is

$$\tilde{u}_i = \max_i\{\tilde{u}_i^*\} - \tilde{u}_i^*, \tag{3.3.11}$$

which can also be substituted into equation (3.3.5) to generate producer-specific estimates of technical efficiency. For large T the estimators in (3.3.9) and (3.3.11) are equivalent. Both are consistent as $I \to +\infty$ and $T \to +\infty$. As in the fixed-effects model, both estimators of technical efficiency in the random-effects model require that at least one producer be 100% technically efficient, with the technical efficiencies of the remaining producers being measured relative to the technically efficient producer(s).

GLS is appropriate when I is large, because consistent estimation of σ_u^2 requires $I \to +\infty$, and when the effects are uncorrelated with the regressors, since uncorrelatedness increases efficiency in estimation. Hausman and Taylor (1981) have developed a test of the uncorrelatedness hypothesis; the test is a Hausman (1978) test of the significance of the difference between the fixed-effects estimator and the GLS estimator. They also developed a similar test of the hypothesis that the u_i are uncorrelated with a subset of the regressors. The primary virtue of GLS, however, is that it allows the presence of time-invariant regressors, the impact of which would be confounded with the impact of variation in technical efficiency in the fixed-effects model. However GLS does require that the u_i be uncorrelated with the regressors, whereas the fixed-effects approach does not.

Maximum Likelihood The preceding methods demonstrate that access to panel data enables one to avoid either the strong distributional assumptions or the equally strong independence assumption usually made in the cross-sectional production frontier literature. Nonetheless, if such assumptions are tenable in a panel data context, maximum likelihood estimation is feasible. Maximum likelihood estimation of a stochastic production frontier panel data model with time-invariant technical efficiency is structurally similar to the same procedure applied to cross-sectional data. This technique is widely used in empirical analysis.

We begin by making the following distributional assumptions on the error components in the stochastic production frontier model given by equation (3.3.1):

(i) $v_{it} \sim$ iid $N(0, \sigma_v^2)$.

(ii) $u_i \sim$ iid $N^+ (0, \sigma_u^2)$.

(iii) u_i and v_{it} are distributed independently of each other, and of the regressors.

These distributional assumptions parallel those employed in the normal–half normal model based on cross-sectional data, except that now the noise component varies through time as well as across producers.

Pitt and Lee (1981) used these assumptions to estimate technical efficiency using panel data. The density function of u, which is independent of time, is given in equation (3.2.12). The density function of $\mathbf{v} = (v_1, \ldots, v_T)'$, which is now time dependent, is given by the following generalization of equation (3.2.20), where producer subscripts are suppressed:

$$f(\mathbf{v}) = \frac{1}{(2\pi)^{T/2} \sigma_v^T} \cdot \exp\left\{ \frac{-\mathbf{v}'\mathbf{v}}{2\sigma_v^2} \right\}. \tag{3.3.12}$$

Given the independence assumption, the joint density function of u and $\mathbf{v}$ is

$$f(u,\mathbf{v}) = \frac{2}{(2\pi)^{(T+1)/2} \sigma_u \sigma_v^T} \cdot \exp\left\{-\frac{u^2}{2\sigma_u^2} - \frac{\mathbf{v}'\mathbf{v}}{2\sigma_v^2}\right\}, \tag{3.3.13}$$

and the joint density function of u and $\varepsilon = (v_1 - u, \ldots, v_T - u)'$ is

$$f(u,\varepsilon) = \frac{2}{(2\pi)^{(T+1)/2} \sigma_u \sigma_v^T} \cdot \exp\left\{-\frac{(u-\mu_*)^2}{2\sigma_*^2} - \frac{\varepsilon'\varepsilon}{2\sigma_v^2} + \frac{\mu_*^2}{2\sigma_*^2}\right\}, \tag{3.3.14}$$

where

$$\mu_* = -\frac{T\sigma_u^2 \bar{\varepsilon}}{\sigma_v^2 + T\sigma_u^2}$$

$$\sigma_*^2 = \frac{\sigma_u^2 \sigma_v^2}{\sigma_v^2 + T\sigma_u^2}$$

$$\bar{\varepsilon} = \frac{1}{T}\sum_t \varepsilon_{it}.$$

Thus the marginal density function of ε is

$$f(\varepsilon) = \int_0^\infty f(u,\varepsilon)\,du$$

$$= \frac{2[1-\Phi(-\mu_*/\sigma_*)]}{(2\pi)^{T/2}\sigma_v^{T-1}(\sigma_v^2+T\sigma_u^2)^{1/2}} \cdot \exp\left\{-\frac{\varepsilon'\varepsilon}{2\sigma_v^2} + \frac{\mu_*^2}{2\sigma_*^2}\right\}. \tag{3.3.15}$$

The log likelihood function for a sample of I producers, each observed for T periods of time, is

$$\ln L = \text{constant} - \frac{I(T-1)}{2}\ln\sigma_v^2 - \frac{I}{2}\ln(\sigma_v^2 + T\sigma_u^2)$$

$$+ \sum_i \ln\left[1-\Phi\left(-\frac{\mu_{*i}}{\sigma_*}\right)\right] - \frac{\Sigma_i \varepsilon_i'\varepsilon_i}{2\sigma_v^2} + \frac{1}{2}\sum_i\left(\frac{\mu_{*i}}{\sigma_*}\right)^2. \tag{3.3.16}$$

This log likelihood function can be maximized with respect to the parameters to obtain maximum likelihood estimates of β, σ_v^2, and σ_u^2.

The next step is to obtain estimates of producer-specific time-invariant technical efficiency. We begin by deriving the conditional distribution $(u|\varepsilon)$, which is

$$f(u|\varepsilon) = \frac{f(u,\varepsilon)}{f(\varepsilon)}$$

$$= \frac{1}{(2\pi)^{1/2}\sigma_*[1 - \Phi(-\mu_*/\sigma_*)]} \cdot \exp\left\{-\frac{(u-\mu_*)^2}{2\sigma_*^2}\right\}, \quad (3.3.17)$$

which is the density function of a variable distributed as $N^+(\mu_*, \sigma_*^2)$. Either the mean or the mode of this distribution can be used as a point estimator of technical efficiency, and we have

$$E(u_i|\varepsilon_i) = \mu_{*i} + \sigma_*\left[\frac{\phi(-\mu_{*i}/\sigma_*)}{1 - \Phi(-\mu_{*i}/\sigma_*)}\right] \quad (3.3.18)$$

and

$$M(u_i|\varepsilon_i) = \begin{cases} \mu_{*i} & \text{if } \varepsilon_i \leq 0, \\ 0 & \text{otherwise.} \end{cases} \quad (3.3.19)$$

The estimators of u_i are consistent as $T \to +\infty$. Either can be substituted into equation (3.3.5) to obtain producer-specific estimates of time-invariant technical efficiency. An alternative estimator is provided by the minimum squared error predictor

$$E(\exp\{-u_i\}|\varepsilon_i) = \frac{1 - \Phi[\sigma_* - (u_{*i}/\sigma_*)]}{1 - \Phi(-u_{*i}/\sigma_*)} \cdot \exp\left\{-\mu_{*i} + \frac{1}{2}\sigma_*^2\right\}.$$

$$(3.3.20)$$

Confidence intervals for any of the three estimators can be constructed exactly as in the cross-sectional maximum likelihood model, with the appropriate changes in notation.

Equations (3.3.12)–(3.3.20) describe the use of maximum likelihood techniques to obtain estimates of producer-specific time-invariant technical efficiency. They are based on the same normal–half normal distributional assumptions that were maintained in the cross-sectional framework analyzed in Section 3.2.2. In that section we also discussed the use of maximum likelihood techniques under alternative distributional assumptions for the one-sided inefficiency error component. Exactly the same alternative distributional assumptions can be maintained in a panel data context. Here we discuss just one alternative, in which the half normal assumption on the u_i is generalized to the truncated normal assumption. The normal–truncated normal specification has been proposed for use in a panel data context by Kumbhakar (1987) and Battese and Coelli (1988).

The log likelihood function for the normal–truncated normal case is given by

$$\ln L = \text{constant} - \frac{I(T-1)}{2}\ln \sigma_v^2 - \frac{I}{2}\ln(\sigma_v^2 + T\sigma_u^2)$$

$$-I\ln\left[1 - \Phi\left(-\frac{\mu}{\sigma_u}\right)\right] + \sum_i \ln\left[1 - \Phi\left(-\frac{\tilde{\mu}_i}{\sigma_*}\right)\right]$$

$$-\frac{\Sigma_i \varepsilon_i' \varepsilon_i}{2\sigma_v^2} - \frac{I}{2}\left(\frac{\mu}{\sigma_u}\right)^2 + \frac{1}{2}\sum_i\left(\frac{\tilde{\mu}_i}{\sigma_*}\right)^2, \qquad (3.3.21)$$

where

$$\tilde{\mu}_i = \frac{\mu\sigma_v^2 - T\bar{\varepsilon}\sigma_u^2}{\sigma_v^2 + T\sigma_u^2},$$

and σ_*^2 and $\bar{\varepsilon}$ are defined beneath equation (3.3.14). Note that $\tilde{\mu}_i = \mu_{*i}$ if $\mu = 0$. The log likelihood function can be maximized with respect to the parameters to obtain maximum likelihood estimates of all parameters.

The conditional distribution $(u|\varepsilon)$ is given by

$$f(u|\varepsilon) = \frac{f(u,\varepsilon)}{f(\varepsilon)}$$

$$= \frac{1}{(2\pi)^{1/2}\sigma_*\left[1 - \Phi(-\tilde{\mu}/\sigma_*)\right]}\cdot\exp\left\{-\frac{(u-\tilde{\mu})^2}{2\sigma_*^2}\right\}, \qquad (3.3.22)$$

which is distributed as $N^+(\tilde{\mu}, \sigma_*^2)$. Either the mean or the mode of this distribution can serve as the basis for a point estimate of producer-specific time-invariant technical efficiency. These are given by

$$E(u_i|\varepsilon_i) = \tilde{\mu}_i + \sigma_*\left[\frac{\phi(-\tilde{\mu}_i/\sigma_*)}{1 - \Phi(-\tilde{\mu}_i/\sigma_*)}\right] \qquad (3.3.23)$$

and

$$M(u_i|\varepsilon_i) = \begin{cases} \tilde{\mu}_i & \text{if } \tilde{\mu}_i \geq 0, \\ 0 & \text{otherwise,} \end{cases} \qquad (3.3.24)$$

respectively, either of which can be substituted into equation (3.3.5) to obtain producer-specific estimates of time-invariant technical efficiency.

An alternative estimator is provided by the minimum squared error predictor

$$E(\exp\{-u_i\}|\varepsilon_i) = \frac{1-\Phi[\sigma_* -(\tilde{\mu}_i/\sigma_*)]}{1-\Phi(-\tilde{\mu}_i/\sigma_*)} \cdot \exp\left\{-\tilde{\mu}_i +\frac{1}{2}\sigma_*^2\right\}, \qquad (3.3.25)$$

which can also be substituted into equation (3.3.5) to obtain producer-specific estimates of time-invariant technical efficiency.

Notice that all formulas in this section collapse to analogous formulas in Section 3.2.2 if $T = 1$.

Are Results Sensitive to the Method of Estimation? We have discussed three alternative approaches to the estimation of a production frontier model when panel data are available: a fixed-effects approach based on LSDV, a random-effects approach based on GLS, and a maximum likelihood approach. The three approaches impose different requirements on the data, and they have different properties. Depending on the circumstances, one might have a preference for one approach over the other two. For example, with large I and small T, or in the presence of time-invariant regressors, a random-effects approach based on GLS is clearly preferred to a fixed-effects approach based on LSDV. And if independence of effects and regressors is a plausible assumption, MLE is generally more efficient than either LSDV or GLS, since it exploits distributional information that the other two do not.

The empirical literature reports several comparisons of the three approaches, and we are interested in whether they generate similar results. On the basis of a series of Monte Carlo experiments, Gong and Sickles (1989) find that the three approaches generate very similar estimates of efficiency, similar in terms of both correlation and rank correlation. This leads them to a preference for the fixed-effects model, due to its relatively weak assumptions and its computational ease. However they also report the worrying finding that as the complexity of the underlying technology increases, the performance of all three approaches deteriorates. Gathon and Perelman (1992) compare results obtained from the three approaches using European railway data ($I = 19$, $T = 28$), and report Spearman rank correlations above 0.8. Bauer, Berger, and Humphrey (1993) compare the results obtained from the three approaches using U.S. banking data ($I = 683$, $T = 12$). They report $R^2 = 0.89$ between fixed-effects and random-effects efficiency estimates, but $R^2 \in (0.38, 0.50)$ between these two estimates and maximum likelihood estimates, presumably because the latter were allowed to be time varying and the former were forced to be time invariant. Bauer and Hancock (1993) compared the three approaches, and four others as well, using U.S. Federal Reserve check processing facilities data ($I = 47$, $T = 12$). They report a high degree of concordance across the seven approaches, particularly within the top and bottom quartiles. Spearman rank correlation coefficients among the three approaches we have considered were on the range $(0.73, 0.99)$, Kendall rank correlation coefficients were on the range $(0.54, 0.94)$, and all were statistically significant at the 99% level. Finally Ahmad and Bravo-Ureta (1996) compared a total of 17 fixed-effects and MLE models, using U.S. dairy farm data ($I = 96$, $T = 14$). For the nine models in which technical efficiency was forced to be time invariant, Spearman rank correlation coefficients were on the range $(0.91, 0.99)$. For the eight models in which technical efficiency was allowed to vary through time, Spearman rank correlation coefficients were on the range $(0.85, 0.99)$. Conflicting evidence no doubt exists, but on the basis of these studies we are inclined to conclude that the three approaches are likely to generate similar efficiency rankings, particularly at the top and the bottom of the distribution, where managerial interest is concentrated.

Technical Change A brief concluding observation concerning technical change is warranted. The longer the panel, the less likely it becomes that technology remains constant. This makes it desirable to include time among the regressors as a proxy for technical change, and doing so causes no unusual problems in estimation. Although this practice is commonplace in the estimation of production *functions* based on panel data, it is relatively uncommon in the estimation of production *frontiers* using panel data. One possible reason for the fact that this practice is relatively uncommon is that production frontier models based on panel data are making increasing use of time-varying technical efficiency specifications, and it may be difficult to disentangle the separate effects of technical change and technical efficiency change when both effects are proxied by the passage of time. We consider the issue of time-varying technical efficiency in Section 3.3.2, and we return to the issue of incorporating technical change into production frontier models in Chapter 8.

3.3.2 Time-Varying Technical Efficiency

The assumption maintained in Section 3.3.1 that technical efficiency is constant through time is a strong one. Particularly if the operating environment is competitive, it is hard to accept the notion that technical inefficiency remains constant through very many time periods. The longer the panel, the more desirable it is to relax this assumption. It is possible to do so, although at the cost of additional parameters to be estimated. As with the time-invariant technical efficiency model, two approaches to the estimation of a time-varying technical efficiency model have been pursued: an approach in which time-varying technical efficiency is modeled using fixed or random effects and a maximum likelihood approach.

Fixed-Effects Models and Random-Effects Models Cornwell, Schmidt, and Sickles (CSS) (1990) and Kumbhakar (1990) were perhaps the first to propose a stochastic production frontier panel data model with time-varying technical efficiency. The model with time-invariant technical efficiency given by equation (3.3.1) becomes

$$\ln y_{it} = \beta_{ot} + \sum_n \beta_n \ln x_{nit} + v_{it} - u_{it}$$
$$= \beta_{it} + \sum_n \beta_n \ln x_{nit} + v_{it}, \tag{3.3.26}$$

where β_{ot} is the production frontier intercept common to all producers in period t, $\beta_{it} = \beta_{ot} - u_{it}$ is the intercept for producer i in period t, and all other variables are as previously defined.

As in all other models, the first objective is to obtain estimates of the parameters describing the structure of production technology, and the second objective is to obtain producer-specific estimates of technical efficiency. Obviously with an $I \times T$ panel it is not possible to obtain estimates of all $I \cdot T$ intercepts β_{it}, the N slope parameters β_n, and σ_v^2. CSS addressed this problem by specifying

$$\beta_{it} = \Omega_{i1} + \Omega_{i2}t + \Omega_{i3}t^2, \tag{3.3.27}$$

which reduces the number of intercept parameters to $I \cdot 3$. Nonetheless it leaves a lot of parameters to be estimated, particularly if the ratio (I/T) is large. The ratio of parameters to be estimated to the number of observations is now $(I \cdot 3 + N + 1)/I \times T$.

This quadratic specification allows technical efficiency to vary through time, and in a different manner for each producer. If $\Omega_{i2} = \Omega_{i3} = 0$ $\forall i$, this model collapses to the time-invariant technical efficiency model described in equation (3.3.1). If $\Omega_{i2} = \Omega_2$ $\forall i$ and $\Omega_{i3} = \Omega_3$ $\forall i$, this model collapses to a fixed-effects model with producer-specific intercepts Ω_{i1} and a quadratic term in time common to all producers given by $(\Omega_2 t + \Omega_3 t^2)$. One interpretation of this restricted version of the model is that technical efficiency is producer specific and varies through time in the same manner for all producers. An alternative interpretation is that technical efficiency is producer specific and time-invariant, with the quadratic time term capturing the effects of technical change. It is not possible to distinguish between the two scenarios.

CSS describe several estimation strategies, including a fixed-effects approach and a random-effects approach. The fixed-effects approach adopts the following strategy. First, either (i) delete u_{it} from equation (3.3.26), estimate the β_ns, from the residuals, and regress the residuals on a constant t and t^2 to obtain estimates of $(\Omega_{i1}, \Omega_{i2}, \Omega_{i3})$ for each producer; or (ii) if I/T is relatively small, include u_{it} in equation (3.3.26), estimate the Ω_{i1} as coefficients of producer dummies, and estimate the Ω_{i2} and Ω_{i3} as coefficients of producer dummies interacted with t and t^2. Then create estimates of the β_{it} and define $\hat{\beta}_{ot} = \max_i\{\hat{\beta}_{it}\}$ as the estimated intercept of the production frontier in period t. The technical efficiency of each producer in period t is then estimated as $TE_{it} = \exp\{-\hat{u}_{it}\}$, where $\hat{u}_{it} = (\hat{\beta}_{ot} - \hat{\beta}_{it})$. Thus in each period at least one producer is estimated to be 100% technically efficient, although the identity of the most technically efficient producer(s) can vary through time.

Time-invariant regressors cannot be included in the fixed-effects model with time-invariant technical efficiency, for the same reason they cannot be included in the CSS time-varying technical efficiency model. CSS therefore developed a GLS random-effects estimator for their time-varying technical efficiency model that can incorporate time-invariant regressors. For fixed T, GLS remains more efficient than the fixed-effects estimator in the time-varying efficiency context. However since GLS also remains inconsistent if the technical efficiencies are correlated with the regressors, CSS also developed an efficient instrumental variables (EIV) estimator that is consistent when efficiencies are correlated with regressors and that allows for the inclusion of time-invariant regressors. For both GLS and EIV approaches, estimation of intercepts and efficiencies proceeds as in the fixed-effects approach discussed previously. The only difference is that different sets of residuals are used.

Lee and Schmidt (1993) proposed an alternative formulation in which the u_{it} in equation (3.3.26) are specified as

$$u_{it} = \beta(t) \cdot u_i, \tag{3.3.28}$$

where the function $\beta(t)$ is specified as a set of time dummy variables β_t. This model, which is reminiscent of the Baltagi and Griffin (1988) formulation of technical change, is in one sense more flexible than the CSS model, since it does not restrict the temporal pattern of the u_{it} to any parametric form. It is also less flexible than the CSS model in another sense, since it restricts the temporal pattern of the u_{it} to be the same (β_t) for all producers. This model is appropriate for short panels, since it requires estimation of $T - 1$ additional parameters (the β_t less one normalizing condition such as $\beta_1 = 1$). If all $\beta_t = 1$, this model collapses to the time-invariant technical efficiency model given by equation (3.3.1).

Lee and Schmidt considered both fixed-effects and random-effects models within which time-varying technical efficiency can be estimated. In both approaches the β_ts are treated as the coefficients of the (fixed or random) effects u_i. Once the β_ts and the u_i are estimated,

$$u_{it} = \max_i \{\hat{\beta}_t \hat{u}_i\} - (\hat{\beta}_t \hat{u}_i), \tag{3.3.29}$$

from which $TE_{it} = \exp\{-\hat{u}_{it}\}$ can be calculated. A generalized method of moments approach to the estimation of the Lee and Schmidt model has been developed by Ahn, Lee, and Schmidt (1994).

Maximum Likelihood If independence and distributional assumptions are tenable, it is also possible to use maximum likelihood techniques to estimate the time-varying technical efficiency model. We begin with the production frontier model (3.2.26) with $u_{it} = \beta_t \cdot u_i$, where $v_{it} \sim$ iid $N(0, \sigma_v^2)$ and $u_i \sim$ iid $N^+(0, \sigma_u^2)$. Defining $\varepsilon_{it} = v_{it} - u_{it} = v_{it} - \beta_t \cdot u_i$ and $\varepsilon_i = (\varepsilon_{i1}, \ldots, \varepsilon_{iT})'$, it follows that

$$f(\varepsilon_i) = \int_0^\infty f(\varepsilon_i, u_i)\, du_i$$

$$= \int_0^\infty \prod_t f(\varepsilon_{it} - \beta_t \cdot u_i)\, f(u_i)\, du_i$$

$$= \frac{2}{(2\pi)^{(T+1)/2}\, \sigma_v^T \sigma_u} \int_0^\infty \exp\left\{ -\frac{1}{2}\left[\frac{\Sigma_t(\varepsilon_{it} - \beta_t \cdot u_i)^2}{\sigma_v^2} + \frac{u_i^2}{\sigma_u^2} \right] \right\} du_i$$

$$= \frac{2\sigma_* \exp\left\{ -\frac{1}{2} a_{*i} \right\}}{(2\pi)^{T/2}\, \sigma_v^T \sigma_u} \int_0^\infty \frac{1}{\sqrt{2\pi}\sigma_*} \exp\left\{ -\frac{1}{2\sigma_*^2}(u_i - \mu_{*i})^2 \right\} du_i,$$

$$(3.3.30)$$

where

$$\int_0^\infty \frac{1}{\sqrt{2\pi}\sigma_*} \exp\left\{ -\frac{1}{2\sigma_*^2}(u_i - \mu_{*i})^2 \right\} du_i = 1 - \Phi\left(-\frac{\mu_{*i}}{\sigma_*} \right),$$

$$\mu_{*i} = \frac{(\Sigma_t \beta_t \cdot \varepsilon_{it})\sigma_v^2}{(\sigma_v^2 + \sigma_u^2 \Sigma_t \beta_t^2)},$$

$$\sigma_*^2 = \frac{\sigma_v^2 \sigma_u^2}{\sigma_v^2 + \sigma_u^2 \Sigma_t \beta_t^2},$$

$$a_{*i} = \frac{1}{\sigma_v^2}\left[\sum_t \varepsilon_{it}^2 - \frac{\sigma_u^2(\Sigma_t \beta_t \cdot \varepsilon_{it})^2}{\sigma_v^2 + \sigma_u^2 \Sigma_t \beta_t^2} \right].$$

The log likelihood function is

$$\ln L = \text{constant} - \frac{I}{2}\ln\sigma_*^2 - \frac{1}{2}\sum_i a_{*i} - \frac{I \cdot T}{2}\ln\sigma_v^2$$

$$- \frac{I}{2}\ln\sigma_u^2 + \sum_i \ln\left[1 - \Phi\left(-\frac{\mu_{*i}}{\sigma_*} \right) \right], \qquad (3.3.31)$$

which can be maximized to obtain maximum likelihood estimates of β, β_t, σ_u^2, and σ_v^2.

From the derivation of the log likelihood function it is easy to show that $u_i | \varepsilon_i \sim N^+(\mu_{*i}, \sigma_*^2)$. An estimator for u_i can be obtained from the mean or the mode of $u_i | \varepsilon_i$, which are given by

$$E(u_i | \varepsilon_i) = \mu_{*i} + \sigma_*\left[\frac{\phi(-\mu_{*i}/\sigma_*)}{1 - \Phi(-\mu_{*i}/\sigma_*)} \right],$$

$$M(u_i | \varepsilon_i) = \begin{cases} u_{*i} & \text{if } \sum_t \beta_t \varepsilon_{it} \geq 0, \\ 0 & \text{otherwise.} \end{cases} \qquad (3.3.32)$$

Once u_i has been estimated, u_{it} can be estimated from $\hat{u}_{it} = \hat{u}_i \cdot \hat{\beta}_t$, where $\hat{u}_i$ is either $E(u_i|\varepsilon_i)$ or $M(u_i|\varepsilon_i)$ and the $\hat{\beta}_t$ are maximum likelihood estimates of β_t, $t = 1, \ldots, T$, subject to a normalization such as $\beta_1 = 1$ or $\beta_T = 1$. The minimum squared error predictor of technical efficiency is

$$E(\exp\{-u_{it}\}|\varepsilon_i) = E(\exp\{-u_i \cdot \beta_t\}|\varepsilon_i)$$
$$= \frac{1 - \Phi(\beta_t \cdot \sigma_* - \mu_{*i}/\sigma_*)}{1 - \Phi(-\mu_{*i}/\sigma_*)}$$
$$\cdot \exp\left\{-\beta_t \cdot \mu_{*i} + \frac{1}{2}\beta_t^2 \cdot \sigma_*^2\right\}. \tag{3.3.33}$$

Two special cases of the preceding model have been considered in the literature. Kumbhakar (1990) specified $\beta(t)$ as the following parametric function of time:

$$\beta(t) = [1 + \exp\{\gamma t + \delta t^2\}]^{-1}. \tag{3.3.34}$$

The Kumbhakar model contains two additional parameters to be estimated, γ and δ, whereas the CSS model contains $I \cdot 3$ additional parameters and the Lee and Schmidt model contains $(T - 1)$ additional parameters. The function $\beta(t)$ satisfies the properties (i) $0 \leq \beta(t) \leq 1$ and (ii) $\beta(t)$ can be monotonically increasing or decreasing, and concave or convex, depending on the signs and magnitudes of the two parameters γ and δ. The hypothesis of time-invariant technical efficiency can be tested by testing the hypothesis that $\gamma = \delta = 0$, in which case $\beta(t) = 1/2$. Kumbhakar proposed maximum likelihood techniques to estimate the model given by equations (3.3.26), (3.3.28), and (3.3.34). Apart from the two additional parameters to be estimated, both the distributional assumptions on v_{it} and u_i and the estimation procedure are the same as in the time-invariant maximum likelihood procedure discussed in Section 3.3.1.

An alternative time-varying technical efficiency model was proposed by Battese and Coelli (1992). Their model consists of equations (3.3.26) and (3.3.28) with

$$\beta(t) = \exp\{-\gamma(t - T)\}, \tag{3.3.35}$$

which has only one additional parameter γ to be estimated. The function $\beta(t)$ satisfies the properties (i) $\beta(t) \geq 0$ and (ii) $\beta(t)$ decreases at an increasing rate if $\gamma > 0$, increases at an increasing rate if $\gamma < 0$, or remains constant if $\gamma = 0$. Battese and Coelli then proceeded to make distributional assumptions (normal for v_{it} and truncated normal for u_i) and used maximum likelihood to obtain estimates of all parameters in the model. The log likelihood function and its partial derivatives are provided in their paper. Based on these distributional assumptions, Battese and Coelli showed that $u_i|\varepsilon_i \sim$ iid $N^+(\mu_{**i}, \sigma_*^2)$, where $\varepsilon_i = \mathbf{v}_i - \beta \cdot u_i$ and

$$\mu_{**i} = \frac{\mu\sigma_v^2 - \beta'\varepsilon_i\sigma_u^2}{\sigma_v^2 + \beta'\beta\sigma_u^2},$$

$$\sigma_*^2 = \frac{\sigma_u^2\sigma_v^2}{\sigma_v^2 + \beta'\beta\sigma_u^2},$$

$$\beta' = (\beta(1), \dots, \beta(T)).$$

Notice that if technical efficiency is time invariant, $\gamma = 0 \Rightarrow \beta(t) = 1$ and $\beta'\beta = T$, and the expressions for μ_{**i} and σ_*^2 collapse to their time-invariant versions given beneath equation (3.3.14).

The minimum mean squared error predictor of technical efficiency is

$$
\begin{aligned}
E(\exp\{-u_{it}\}|\varepsilon_i) &= E(\exp\{\beta(t)\cdot u_i\}|\varepsilon_i) \\
&= \frac{1 - \Phi(\beta(t)\sigma_* - \mu_{*i}/\sigma_*)}{1 - \Phi(-\mu_{*i}/\sigma_*)} \\
&\quad \cdot \exp\left\{-\beta(t)\mu_{*i} + \frac{1}{2}\beta(t)^2\sigma_*^2\right\}.
\end{aligned}
\tag{3.3.36}
$$

Method of Moments It is also possible to estimate the production frontier model given in equations (3.3.26) and (3.3.28) using a method of moments approach. We begin by rewriting equation (3.3.26) as

$$
\begin{aligned}
\ln y_{it} &= \beta_o - \beta_t \cdot \sqrt{\frac{2}{\pi}}\sigma_u + \sum_n \beta_n \ln x_{nit} + v_{it} - (u_{it} - E(u_{it})) \\
&= \beta_t^* + \sum_n \beta_n \ln x_{nit} + v_{it} - u_{it}^*,
\end{aligned}
\tag{3.3.37}
$$

where $u_{it} = u_i \cdot \beta_t$ and $E(u_{it}) = \beta_t \cdot \sqrt{2/\pi} \cdot \sigma_u$. In the first step OLS is performed on equation (3.3.37) with time dummies added. The coefficients of the time dummies are the β_t^*s. In the second step the residuals of the first-step OLS regression (which are estimates of $\varepsilon_{it}^* = v_{it} - u_{it}^*$) are used to compute third moments for each t. These are given by $m_{3t} = \beta_t^3 \cdot E(u_i - E(u_i))^3 = \beta_t^3 \cdot \sigma_u^3 \cdot [\sqrt{2/\pi}(1 - 4/\pi)]$, from which

$$\beta_t \sigma_u = \left[\frac{m_{3t}}{\sqrt{2/\pi}} \left(1 - \frac{4}{\pi}\right)^{-1} \right]^{1/3}, \qquad t = 1, \ldots, T. \tag{3.3.38}$$

The normalization $\beta_1 = 1$ allows one to obtain estimates of σ_u and β_t, $t = 2, \ldots, T$, from equation (3.3.38). An estimate of β_o can be obtained from $\hat{\beta}_o = (1/T)\Sigma_t\hat{\beta}_t^* + \hat{\beta}_t\hat{\sigma}_u\sqrt{2/\pi}$. In the third step σ_v^2 is estimated. Since the variance of ε_{it}^* is $[\sigma_v^2 + \beta_t^2\sigma_u^2 (1 - 2/\pi)]$, σ_v^2 can be estimated as

$$\sigma_v^2 = \frac{1}{I \cdot T} \sum_i \sum_t \hat{\varepsilon}_{it}^{*2} - \frac{1}{T}\hat{\sigma}_u^2\left(1 - \frac{2}{\pi}\right)\sum_t \hat{\beta}_t^2. \tag{3.3.39}$$

In the fourth step the estimated values of β, β_t, σ_v^2, and σ_u^2 are used to obtain estimates of u_i from either $E(u_i|\varepsilon_i)$ or $M(u_i|\varepsilon_i)$. Estimates of u_{it} are then obtained from $\hat{u}_{it} = E(u_i|\varepsilon_i) \cdot \hat{\beta}_t$ or $\hat{u}_{it} = M(u_i|\varepsilon_i) \cdot \hat{\beta}_t$. One can also calculate the minimum mean squared error predictor $E(\exp\{-u_{it}\}|\varepsilon_i)$ using equation (3.3.36).

Still another specification of the time-varying technical efficiency model given by equation (3.3.26) was proposed by Kumbhakar and Hjalmarsson (1993). In their model u_{it} in equation (3.3.26) is broken down into two components: a producer-specific component capturing producer heterogeneity (due perhaps to omitted time-invariant inputs) and a producer- and time-specific component representing technical inefficiency. Thus equation (3.3.28) is replaced by

$$u_{it} = \tau_i + \xi_{it}, \tag{3.3.40}$$

where the technical inefficiency component ξ_{it} is assumed to be distributed as $N^+(0, \sigma_\xi^2)$. Since ξ_{it} is nonnegative, its parameter can be separately identified from that of v_{it}, which is assumed to be distributed as $N(0, \sigma_v^2)$. The producer-specific error components τ_i are also identified, since they are time-invariant (fixed or random) effects. Estimation of this model proceeds in two steps. In the first-step either a fixed-effects model or a random-effects model is used to obtain estimates of all parameters but $(\beta_o + \tau_i)$ and the parameters associated with ξ_{it} and v_{it}. The first step does not impose distributional assumptions on the error components. In the second step distributional assumptions are imposed on ξ_{it} and v_{it}, and the fixed effects $(\beta_o + \tau_i)$ and the parameters associated with ξ_{it} and v_{it} are estimated by conditional (on the first-stage parameter estimates) maximum likelihood.

The virtue of this approach is that it avoids imposing distributional assumptions until the second step. The problem with this approach is that any time-invariant component of technical inefficiency is captured by the fixed effects, rather than by the one-sided error component, where it belongs. This issue is discussed by Heshmati and Kumbhakar (1994) and Kumbhakar and Heshmati (1995).

Just as long panels make a time-varying specification of technical efficiency desirable, they also make it desirable to allow for technical change. A time indicator can be included among the regressors in a time-varying technical efficiency model, just as it can in a time-invariant technical efficiency model, enabling one to disentangle the effect of technical change from that of technical efficiency change. This has been accomplished analytically by Kumbhakar (1990), and implemented empirically by Battese and Coelli (1992) and many others.

3.4 STOCHASTIC PRODUCTION FRONTIER MODELS WITH HETEROSKEDASTICITY

In a classical linear regression model it is typically assumed that the error term is *homoskedastic*, that is, has constant variance. However in many cases the error term may be *heteroskedastic*, with variance positively correlated with size-related characteristics of the observations. In this context the consequences of heteroskedasticity are not particularly severe; estimators are unbiased and consistent, although they are not efficient.

The heteroskedasticity problem is potentially more severe in a stochastic production frontier context. Heteroskedasticity can appear in either error component, and it can affect inferences concerning production technology parameters, as well as the parameters of either error component. Consequently it can affect inferences concerning technical efficiency. In this section we consider the effects of heteroskedasticity in a stochastic production frontier context. We consider cross-sectional models in Section 3.4.1, and we turn to panel data models in Sections 3.4.2 and 3.4.3.

3.4.1 Heteroskedastic Cross-Sectional Models

Among the assumptions underlying the stochastic production frontier model discussed in Section 3.2.2 is that of homoskedasticity of both error components. But the symmetric noise error component might be heteroskedastic if the sources of noise vary with the size of producers. And the one-sided technical inefficiency error component might be heteroskedastic if, as some suspect, the sources of inefficiency vary with the size of producers. It is therefore desirable to investigate the consequences of heteroskedasticity in either error component. Since the composed error is asymmetric, we have reason to believe that the consequences of heteroskedasticity, especially in the one-sided inefficiency error component, will differ from its consequences in a classical linear regression model. Heteroskedasticity in the one-sided technical inefficiency error component has been analyzed by Caudill and Ford (1993) and Caudill, Ford, and Gropper (1995). Here we consider heteroskedasticity in either or both of the two error components.

v **Is Heteroskedastic** If heteroskedasticity appears in the symmetric noise error component, we still obtain unbiased estimates of all parameters describing the structure of the production frontier [except for the intercept, since $E(u) \neq 0$], even if heteroskedasticity is ignored. To see this, let the stochastic production frontier model be

$$\ln y_i = \beta_o + \sum_n \beta_n \ln x_{ni} + v_i - u_i, \qquad (3.4.1)$$

and if we assume that $v_i \sim N(0, \sigma_{vi}^2)$ and $u_i \sim N^+(0, \sigma_u^2)$, we have

$$E(\ln y_i) = [\beta_o - \sqrt{2/\pi}\,\sigma_u] + \sum_n \beta_n \ln x_{ni}. \qquad (3.4.2)$$

Thus heteroskedasticity in v generates unbiased estimates of the β_ns and a downward-biased estimate of β_o, exactly as in the homoskedastic case. However the bias in the estimated intercept can be corrected once σ_u is estimated.

The effect of heteroskedasticity in v on maximum likelihood estimates of technical efficiency is not so benign. To examine this effect, we base our estimate of technical efficiency on the conditional mode $M(u_i|\varepsilon_i)$. The analysis would be structurally similar, but analytically more complicated, if we based our estimate of technical efficiency on the conditional mean. In the presence of heteroskedasticity in v, equation (3.2.29) becomes

$$M(u_i|\varepsilon_i) = \begin{cases} -\varepsilon_i \left[\dfrac{1}{1+\sigma_{vi}^2/\sigma_u^2} \right] & \text{if } \varepsilon_i \leq 0, \\ 0 & \text{otherwise.} \end{cases} \quad (3.4.3)$$

In contrast to the homoskedastic version of equation (3.4.3) given in equation (3.2.29), there are now two sources of variation in estimated technical efficiency. The first is the residual itself. The second is the weight attached to the residual, which now has a noise component with nonconstant variance. Thus if two producers have the same residual, their estimated technical efficiency will still differ unless they also have the same noise component variance. In the likely event that σ_{vi}^2 varies directly with the size of producers (as measured, say, by their output), then an unwarranted assumption of homoskedasticity causes a downward bias in $M(u_i|\varepsilon_i)$ for relatively small producers and an upward bias in $M(u_i|\varepsilon_i)$ for relatively large producers. This in turn causes estimates of technical efficiency to be biased upward for relatively small producers and to be biased downward for relatively large producers, since heteroskedasticity is improperly attributed to technical inefficiency.

When only cross-sectional data are available, it is of course not possible to estimate a full set of producer-specific variance parameters σ_{vi}^2, in addition to the other parameters σ_u^2 and β common to all producers. Thus a model incorporating heteroskedasticity in v must conserve on parameters by expressing σ_{vi}^2 as a function of a vector of producer-specific size-related variables z_i, such as $\sigma_{vi}^2 = g_1(z_i; \delta_1)$. Such a model can be estimated using either maximum likelihood techniques or a method of moments approach, each of which generalizes material introduced in Section 3.2.2.

Maximum likelihood estimation of the model given in equations

(3.4.1) and (3.4.2) is based on the distributional assumptions $v_i \sim N(0, \sigma_{vi}^2)$ with $\sigma_{vi}^2 = g_1(z_i; \delta_1)$, and $u_i \sim$ iid $N^+(0, \sigma_u^2)$. Following the procedures outlined in Section 3.2.2, the log likelihood function in equation (3.2.26) can be generalized in the case in which v is heteroskedastic to

$$\ln L = \text{constant} - \frac{1}{2} \sum_i \ln[g_1(z_i; \delta_1) + \sigma_u^2]$$

$$+ \sum_i \ln \Phi\left(-\frac{\varepsilon_i \lambda_i}{\sigma_i}\right) - \frac{1}{2} \sum_i \frac{\varepsilon_i^2}{\sigma_i^2}, \tag{3.4.4}$$

where

$$\sigma_i^2 = \sigma_u^2 + \sigma_{vi}^2 = \sigma_u^2 + g_1(z_i; \delta_1),$$

$$\lambda_i = \frac{\sigma_u}{\sigma_{vi}} = \frac{\sigma_u}{\sqrt{g_1(z_i; \delta_1)}}.$$

The log likelihood function can be maximized to obtain estimates of β, σ_u^2, and δ_1. The estimate of δ_1 can then be used to obtain estimates of σ_{vi}^2 by means of $\hat{\sigma}_{vi}^2 = g_1(z_i; \hat{\delta}_1)$, which can be substituted with $\hat{\sigma}_u^2$ into equation (3.4.3), which is then substituted into equation (3.3.5) to obtain estimates of the technical efficiency of each producer.

A method of moments approach to estimation of the model given in equation (3.4.1) consists of three steps. In the first step, equation (3.4.1) is estimated by OLS to obtain residuals $\hat{\varepsilon}_i$. Since $\hat{\varepsilon}_i$ serves as a proxy for $[v_i - (u_i - E(u_i))]$, we use the third moment m_3 of $\hat{\varepsilon}_i$ to estimate σ_u^2 as in equation (3.2.63). The second step utilizes the fact that $\text{Var}[v_i - (u_i - E(u_i))] = \sigma_{vi}^2 + [(\pi - 2)/\pi]\sigma_u^2 = g_1(z_i; \delta_1) + [(\pi - 2)/\pi]\sigma_u^2$. We then regress $[\hat{\varepsilon}_i^2 - ((\pi - 2)/\pi)\hat{\sigma}_u^2]$ on $g_1(z_i; \delta_1)$ to obtain a consistent estimate of δ_1. The third step is optional. Using the estimated values of $\hat{\sigma}_{vi}^2 = g_1(z_i; \hat{\delta}_1)$ and $\hat{\sigma}_u^2$, it is possible to improve the estimates of β obtained in the first step by performing GLS/weighted least squares. These GLS estimates of β can be reused in the second step to replace the OLS residuals $\hat{\varepsilon}_i$ with the GLS residuals $\tilde{\varepsilon}_i$ in the regression to estimate δ_1.

u Is Heteroskedastic If there are producer-specific factors that influence technical efficiency, then their effect will show up as producer-specific parameters of the distribution of u. This makes matters worse than when heteroskedasticity appears in the symmetric noise error component v. In this case both the estimates of the parameters describing the structure of the production frontier and the estimates of technical efficiency will be adversely affected by neglected heteroskedasticity. To see this, suppose that the variance of u is producer specific, and consider as before the normal–half normal model. Then equation (3.4.2) becomes

$$E(\ln y_i) = \left[\beta_o - \sqrt{\frac{2}{\pi}}\sigma_{ui}\right] + \sum_n \beta_n \ln x_{ni}. \tag{3.4.5}$$

Thus heteroskedasticity in u generates producer-specific intercepts, estimates of which are biased if heteroskedasticity is ignored. Consequently estimates of the remaining technology parameters are also biased by the neglect of heteroskedasticity.

The effect of heteroskedasticity in u on estimates of technical efficiency is determined by substituting σ_{ui}^2 into $M(u_i|\varepsilon_i)$ to obtain

$$M(u_i|\varepsilon_i) = \begin{cases} -\varepsilon_i\left[\dfrac{1}{1+\sigma_v^2/\sigma_{ui}^2}\right] & \text{if } \varepsilon_i \leq 0, \\ 0 & \text{otherwise.} \end{cases} \tag{3.4.6}$$

Once again, estimates of technical efficiency have two sources of variation. As before, one is the residual, and the other is the weight attached to the residual, but this time variation in the weight is attributed to heteroskedasticity in u. If heteroskedasticity in u varies directly with producer size, then its neglect causes an upward bias in the estimate of $M(u_i|\varepsilon_i)$ for relatively small producers and a downward bias in the estimate of $M(u_i|\varepsilon_i)$ for relatively large producers. This in turn causes estimates of the technical efficiency of relatively small producers to be biased downward and estimates of the technical efficiency of relatively large producers to be biased upward. Thus the effect of neglected heteroskedasticity in u is in the opposite direction as the effect of neglected heteroskedasticity in v.

Of course it is not possible to estimate σ_{ui}^2 for each producer in a single cross section, and so σ_{ui}^2 must be expressed as a function of producer-specific variables z_i and estimated by generalizing the maximum likelihood techniques developed in Section 3.2.2. We make the distributional assumptions $u_i \sim N^+(0, \sigma_{ui}^2)$ with $\sigma_{ui}^2 = g_2(z_i; \delta_2)$ and $v_i \sim$ iid $N(0, \sigma_v^2)$. The log likelihood function for the model in which u is heteroskedastic is

$$\ln L = \text{constant} - \frac{1}{2}\sum_i \ln[g_2(z_i;\delta_2) + \sigma_v^2]$$

$$+ \sum_i \ln \Phi\left(-\frac{\varepsilon_i \lambda_i}{\sigma_i}\right) - \frac{1}{2}\sum_i \frac{\varepsilon_i^2}{\sigma_i^2}, \tag{3.4.7}$$

where

$$\sigma_i^2 = \sigma_v^2 + \sigma_{ui}^2 = \sigma_v^2 + g_2(z_i;\delta_2),$$

$$\lambda_i = \frac{\sigma_{ui}}{\sigma_v} = \frac{\sqrt{g_2(z_i;\delta_2)}}{\sigma_v}.$$

The log likelihood function can be maximized to obtain estimates of β, σ_v^2, and δ_2. An estimate of σ_{ui}^2 can then be obtained from $\hat{\sigma}_{ui}^2 = g_2(z_i; \hat{\delta}_2)$. After estimation, estimated values of σ_v^2 and σ_{ui}^2 can be substituted into equation (3.4.6), which is then substituted into equation (3.3.5), to obtain unbiased estimates of the technical efficiency of each producer.

In order to implement the maximum likelihood procedure, a parametric specification for $g_2(z_i; \delta_2)$ must be supplied, and a few specifications have been proposed in the literature. Reifschneider and Stevenson (1991) suggested the additive formulation $\sigma_{ui} = \sigma_{uo} + g(z_i; \gamma)$ with $g(z_i; \gamma) \geq 0$, but they did not estimate such a model. Simar, Lovell, and Vanden Eeckaut (1994) proposed the specification $u_i = \exp\{\gamma' z_i\} \cdot \eta_i$, where the η_i are iid with $\eta_i \geq 0$, $E(\eta_i) = 1$, $\sigma_{\eta i}^2 = \sigma_\eta^2$. It follows that $E(u_i) = \exp\{\gamma' z_i\} \geq 0$ as required and that σ_{ui}^2 has the multiplicative form $\sigma_{ui}^2 = \exp\{2\gamma' z_i\} \cdot \sigma_\eta^2$. They showed how to estimate such a model by nonlinear least squares and by maximum likelihood, although they did not implement their model empirically. Caudill, Ford, and Gropper independently developed and estimated (by MLE) the same multiplicative model, and performed a likelihood ratio test of the homoskedasticity restriction.

When u is heteroskedastic estimation by maximum likelihood is the only option, because the method of moments approach does not work. The first-step OLS regression is

$$\ln y_i = \beta_{oi} + \sum_n \beta_n \ln x_{ni} + v_i - (u_i - E(u_i)), \tag{3.4.8}$$

where $\beta_{oi} = \beta_o - E(u_i) = \beta_o - \sqrt{(2/\pi)g_2(z_i;\delta_2)}$. The intercept is now producer specific, and nonlinear in the parameters β_o and δ_2. Consequently OLS produces biased estimates of all first-step parameters. There is also a difficulty with the second-step regression used to estimate δ_2. If $\hat{\varepsilon}_i^2$ is regressed on $[\sigma_v^2 + ((\pi - 2)/\pi)g_2(z_i; \delta_2)]$, which is the variance of $[v_i - (u_i - E(u_i))]$, σ_v^2 cannot be separated from $g_2(z_i; \delta_2)$ if $g_2(z_i; \delta_2)$ contains an intercept term. Neither of these difficulties arises when v is heteroskedastic.

Both u and v Are Heteroskedastic This model is a straightforward combination of the two models just described. We have seen that maximum likelihood estimates of the parameters describing the structure of the production frontier are biased by the neglect of heteroskedasticity in u, and that maximum likelihood estimates of technical efficiency are biased by the neglect of heteroskedasticity in *either v or u*. The effect of heteroskedasticity in *both v and u* on maximum likelihood estimates of technical efficiency can be seen by assuming a normal–half normal model and using the conditional mode to generate

$$
M(u_i|\varepsilon_i) = \begin{cases} -\varepsilon_i \left[\dfrac{1}{1 + \sigma_{vi}^2 / \sigma_{ui}^2} \right] & \text{if } \varepsilon_i \le 0, \\ 0 & \text{otherwise.} \end{cases}
\tag{3.4.9}
$$

Thus the bias in estimated values of $M(u_i|\varepsilon_i)$ depends on the variance ratio $(\sigma_{vi}^2/\sigma_{ui}^2)$. Only if $(\sigma_{vi}^2/\sigma_{ui}^2)$ is constant across producers are estimates of $M(u_i|\varepsilon_i)$ unbiased when based on the assumption of homoskedasticity. In the absence of constancy, the use of equation (3.4.9) requires that producer-specific estimates of both variance components be obtained using maximum likelihood techniques. Once again estimation by maximum likelihood is the only option; since the method of moments approach does not work when u is heteroskedastic, it does not work when both v and u are heteroskedastic.

We make the distributional assumptions $v_i \sim N(0, \sigma_{vi}^2)$ with $\sigma_{vi}^2 = g_1(z_i; \delta_1)$ and $u_i \sim N^+(0, \sigma_{ui}^2)$ with $\sigma_{ui}^2 = g_2(z_i; \delta_2)$. The log likelihood function is

$$
\ln L = \text{constant} - \frac{1}{2} \sum_i \ln[g_1(z_i; \delta_1) + g_2(z_i; \delta_2)]
$$
$$
+ \sum_i \ln \Phi\left(-\frac{\varepsilon_i \lambda_i}{\sigma_i} \right) - \frac{1}{2} \sum_i \frac{\varepsilon_i^2}{\sigma_i^2},
\tag{3.4.10}
$$

where

$$\sigma_i^2 = \sigma_{vi}^2 + \sigma_{ui}^2 = g_1(z_i; \delta_1) + g_2(z_i; \delta_2),$$

$$\lambda_i = \frac{\sigma_{ui}}{\sigma_{vi}} = \sqrt{\frac{g_2(z_i; \delta_2)}{g_1(z_i; \delta_1)}}.$$

The log likelihood function can be maximized to obtain estimates of β, δ_1, and δ_2. This provides estimates of the two functions $g_1(z_i; \delta_1)$ and $g_2(z_i; \delta_2)$, which can be substituted into equation (3.4.9), which in turn can be substituted into equation (3.3.5) to obtain producer-specific estimates of technical efficiency.

From the three cases just discussed, it follows that (i) unmodeled heteroskedasticity in v does not lead to bias in estimates of parameters describing the structure of the production frontier, although it does lead to bias in estimates of technical efficiency; (ii) ignoring heteroskedasticity in u has more serious consequences, since it causes bias in both estimates of the parameters describing the structure of the production frontier and estimates of technical efficiency; and (iii) unmodeled heteroskedasticity in both error components causes biases in opposite directions, so if heteroskedasticity occurs in both error components there is hope that the overall bias may be small. From an empirical standpoint, the proper procedure is to start with a model that incorporates heteroskedasticity in both error components by means of the functions $g_1(z_i; \delta_1)$ and $g_2(z_i; \delta_2)$, and to test the homoskedasticity restrictions that $\delta_1 = 0$ and/or $\delta_2 = 0$. However a potential problem is that the results might be sensitive to the arguments and functional forms of the two heteroskedasticity relationships, and there is no way of getting around this problem in a cross-sectional model.

3.4.2 Heteroskedastic Panel Data Models with Time-Invariant Technical Efficiency

As in cross-sectional models, three possibilities exist: heteroskedasticity can appear in either or both of the error components. We consider each of these possibilities in turn.

***v* Is Heteroskedastic** Consider the simple panel data production frontier model with time-invariant technical efficiency given by

$$\ln y_{it} = \beta_o + \sum_n \beta_n \ln x_{nit} + v_{it} - u_i. \tag{3.4.11}$$

If we consider a fixed-effects approach, the only way to introduce heteroskedasticity into the model is through the v_{it}. If we assume that the v_{it} are iid $(0, \sigma_{vi}^2)$ and that the $u_i \geq 0$, an LSDV estimator gives unbiased estimates of $\beta_{oi} = (\beta_o - u_i)$ and the β_ns, as in the homoskedastic case discussed in Section 3.3.1. A consistent (in I and T) estimator for u_i is provided by $\hat{u}_i = \max_i \{\hat{\beta}_{oi}\} - \hat{\beta}_{oi}$. Thus neglecting heteroskedasticity in the noise component of the fixed-effects model does not create a serious problem; all production frontier parameters and producer-specific technical efficiency are consistently estimated.

An alternative to the LSDV approach that accounts for heteroskedasticity in v is the GLS approach, which does not require distributional assumptions on either error component, and which is more efficient than LSDV. To implement the GLS procedure, we assume that $v_{it} \sim (0, \sigma_{vi}^2)$ and $u_i \sim$ iid $(0, \sigma_u^2)$ with $u_i \geq 0$. The model can then be written as in equation (3.3.7), which looks like a standard panel data model with the exception that v is heteroskedastic across producers. The most efficient estimator in this context is GLS, which can be implemented if σ_u^2 and σ_{vi}^2 are either known or can be estimated. In the present case σ_{vi}^2 can be estimated from the residuals of a within-transformed model (which is equivalent to LSDV) by means of $\hat{\sigma}_{vi}^2 = (1/T)\Sigma_t \hat{\epsilon}_{it}^2$, where the $\hat{\epsilon}_{it}$ are the residuals of the within-transformed model. An estimate of the variance of u can then be obtained from the residuals in equation (3.4.11) using the within estimates of the β_ns. Once the σ_{vi}^2 and the variance of u have been estimated, the model in equation (3.3.7) can be estimated using GLS. The resulting GLS estimates of β can then be used to estimate $\hat{u}_i = \max\{\bar{\epsilon}_i\} - \bar{\bar{\epsilon}}_i$, where $\bar{\bar{\epsilon}}_i = (1/T)\Sigma_t [\ln y_{it} - \hat{\beta}_o - \Sigma_n \hat{\beta}_n \ln x_{nit}]$ and the $\hat{\beta}_n, n = 0, 1, \ldots, N$, are the GLS estimates of the β_ns. It is also possible to use the best linear unbiased predictor of u_i.

Thus the consistency of estimates of parameters describing the structure of the production frontier and of the technical efficiency of each producer are preserved (as $I \to +\infty$ and $T \to +\infty$) under both fixed-effects and random-effects approaches. Heteroskedasticity in v causes much less serious problems in a panel data context than in a cross-sectional context.

It is also possible to make distributional assumptions and estimate the model using maximum likelihood techniques or a method of moments approach. If we assume that $v_{it} \sim N(0, \sigma_{vi}^2)$ and that $u_i \sim N^+(0, \sigma_u^2)$, the log likelihood function becomes

$$\ln L = \text{constant} - \left(\frac{T-1}{2}\right)\sum_i \ln \sigma_{vi}^2 - \frac{1}{2}\sum_i \ln(\sigma_{vi}^2 + T\sigma_u^2)$$
$$+ \sum_i \ln\left[1 - \Phi\left(-\frac{\mu_{*i}}{\sigma_{*i}}\right)\right] - \frac{1}{2}\sum_i \frac{\varepsilon_i' \varepsilon_i}{\sigma_{vi}^2}$$
$$+ \frac{1}{2}\sum_i \left(\frac{\mu_{*i}}{\sigma_{*i}}\right)^2, \tag{3.4.12}$$

where

$$\frac{\mu_{*i}}{\sigma_{*i}} = \frac{-T\bar{\varepsilon}_i \sigma_u}{\sigma_{vi}(\sigma_{vi}^2 + T\sigma_u^2)^{1/2}}.$$

The parameters to be estimated are $(I + N + 2)$ in number, β, σ_u^2, and σ_{vi}^2, $i = 1, \ldots, I$. Consequently maximum likelihood is impractical unless T is large relative to I. If maximum likelihood estimates can be obtained, however, then estimates of producer-specific technical inefficiency can be obtained from equation (3.3.18) or (3.3.19), and estimates of producer-specific technical efficiency can be obtained from equation (3.3.20).

A method of moments approach is more likely to be practical than a maximum likelihood approach. In the first step we perform OLS and then use equation (3.2.63) to obtain an estimate of σ_u^2 from the third moment of the OLS residuals. In the second step we estimate the within-transformed model given in equation (3.3.7) to obtain estimates of the σ_{vi}^2 by means of $\hat{\sigma}_{vi}^2 = (1/T)\Sigma_t \tilde{\varepsilon}_{it}^2$, where the $\tilde{\varepsilon}_{it}^2$ are residuals of the within-transformed model. To improve on the within estimators of the β_ns, we make the heteroskedasticity correction (using GLS/weighted least squares) on the within-transformed model. We then recalculate the residuals of the within-transformed model using the GLS β_ns and reestimate the σ_{vi}^2. In the third step we substitute the estimates of σ_u^2 and the σ_{vi}^2 into equation (3.3.18) or (3.3.19) to obtain producer-specific estimates of u_i, and then we substitute these estimates into equation (3.3.20) to obtain producer-specific estimates of technical efficiency.

***u* Is Heteroskedastic** This specification precludes the use of a fixed-effects model, since the u_i cannot be fixed and heteroskedastic. A random-effects approach is also impractical. To see why, suppose that $u_i \sim (0, \sigma_{ui}^2)$ with $u_i \geq 0$ and $v_{it} \sim$ iid $(0, \sigma_v^2)$ and consider equation (3.3.7). Since $u_i \geq 0$, $E(u_i)$ depends on its variance, which is not a constant. Consequently the intercept term $[\beta_o - E(u_i)]$ is firm specific, the form of which depends on the distribution of u_i. Its parameters are β_o and $\sigma_{ui}^2, i = 1, \ldots, I$. σ_{ui}^2 also appears in the variance–covariance matrix of $(v_{it} - u_i^*)$. Thus OLS with a constant intercept generates biased and inconsistent parameter estimates (as the method of moments approach does in a cross-sectional model). Consequently GLS cannot be performed because it requires prior estimates of σ_{ui}^2 and σ_v^2.

It is in principle possible to use maximum likelihood techniques to estimate the model when u is heteroskedastic. However this approach is unlikely to be practical, for the same reason MLE is unlikely to be practical when v is heteroskedastic. Estimation of $(I + N + 2)$ parameters β, σ_v^2, and $\sigma_{ui}^2, i = 1, \ldots, I$, requires that T be large relative to I.

Fortunately a method of moments approach is practical in this case, and it works essentially as it does in the case in which v is heteroskedastic. In the first step OLS is used to obtain estimates of the β_ns and σ_v^2 from the within-transformed model. No distributional assumptions on u_i and the v_{it} are required. In the second step we exploit the facts that $\ln y_{it} - \Sigma_n \beta_n \ln x_{nit} = \beta_o + v_{it} - u_i$, and that $\text{Var}(\beta_o + v_{it} - u_i) = \sigma_v^2 + [(\pi - 2)/\pi]\sigma_{ui}^2$. Consistent estimators of σ_{ui}^2 can thus be obtained from $\hat{\sigma}_{ui}^2 = [\pi/(\pi - 2)] \cdot [(1/T)\Sigma_t \{\ln y_{it} - \Sigma_n \hat{\beta}_n \ln x_{nit}\}^2 - \hat{\sigma}_v^2]$, where the $\hat{\beta}_n$s are LSDV estimates of the β_ns and $\hat{\sigma}_v^2 = (1/I \times T)\Sigma_i \Sigma_t \tilde{\varepsilon}_{it}^2$, $\tilde{\varepsilon}_{it}$ being the residuals of the within-transformed model. The $\hat{\beta}_n$s and $\hat{\sigma}_v^2$ are consistent. In the third step we substitute the estimates of β, σ_v^2, and the σ_{ui}^2 into equation (3.3.18) or (3.3.19), which in turn is substituted into equation (3.3.20) to obtain producer-specific estimates of technical efficiency.

Both *u* and *v* Are Heteroskedastic In this case we have

$$
\begin{aligned}
E(\ln y_{it}) &= \left[\beta_o - \sqrt{\frac{2}{\pi}}\sigma_{ui}\right] + \sum_n \beta_n \ln x_{nit} \\
&= \beta_{oi} + \sum_n \beta_n \ln x_{nit}.
\end{aligned}
\tag{3.4.13}
$$

Estimation difficulties and their solution are essentially the same as in the case in which only u is heteroskedastic. Fixed-effects and random-effects approaches are not practical in this case, for the same reasons they are not practical in the case in which only u is heteroskedastic. Maximum likelihood is feasible in principle, but with both v and u being heteroskedastic there are simply too many parameters ($N + 1$ technology parameters and $2 \times I$ variance parameters) to be estimated for a maximum likelihood approach to be empirically practical.

Fortunately a method of moments approach is empirically feasible when both v and u are heteroskedastic. In the first step we obtain a heteroskedasticity-corrected within estimate of β, as in the second step of the model in which only v is heteroskedastic. We use these estimates of β to calculate residuals of the within-transformed model, from which we obtain estimates of the σ_{vi}^2 by means of $\hat{\sigma}_{vi}^2 = (1/T)\Sigma_t\tilde{\varepsilon}_{it}^2$, $i = 1, \ldots, I$, where the $\tilde{\varepsilon}_{it}$ are the residuals of the within-transformed model. As before, no distributional assumptions are required. In the second step we use the estimate of β obtained in the first step to obtain residuals of the original untransformed model. These residuals $\hat{\varepsilon}_{it}$ can be viewed as estimators of $(\beta_o + v_{it} - u_i)$. We then calculate the third central moment m_{3i} of $\hat{\varepsilon}_{it}$ for each i, and obtain estimates of the $\hat{\sigma}_{ui}^2$ by means of $\hat{\sigma}_{ui}^2 = [m_{3i}/\sqrt{2/\pi}(1 - 4/\pi)]^{2/3}$. In the third step we obtain an estimator for β_o from the first moment of ε_{it} by means of $\hat{\beta}_o = [(1/I \times T)\Sigma_i\Sigma_t\hat{\varepsilon}_{it} + (1/I)\sqrt{2/\pi}\Sigma_i\hat{\sigma}_{ui}]$. Finally, we substitute these estimates into equation (3.3.18) or (3.3.19), which is then substituted into equation (3.3.20) to obtain producer-specific estimates of technical efficiency.

3.4.3 Heteroskedastic Panel Data Models with Time-Varying Technical Efficiency

v Is Heteroskedastic   The basic model is now written as

$$\ln y_{it} = \beta_o + \sum_n \beta_n \ln x_{nit} + v_{it} - u_{it}$$

$$= \beta_{it} + \sum_n \beta_n \ln x_{nit} + v_{it}, \tag{3.4.14}$$

where $\beta_{it} = \beta_o - u_{it}$. The only difference between the present models and those considered in Section 3.3.2 is that now the noise error component is heteroskedastic, and the only difference between the present models and those considered in Section 3.4.2 is that now the technical inefficiency error component is time varying. We consider three possible cases; the first is the Cornwell, Schmidt, and Sickles (CSS) (1990) formulation, the second is the Lee and Schmidt (1993) formulation, and the third is the formulation proposed by Kumbhakar (1990) and Battese and Coelli (1992). Each was introduced in Section 3.3.2 under the assumption that both error components are homoskedastic.

In the CSS formulation $\beta_{it} = \Omega_{i1} + \Omega_{i2}t + \Omega_{i3}t^2$ [equation (3.3.27)]. Estimation of the model in equation (3.4.14) proceeds as follows. In the first step we introduce producer dummies and their interactions with t and t^2 in equation (3.4.14) and estimate it using OLS. [An alternative strategy would be to use the generalized within transformation in which the β_{it} terms fall out of equation (3.4.14) and are recovered from the generalized residuals.] An estimate of σ_{vi}^2 is obtained from the sum of squared residuals calculated for each i, $i = 1, \ldots, I$. In the second step we correct for heteroskedasticity using the estimate of σ_{vi}^2 obtained in the first step and reestimate equation (3.4.14). We then estimate $\beta_{it} = \Omega_{i1} + \Omega_{i2}t + \Omega_{i3}t^2$. Finally we obtain an estimate of u_{it} from $\hat{u}_{it} = \max_i\{\hat{\beta}_{it}\} - \hat{\beta}_{it}$ for $t = 1, \ldots, T$. Defining u_{it} in this way allows the production frontier intercept to change through time.

In the Lee and Schmidt formulation $\beta_{it} = \beta_t \cdot u_i$, where the u_i are time-invariant fixed effects and the β_t are parameters to be estimated [equation (3.3.28)]. In the first step we use nonlinear least squares to estimate equation (3.4.14) with producer dummies and time dummies or, alternatively, perform the generalized within transformation and estimate β. Estimates of the β_t and the u_i are obtained from the coefficients of the time and producer dummies, respectively, from the residuals. In the second step we estimate σ_{vi}^2 from the mean squared residuals for each i, $i = 1, \ldots, I$, obtained from the first-step regression. In the third step we repeat the first step after the heteroskedasticity correction to obtain new estimates of the coefficients. Finally, we estimate u_{it} from $\hat{u}_{it} = \hat{\beta}_t \cdot \hat{u}_i$.

In the Kumbhakar and the Battese and Coelli formulations $\beta_{it} = \beta(t) \cdot u_i$ [equations (3.3.30) and (3.3.31)]. In these formulations u_i and v_{it} are random effects, and we make distributional assumptions on them. In addition, $\beta(t)$ may be a parametric function of time with few parameters [as in equations (3.3.30) and (3.3.31)] or a set of $T - 1$ coefficients of time dummies as in the Lee and Schmidt formulation. Two estimation strategies can be followed.

A maximum likelihood approach is based on the usual distributional assumptions $v_{it} \sim N(0, \sigma_{vi}^2)$ and $u_i \sim N^+(0, \sigma_u^2)$. However this approach is apt to be impractical if *either I or T* is large, since there are I variance parameters to be estimated and $T - 1$ efficiency parameters to be estimated. Consequently we do not pursue the MLE approach.

To use the method of moments approach, we begin by rewriting the model in equation (3.4.14) as

$$\ln y_{it} = \beta_t^* + \sum_n \beta_n \ln x_{nit} + v_{it} - u_{it}^*, \tag{3.4.15}$$

where

$$\beta_t^* = \beta_o - E(u_{it}) = \beta_o - \beta_t \sqrt{\frac{2}{\pi}} \sigma_u,$$

$$u_{it}^* = u_{it} - E(u_{it}).$$

The first and second steps are the same as in the homoskedastic case discussed in Section 3.3.2. The third step is based on the fact that $\mathrm{Var}(\varepsilon_{it}^*) = \sigma_{vi}^2 + \beta_t^2 \cdot (\pi - 2/\pi) \cdot \sigma_u^2$, where $\varepsilon_{it}^* = v_{it} - u_{it}$, which enables us to estimate σ_{vi}^2 from $\hat{\sigma}_{vi}^2 = (1/T)\Sigma_t \hat{\varepsilon}_{it}^{*2} - (1/T) \cdot ((\pi - 2)/\pi) \cdot \Sigma_t \hat{\beta}_t^2 \cdot \hat{\sigma}_u^2$. In the fourth step we estimate u_i using either $E(u_i|\varepsilon_i)$ or $M(u_i|\varepsilon_i)$, from which we obtain estimates of $\hat{u}_{it} = \hat{u}_i \cdot \hat{\beta}_t$. These formulas are the same as in the homoskedastic case except for the fact that σ_v^2 is replaced by σ_{vi}^2.

u Is Heteroskedastic Here we consider only the Kumbhakar and the Battese and Coelli formulations, since the CSS and the Lee and Schmidt formulations treat the u_i as fixed effects, and it is not possible for u_{it} to be heteroskedastic if the u_i are fixed effects. [However if u_{it} is random with form $u_{it} = \beta_t \cdot u_i$, then $\mathrm{Var}(u_{it}) = \beta_t^2 \cdot \sigma_{ui}^2$, which is heteroskedastic in the time dimension even if $\sigma_{ui}^2 = \sigma_u^2$. Here we are dealing with the case in which σ_{ui}^2 varies with I.] As in the case when v is heteroskedastic, it is possible to use the method of moments approach to estimate the parameters, and then the JLMS technique to estimate technical efficiency.

Heteroskedasticity in u_{it} can also be introduced some other ways.

One way is to express u_{it} as the parametric function $u_{it} = g(z_{it}; \gamma) + w_{it}$. The requirement that $u_{it} \geq 0$ implies that $w_{it} \geq -g(z_{it}; \gamma)$. In this framework $g(z_{it}; \gamma)$ can be viewed as the deterministic component of technical inefficiency (which is explained by the z_{it} variables), and the w_{it} are the residual components. An alternative to this is to assume that $u_{it} = g(z_{it}; \gamma) \cdot w_{it}$, where $w_{it} \sim N^+(0, \sigma_w^2)$ and $g(z_{it}; \gamma) \geq 0$. A common feature of each of these models is that both the mean and the variance of u_{it} are functions of the z variables. However the exact nature of the heteroskedasticity differs across these formulations.

For example, consider the model proposed by Kumbhakar, Ghosh, and McGuckin (1991) and by Battese and Coelli (1995), in which $u_{it} \sim N^+(z'_{it}\delta, \sigma_u^2)$. In this model

$$E(\ln y_{it}) = \beta_o + \sum_n \beta_n \ln x_{nit} + E(v_{it}) - E(u_{it})$$

$$= \beta_o + \sum_n \beta_n \ln x_{nit} - \left\{ z'_{it}\delta + \frac{\phi(z'_{it}\delta/\sigma_u)}{\Phi(z'_{it}\delta/\sigma_u)} \right\}, \qquad (3.4.16)$$

where $\phi(\cdot)$ and $\Phi(\cdot)$ are the density function and the cumulative distribution function of a standard normal variable. It can be easily seen that neglecting heteroskedasticity will lead to biased estimates of the parameters describing the structure of the production frontier, especially if the z_{it} variables are a subset of the x_{it} variables, or if the z_{it} variables are highly correlated with the x_{it} variables.

Each of these models can be estimated by extending the ALS approach, by replacing the half normal assumption on u with a truncated normal assumption, the truncation point being both firm and time specific. Since the truncation point is both firm and time specific, the variance of the truncated normal distribution depends on the truncation point, making the model heteroskedastic. Once the parameters of the model are estimated using the ALS maximum likelihood method, the JLMS method can be used to estimate producer-specific technical efficiency.

Both u and v Are Heteroskedastic In this case we assume that $v_{it} \sim N(0, \sigma_{vi}^2)$ and that $u_{it} = \beta_t \cdot u_i$ with $u_i \sim N^+(0, \sigma_{ui}^2)$. For reasons discussed previously, maximum likelihood is unlikely to be practical empirically, and so we consider only a method of moments approach. The production frontier is expressed in exactly the same manner as in the case in which only u is heteroskedastic. The first step is also the same. The second step is modified slightly to account for the heteroskedasticity in v. Since $\text{Var}(\varepsilon_{it}^*) = \sigma_{vi}^2 + [(\pi - 2)/\pi] \cdot \beta_t^2 \cdot \sigma_{ui}^2$, σ_{vi}^2 can be estimated from $\hat{\sigma}_{vi}^2 = (1/T)\Sigma_t\varepsilon_{it}^{*2} - (1/T)\cdot[(\pi - 2)/\pi]\cdot\Sigma_t\hat{\beta}_t^2 \cdot \hat{\sigma}_{ui}^2$. In the third step the estimates obtained from the first two steps are substituted into equations (3.3.18)–(3.3.20) to obtain consistent producer-specific estimates of technical efficiency.

3.5 A GUIDE TO THE LITERATURE

The estimation of technical efficiency is a collection of analytical techniques, and these techniques have been applied to virtually every field in economics. Theoretical developments and empirical applications have appeared in the *Journal of Econometrics* and the *Journal of Productivity Analysis*, and empirical applications have appeared in virtually every other journal in the profession. Rather than refer the reader to specific developments and applications, we mention several recent surveys of the field. Among the better surveys are those by Schmidt (1985–1986), Bauer (1990b), Battese (1992), Greene (1993, 1997) (who provides a useful empirical application illustrating how various techniques work), and Cornwell and Schmidt (1996). Special issues of journals devoted to efficiency measurement have been edited by Aigner and Schmidt (1980), Lewin and Lovell (1990, 1995), Gulledge and Lovell (1992), Simioni (1994), Olesen, Petersen, and Lovell (1996), Berger et al. (1997), Battese and Coelli (1997), and Tulkens (1998). Efficiency measurement techniques and applications are surveyed in books edited by Fried, Lovell, and Schmidt (1993) and Coelli, Rao, and Battese (1998). Many of these references survey noneconometric as well as econometric approaches to efficiency measurement.

4 The Estimation and Decomposition of Cost Efficiency

4.1 INTRODUCTION

In Chapter 3 we considered various approaches to the estimation of technical efficiency. The standard against which technical efficiency was estimated was provided by the production frontier, and we adopted an *output-oriented* approach to the estimation of technical efficiency. In this chapter we consider various approaches to the estimation of cost efficiency. The standard against which cost efficiency is estimated is provided by the cost frontier, and we adopt an *input-oriented* approach to the estimation of cost efficiency.

Several significant differences between the estimation of output-oriented technical efficiency and the estimation of input-oriented cost efficiency should be noted.

The first difference concerns data requirements. The estimation of technical efficiency requires information on input use and output provision, whereas the estimation of cost efficiency requires information on input prices, output quantities, and total expenditure on the inputs used, and depending on the model, perhaps input quantities or input cost shares as well. The data requirements for the estimation of cost efficiency are more onerous in some situations and less onerous in others.

The second difference concerns the number of outputs. Estimation of a cost frontier can be accomplished in situations in which producers produce multiple outputs, whereas estimation of a production frontier requires that producers produce a single output. To use

131

quantity data on multiple inputs and multiple outputs to estimate technical efficiency requires the estimation of either of the two distance functions introduced in Section 2.2.3. An output distance function, which is dual to a revenue frontier, can be used to estimate output-oriented technical efficiency, as in Section 3.2.3. Alternatively, an input distance function, which is dual to a cost frontier, can be used to estimate input-oriented technical efficiency.

The third difference concerns quasi-fixed inputs. In the estimation of a stochastic production frontier, efficiency measurement is output oriented and all inputs are treated equally. No distinction is made between variable inputs and quasi-fixed inputs, and so knowledge that some inputs are not variable during the time period under consideration is not exploited. However in the estimation of a stochastic cost frontier, efficiency measurement is input oriented and it is possible to treat variable and quasi-fixed inputs differently. In this way knowledge concerning quasi-fixity of some inputs is exploited by replacing a cost frontier with a variable cost frontier.

The fourth difference concerns behavioral assumptions. The estimation of technical efficiency does not require the imposition of a behavioral objective on producers, whereas the estimation of cost efficiency does. Such an objective may be inappropriate, although it is hard to conceive of many situations in which it is. It may also be unrealistic, if producers are constrained in their ability to freely adjust their use of inputs, and such constraints are not explicitly modeled. However if not all inputs are variable, due perhaps to short-run fixity or to contractual arrangement, then as we just mentioned a variable cost frontier can be used to estimate variable cost efficiency. In our view the (total or variable) cost minimization objective is an appropriate objective in many environments. It is particularly appropriate in competitive environments in which input prices (rather than input quantities) are exogenous, and in which output is demand driven, and so also can be considered to be exogenous. The more competitive the operating environment, the more appropriate the cost efficiency criterion becomes. Ironically, many regulated industries also satisfy these exogeneity criteria, despite the facts that they are generally noncompetitive and that the regulatory constraints are rarely incorporated into models of cost efficiency. Moreover, in many industries (such as electricity generation, for example) output is not storable, and so the output maximization objective that underlies the estimation of output-oriented technical efficiency would be inappropriate.

The final difference concerns the information that can be obtained from the efficiency estimation exercise. Whereas technical efficiency cannot be decomposed, cost efficiency can be decomposed, and in many circumstances it is desirable to do so. As we indicated in Section 2.4.1, any departure from cost efficiency has two potential sources, input-oriented technical inefficiency and input allocative inefficiency. To the extent that technical and allocative inefficiency have different causes, a determination of which of the two constitutes the main source of cost inefficiency can be a very useful exercise. Thus there are two significant differences between the performance evaluation explored in this chapter and that explored in Chapter 3. First, since input-oriented technical efficiency is necessary, but not sufficient, for cost efficiency, the degree of cost efficiency is not greater than the magnitude of input-oriented technical efficiency, the difference being the extent of input allocative efficiency. Second, measures of input-oriented technical efficiency can differ from measures of output-oriented technical efficiency. As we indicated in Section 2.3.1, the two measures are equal if either measure equals one, so that production is technically efficient, or if production is technically inefficient and production technology satisfies constant returns to scale. If neither condition holds, then input-oriented technical efficiency is greater than or less than output-oriented technical efficiency according as returns to scale are increasing or decreasing over the relevant region of production technology. What this means is that any comparison of producer performance based on technical efficiency estimates obtained from the models developed in Chapter 3, and technical efficiency estimates obtained from the models to be developed in this chapter, must be treated with caution.

This chapter is organized as follows.

In Section 4.2 we consider the estimation of cost efficiency when only cross-sectional data are available.

In Section 4.2.1 we develop single-equation cost frontier models. These models are based on expenditure, output quantity, and input price data; they do not utilize input quantity data in their estimation. They can be used to estimate cost efficiency, or they can be used to estimate input-oriented technical efficiency if an assumption of input allocative efficiency is maintained. In the latter case a direct link between the material in Chapter 3 and that in Chapter 4 is established, subject to the qualification concerning the different orientations. It is not possible to decompose estimated cost efficiency into estimates of technical and allocative efficiency with a single-equation model. In Section 4.2.1.1 we consider the case in which producers produce a single output, and we use a Cobb–Douglas cost frontier as the standard against which to estimate cost efficiency. The advantage of the Cobb–Douglas specification is its self-duality property, which enables us to go back and forth between the cost frontier and the production frontier. In Section 4.2.1.2 we consider the case in which producers produce multiple outputs, and we use a translog cost frontier as the standard against which to measure cost efficiency. The translog functional form is not self-dual; indeed it has no known dual. However it has the advantages of flexibility, which reduces the likelihood of confounding the structure of the cost frontier with variation in cost efficiency, and an ability to incorporate multiple outputs into the analysis. In Section 4.2.1.3 we consider the case in which producers use multiple inputs to produce a single output, and in which some of the inputs are quasi-fixed. We use a translog variable cost frontier as the standard against which to measure variable cost efficiency. The techniques developed in Chapter 3 for the estimation of technical efficiency can be applied with only minor modification to the problem of estimating cost efficiency within a single-equation framework.

In Section 4.2.2 we develop simultaneous-equation cost frontier models. These models are based on expenditure, output quantity, input price, and either input quantity or input cost share data. The chief advantage of these models is that, since they exploit additional information, they can be used to decompose estimated cost efficiency into estimates of the cost of input-oriented technical efficiency and the cost of input allocative efficiency. In Section 4.2.2.1, which extends Section 4.2.1.1, we consider the case in which producers produce a single output, and we use a Cobb–Douglas cost frontier as the standard against which to estimate and decompose cost efficiency. As a result of the self-duality property of the Cobb–Douglas functional form, a variety of equation systems can be developed for the purpose of estimating and decomposing cost efficiency. One such system, which we explore in some detail, consists of the first-order conditions for cost minimization. In Section 4.2.2.2, which extends Section 4.2.1.2, we consider the case in which producers produce multiple outputs, and we use a translog cost frontier as the standard against which to estimate and decompose cost efficiency. Since the translog functional form is not self-dual, the choice of equation systems to estimate is limited. In this case the system of equations to be estimated typically consists of the cost frontier and $(N - 1)$ of the input cost share equations.

In Section 4.2.3 we consider the problem of decomposing cost efficiency in greater detail than in previous sections. A decomposition of estimated cost efficiency into estimates of the cost of input-oriented technical efficiency and the cost of input allocative efficiency requires that either input quantity or input cost share data be available, in addition to input price, output quantity, and expenditure data. The decomposition is based on a simultaneous-equation model that utilizes the additional data in the estimation stage.

In Section 4.3 we consider the estimation of cost efficiency when panel data are available. As was the case with the estimation of output-oriented technical efficiency in Chapter 3, the availability of panel data provides many advantages in the estimation of cost efficiency.

In Section 4.3.1 we develop single-equation panel data cost frontier models. As in a cross-sectional context, these models can be used to estimate cost efficiency, or if an assumption of allocative efficiency is maintained they can be used to estimate the magnitude and cost of technical efficiency. These panel data models are structurally similar to the single-equation models developed for use with cross-sectional data in Section 4.2.1. The material presented in this section largely parallels the material presented in Section 3.3.

In Section 4.3.2 we develop simultaneous-equation panel data cost frontier models. These models are structurally similar to the simultaneous-equation models developed for use with cross-sectional data in Section 4.2.2. The material presented in this section has no counterpart in Chapter 3.

In Section 4.4 we discuss a pair of very different approaches to the estimation of cost efficiency. These two approaches are less ambitious, and less formally structured, than the approaches developed in Sections 4.2 and 4.3, but they both generate a modest amount of useful information with a minimum of effort. The first approach is labeled "thick frontier analysis," and can be applied to either cross-sectional data or panel data. The second approach is referred to as a "distribution-free approach," and requires panel data.

We do not analyze the problem of heteroskedasticity in this

chapter, despite the fact that it is apt to be at least as serious a problem in a cost frontier context as in a production frontier context. The techniques developed in Section 3.4 can be applied to the problem of heteroskedasticity in a single-equation cost frontier model, with nothing more than a few sign changes. In addition, Kumbhakar (1996d) provides a detailed analytical and empirical treatment of heteroskedasticity within a simultaneous-equation panel data cost frontier model of the type we discuss in Section 4.3.2.

Section 4.5 concludes with a guide to the relevant literature.

4.2 CROSS-SECTIONAL COST FRONTIER MODELS

A cost frontier can be treated as a single-equation model, just as a production frontier was in Chapter 3. In this case it is possible to obtain estimates of the parameters describing the structure of the cost frontier, as well as producer-specific estimates of cost efficiency. However if input quantity data or input cost share data are available, and if Shephard's lemma is invoked, a cost frontier can be treated as a component of a simultaneous-equation model. In this case it is possible to obtain estimates of the parameters describing the structure of the cost frontier and producer-specific estimates of cost efficiency, as in the single-equation case, and it is also possible to obtain producer-specific estimates of the magnitude and cost of technical efficiency and the magnitude and cost of input allocative efficiency as well. Thus moving from a single-equation model to a simultaneous-equation model requires more data and involves a more complicated estimation problem, but it offers the possibility of gaining more insight into the nature of cost efficiency. We consider single-equation cost frontier models in Section 4.2.1, and we consider simultaneous-equation cost frontier models in Section 4.2.2. In Section 4.2.3 we show how the availability of input quantity data enables one to decompose cost efficiency into its two components.

4.2.1 Single-Equation Cost Frontier Models

In this section we assume that cross-sectional data on the prices of inputs employed, the quantities of outputs produced, and total expenditure are available for each of I producers. The analysis is based on a cost frontier, which can be expressed as

$$E_i \geq c(y_i, w_i; \beta), \qquad i = 1, \ldots, I, \tag{4.2.1}$$

where $E_i = w_i^T x_i = \Sigma_n w_{ni} x_{ni}$ is the expenditure incurred by producer i, $y_i = (y_{1i}, \ldots, y_{Mi}) \geq 0$ is a vector of outputs produced by producer i, $w_i = (w_{1i}, \ldots, w_{Ni}) > 0$ is a vector of input prices faced by producer i, $c(y_i, w_i; \beta)$ is the cost frontier common to all producers, and β is a vector of technology parameters to be estimated. Notice that the input vector x_i used by producer i is not necessarily observed. If it is not observed, cost efficiency cannot be decomposed into the cost of input-oriented technical inefficiency and the cost of input allocative inefficiency. If it is observed, the decomposition can be achieved. We defer discussion of the decomposition of cost efficiency to Sections 4.2.2 and 4.2.3.

In Chapter 2 we expressed the cost efficiency of a producer as $CE(y, x, w)$. Here we write cost efficiency as CE_i, replacing the arguments with a producer identifier. Since CE_i is the cost efficiency of producer i, we have from equation (4.2.1)

$$CE_i = \frac{c(y_i, w_i; \beta)}{E_i}, \tag{4.2.2}$$

which defines cost efficiency as the ratio of minimum feasible cost to observed expenditure. Since $E_i \geq c(y_i, w_i; \beta)$, it follows that $CE_i \leq 1$. $CE_i = 1$ if, and only if, $x_{ni} = x_{ni}(y_i, w_i; \beta)$ $\forall n$ so that $E_i = \Sigma_n w_{ni} x_{ni}(y_i, w_i; \beta)$ attains its minimum feasible value of $c(y_i, w_i; \beta)$. Otherwise $CE_i < 1$ provides a measure of the ratio of minimum cost to observed expenditure.

In equation (4.2.1) the cost frontier $c(y_i, w_i; \beta)$ is deterministic, and so in equation (4.2.2) the entire excess of observed expenditure over minimum feasible cost is attributed to cost inefficiency. Such a formulation ignores the fact that expenditure may be affected by random shocks not under the control of producers. A stochastic cost frontier can be written as

$$E_i \geq c(y_i, w_i; \beta) \cdot \exp\{v_i\}, \tag{4.2.3}$$

where $[c(y_i, w_i; \beta) \cdot \exp\{v_i\}]$ is the stochastic cost frontier. The stochastic cost frontier consists of two parts: a deterministic part $c(y_i, w_i; \beta)$ common to all producers and a producer-specific random part $\exp\{v_i\}$, which captures the effects of random shocks on each producer. If the cost frontier is specified as being stochastic, the appropriate measure of cost efficiency becomes

$$CE_i = \frac{c(y_i, w_i; \beta) \cdot \exp\{v_i\}}{E_i}, \tag{4.2.4}$$

which defines cost efficiency as the ratio of minimum cost attainable in an environment characterized by $\exp\{v_i\}$ to observed expenditure. $CE_i \leq 1$, with $CE_i = 1$ if, and only if, $E_i = c(y_i, w_i; \beta) \cdot \exp\{v_i\}$. Otherwise $CE_i < 1$ provides a measure of the ratio of minimum feasible cost to observed expenditure.

The estimation of cost efficiency can be based on either equation (4.2.1) or equation (4.2.3). Estimation based on equation (4.2.1) would follow procedures analogous to those developed in Section 3.2.1 for the estimation of technical efficiency relative to a deterministic production frontier. Goal programming, corrected OLS, and modified OLS have all been used to estimate deterministic cost frontiers. However since these procedures have already been developed, but more importantly because we are not enamored of deterministic frontiers of any type, we do not consider the estimation of deterministic cost frontiers. We focus our attention on the estimation of stochastic cost frontier models based on equation (4.2.3). In Section 4.2.1 we consider single-equation models in which cost efficiency is estimated, but cannot be decomposed. The techniques for the estimation of these single-equation models are analogous to the techniques developed in Section 3.2.2 for the estimation of output-oriented technical efficiency. Maximum likelihood and method of moments approaches can both be applied to the estimation of cost efficiency in a single-equation model. In Section 4.2.2 we consider simultaneous-equation models in which cost efficiency can be estimated and decomposed. There is no analogue to these models in Chapter 3. In Section 4.2.3 we consider the decomposition of cost inefficiency in greater detail. We consider simultaneous-equation models in which a decomposition of cost inefficiency is made possible by the availability of input quantity or input cost share data.

4.2.1.1 The Single-Output Cobb–Douglas Cost Frontier

If we assume that the deterministic kernel $c(y_i, w_i; \beta)$ of the single-output cost frontier takes the log-linear Cobb–Douglas functional form, then the stochastic cost frontier model given in equation (4.2.3) can be written as

$$\ln E_i \geq \beta_o + \beta_y \ln y_i + \sum_n \beta_n \ln w_{ni} + v_i$$

$$= \beta_o + \beta_y \ln y_i + \sum_n \beta_n \ln w_{ni} + v_i + u_i, \qquad (4.2.5)$$

where v_i is the two-sided random-noise component, and u_i is the nonnegative cost inefficiency component, of the composed error term $\varepsilon_i = v_i + u_i$. Since a cost frontier must be linearly homogeneous in input prices, $c(y_i, \lambda w_i; \beta) = \lambda c(y_i, w_i; \beta)$, $\lambda > 0$, and either the parameter restriction $\beta_k = 1 - \sum_{n \neq k} \beta_n$ must be imposed prior to estimation, or equation (4.2.5) must be reformulated as

$$\ln\left(\frac{E_i}{w_{ki}}\right) = \beta_o + \beta_y \ln y_i + \sum_{n \neq k} \beta_n \ln\left(\frac{w_{ni}}{w_{ki}}\right) + v_i + u_i. \qquad (4.2.6)$$

Using equation (4.2.4), a measure of cost efficiency is provided by

$$CE_i = \exp\{-u_i\}. \qquad (4.2.7)$$

In both formulations of the stochastic cost frontier, the error term $\varepsilon_i = v_i + u_i$ is asymmetric, being positively skewed since $u_i \geq 0$. Apart from the homogeneity restriction on the β_ns and the direction of the skewness of the error term, the stochastic cost frontier model given by equation (4.2.5) or equation (4.2.6) is structurally indistinguishable from the stochastic production frontier model given by equation (3.2.18). Thus apart from some sign changes, the entire analysis of Section 3.2.2 applies with equal force to the estimation of a stochastic cost frontier. If maximum likelihood techniques are employed to obtain estimates of β and the parameters of the two error components, the same distributional assumptions can be made for the error components in equation (4.2.5) or equation (4.2.6). It is also possible to use method of moments estimation techniques to obtain estimates of β and the parameters of the two error components. In either case the JLMS decomposition can be used to separate noise from cost inefficiency in the residuals. The estimated cost inefficiency component can then be substituted into equation (4.2.7) to obtain producer-specific estimates of cost efficiency.

We now illustrate the use of maximum likelihood techniques to estimate the stochastic Cobb–Douglas cost frontier given in equation (4.2.6). We make the following distributional assumptions:

(i) $v_i \sim$ iid $N(0, \sigma_v^2)$.

(ii) $u_i \sim$ iid $N^+(0, \sigma_u^2)$.

(iii) v_i and u_i are distributed independently of each other, and of the regressors.

The density function of $u \geq 0$ is given in equation (3.2.12). The density function of v is given in equation (3.2.20). The marginal density function of $\varepsilon = v + u$ is

$$f(\varepsilon) = \int_o^\infty f(u, \varepsilon)\, du$$

$$= \int_o^\infty \frac{2}{2\pi\sigma_u\sigma_v} \cdot \exp\left\{ \frac{-u^2}{2\sigma_u^2} - \frac{(\varepsilon - u)^2}{2\sigma_v^2} \right\} du$$

$$= \frac{2}{\sqrt{2\pi}\sigma} \cdot \left[1 - \Phi\left(\frac{-\varepsilon\lambda}{\sigma} \right) \right] \cdot \exp\left\{ -\frac{\varepsilon^2}{2\sigma^2} \right\}$$

$$= \frac{2}{\sigma} \cdot \phi\left(\frac{\varepsilon}{\sigma} \right) \cdot \Phi\left(\frac{\varepsilon\lambda}{\sigma} \right), \tag{4.2.8}$$

where $\sigma = (\sigma_u^2 + \sigma_v^2)^{1/2}$, $\lambda = \sigma_u/\sigma_v$, and $\Phi(\cdot)$ and $\phi(\cdot)$ are the standard normal cumulative distribution and density functions. As $\lambda \to 0$ either $\sigma_v^2 \to +\infty$ or $\sigma_u^2 \to 0$, and the symmetric error component dominates the one-sided error component in the determination of ε. As $\lambda \to +\infty$ either $\sigma_u^2 \to +\infty$ or $\sigma_v^2 \to 0$ and the one-sided error component dominates the symmetric error component in the determination of ε. In the former case the stochastic cost frontier model collapses to an OLS cost function model with no variation in cost efficiency, whereas in the latter case the model collapses to a deterministic cost frontier model with no noise. As in Chapter 3, it is possible to conduct a likelihood ratio test of the hypothesis that $\lambda = 0$.

The marginal density function $f(\varepsilon)$ is asymmetrically distributed, with mean and variance

$$E(\varepsilon) = E(u) = \sigma_u \sqrt{\frac{2}{\pi}},$$

$$V(\varepsilon) = \frac{\pi - 2}{\pi}\sigma_u^2 + \sigma_v^2. \tag{4.2.9}$$

Geometrically, $f(\varepsilon)$ looks just like the densities appearing in Figure 3.3, except that the direction of the skewness is reversed.

Using equation (4.2.8), the log likelihood function for a sample of I producers is

$$\ln L = \text{constant} - I \ln \sigma + \sum_i \ln \Phi\left(\frac{\varepsilon_i \lambda}{\sigma}\right) - \frac{1}{2\sigma^2}\sum_i \varepsilon_i^2. \qquad (4.2.10)$$

The log likelihood function can be maximized with respect to the parameters to obtain maximum likelihood estimates of all parameters.

The next step is to obtain estimates of the cost efficiency of each producer. We have estimates of $\varepsilon_i = v_i + u_i$, which obviously contain information on u_i. If $\varepsilon_i < 0$, chances are that u_i is not large [since $E(v_i) = 0$], which suggests that this producer is relatively cost efficient, whereas if $\varepsilon_i > 0$, chances are that u_i is large, which suggests that this producer is relatively cost inefficient. The problem is to extract the information that ε_i contains on u_i. A solution to the problem is obtained from the conditional distribution of u_i given ε_i, which contains whatever information ε_i contains concerning u_i. Adapting the JLMS procedure to the estimation of cost efficiency when $u_i \sim N^+(0, \sigma_u^2)$, the conditional distribution of u given ε is

$$f(u|\varepsilon) = \frac{f(u,\varepsilon)}{f(\varepsilon)}$$

$$= \frac{1}{\sqrt{2\pi}\sigma_*} \cdot \exp\left\{-\frac{(u-\mu_*)^2}{2\sigma_*^2}\right\} \Big/ \left[1 - \Phi\left(\frac{-\mu_*}{\sigma_*}\right)\right], \qquad (4.2.11)$$

where $\mu_* = \varepsilon\sigma_u^2/\sigma^2$ and $\sigma_*^2 = \sigma_u^2\sigma_v^2/\sigma^2$. Since $f(u|\varepsilon)$ is distributed as $N^+(\mu_*, \sigma_*^2)$, either the mean or the mode of this distribution can serve as a point estimator for u_i. They are given by

$$E(u_i|\varepsilon_i) = \mu_{*i} + \sigma_*\left[\frac{\phi(-\mu_{*i}/\sigma_*)}{1 - \Phi(-\mu_{*i}/\sigma_*)}\right]$$

$$= \sigma_*\left[\frac{\phi(\varepsilon_i\lambda/\sigma)}{1 - \Phi(-\varepsilon_i\lambda/\sigma)} + \left(\frac{\varepsilon_i\lambda}{\sigma}\right)\right], \qquad (4.2.12)$$

and

$$M(u_i|\varepsilon_i) = \begin{cases} \varepsilon_i\left(\dfrac{\sigma_u^2}{\sigma^2}\right) & \text{if } \varepsilon_i \geq 0, \\ 0 & \text{otherwise,} \end{cases} \qquad (4.2.13)$$

respectively. Once point estimates of u_i are obtained, estimates of the cost efficiency of each producer can be obtained by substituting either $E(u_i|\varepsilon_i)$ or $M(u_i|\varepsilon_i)$ into equation (4.2.7). It is also possible to adapt the Battese and Coelli (1988) point estimator

$$CE_i = E(\exp\{-u_i\}|\varepsilon_i) = \left[\frac{1-\Phi(\sigma_*-\mu_{*i}/\sigma_*)}{1-\Phi(-\mu_{*i}/\sigma_*)}\right] \cdot \exp\left\{-\mu_{*i}+\frac{1}{2}\sigma_*^2\right\}.$$

(4.2.14)

The point estimators of CE_i obtained by substituting equations (4.2.12) and (4.2.14) into equation (4.2.7) can give different results, since $\exp\{E(u_i|\varepsilon_i)\} \neq E[\exp\{u_i\}|\varepsilon_i]$. We prefer the Battese and Coelli point estimator to the JLMS point estimator for the same reasons we did in Chapter 3; the latter is a first-order approximation to the former. Regardless of which estimator is used, however, the estimates of cost efficiency are inconsistent because the variation associated with the distribution of $(u_i|\varepsilon_i)$ is independent of i. It is also possible to obtain confidence intervals for the point estimates of cost efficiency, by exploiting the fact that the density of $(u_i|\varepsilon_i)$ is known to be that of an $N^+(\mu_*, \sigma_*^2)$. Horrace and Schmidt (1995, 1996), Bera and Sharma (1996), and Hjalmarsson, Kumbhakar, and Heshmati (1996) have derived upper and lower bounds on $(u_i|\varepsilon_i)$, which imply lower and upper bounds on $(\exp\{u_i\}|\varepsilon_i)$.

Three final points deserve mentioning. First, equations (4.2.8)–(4.2.14) are the same as the corresponding equations in Chapter 3, apart from some sign changes to reflect the fact that here $\varepsilon_i = v_i + u_i$, whereas in Chapter 3 $\varepsilon_i = v_i - u_i$. Second, it is not necessary to specify the deterministic kernel of the stochastic cost frontier as having a Cobb–Douglas functional form. This form was used for illustrative purposes only, and other forms may be used in its place. Third, regardless of the functional form used, the efficiency information that emerges from the analysis is limited to producer-specific estimates of the cost of inefficiency. With a single-equation model, and without input quantity or input cost share data, it is not possible to decompose these estimates into estimates of the cost of input-oriented technical inefficiency and the cost of input allocative inefficiency. A decomposition requires additional data and a simultaneous-equation model.

4.2.1.2 The Multiple-Output Translog Cost Frontier

A great virtue of the Cobb–Douglas functional form is that its simplicity enables us to focus our attention where it belongs, on the error term, which contains information on the cost of inefficiency. As an empirical matter, however, the simplicity of the Cobb–Douglas functional form creates two problems. As Hasenkamp (1976) noted long ago, in a commentary on Klein's (1947) famous railroad study, a function (or frontier) having the Cobb–Douglas form cannot accommodate multiple outputs without violating the requisite curvature properties in output space. In addition, if the true structure of (single-output) production technology is more complex than its Cobb–Douglas representation, the unmodeled complexity will show up in the error term, perhaps leading to biased estimates of the cost of inefficiency. For these reasons we now introduce the translog functional form, due originally to Christensen, Jorgenson, and Lau (1971). The translog cost frontier has several virtues: (i) It accommodates multiple outputs without necessarily violating curvature conditions; (ii) it is flexible, in the sense that it provides a second-order approximation to any well-behaved underlying cost frontier at the mean of the data; and (iii) it forms the basis of much of the empirical estimation and decomposition of cost efficiency based on a system of equations.

If we assume that the deterministic kernel $c(y_i, w_i; \beta)$ of the multiple-output cost frontier takes the log-quadratic translog functional form, then the stochastic cost frontier model given in equation (4.2.5) can be written as

$$
\begin{aligned}
\ln E_i \geq \beta_o &+ \sum_m \alpha_m \ln y_{mi} + \sum_n \beta_n \ln w_{ni} + \frac{1}{2} \sum_m \sum_j \alpha_{mj} \ln y_{mi} \ln y_{ji} \\
&+ \frac{1}{2} \sum_n \sum_k \beta_{nk} \ln w_{ni} \ln w_{ki} + \sum_n \sum_m \gamma_{nm} \ln w_{ni} \ln y_{mi} + v_i \\
= \beta_o &+ \sum_m \alpha_m \ln y_{mi} + \sum_n \beta_n \ln w_{ni} + \frac{1}{2} \sum_m \sum_j \alpha_{mj} \ln y_{mi} \ln y_{ji} \\
&+ \frac{1}{2} \sum_n \sum_k \beta_{nk} \ln w_{ni} \ln w_{ki} + \sum_n \sum_m \gamma_{nm} \ln w_{ni} \ln y_{mi} + v_i + u_i,
\end{aligned}
$$

$$(4.2.15)$$

where Young's theorem requires that the symmetry restrictions $\alpha_{nk} = \alpha_{kn}$ and $\beta_{mj} = \beta_{jm}$ be imposed, and homogeneity of degree $+1$ in input prices requires imposition of the additional restrictions $\Sigma_n\beta_n = 1$, $\Sigma_n\beta_{nk} = 0 \ \forall k$, and $\Sigma_n\gamma_{nm} = 0 \ \forall m$. As usual, v_i is the two-sided noise component, and u_i is the nonnegative cost inefficiency component, of the composed error term $\varepsilon_i = v_i + u_i$. The one-sided error component u_i captures the composite cost of input-oriented technical inefficiency and input allocative inefficiency; if technical inefficiency had an output orientation, it would also interact with the regressors in equation (4.2.15). If $M = 1$, equation (4.2.15) collapses to a single-output translog cost frontier. If, in addition, $\beta_{nk} = \gamma_n = 0 \ \forall n, k$, then the translog cost frontier collapses to the Cobb–Douglas cost frontier given in equation (4.2.5). These and other parametric restrictions are testable.

It is possible to estimate a translog cost frontier and to obtain producer-specific estimates of cost efficiency, by following the procedures described in Section 4.2.1.1 for the estimation of a Cobb–Douglas cost frontier. Nothing changes, except for the functional form of $c(y_i, w_i; \beta)$. However if either M or N is large, a large sample size will be required. Moreover, multicollinearity among the regressors is likely to lead to imprecise estimates of many parameters in the model, possibly including those characterizing the two error components. Thus the benefit of flexibility is likely to be offset by the cost of statistically insignificant parameter estimates. For this reason the translog cost frontier is infrequently estimated as a single-equation model. We return to the translog cost frontier in a simultaneous-equation setting in Section 4.2.2.2.

4.2.1.3 The Single-Output Translog Variable Cost Frontier

Suppose that a sample of $i = 1, \ldots, I$ producers each use a vector of variable inputs $x_i = (x_{1i}, \ldots, x_{Ni}) > 0$, available at prices $w_i = (w_{1i}, \ldots, w_{Ni}) > 0$, and a vector of quasi-fixed inputs $z_i = (z_{1i}, \ldots, z_{Qi}) > 0$, to produce a single output $y_i > 0$. Producers incur variable expense $VE_i = \Sigma_n w_{ni}x_{ni}$ in the process. Then the relevant frontier against which to measure their efficiency is the stochastic variable cost frontier $vc(y_i, w_i, z_i; \beta) \cdot \exp\{v_i + u_i\}$, where $v_i \sim N(0, \sigma_v^2)$ captures the effects of statistical noise and $u_i \geq 0$ reflects the cost of inefficiency in the allocation of variable inputs. If the deterministic kernel of this frontier takes the translog functional form, then we have

$$\ln VE_i = \beta_o + \beta_y \ln y_i + \sum_n \alpha_n \ln w_{ni} + \sum_q \beta_q \ln z_{qi} + \frac{1}{2}\beta_{yy}(\ln y_i)^2$$

$$+ \frac{1}{2}\sum_n \sum_k \alpha_{nk} \ln w_{ni} \ln w_{ki} + \frac{1}{2}\sum_q \sum_r \beta_{qr} \ln z_{qi} \ln z_{ri}$$

$$+ \sum_n \sum_q \gamma_{nq} \ln w_{ni} \ln z_{qi} + \sum_n \alpha_{yn} \ln y_i \ln w_{ni}$$

$$+ \sum_q \beta_{yq} \ln y_i \ln z_{qi} + v_i + u_i. \qquad (4.2.16)$$

The usual symmetry and linear homogeneity parameter restrictions can be imposed prior to estimation. The remaining regularity conditions, including those involving z_i, can be tested after estimation. The regularity conditions involving z_i depend on the properties satisfied by GR discussed in Chapter 2. Under the strong monotonicity property $G6$, $vc(y_i, w_i, z_i; \beta)$ is nonincreasing in z_i. Under the convexity property $G7$, $vc(y_i, w_i, z_i; \beta)$ is a convex function in (y_i, z_i). Finally if GR is a cone [so that technology exhibits constant returns to scale in (y_i, x_i, z_i)], $vc(y_i, w_i, z_i; \beta)$ is linearly homogeneous in (y_i, z_i).

If independence assumptions are maintained and if a distributional assumption (e.g., half normal) is imposed on u_i, equation (4.2.16) can be estimated by maximum likelihood. Estimation proceeds exactly as in Sections 4.2.1.1 and 4.2.1.2, so we do not repeat the details here. We do note, however, that the independence assumptions become more restrictive in this model, since now v_i and u_i must be distributed independently of each other and of the regressors, which now include the quasi-fixed input quantities.

The great advantage of equation (4.2.16) is that it exploits information (quasi-fixity of some inputs), which a stochastic production frontier cannot. Moreover, after estimation of equation (4.2.16), shadow prices of each quasi-fixed input can be calculated by means of

$$\frac{-\partial VE_i}{\partial z_{qi}} = \frac{\widetilde{VE_i}}{z_{qi}} \cdot \left(\hat{\beta}_q + \sum_r \hat{\beta}_{qr} \ln z_{ri} + \sum_n \hat{\gamma}_{qn} \ln w_{ni} + \hat{\beta}_{yq} \ln y_i \right),$$

$$q = 1, \dots, Q, \qquad (4.2.17)$$

where $\widetilde{VE}_i = \hat{VE}_i \cdot \exp\{-\hat{u}_i\}$ is the predicted cost-efficient value of VE_i. If prices $p_i = (p_{1i}, \ldots, p_{Qi}) > 0$ of the quasi-fixed inputs are known, a comparison of predicted shadow prices with actual prices provides an indication of which quasi-fixed inputs are over- or underutilized, given the observed values of (y_i, w_i, z_i). Quasi-fixed input z_{qi} is efficiently utilized if $(-\partial VE_i/\partial z_{qi}) = p_{qi}$, and overutilized (underutilized) if $(-\partial VE_i/\partial z_{qi}) < (>) \, p_{qi}$.

Since total cost is minimized when both variable cost and quasi-fixed cost are minimized, misallocation of quasi-fixed inputs constitutes another type of cost inefficiency. The cost of over- or underutilization of quasi-fixed inputs can be determined as follows. First, set the predicted quasi-fixed input shadow prices given in equation (4.2.17) equal to their actual prices, a necessary condition for total cost minimization. Next, solve this system of Q equations for optimal values z_{qi}^* of the quasi-fixed inputs. Finally, calculate the ratio of (or the difference between) the actual cost $\Sigma_q p_{qi} z_{qi}$ of the quasi-fixed inputs to the cost of an efficient combination of quasi-fixed inputs $\Sigma_q p_{qi} z_{qi}^*$.

4.2.2 Simultaneous-Equation Cost Frontier Models

Single-equation cost frontier models are easy to estimate, but they generate limited information. If all that is desired is producer-specific estimates of cost efficiency, single-equation models are adequate for the task, although degrees of freedom problems are likely to plague the estimation of a flexible cost frontier. However if a decomposition of cost inefficiency into its technical and allocative components is desired, it is necessary to employ data on either input quantities or input cost shares in the estimation of a system of equations. The question is: which system? The obvious answer would be to invoke Shephard's lemma and estimate a system consisting of the cost frontier and the associated cost-minimizing input demand equations, or the natural logarithm of the cost frontier and the associated cost-minimizing input share equations. This is indeed the approach adopted when the translog functional form is specified, but when the Cobb–Douglas functional form is specified, its property of self-duality makes other approaches feasible. We begin by considering the single-output Cobb–Douglas cost frontier in Section 4.2.2.1, and we then move on to the multiple-output translog cost frontier in Section 4.2.2.2.

4.2.2.1 Single-Output Cobb–Douglas Cost Systems

We begin by following Schmidt and Lovell (1979), who first developed a stochastic cost frontier model designed to provide estimates of input-oriented technical efficiency and input allocative efficiency. Their approach exploits the self-duality of the Cobb–Douglas functional form. The stochastic Cobb–Douglas production frontier is

$$\ln y = \beta_o + \sum_n \beta_n \ln x_n + v - u, \tag{4.2.18}$$

where producer subscripts are omitted for the moment. As always, $[\beta_o + \Sigma_n\beta_n\ln x_n]$ represents the deterministic kernel of the stochastic production frontier $[\beta_o + \Sigma_n\beta_n\ln x_n + v]$, and $u \geq 0$ represents output-oriented technical inefficiency. If the producer is assumed to seek to minimize the cost $E = \Sigma_n w_n x_n$ of producing its chosen rate of output, then the first-order conditions for the cost minimization problem can be expressed as the system of equations consisting of equation (4.2.18) and the $(N-1)$ first-order conditions

$$\ln\left(\frac{x_1}{x_n}\right) = \ln\left(\frac{\beta_1 w_n}{\beta_n w_1}\right), \qquad n = 2, \ldots, N. \tag{4.2.19}$$

Input allocative inefficiency can be introduced by converting equation (4.2.19) to

$$\ln\left(\frac{x_1}{x_n}\right) = \ln\left(\frac{\beta_1 w_n}{\beta_n w_1}\right) + \eta_n, \qquad n = 2, \ldots, N. \tag{4.2.20}$$

The terms η_n represent input allocative inefficiency for the input pair x_1 and x_n. Since an input can be over- or underutilized relative to input x_1, individual η_ns can take on positive, zero, or negative values. The direction and magnitude of the input allocative inefficiency involving inputs x_n and x_k is given by the ratio (η_n/η_k). A producer is allocatively efficient in its input use if, and only if, $\eta_n = 0$, $n = 2, \ldots, N$.

Equations (4.2.18) and (4.2.20) incorporate both output-oriented technical inefficiency and input allocative inefficiency, and they can be used to solve for the input demand equations, which are given by

$$\ln x_1 = \ln k_1 + \frac{1}{r}\ln y + \frac{1}{r}\sum_{n>1}\beta_n \ln\left(\frac{w_n}{w_1}\right)$$

$$+ \sum_{n>1}\left(\frac{\beta_n}{r}\right)\eta_n - \frac{1}{r}(v-u)$$

$$\vdots$$

$$\ln x_n = \ln k_n + \frac{1}{r}\ln y + \frac{1}{r}\sum_{n>1}\beta_n \ln\left(\frac{w_n}{w_1}\right)$$

$$+ \sum_{n>1}\left(\frac{\beta_n}{r}\right)\eta_n - \eta_n - \frac{1}{r}(v-u), \qquad n = 2,\ldots, N, \qquad (4.2.21)$$

where $r = \Sigma_n\beta_n$ provides a measure of returns to scale in production and

$$k_n = \beta_n\left[\exp\{\beta_o\}\prod_n\beta_n^{\beta_n}\right]^{-1/r}, \qquad n = 1,\ldots, N.$$

The first three terms on the right-hand sides of equations (4.2.21) are the deterministic kernels $\ln x_1(\ln y, \ln w; \beta)$ and $\ln x_n(\ln y, \ln w; \beta)$, $n = 2,\ldots, N$, respectively, of the stochastic cost-minimizing input demand equations. The stochastic cost-minimizing input demand equations are given by $[\ln x_1(\ln y, \ln w; \beta) - v/r]$ and $[\ln x_n(\ln y, \ln w; \beta) - v/r]$, $n = 2,\ldots, N$, respectively. Actual input demands differ from stochastic cost-minimizing input demands due to the presence of both technical inefficiency and input allocative inefficiency.

The impact of technical inefficiency on input demands is given by the terms $(+u/r)$ in each demand equation. Since $u \geq 0$, technical inefficiency increases demand for each input by $(+u/r)$ percent. Technical inefficiency being neutral with respect to input usage, its impact is uniform across input demands. Notice that the output-oriented technical inefficiency $(-u)$ appearing in the production frontier introduced in equation (4.2.18) has been converted to input-oriented technical inefficiency $(+u/r)$ in the input demand equations derived in equations (4.2.21), with the conversion factor being provided by the reciprocal of the magnitude of scale economies, as measured by the degree of homogeneity of the production frontier. The change of sign reflects the fact that production of *less* than maximum output corresponds to usage of *more* than minimum inputs.

The impact of input allocative inefficiency on input demand is given by the term $[\Sigma_{n>1}(\beta_n/r)\eta_n]$ in the demand equation for x_1, and by the term $[\Sigma_{n>1}(\beta_n/r)\eta_n - \eta_n]$ in the demand equations for the remaining inputs. Since the signs of individual η_ns are not known a priori, it is not possible to say whether demand for a particular input will be increased or reduced by input allocative inefficiency. This can be determined only by estimating the η_ns.

From the input demand equations (4.2.21) we derive an expression for total expenditure $E = \Sigma_n w_n x_n$. This expression incorporates both the cost of technical inefficiency and the cost of input allocative inefficiency, and is given by

$$\ln E = K + \frac{1}{r}\ln y + \sum_n \left(\frac{\beta_n}{r}\right)\ln w_n - \frac{1}{r}(v - u) + (A - \ln r), \qquad (4.2.22)$$

where

$$K = \ln\left[\sum_n k_n\right] = \ln r - \frac{\beta_o}{r} - \frac{1}{r}\ln\left[\prod_n \beta_n^{\beta_n}\right],$$

$$A = \sum_{n>1}\left(\frac{\beta_n}{r}\right)\eta_n + \ln\left[\beta_1 + \sum_{n>1}\beta_n \exp\{-\eta_n\}\right].$$

The first three terms on the right-hand side of equation (4.2.22) constitute the deterministic kernel $\ln c(\ln y, \ln w; \beta)$ of the stochastic cost frontier $[\ln c(\ln y, \ln w; \beta) - v/r]$. Actual expenditure exceeds minimum cost for either or both of two reasons. The term $(+u/r) \geq 0$ measures the cost of output-oriented technical inefficiency, and attains its minimum value if, and only if, $u = 0$. The term $(A - \ln r) \geq 0$ measures the cost of input allocative inefficiency, and attains its minimum value if, and only if, $\eta_2 = \cdots = \eta_N = 0$.

We now consider how to estimate the magnitudes and costs of technical and input allocative inefficiency in the Cobb–Douglas model. It is possible to estimate the cost frontier given in equation (4.2.22), and to use the JLMS technique to estimate the separate effects on expenditure of *total* cost inefficiency $[(u/r) + (A - \ln r)]$ and noise. But it is not possible to disentangle the contribution of technical inefficiency from that of input allocative inefficiency; the composed error term is simply intractable. It is also possible to estimate the system of input demand equations given in equations (4.2.21), but the error terms in these equations are also so complicated as to make it impossible to disentangle the effects of technical and input allocative inefficiency. The procedure suggested by Schmidt and Lovell is to estimate the system of first-order conditions for cost minimization given in equations (4.2.18) and (4.2.20), since the error terms in these equations are simple. Adding a producer subscript and rearranging equations (4.2.20), this system becomes

$$\ln y_i = \beta_o + \sum_n \beta_n \ln x_{ni} + v_i - u_i$$

$$\ln\left(\frac{x_{ni}}{x_{1i}}\right) = \ln\left(\frac{\beta_n}{\beta_1}\right) - \ln\left(\frac{w_{ni}}{w_{1i}}\right) - \eta_{ni},$$

$$n = 2, \ldots, N, \ i = 1, \ldots, I. \tag{4.2.23}$$

This system is estimated using maximum likelihood techniques, since the error term in the production frontier is composed of noise and technical inefficiency, and as we saw in Chapter 3, decomposition of this error term is facilitated by the imposition of distributional assumptions on its two components. Four features of this system are noteworthy: (i) Inputs are endogenous, and output and input prices are exogenous; (ii) technical inefficiency is producer specific, and input allocative efficiency is also producer specific for each input pair; (iii) technical inefficiency is not transmitted to the last $(N - 1)$ first-order conditions; and (iv) noise does not appear in the input mix equations. Although technical inefficiency increases the demand for all inputs, it does so equiproportionately, so that the ratios of input demands in the first-order conditions are unaffected by technical inefficiency. Consequently we shall assume that the error term in the production frontier is statistically independent of the error terms in the first-order conditions.

We make the following distributional assumptions on the error terms:

(i) $v_i \sim$ iid $N(0, \sigma_v^2)$.

(ii) $u_i \sim$ iid $N^+(0, \sigma_u^2)$.

(iii) $\eta_i = (\eta_{2i}, \ldots, \eta_{Ni})' \sim$ iid $N(0, \Sigma)$.

(iv) v_i is distributed independently of u_i, and each of them is distributed independently of the elements of η_i.

With these distributional assumptions, the joint density function of the error vector $[(v - u), \eta']'$ for a single observation can be written as $f(\varepsilon, \eta) = f_\varepsilon(\varepsilon) \cdot f_\eta(\eta)$, where $\varepsilon = v - u$, the density function $f_\varepsilon(\varepsilon)$ is given in equation (3.2.23), and $f_\eta(\eta)$ is the density function of a multivariate normal variable given by

$$f_\eta(\eta) = (2\pi)^{-(N-1)/2} |\Sigma|^{-1/2} \exp\left\{-\frac{1}{2}(\eta'\Sigma^{-1}\eta)\right\}. \tag{4.2.24}$$

Thus the log likelihood function is

$$\ln L = \text{constant} + \sum_i \ln f_\varepsilon(\varepsilon_i) + \sum_i \ln f_\eta(\eta_i) + I \ln r$$

$$= \text{constant} - I \ln \sigma - \frac{I}{2}\ln|\Sigma| + I \ln r$$

$$- \frac{1}{2}\sum_i \left[\eta_i'\Sigma^{-1}\eta_i + \left(\frac{1}{\sigma^2}\right)\varepsilon_i^2\right] + \sum_i \left[1 - \Phi\left(\frac{\varepsilon_i\lambda}{\sigma}\right)\right], \tag{4.2.25}$$

where

$$\eta_i = \begin{bmatrix} -\ln\left(\dfrac{x_{2i}}{x_{1i}}\right) + \ln\left(\dfrac{\beta_2}{\beta_1}\right) - \ln\left(\dfrac{w_{2i}}{w_{1i}}\right) \\ \vdots \\ -\ln\left(\dfrac{x_{Ni}}{x_{1i}}\right) + \ln\left(\dfrac{\beta_N}{\beta_1}\right) - \ln\left(\dfrac{w_{Ni}}{w_{1i}}\right) \end{bmatrix},$$

$$\varepsilon_i = \ln y_i - \beta_o - \sum_n \beta_n \ln x_{ni},$$

and $r = \Sigma_n\beta_n$ is the Jacobian of the transformation from (ε, η) to $(\ln x_1, \ldots, \ln x_N)$. As in Chapter 3, $\lambda = \sigma_u/\sigma_v$, $\sigma = (\sigma_u^2 + \sigma_v^2)^{1/2}$, and $\Phi(\cdot)$ is the cumulative distribution function of a standard normal variable. This log likelihood function can be maximized with respect to the parameters to obtain maximum likelihood estimates of all parameters in the model.

Once the parameters have been estimated, information of two sorts is provided. The structure of production technology is characterized by estimated values of β_o and the β_ns, and the nature of inefficiency is characterized by estimates of u_i and the η_{ni}s. Producer-specific estimates of technical inefficiency can be extracted from the residuals of the production frontier in equations (4.2.23). Following

JLMS, either the mean or the mode of $(u_i | \varepsilon_i)$ can be used to provide an estimate of technical inefficiency, which is then substituted into $TE_i = \exp\{-u_i\}$ as usual. Producer-specific estimates of the cost of technical inefficiency are obtained from equation (4.2.22) by means of $CTE_i = \exp\{u_i/r\}$. Producer-specific estimates of allocative inefficiency are obtained from the residuals of the input mix equations in equations (4.2.23). These residuals are then substituted into the input demand equations (4.2.21) to provide estimates of the impact of allocative inefficiency on the usage of each input. Producer-specific estimates of the cost of allocative inefficiency are obtained by substituting these same residuals into the expression for $(A - \ln r)$ in equation (4.2.22) to obtain $CAE_i = \exp\{A - \ln r\}$.

In the system given by equations (4.2.23), the input allocative inefficiencies are treated as elements of a random error vector having zero mean. Thus it is expected that mean input allocative inefficiencies are zero, and this is in contrast to the expectation that mean technical inefficiency is positive, since $E(u) = \sqrt{2/\pi}\sigma_u$. It is possible to generalize this model to allow the input mix system error vector to have nonzero mean, in which case the input allocative inefficiencies (and their cost) have nonzero expectation. One motivation for such a generalization would be that the data were generated by an environment in which it is to be expected that input allocative inefficiency of a particular type might be present. An example is provided by utilities subject to rate of return regulation, which according to the Averch–Johnson (1962) hypothesis induces them to overinvest in their rate base (capital) inputs relative to their other inputs. Another example is provided by agriculture, in which evidence suggests that in a wide variety of environments farmers use excessive amounts of fertilizers and pesticides relative to other inputs. In each of these situations, and in others as well, it is desirable to allow input allocative inefficiency to be systematic, and then to test the hypothesis that it is not.

We retain the system of equations (4.2.23), and we retain the distributional assumptions imposed previously, with one exception. We replace (iii) with

(iiis) $\eta_i \sim$ iid $N(\mu, \Sigma)$,

and we follow the same estimation strategy as before. The log likelihood function given in equation (4.2.25) becomes

$$\ln L = \text{constant} - I \ln \sigma - \frac{I}{2} \ln |\Sigma| + I \ln r$$

$$- \frac{1}{2} \sum_i \left[(\eta_i - \mu)' \Sigma^{-1} (\eta_i - \mu) + \left(\frac{1}{\sigma^2} \right) \varepsilon_i^2 \right] + \sum_i \left[1 - \Phi \left(\frac{\varepsilon_i \lambda}{\sigma} \right) \right],$$

(4.2.26)

which collapses to the log likelihood function given in equation (4.2.25) if $\mu = 0$. This log likelihood function can be maximized with respect to the parameters to obtain maximum likelihood estimates of all parameters, now including the elements of the systematic input misallocation vector μ. The hypothesis that $\mu = 0$, or that any subset of the μs is zero, can be tested by computing a likelihood ratio test statistic in the usual manner. The magnitudes and costs of technical and systematic input allocative inefficiency are calculated as before, recalling that now the η_ns have means of μ_n, $n = 2, \ldots, N$.

In both of the preceding models we assumed that the two error components in the production frontier were statistically independent of each other, and of the error terms in the input mix equations. Since v represents the influence of factors beyond the control of producers, it makes sense to assume that v is independent of u and η. However independence of u and η is a different matter. It is possible to relax this assumption also, and to test the independence between u and η, if there is reason to believe that producers who are relatively technically inefficient are also relatively inefficient in their allocation of inputs, and vice versa. Schmidt and Lovell (1980) developed a model in which technical and input allocative inefficiencies are allowed to be correlated. In such a model distributional assumptions (i) and (ii) are retained, but (iiis) [or its restricted version (iii)] and (iv) are replaced by

(v) $\begin{bmatrix} |u| \\ \eta \end{bmatrix} \sim N \left[\begin{pmatrix} 0 \\ \mu \end{pmatrix}, \Sigma \right],$

where

$$\Sigma = \begin{bmatrix} \sigma_u^2 & \Sigma_{u\eta} \\ \Sigma_{u\eta}' & \Sigma_{\eta\eta} \end{bmatrix}.$$

Notice that u is allowed to be correlated not with the η_ns, but with the absolute values of the η_ns. If $\Sigma_{u\eta} \neq 0$, then $|u|$ and η are correlated, which implies that u is uncorrelated with η_n. However u is positively correlated with $|\eta_n|$, and this positive correlation holds regardless of the sign of the nth element of $\Sigma_{u\eta}$. If $\Sigma_{u\eta} = 0$, then u is uncorrelated with the $|\eta_n|$, and we are back to the previous model in which technical and allocative inefficiencies are independently distributed over the sample. This is a testable hypothesis.

In this framework producers who are relatively technically inefficient are also relatively allocatively inefficient, in the sense that their input mixes are farther off their least cost expansion paths, in either direction, than are those of producers who are relatively technically efficient. What matters in this framework is not the directions of allocative inefficiencies, but their magnitudes, because it is the magnitudes of allocative inefficiencies which, like technical inefficiency, raise cost.

4.2.2.2 *The Multiple-Output Translog Cost System*

In the single-output Cobb–Douglas cost system we did not exploit duality theory in the efficiency estimation exercise; we estimated the system of first-order conditions for cost minimization, which were obtained directly from the production frontier. Instead we exploited the self-duality property of the Cobb–Douglas functional form in the efficiency estimation exercise. The ability to express the impact of technical and allocative inefficiency on input demand and total expenditure was the consequence of our ability to express the expenditure and input demand relationships in closed form in terms of the parameters of the production relationship. Very few functional forms have a dual that can be obtained directly from them, and so the strategy adopted in Section 4.2.2.1 is not generally applicable.

In this section we develop a different strategy, one that is based on the (nonfrontier) strategy originally proposed by Christensen and Greene (1976) for estimating the parameters of a translog cost *function*. We begin by reviewing their strategy, which involves estimating a system of equations based on the cost function and its associated input share equations, and then using the estimated cost function parameters to draw inferences concerning the structure of the underlying, but unknown, production technology. The underlying production technology is unknown because, like most flexible functional forms, the translog cost function has no closed-form dual production or transformation function. We then develop a strategy for converting their cost function to a cost frontier by introducing technical and input allocative inefficiency into the system.

The translog cost function and its associated input cost share equations can be written in deterministic form as

$$\ln E_i = \beta_o + \sum_m \alpha_m \ln y_{mi} + \sum_n \beta_n \ln w_{ni} + \frac{1}{2}\sum_m \sum_j \alpha_{mj} \ln y_{mi} \ln y_{ji}$$

$$+\frac{1}{2}\sum_n \sum_k \beta_{nk} \ln w_{ni} \ln w_{ki} + \sum_n \sum_m \gamma_{nm} \ln w_{ni} \ln y_{mi},$$

$$S_{ni} = \beta_n + \sum_k \beta_{nk} \ln w_{ki} + \sum_m \gamma_{nm} \ln y_{mi}, \qquad n = 1, \ldots, N,$$

$$(4.2.27)$$

where $S_{ni} = \partial \ln E_i/\partial \ln w_{ni} = w_{ni}x_{ni}/E_i$ from Shephard's lemma.

Estimation of the system, rather than just the cost function, adds degrees of freedom and results in more efficient parameter estimates. The system can be estimated by imposing the symmetry and linear homogeneity restrictions listed beneath equation (4.2.15), deleting one input cost share equation (since they sum to unity for each producer), appending additive jointly normally distributed error terms for each remaining equation, and iterating on seemingly unrelated regressions (SUR) until convergence is achieved. Kmenta and Gilbert (1968) have demonstrated that this procedure generates maximum likelihood estimates, and Barten (1969) has demonstrated that these estimates are invariant to which share equation is deleted.

The problem now is to reformulate the system given in equations (4.2.27) into a frontier context. We begin by deleting the first input cost share equation and rewriting the system of N equations as

$$\ln E_i = \ln c(y_i, w_i; \beta) + v_i + u_i,$$

$$S_{ni} = S_{ni}(y_i, w_i; \beta) + \eta_{ni}, \qquad n = 2, \ldots, N \qquad (4.2.28)$$

where $\ln c(y_i, w_i; \beta)$ is the deterministic kernel of the stochastic translog cost frontier, the $S_{ni}(y_i, w_i; \beta)$ are the deterministic kernels of the stochastic translog input cost share equations, and β represents the set of all technology parameters appearing in the cost frontier in equations (4.2.27). The error component u_i captures the effect on expenditure of inefficiency, either technical inefficiency or input allocative inefficiency or both, depending on how the N error terms u_i and the η_{ni} are interpreted and related. We begin by making the following distributional assumptions on the error terms:

(i) $v_i \sim$ iid $N(0, \sigma_v^2)$.

(ii) $u_i \sim$ iid $N^+(0, \sigma_u^2)$.

(iii) $\eta_i = (\eta_{2i}, \ldots, \eta_{Ni})' \sim N(0, \Sigma)$.

(iv) v_i and u_i are distributed independently of each other, and of the elements of η_i.

These assumptions make sense only if allocative efficiency is assumed, so that v_i and η_i represent statistical noise. This is because if η_i represents allocative inefficiency, it cannot be distributed independently of u_i, since allocative inefficiency raises cost. However if η_i represents statistical noise, then u_i captures the cost, which is equivalent to the magnitude, of input-oriented technical inefficiency. Consequently under this assumption the system of equations (4.2.28) provides no more information than does its cost frontier component. Including the share equations provides more efficient parameter estimates, but they may very well be biased by an inappropriate assumption of allocative efficiency. On the other hand, if it is assumed that η_i represents allocative inefficiency, then u_i captures the cost of both technical and allocative inefficiency. Unfortunately, in this case the distributional assumption (iv) makes no sense, because the cost of allocative inefficiency must vary directly with its magnitude, in which case u_i and η_i cannot be statistically independent. It is of course possible to maintain the independence assumption and estimate the model, but failure of independence is likely to lead to inconsistent parameter estimates. And even then, it is not possible to decompose the cost of inefficiency into its two sources.

The dilemma in the preceding paragraph was first noted by Greene (1980b), and so the problem of specifying a sensible translog system that incorporates both technical and allocative inefficiency has come to be known as "the Greene problem." Schmidt (1984) was the first to propose a solution to the problem. He interpreted $\eta \sim N(0, \Sigma)$ as reflecting allocative inefficiency, and he interpreted $u = u_T + u_A$ as reflecting the cost of technical (u_T) and allocative (u_A) inefficiency, with $u_T \sim N^+(0, \sigma_T^2)$. Rather than making a separate distributional assumption on u_A, he specified the cost of allocative inefficiency as a function of η. Schmidt proposed $u_A = \eta'A\eta$, with A an $N \times N$ positive semidefinite matrix. In this formulation $u_A = 0$ when $\eta = 0$, $u_A > 0$

when $\eta \neq 0$, and u_A is positively correlated with the absolute value of each element of η. No distributional assumption needs to be made for u_A, since an estimate of u_A is obtained from estimates of η and estimates of the elements of A. (Although only $N - 1$ share equations are included in the system to be estimated, the elements of η sum to zero, so the missing element can be derived residually.) Schmidt proposed $A = D^{1/(N-1)}\Sigma^+$, where D is the product of the nonzero eigenvalues of Σ, and Σ^+ is the generalized inverse of Σ. With this specification of A, maximum likelihood techniques can be used to provide estimates of the parameters of the cost frontier, the magnitudes of allocative inefficiency, and the cost of technical and allocative inefficiency. Schmidt did not provide an empirical application of his procedure.

Melfi (1984) and Bauer (1985) implemented Schmidt's procedure empirically, but to do so they had to simplify the specification of A. Melfi assumed $A = I$, so that u_A is the sum of squared input share equation errors. An obvious drawback of this specification is that u_A is forced toward zero. Bauer generalized Melfi's specification by allowing A to be a positive semidefinite diagonal matrix whose elements are treated as $(N - 1)$ additional parameters to be estimated; in this formulation u_A is a weighted sum of squared input share equation errors. Once distributional assumptions are made for v, u_T, and η, the translog cost frontier system can be estimated by maximum likelihood; the log likelihood function appears in Bauer (1990b).

Kumbhakar (1991) suggested a specification similar to Bauer's, but which incorporates no additional parameters to be estimated. He required that $\eta_n = \partial u_A / \partial \ln w_n$, $n = 2, \ldots, N$, so that input share equation errors are related to the cost of input allocative inefficiency, just as the input share equations themselves are related to the cost frontier, by way of Shephard's lemma. He then showed that the relationship $u_A = \eta' A \eta$ can be written as $u_A = \eta^{*\prime} K \eta^*$, where $\eta^* = (\eta_1, \ldots, \eta_{N-1})$ and K is a symmetric $(N - 1) \times (N - 1)$ matrix. Now $\partial(\eta^{*\prime} K \eta^*)/\partial \ln w_n = \eta_n$ if

$$-\sum_n k_{kn}\beta^*_{kn} = -\frac{1}{2} \quad \text{and} \quad \sum_n k_{hn}\beta^*_{kn} = 0, \qquad h \neq k, \qquad (4.2.29)$$

where $[k_{hn}]$ is the K matrix and $[\beta^*_{kn}]$ is the matrix of coefficients on $[\ln w_k \ln w_n]$ in the translog cost frontier, with the last row and column deleted. These conditions can be expressed in matrix form as $K\beta^* =$

$-(1/2)I$, where β^* is the $[\beta^*_{kn}]$ matrix and I is the identity matrix of order $(N-1)$. Thus the solution for K is $K = -(1/2)\beta^{*-1}$ and we have $u_A = -(1/2)\eta^{*'}\beta^{*-1}\eta^*$. In contrast to the previous specifications, there are no additional parameters to be estimated. However for K to be a positive semidefinite matrix, β^{*-1} must be negative semidefinite, and even concavity of the cost frontier in input prices does not guarantee that β^{*-1} is negative semidefinite.

An obvious drawback of all three specifications is that η represents pure allocative inefficiency; there is no noise in the input share equations. Ferrier and Lovell (1990) provided an extension of Bauer's specification by allowing $\eta_{ni} = \eta_n + \xi_{ni}$. In their specification η_{ni} is the error in the nth share equation, η_n represents allocative inefficiency in the use of the nth input, and ξ_{ni} represents noise in the nth input share equation. Unfortunately in this specification allocative inefficiency varies across inputs, but not across producers; this is the price to be paid for introducing noise into the input share equations. Consequently in this specification the cost of allocative inefficiency, $u_A = \eta'A\eta$, is the same for all producers. If distributional assumptions are made for v, u_T, and η, and if A is specified as an $N \times N$ positive semidefinite diagonal matrix, maximum likelihood techniques can be used to obtain estimates of all parameters in the model, and to estimate magnitudes and costs of producer-specific technical inefficiency and allocative inefficiency, which is common to all producers. Ferrier and Lovell assumed that $u_{Ti} \sim N^+(0, \sigma_T^2)$ and $\eta_{ni} \sim N(\eta_n, \sigma_\eta^2)$. An alternative way of introducing persistent allocative inefficiency into the model would be to delete the cross-equation parameter equality restrictions on the β_n in equations (4.2.27). This would leave the β_n in the expenditure equation, but the intercept in the nth input cost share equation would become $(\beta_n + \eta_n)$, $n = 2$, ..., N. It would then be possible to test the hypothesis of no allocative inefficiency by testing the hypothesis that the $N - 1$ input cost share equation intercepts are jointly equal to the corresponding expenditure equation slope parameters.

4.2.3 Decomposing Cost Inefficiency

In Section 4.2.1 we showed that in a single-equation cost frontier model it is possible to estimate the cost of overall (the sum of technical and input allocative) inefficiency, but that it is not possible to decompose estimated cost inefficiency into its technical and allocative components. In Section 4.2.2 we showed that, under certain conditions, in a simultaneous-equation cost frontier model it is possible to estimate the magnitude as well as the cost of input allocative inefficiency, and to estimate both the cost and the magnitude of technical inefficiency. The conditions sufficient for a decomposition include either restrictions on the number of outputs and the functional form of the cost frontier (the self-dual, single-output Cobb–Douglas form considered in Section 4.2.2.1) or restrictions on the structure of the disturbance terms in the model (the multiple-output translog cost frontier considered in Section 4.2.2.2). In both cases the ability to decompose the estimated cost of overall inefficiency into its sources comes not from having a system of equations rather than a single equation, but from imposing restrictive assumptions and having additional data, the input quantities or the input cost shares. This suggests that with such data in hand, it may *always* be possible to decompose cost inefficiency, without having to make such restrictive assumptions. Färe and Primont (1996) have demonstrated that this is indeed true analytically, and several authors have achieved such an analytical decomposition within a translog stochastic cost frontier framework. However successful empirical implementation of the decomposition has proved elusive.

The argument that the availability of input quantity or cost share data does permit the decomposition of cost inefficiency originated with Kopp and Diewert (1982) and Zieschang (1983), and was revisited by Mensah (1994). Their argument is intuitively appealing and analytically correct. However as a practical matter their argument is flawed. We will return to the flaw after outlining their analytical argument.

Figure 4.1 provides an illustration of the problem. A producer uses input vector x to produce output vector y, and faces input price vector w. The producer's actual cost is $E = w^T x$, and the producer's minimum cost is $c(y, w; \beta) = w^T x^*$. The producer's cost efficiency is thus $CE = w^T x^*/w^T x = c(y, w; \beta)/w^T x$. The problem is to decompose cost inefficiency into its technical and allocative components. The cost (and magnitude) of input-oriented technical inefficiency is $CTI = w^T x'/w^T x$, and the cost of allocative inefficiency is $CAI = w^T x^*/w^T x' = c(y, w; \beta)/w^T x'$. Thus the decomposition problem boils down to one of finding the two unobserved input quantity vectors x^* and x'.

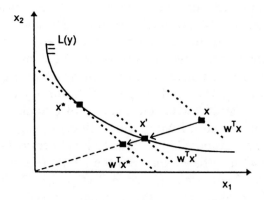

Figure 4.1 The Decomposition of Cost Inefficiency ($N = 2$)

Finding the cost-efficient input quantity vector x^* is easy. From Shephard's lemma, $x^* = \nabla_w c(y, w; \beta)$, and this can be determined even in a single-equation model and even without input quantity data. Finding the technically efficient, but allocatively inefficient, input quantity vector x' is the problem. However it is clear from Figure 4.1 that $x' = \nabla_w c(y, w'; \beta)$ for some unobserved input price vector w'. Now the decomposition problem boils down to one of finding the unobserved input price vector w', from which Shephard's lemma generates the unobserved input quantity vector x'.

Kopp and Diewert demonstrated that w' and x' can be derived by solving the system of $(2N - 1)$ equations

$$\frac{x'_n}{x'_1} - \frac{x_n}{x_1} = 0, \qquad n = 2, \ldots, N,$$
$$x' - \nabla_{w'} c(y, w'; \beta) = 0 \qquad\qquad (4.2.30)$$

in the $2N$ variables (w', x'). The first set of conditions requires x' to have the same input mix as x, and the second set of conditions requires $x' \in \text{Isoq } L(y)$. The system is closed with a normalizing condition on w', such as $w'_1 = 1$, since only relative input prices are required to determine x'. Kopp and Diewert obtained a solution to the system of equations (4.2.30) by using numerical techniques to find the values of the unknown variables (w', x') that minimize the sum of squared differences.

Zieschang simplified the system of $(2N - 1)$ equations to the system of $(N - 1)$ equations

$$\frac{\partial c(y,w';\beta)/\partial w'_n}{\partial c(y,w';\beta)/\partial w'_1} - \frac{x_n}{x_1} = 0, \qquad n = 2, \ldots, N, \tag{4.2.31}$$

which is to be solved for (w'_n/w'_1). Once the (w'_n/w'_1) are determined, it follows that $w' = (1, w'_2/w'_1, \ldots, w'_N/w'_1)/[x_1 + \Sigma_{n>1}(w'_n/w'_1)x_n)]$. Finally, $x' = \nabla_{w'}c(y, w'; \beta)$. The computational advantage of the system (4.2.31) over the system (4.2.30) increases with N.

Mensah showed that the unknown input price vector w', and hence the unknown input quantity vector x', could be obtained by solving the system of N equations

$$w'_n - w_n \cdot \left[\frac{\partial \ln c(y,w';\beta)/\partial \ln w'_n}{w_n x_n / w^T x}\right] = 0, \qquad n = 1, \ldots, N. \tag{4.2.32}$$

Thus the Mensah approach involves inferring w' from w by scaling each element of w by the ratio of its cost-minimizing input share when input prices are w' to its actual cost share when input prices are w.

Each of these solution procedures is analytically elegant, although each procedure requires the numerical solution of a system of nonlinear equations to derive an estimate of the unobserved input price vector w'. Particularly as N and M become large, concerns about the rate at which the system converges to a solution, about the nonnegativity of the solution, and about the existence of multiple local optimal solutions become relevant. There is some empirical evidence that solutions for w' can contain negative elements, or can generate negative costs of either technical or allocative inefficiency, neither of which makes any economic sense. An example of the former problem is reported by Kopp and Diewert, and several examples of the latter problem are reported by Berger and Humphrey (1991). As a way of avoiding such difficulties, Mensah proposed a linear approximation to the nonlinear system (4.2.32). The linear approximation is given by

$$w'_n - w_n \cdot \left[\frac{\partial \ln c(y,w;\beta)/\partial \ln w_n}{w_n x_n / w^T x}\right] \cong 0, \qquad n = 1, \ldots, N. \tag{4.2.33}$$

The approximation replaces cost-minimizing input cost shares when input prices are w' with cost-minimizing input cost shares when input prices are w. Mensah reports empirical evidence that the approximate solution for w' obtained from equation (4.2.33), and the implied decomposition of cost inefficiency into its technical and allocative components, are very close to the nonlinear solution for w' obtained from equation (4.2.32) and its implied decomposition.

Unfortunately each of the procedures outlined previously has an additional empirical shortcoming: Each is based on a knowledge of the cost frontier $c(y, w; \beta)$, perhaps with w' replacing w. However $c(y, w; \beta)$ is unknown, and must be estimated prior to the decomposition of cost inefficiency, and estimation of $c(y, w; \beta)$ when both technical and allocative inefficiency are present is a formidable problem, as we have indicated. Indeed this problem may be the source of the numerical difficulties mentioned previously. Thus although these "solutions" are analytically correct, they do not solve the fundamental econometric problem of formulating and estimating a translog cost system in the presence of both types of inefficiency because they fail to incorporate statistical noise in an econometrically consistent fashion. The Greene problem is an econometric problem, not an analytical problem. These three studies demonstrate that the analytical problem has been solved. However the econometric problem remains.

In the models discussed in Section 4.2.2.2 allocative inefficiency is modeled in an ad hoc fashion. Each of these specifications appeals to the fact that allocative inefficiency increases cost, and a quadratic expression involving allocative inefficiency is added to the expenditure equation to represent the cost increase due to allocative inefficiency. In these specifications the cost of allocative inefficiency is independent of output quantities and input prices. Kumbhakar (1997) has introduced allocative inefficiency in a theoretically and econometrically consistent manner, by adapting the Schmidt and Lovell (1979) Cobb–Douglas production frontier specification to the translog cost frontier framework. Although he worked out the details for a translog cost frontier system, his approach is applicable to any cost frontier.

A cost frontier incorporating both technical and allocative inefficiency can be expressed as

$$\ln E = \ln c(y, w; \beta) + v + u_T + u_A, \qquad (4.2.34)$$

where $c(y, w; \beta)$ is the deterministic kernel of the stochastic cost frontier, v is a stochastic noise error component, the error component $u_T \geq 0$ represents the cost of input-oriented technical inefficiency, and the error component $u_A \geq 0$ represents the cost of input allocative inefficiency. The latter can be modeled as departures of marginal rates of substitution from input price ratios, and so

$$\frac{f_n(x;\beta)}{f_1(x;\beta)} = \frac{w_n}{w_1} \cdot \exp\{\eta_n\} = \frac{w_n^*}{w_1}, \qquad n = 2, \ldots, N, \tag{4.2.35}$$

where $f(x;\beta)$ is the production frontier dual to $c(y, w; \beta)$. It can be shown that

$$u_A = \ln c\big(y, w^*; \beta\big) - \ln c(y, w; \beta) + \ln G, \tag{4.2.36}$$

where $w^* = (w_1, w_2^*, \ldots, w_N^*)$ and

$$G = \sum_n \left[\frac{\partial \ln c(y, w^*; \beta)}{\partial \ln w_n^*} \right] \cdot \exp\{-\eta_n\} = \sum_n S_n(y, w^*; \beta) \cdot \exp\{-\eta_n\}.$$

The input cost share equations associated with the expenditure equation (4.2.34) are

$$\frac{w_n x_n}{E} = \frac{S_n(y, w^*; \beta)}{G \cdot \exp\{\eta_n\}} = S_n(y, w; \beta) + A\eta_n, \tag{4.2.37}$$

where

$$A\eta_n = \frac{S_n(y, w^*; \beta)}{G \cdot \exp\{\eta_n\}} - S_n(y, w; \beta) \qquad n = 1, \ldots, N.$$

If $c(y, w^*; \beta)$ is assumed to take the translog form, then

$$u_A = \ln G + \sum_n \beta_n \eta_n + \sum_n \sum_k \beta_{nk} \ln w_k \eta_n$$

$$+ \frac{1}{2} \sum_n \sum_k \beta_{nk} \eta_n \eta_k + \sum_n \sum_m \gamma_{nm} \ln y_m \eta_n, \tag{4.2.38}$$

where

$$A\eta_n = \left[S_n(y, w; \beta) \cdot (1 - G \cdot \exp\{\eta_n\}) + \sum_m \beta_{nm} \eta_m \right] \Big/ G \cdot \exp\{\eta_n\},$$

$$n = 1, \ldots, N,$$

$$G = \sum_n \left(\beta_n + \sum_k \beta_{nk} \ln w_k^* + \sum_m \gamma_{nm} \ln y_m \right) \cdot \exp\{-\eta_n\}.$$

$$\tag{4.2.39}$$

Although this translog cost system looks like the other translog cost systems considered previously, it differs in that it treats allocative inefficiency in a consistent fashion. Several features of this system should be noted. (1) Both the impact of allocative inefficiency on input cost shares [the $A\eta_n$s in equations (4.2.39)] and the cost of allocative inefficiency [u_A in equation (4.2.37)] are influenced by output quantities and input prices. This implies that if the η_n are assumed to be random, all error terms are heteroskedastic unless parameter restrictions sufficient to collapse the cost frontier to a Cobb–Douglas form are imposed. (2) Since u_A depends on output quantities and input prices, an assumption that overall cost inefficiency ($u_T + u_A$) is iid in a single-equation translog cost frontier model would be inappropriate. (3) The magnitudes of allocative inefficiencies (the η_ns), the impacts of allocative inefficiencies on input cost shares (the $A\eta_n$s), and the cost of allocative inefficiency (u_A) are all identified. It is not necessary to assume a self-dual production frontier, as Schmidt and Lovell did, to identify each of these effects. (4) It is straightforward to show that $u_A = 0 \Leftrightarrow \eta = 0$ and that $u_A > 0$ if $\eta \neq 0$. These parametric restrictions are testable.

Estimation remains a problem. If allocative inefficiency is assumed to be random, and allowed to be both input and producer specific, the translog cost system becomes extremely difficult to estimate. The difficulty arises from the fact that the $A\eta_n$s are highly nonlinear functions of the η_ns, and it is impossible to derive distributions for the $A\eta_n$s starting from a joint distribution for the allocative inefficiency vector η. It is possible, however, to overcome this difficulty by making the restrictive assumption that the magnitudes of allocative inefficiency are input specific but do not vary across producers. The advantage of this assumption, noted by Ferrier and Lovell, is that stochastic noise components ξ_{ni} can be added to the nth input cost share equation for the ith producer. Thus the effects of random noise can be accommodated in the expenditure equation and the input cost share equations, which become

$$\frac{w_n x_n}{E} = S_n(y, w; \beta) + A\eta_n + \xi_n, \qquad n = 1, \ldots, N, \qquad (4.2.40)$$

where the $A\eta_n$ are defined in equations (4.2.39). Note that the $A\eta_n$ are functions of data and parameters to be estimated and that the ξ_n are both input and producer specific.

The translog cost system can be estimated using maximum likelihood techniques under the distributional assumptions:

(i) $v \sim$ iid $N(0, \sigma_v^2)$.

(ii) $u_T \sim$ iid $N^+(0, \sigma_u^2)$.

(iii) $\xi \sim$ iid $N(0, \Sigma_\xi)$.

Here $\xi = (\xi_1, \ldots, \xi_N)'$ and Σ_ξ is an $N \times N$ positive semidefinite matrix. Although these distributional assumptions were also made by Ferrier and Lovell, the present model incorporates allocative inefficiency in a more sophisticated fashion than does their model.

Once the parameters are estimated, estimates of the cost of allocative inefficiency can be obtained from u_A in equation (4.2.37). Note that although the magnitudes of allocative inefficiency are assumed to be invariant across producers, estimates of the cost of allocative inefficiency are producer specific. This is because u_A depends on output quantities and input prices. Estimates of u_T, which is also producer specific, can be obtained from estimates of $(v + u_T)$ using the JLMS decomposition.

A less efficient but computationally simpler way of estimating the translog cost system is to use a two-step procedure. In the first step the input cost share equations are estimated using iterated SUR. This procedure does not require the normality assumption on ξ. However the input cost share equations do not contain all the parameters of the translog cost frontier. The remaining parameters, and the parameters associated with the distributions of v and u_T, are estimated in the second step. In the second step distributional assumptions are imposed on v and u_T, and maximum likelihood techniques are used to estimate the remaining parameters.

We conclude this section on a somewhat pessimistic note. It appears that the Greene problem has yet to be satisfactorily resolved. The strategy initiated by Schmidt (1984), and modified by Melfi (1984), Bauer (1985), and Kumbhakar (1991), provides a solution to the problem, but at the cost of assuming that there is no noise in the input share equations. The strategy proposed by Ferrier and Lovell (1990) also provides a solution to the problem, but at the considerable cost of assuming that allocative inefficiency and its cost vary across inputs but not across producers. The strategy proposed by Kopp and Diewert (1982), Zieschang (1983), and Mensah (1994) does not embed the translog system within a sensible stochastic frame-work, and requires the numerical solution of a system of nonlinear equations. The procedure developed by Kumbhakar (1997) is analyt-ically elegant and econometrically tractable. At the cost of assuming that the magnitudes of allocative inefficiency are invariant across producers, the model accommodates random noise in the input cost share equations as well as in the cost frontier equation. And although the magnitudes of allocative inefficiency are invariant across pro-ducers, their impacts on input cost shares and on expenditure do vary across producers.

4.3 PANEL DATA COST FRONTIER MODELS

The disadvantages of having only cross-sectional data with which to estimate technical efficiency relative to a stochastic production frontier were noted at the beginning of Section 3.3. Each of these disadvantages carries over to the estimation of cost efficiency relative to a stochastic cost frontier in a single-equation model. The fundamental problem is that in a single cross section we get to observe each producer only once, and this severely limits the confidence we have in our (technical or cost) efficiency estimates. In the cross-sectional environment of Section 4.2, data limitations required the imposition of two types of assumptions and still left us with problems:

(i) Maximum likelihood estimation of a stochastic cost frontier, and the subsequent decomposition of the residual into cost inefficiency and statistical noise, both rest on strong distribu-tional assumptions on each error component.

(ii) Maximum likelihood estimation also requires an assumption that the cost inefficiency error component be independent of the regressors – output quantities and input prices, and perhaps quasi-fixed input quantities as well. However it is frequently argued that a principal cause of cost inefficiency is large size; if this is true, it would call into question the validity of the independence assumption.

(iii) The JLMS technique can be applied to the estimation of cost efficiency, but the estimator is not consistent as $I \rightarrow +\infty$.

It is possible to overcome each of these problems if we have access to panel data. The expanded range of estimation procedures discussed in Section 3.3 is equally applicable to the estimation of stochastic cost frontier models. Maximum likelihood estimation remains feasible, and it is a popular option, its distributional and independence assumptions notwithstanding. However fixed-effects and random-effects approaches are also available in a panel data context, and they have certain advantages over maximum likelihood techniques.

Strategies for the estimation of single-equation stochastic cost frontier models in the presence of panel data are virtually identical to those developed for the estimation of stochastic production frontier models. All that is required is to change the sign of the appropriate error component. Consequently Section 4.3.1 is brief, since all essential details appear in Section 3.3. There is no counterpart in Chapter 3 to simultaneous-equation cost frontier models. Consequently Section 4.3.2 is new, although the extension of cross-sectional cost frontier systems to panel data cost frontier systems is straightforward.

4.3.1 Single-Equation Cost Frontier Models

We assume that we have observations on a panel of I producers through T time periods. The panel need not be balanced, although to conserve on notation we shall assume that it is. Also to conserve on notation, we assume that the deterministic kernel of the stochastic cost frontier takes the single-output Cobb–Douglas form. The extension to multiple outputs and to flexible functional forms is straightforward. Finally, we assume initially that cost efficiency is time invariant. Armed with these assumptions, we express the cost frontier model as

$$\ln E_{it} = \beta_o + \beta_y \ln y_{it} + \Sigma_n \beta_n \ln w_{nit} + v_{it} + u_i, \qquad (4.3.1)$$

where v_{it} represents random statistical noise, $u_i \geq 0$ represents time-invariant cost inefficiency, and $\Sigma_n \beta_n = 1$ ensures homogeneity of degree +1 of the cost frontier in input prices.

If we assume that the v_{it} are iid $(0, \sigma_v^2)$ and are uncorrelated with the regressors, none of which is time invariant, and if we make no distributional or independence assumption on the u_i, equation (4.3.1) can be estimated by means of a fixed-effects approach. Rewriting equation (4.3.1) as

$$\ln E_{it} = \beta_{oi} + \beta_y \ln y_{it} + \Sigma_n \beta_n \ln w_{nit} + v_{it}, \qquad (4.3.2)$$

where the $\beta_{oi} = \beta_o + u_i$ are producer-specific intercepts, the model can be estimated by LSDV. After estimation the cost frontier intercept is estimated as $\hat{\beta}_o = \min_i\{\hat{\beta}_{oi}\}$ and the u_i are estimated from $\hat{u}_i = \hat{\beta}_{oi} - \hat{\beta}_o \geq 0$. Finally, producer-specific estimates of cost efficiency are obtained from $CE_i = \exp\{-\hat{u}_i\}$. In the fixed-effects model at least one producer has $CE_i = 1$, and the remaining producers have $CE_i < 1$. Estimates of cost efficiency are consistent as $I \rightarrow +\infty$ and $T \rightarrow +\infty$.

If instead we assume that the u_i are randomly distributed with constant mean and variance, but are uncorrelated with the v_{it} and with the regressors, and if we assume that the v_{it} have zero expectation and constant variance, we can incorporate time-invariant regressors into the model and use a random-effects approach to estimate equation (4.3.1). Rewriting equation (4.3.1) as

$$\ln E_{it} = \beta_o^* + \beta_y \ln y_{it} + \Sigma_n \beta_n \ln w_{nit} + v_{it} + u_i^*, \qquad (4.3.3)$$

where $\beta_o^* = [\beta_o + E(u_i)]$ and $E(u_i^*) = E[u_i - E(u_i)] = 0$, the model can be estimated by GLS. After estimation of equation (4.3.3), an estimate of u_i^* is obtained from the regression residuals by means of $\hat{u}_i^* = (1/T)\Sigma_t(\ln E_{it} - \hat{\beta}_o^* - \hat{\beta}_y \ln y_{it} - \Sigma_n \hat{\beta}_n \ln w_{nit})$, from which we obtain $\hat{u}_i = \hat{u}_i^* - \min_i\{\hat{u}_i^*\} \geq 0$ and $CE_i = \exp\{-\hat{u}_i\}$. These estimates are also consistent as $I \rightarrow +\infty$ and $T \rightarrow +\infty$.

The GLS estimator hinges on the assumption that the random effects (the u_i) are uncorrelated with the regressors, whereas the LSDV estimator does not. However since GLS allows for the inclusion of time-invariant regressors, it is desirable to test the independence hypothesis. As in Chapter 3, a Hausman–Taylor (1981) test procedure can be applied here. If an independence assumption is warranted, and if one is willing to make distributional assumptions on v and u, maximum likelihood techniques can be employed to estimate the parameters of equation (4.3.1). The appeal of MLE is that it should produce more efficient parameter estimates than either LSDV or GLS, since it exploits distributional information that the other estimators do not. MLE proceeds exactly as in Section 3.3.1 (with many sign changes, since here $\varepsilon = v + u$, whereas there

$\varepsilon = v - u$) and exactly as in Section 4.2.1 (with time subscripts added to producer subscripts where appropriate).

We now sketch the MLE procedure, omitting details. We make the following assumptions on the error components in the stochastic cost frontier model given in equation (4.3.1):

(i) $v_{it} \sim$ iid $N(0, \sigma_v^2)$

(ii) $u_i \sim$ iid $N^+(0, \sigma_u^2)$

(iii) u_i and v_{it} are distributed independently of each other, and of the regressors.

The marginal density function $f(\varepsilon) = f(v + u)$ is the same as the marginal density function $f(\varepsilon) = f(v - u)$ given in equation (3.3.15), apart from a change in sign in the definition of μ_*. The log likelihood function for a sample of I producers, each observed for T periods of time, becomes

$$\ln L = \text{constant} - \frac{I(T-1)}{2} \ln \sigma_v^2 - \frac{I}{2} \ln(\sigma_v^2 + T\sigma_u^2)$$

$$+ \sum_i \ln\left[1 - \Phi\left(-\frac{\mu_{*i}}{\sigma_*}\right)\right] - \left(\frac{\varepsilon'\varepsilon}{2\sigma_v^2}\right) + \frac{1}{2}\sum_i \left(\frac{\mu_{*i}}{\sigma_*}\right)^2, \qquad (4.3.4)$$

where $\mu_{*i} = T\sigma_u^2\bar{\varepsilon}_i/(\sigma_v^2 + T\sigma_u^2)$ and $\sigma_*^2 = \sigma_u^2\sigma_v^2/(\sigma_v^2 + T\sigma_u^2)$. This log likelihood function can be maximized with respect to the parameters to obtain maximum likelihood estimates of β, σ_v^2, and σ_u^2.

The conditional distribution of $(u|\varepsilon)$ is

$$f(u|\varepsilon) = \frac{1}{(2\pi)^{1/2}\sigma_*[1 - \Phi(-\mu_*/\sigma_*)]} \cdot \exp\left\{-\frac{(u-\mu_*)^2}{2\sigma_*^2}\right\}, \qquad (4.3.5)$$

which is the density function of a variable distributed as $N^+(\mu_*, \sigma_*^2)$. Either the mean or the mode of this distribution can be used as a point estimator of cost efficiency, and we have

$$E(u_i|\varepsilon_i) = \mu_{*i} + \sigma_*\left[\frac{\phi(-\mu_{*i}/\sigma_*)}{1 - \Phi(-\mu_{*i}/\sigma_*)}\right] \qquad (4.3.6)$$

and

$$M(u_i|\varepsilon_i) = \begin{cases} \mu_{*i} & \text{if } \varepsilon_i \geq 0, \\ 0 & \text{otherwise,} \end{cases} \qquad (4.3.7)$$

respectively. These estimators are consistent as $T \to +\infty$. Either can be substituted into $CE_i = \exp\{-u_i\}$ to obtain producer-specific estimates of time-invariant cost efficiency. An alternative estimator is provided by the minimum squared error predictor

$$E(\exp\{-u_i\}|\varepsilon_i) = \frac{1 - \Phi[\sigma_* - (\mu_{*i}/\sigma_*)]}{1 - \Phi(-\mu_{*i}/\sigma_*)} \cdot \exp\left\{-\mu_{*i} + \frac{1}{2}\sigma_*^2\right\}. \qquad (4.3.8)$$

Confidence intervals for any of these estimators can be constructed exactly as in the cross-sectional maximum likelihood model, with the appropriate changes in notation.

   The longer the panel, the less tenable is the assumption that cost efficiency is time invariant. All three estimation procedures, LSDV, GLS, and MLE, can be modified to accommodate time-varying cost efficiency, exactly as they were in Section 3.3.2 in the estimation of technical efficiency. The only changes involve raising instead of lowering intercepts for cost-inefficient producers in the case of LSDV and GLS, and some sign changes in the case of MLE. We leave the details to the reader.

4.3.2 Simultaneous-Equation Cost Frontier Models

As we noted at the outset of Section 4.2.2 in a cross-sectional context, simultaneous-equation cost frontier models offer the possibility of generating more information than single-equation cost frontier models. While single-equation models can provide estimates of the cost of input-oriented inefficiency, simultaneous-equation models can *in principle* provide estimates of the separate costs of technical and allocative inefficiency. However we also noted that a fully satisfactory *econometric* specification of a simultaneous-equation model remains to be developed. We also noted at the outset of Section 4.3 that the advantage of having access to panel data is that we get to observe producers more than once. This enables us to relax restrictive distributional and independence assumptions, and to obtain consistent estimates of cost efficiency. Consequently having access to panel data with which to estimate a simultaneous-equation cost frontier system combines the best of both worlds, and offers the best opportunity to solve the Greene problem.

We consider two models, the single-output Cobb–Douglas model discussed in Section 4.2.2.1 and the multiple-output translog model discussed in Section 4.2.2.2. The Cobb–Douglas model given in equations (4.2.23) is not entirely satisfactory because the input mix equation errors consist entirely of allocative inefficiency; no statistical noise appears in these equations. None of the translog systems is embedded in a stochastic framework that is both econometrically sensible and estimable. Perhaps having access to panel data will help to resolve either or both difficulties.

Cobb–Douglas With panel data covering I producers through T time periods, the Cobb–Douglas system (4.2.23) can be slightly rearranged and written as

$$\ln y_{it} = \beta_o + \sum_n \beta_n \ln x_{nit} + v_{it} - u_i,$$

$$\ln x_{1it} - \ln x_{nit} + \ln\left(\frac{\beta_n}{\beta_1}\right) = \ln\left(\frac{w_{nit}}{w_{1it}}\right) + \eta_{ni} + \xi_{nit}, \qquad n = 2, \ldots, N.$$

$$(4.3.9)$$

The essential difference between equations (4.3.9) and equations (4.2.23), apart from the addition of time subscripts, is the appearance of statistical noise, captured by the ξ_{nit}, in the input mix equations contained in equations (4.3.9). With panel data it is possible to separate allocative inefficiency from noise. Notice that both the cost of technical inefficiency (represented by the u_i) and the magnitudes of allocative inefficiency (represented by the η_{ni}) are producer specific but time invariant.

This model can be estimated in two ways, depending on whether the u_i are assumed to be fixed or random effects. If the u_i are assumed to be fixed effects, no distributional assumption is needed, and a fixed-effects approach is feasible. Solving equations (4.3.9) for the natural logarithms of the inputs, we obtain

$$\ln x_{kit} = \alpha_k + \sum_{n>1}\left(\frac{\beta_n}{r} - \delta_{nk}\right)\eta_{ki} + \frac{1}{r}\ln y_{it} + \sum_{n>1}\left(\frac{\beta_n}{r}\right)\ln\left(\frac{w_{nit}}{w_{kit}}\right)$$

$$+ \sum_{n>1}\left(\frac{\beta_n}{r} - \delta_{nk}\right)\xi_{nit} + \frac{1}{r}u_i - \frac{1}{r}v_{it}, \qquad k = 1, \ldots, N, \quad (4.3.10)$$

where $r = \Sigma_n \beta_n$ and

$$\alpha_k = \ln\beta_k - \frac{1}{r}\left[\beta_o + \sum_n \beta_n \ln\beta_n\right],$$

$$\delta_{nk} = \begin{cases} 1 & \text{if } k = n, \\ 0 & \text{otherwise.} \end{cases}$$

Applying a within transformation to equations (4.3.10) eliminates the time-invariant terms α_k, η_{ki}, and u_i. This allows nonlinear SUR to be applied to the transformed system of input demand equations to obtain estimates of the β_ks. These estimates can then be inserted into equations (4.3.9) to generate estimates of the η_{ni} and u_i by means of

$$\hat{\eta}_{ni} = \overline{\ln\left(\frac{x_{1i}}{x_{ni}}\right)} + \overline{\ln\left(\frac{w_{1i}}{w_{ni}}\right)} + \ln\left(\frac{\hat{\beta}_n}{\hat{\beta}_1}\right),$$

$$\hat{u}_i = \max_i(\bar{e}_i) - \bar{e}_i, \tag{4.3.11}$$

where $\bar{e}_i = (1/T)\Sigma_t(\ln y_{it} - \hat{\beta}_o - \Sigma_n\hat{\beta}_n\ln x_{nit})$ and a bar over a variable indicates the temporal mean of the variable.

If the u_i are assumed to be random effects, we can use MLE to obtain estimates of the parameters of the model. We make the following assumptions:

(i) $v_{it} \sim$ iid $N(0, \sigma_v^2)$.

(ii) $u_i \sim$ iid $N^+(0, \sigma_u^2)$.

(iii) $\xi_{nit} \sim$ iid $N(0, \Sigma)$.

(iv) u_i, v_{it}, and ξ_{nit} are distributed independently of each other, and of the regressors.

With these distributional assumptions, the log likelihood function for equations (4.3.9) is

$$\ln L = \text{constant} - \frac{1}{2}I(T-1)\ln\sigma_v^2 - \frac{I}{2}\ln(\sigma_v^2 + T\sigma_u^2)$$

$$-\frac{1}{2\sigma_v^2}\sum_i(\varepsilon_i'A\varepsilon_i) + \sum_i\ln\Phi(a_i) + IT\ln r$$

$$-\frac{1}{2}IT\ln|\Sigma| - \frac{1}{2}\sum_i\sum_t z_{it}'\Sigma^{-1}z_{it}, \tag{4.3.12}$$

where

$$A = I_T - \frac{\sigma_u^2 \iota \iota'}{\sigma_v^2 + T\sigma_u^2},$$

$$\iota_{N \times 1} = (1, \ldots, 1)',$$

I_T is a $T \times T$ identity matrix,

$$\varepsilon_i = (\varepsilon_{I1}, \ldots, \varepsilon_{iT})' = \varpi_i - \iota u_i, \qquad i = 1, \ldots, I,$$

$$a_i = \frac{\sigma_u}{\sigma_v} \frac{\sum_t \varepsilon_{it}}{\sqrt{(\sigma_v^2 + T\sigma_u^2)}}, \qquad i = 1, \ldots, I,$$

$$z_{it} = \begin{bmatrix} \ln x_{1it} - \ln x_{2it} - \ln w_{2it} + \ln w_{1it} - \ln \beta_1 + \ln \beta_2 - \eta_{2i} \\ \vdots \\ \ln x_{1it} - \ln x_{Nit} - \ln w_{Nit} + \ln w_{1it} - \ln \beta_1 + \ln \beta_N - \eta_{Ni} \end{bmatrix}.$$

The computational burden of obtaining parameter estimates can be substantially reduced by concentrating the log likelihood function with respect to η_{ni} and Σ. At the maximum of $\ln L$ we have

$$\eta_{ni} = \overline{\ln x_{1i}} - \overline{\ln x_{ni}} - \overline{\ln w_{ni}} + \overline{\ln w_{1i}} - \ln \beta_1 + \ln \beta_n, \qquad n = 1, \ldots, N,$$

$$\Sigma = \frac{1}{I \cdot T} \sum_i \sum_t z_{it}^* z_{it}^{*\prime},$$

where $z_{it}^* = z_{it} - \iota \bar{z}_i$. Substituting these values back into the log likelihood function yields the concentrated log likelihood function

$$\ln L = \text{constant} - \frac{1}{2} I(T-1) \ln \sigma_v^2 - \frac{I}{2} \ln(\sigma_v^2 + T\sigma_u^2) - \frac{1}{2\sigma_v^2} \sum_i (\varepsilon_i' A \varepsilon_i)$$

$$+ \sum_i \ln \Phi(a_i) + IT \ln r - \frac{1}{2} IT \ln \left| \frac{1}{IT} \sum_i \sum_t z_{it}^* z_{it}^{*\prime} \right|, \qquad (4.3.13)$$

which can be maximized to obtain estimates of $\beta_o, \beta_1, \ldots, \beta_N, \sigma_v^2$, and σ_u^2. The simplification of the concentrated log likelihood function results from the fact that the z_{it}^* do not depend on any parameters, a typical element of z_{it}^* having the form $z_{kit}^* = \overline{\ln x_{1it}} - \overline{\ln x_{kit}} + \overline{\ln w_{1it}} - \overline{\ln w_{kit}}$. Consequently the last term in the concentrated log likelihood function is a constant.

The next step is to obtain estimates of technical efficiency. A minor modification of analogous results in Section 3.3.1 can be used to demonstrate that the conditional distribution of $(u_i | \varepsilon_{it})$ is $N^+(\mu_{*i}, \sigma_*^2)$, where

$$\mu_{*i} = \frac{\sigma_u^2}{\sigma_v^2 + T\sigma_u^2} \sum_t \varepsilon_{it},$$

$$\sigma_*^2 = \frac{\sigma_u^2 \sigma_v^2}{\sigma_v^2 + T\sigma_u^2}.$$

Thus either the mean or the mode of $(u_i | \varepsilon_i)$, where $\varepsilon_i = (\varepsilon_{i1}, \ldots, \varepsilon_{iT})'$, can be used as a point estimator of u_i, and we have

$$E(u_i | \varepsilon_{it}) = \sigma_* \left[\frac{\mu_{*i}}{\sigma_*} + \frac{\phi(\mu_{*i}/\sigma_*)}{\Phi(\mu_{*i}/\sigma_*)} \right],$$

$$M(u_i | \varepsilon_{it}) = \begin{cases} \mu_{*i} & \text{if } \sum_t \varepsilon_{it} \geq 0, \\ 0 & \text{otherwise.} \end{cases} \tag{4.3.14}$$

The final step is to obtain estimates of allocative inefficiency. This requires estimates of the η_{ni}, which are provided in equation (4.3.11).

Translog With panel data covering I producers through T time periods, the translog cost system given in equations (4.2.34) and (4.2.38) can be written as

$$\ln E_{it} = \ln c(y_{it}, w_{it}; \beta) + v_{it} + u_{Ti} + u_{Ait},$$

$$\frac{w_{nit} x_{nit}}{E_{it}} = S_{nit}(y_{it}, w_{it}; \beta) + A\eta_{ni} + \xi_{nit}, \qquad n = 2, \ldots, N, \tag{4.3.15}$$

where u_{Ait} generalizes the expression in equation (4.2.37) and the $A\eta_{ni}$ generalize the expressions in equation (4.2.39). The essential difference between the translog cost system in equations (4.2.34) and (4.2.38) and the system in equation (4.3.15), apart from the addition of time subscripts, is that in the present panel data formulation the magnitudes of allocative inefficiency (the η_{ni}) are parameters to be estimated, and are both input and producer specific, although they are time invariant. However the impact of allocative inefficiency on input cost shares (the $A\eta_{ni}$) and on cost (u_{Ait}) is time varying, because both expressions depend on time-varying data. This increased flexibility is yet another illustration of the advantage of having access to panel data. It is also possible to introduce some form of time dependence into the magnitudes of allocative inefficiency, for example by specifying $\eta_{nit} = \eta_{ni} \cdot \gamma(t)$, where $\gamma(t)$ is a parametric function of time and the η_{ni} are fixed parameters.

Under the distributional assumptions that $v_{it} \sim$ iid $N(0, \sigma_v^2)$, $u_{Ti} \sim$ iid $N^+(0, \sigma_u^2)$, and $\xi_{it} \sim$ iid $N(0, \Sigma_\zeta)$, the log likelihood function can be written as

$$\ln L = \sum_i \ln f(\varepsilon_i) + \sum_i \ln f(\xi_i), \qquad (4.3.16)$$

where $\varepsilon_i = (\varepsilon_{i1}, \ldots, \varepsilon_{iT})'$, $\varepsilon_{it} = v_{it} + u_{Ti}$, and

$$f(\xi_i) = (2\pi)^{-NT/2} \cdot |\Sigma_\xi|^{-T/2} \cdot \exp\left\{ -\frac{1}{2} \sum_t \xi'_{it} \Sigma_\xi^{-1} \xi_{it} \right\},$$

and $\xi_{it} = (\xi_{i1t}, \ldots, \xi_{iNt})'$. Estimation of u_{Ti} for each producer is the same as in equation (4.3.6) or (4.3.7), and estimates of CE_i can be obtained from equation (4.3.8). Finally, estimates of u_{Ait} can be obtained from the estimated values of the parameters in the definition of u_{Ait}.

4.4 TWO ADDITIONAL APPROACHES TO THE ESTIMATION OF COST EFFICIENCY

Two novel approaches to the estimation of cost efficiency have recently been developed. Both can be based on a translog system consisting of a cost equation and its associated input cost share equations. However neither approach attempts to decompose estimated cost inefficiency into its technical and allocative components. The first approach is an admittedly ad hoc approach dubbed "thick frontier analysis," TFA for short. TFA does not require a one-sided error term, and so is not really a frontier approach to the estimation of cost efficiency. However in contrast to some of the more sophisticated approaches discussed in previous sections, TFA is easy to implement, using either cross-sectional data or panel data. The price to be paid for its simplicity is the extreme paucity of information it generates. We consider TFA in Section 4.4.1. The second approach is dubbed a "distribution-free approach," DFA for short, because although it contains a one-sided error term representing cost inefficiency, it imposes no distributional assumptions on it. DFA requires panel data, and is structurally similar to the GLS approach discussed in Section 4.3. We consider DFA in Section 4.4.2.

4.4.1 Thick Frontier Analysis

Thick frontier analysis was developed by Berger and Humphrey (1991, 1992) as a way of avoiding the restrictive assumptions required in conventional approaches to the estimation of cost efficiency. TFA is much less structured than conventional approaches, and so it generates less information, but it always "works." It can be employed within a single cross section or a panel. We discuss TFA within a cross-sectional context.

We begin by assuming that we have observations on total expenditure E_i incurred, a vector $y_i \geq 0$ of outputs produced, and a vector $w_i > 0$ of input prices faced, by a sample of producers indexed $i = 1$, ..., I. Next we identify producers located in the top and bottom quartiles (or quintiles or whatever) of the average cost distribution. (If producers produce multiple outputs, average cost can be proxied by total cost divided by the Euclidean norm of the output vector, or by assets or employment.) Producers located in the bottom quartile are presumed to be relatively cost efficient as a group, and together they define a *thick frontier*. Producers located in the top quartile are presumed to be cost inefficient relative to the thick frontier. If differences in average cost are also thought to be scale related, it is possible to control for this influence by stratifying the sample into size classes (if the sample size permits) before forming the quartiles; this ensures that a range of producers is represented within each quartile. Variation in input prices is handled in a different way, described later.

The next step is to estimate separate cost functions (not frontiers) for the top and bottom average cost quartiles. Variation in residuals *within* each quartile is assumed to reflect only random statistical noise, whereas differences in the average level of predicted costs *between* the top and bottom quartiles is assumed to reflect only a combination of exogenous influences and cost inefficiency within the top quartile. While it is unlikely that these assumptions hold exactly, and consequently it is unlikely that TFA yields precise estimates of cost efficiency, the objective of TFA is not econometric rigor, but reliable insight into the probable magnitude of the problem.

Suppose that the cost functions within each quartile have translog form. Then we can estimate the structure of technology within each quartile by estimating the system of equations

$$\ln E_i = \ln c(y_i, w_i; \beta) + v_i,$$

$$\frac{w_{ni} x_{ni}}{E_i} = S_{ni}(y_i, w_i; \beta) + v_{ni}, \qquad n = 2, \ldots, N. \tag{4.4.1}$$

This system is estimated twice, once for each quartile. On the assumption that $[v_i, v_{ni}']' \sim N(0, \Sigma)$, this system may be estimated by SUR, as in Christensen and Greene (1976). Denote the estimated parameter vectors for the first and fourth quartiles β^1 and β^4, and denote the predicted average costs at the mean values of (y_i, w_i) within each quartile by $[c(y, w; \beta^1)/y]^{Q1}$ and $[c(y, w; \beta^4)/y]^{Q4}$, where if y is not a scalar one of the proxies mentioned previously is used.

The difference between the two quartile predicted average costs can be expressed and decomposed as

$$\frac{[c(y, w; \beta^4)/y]^{Q4} - [c(y, w; \beta^1)/y]^{Q1}}{[c(y, w; \beta^1)/y]^{Q1}}$$

$$= \frac{[c(y, w; \beta^4)/y]^{Q4} - [c(y, w; \beta^1)/y]^{Q4}}{[c(y, w; \beta^1)/y]^{Q1}}$$

$$+ \frac{[c(y, w; \beta^1)/y]^{Q4} - [c(y, w; \beta^1)/y]^{Q1}}{[c(y, w; \beta^1)/y]^{Q1}}. \tag{4.4.2}$$

The left-hand side of equation (4.4.2) provides an estimate of the percentage difference between the predicted average costs of producers located in quartiles $Q4$ and $Q1$. Since cost functions are estimated separately for the two quartiles, estimated parameter vectors β^4 and β^1 are allowed to differ. Differences between β^4 and β^1, particularly but not exclusively differences between the two intercepts, are intended to reflect differences in cost efficiency between the two quartiles. The first term on the right-hand side provides an estimate of the cost inefficiency of producers located in $Q4$. Here cost inefficiency is estimated as the difference between predicted average cost in $Q4$ using the inefficient $Q4$ technology represented by β^4 and predicted average cost in $Q4$ using the efficient $Q1$ technology represented by β^1, expressed as a percentage of predicted average cost in $Q1$. There is no cost efficiency differential if $[c(y, w; \beta^4)/y]^{Q4} = [c(y, w; \beta^1)/y]^{Q4}$, a sufficient condition for which is $\beta^4 = \beta^1$. The second term on the right-hand side provides an estimate of the average cost difference attributable not to cost inefficiency but to heterogeneity in the markets in which inefficient and efficient producers operate. Equal cost efficiency is enforced by giving producers in both quartiles the same estimated β^1 technology. The market heterogeneity may be reflected in differences between $(y, w)^{Q4}$ and $(y, w)^{Q1}$.

It is important to emphasize that the decomposition in equation (4.4.2) is applied not to individual producers in either quartile, but to hypothetical mean producers in each quartile. It is in this sense that TFA provides limited information. However since TFA associates cost inefficiency with differences between β^4 and β^1, the following expression can be used to provide an estimate of the average cost inefficiency (ACI_i) of individual producers in $Q4$:

$$ACI_i = \frac{[c(y_i, w_i; \beta^4)/y_i]^{Q4} - [c(y_i, w_i; \beta^1)/y_i]^{Q4}}{[c(y_i, w_i; \beta^1)/y_i]^{Q4}}. \tag{4.4.3}$$

ACI_i indicates the percentage by which average cost is raised using inefficient technology represented by β^4 rather than efficient technology represented by β^1.

The TFA approach has some nice features. Unlike an explicit cost frontier approach, TFA does not require restrictive distributional and independence assumptions on error components; indeed it has no one-sided error component. It is based on an estimable version of the translog cost system with a conventional error structure, and so it is not susceptible to the "Greene problem" that plagues the translog cost frontier system. It does not look for evidence of inefficiency in one-sided error components, which can be difficult to identify; instead it associates inefficiency with differences between easily estimated quartile parameter vectors. Finally, Bauer, Berger, and Humphrey (1993) report evidence based on U.S. banking data suggesting that TFA generates cost efficiency estimates that are similar in magnitude to estimates generated by stochastic frontier techniques.

However TFA has some rather serious shortcomings. First, it is arbitrarily based on average cost quartiles, and estimated cost inefficiency would increase if equally arbitrary quintiles were used instead. Second, it uses only half of the data (or 40% of the data if quintiles are used), and not many researchers are so well endowed with degrees of freedom that they can discard half of their observations. Most importantly, TFA does not generate cost efficiency estimates for each producer in the sample. It generates only one cost efficiency estimate, for the hypothetical mean producer in the high-cost quartile relative to the hypothetical mean producer in the low-cost quartile. (Of course if the observations are stratified into S size classes, TFA would generate S such cost efficiency estimates.) Thus TFA is likely to be useless to management and of limited value to policy-makers.

4.4.2 A Distribution-Free Approach

The distribution-free approach was introduced by Berger (1993). DFA requires panel data, and is structurally similar to the GLS approach discussed in Section 4.3. It is based on a translog system of cost and input cost share equations, and it generates estimates of cost inefficiency for each producer in each time period.

Suppose we observe a sample of producers indexed $i = 1, \ldots, I$ in each of T time periods indexed $t = 1, \ldots, T$. For each producer we observe total expenditure E_{it}, a vector y_{it} of outputs produced, and a vector w_{it} of input prices paid. Then a translog system consisting of a cost equation and its associated input cost share equations can be written as

$$\ln E_{it} = \ln c(y_{it}, w_{it}; \beta^t) + v_{it} + u_i,$$

$$\frac{w_{nit} x_{nit}}{E_{it}} = s_{nit}(y_{it}, w_{it}; \beta^t) + v_{nit}, \qquad n = 2, \ldots, N. \qquad (4.4.4)$$

This system is estimated separately for each time period, and so the technology parameter vector has a time superscript. Within each time period the error vector $[v_{it}, v_{nit}']'$ captures the effects of random statistical noise, and the error component $u_i \geq 0$ measures the cost of producer-specific cost inefficiency. Since $E(v_{nit}) = 0$, allocative efficiency is imposed, and so u_i captures the cost of technical inefficiency only.

The system of equations (4.4.4) is estimated using SUR a total of T times, once for each time period. Thus it is assumed that the u_i are random effects distributed independently of the regressors. For each producer the cost equation residuals $\hat{\varepsilon}_{it} = \hat{v}_{it} + \hat{u}_i$ are averaged over time to obtain $\hat{\varepsilon}_i = (1/T)\Sigma_t\hat{\varepsilon}_{it}$. On the assumption that the random-noise error component v_{it} should tend to average zero over time, $\hat{\varepsilon}_i = (1/T)\Sigma_t\hat{\varepsilon}_{it} \cong \hat{u}_i$ provides an estimate of the cost inefficiency error component. To ensure that estimated cost inefficiency is nonnegative, $\hat{\varepsilon}_i$ is normalized on the smallest value, and we obtain

$$\hat{CE}_i = \exp\{-[\hat{\varepsilon}_i - \min_i(\hat{\varepsilon}_i)]\}. \tag{4.4.5}$$

This estimator is similar to the GLS panel data estimator in which u_i is treated as a random effect, and this similarity suggests that it is appropriate when I is large relative to T and when the u_i are orthogonal to the regressors. However it differs from GLS in that the structure of the underlying production technology is allowed to vary through time. Berger also noted that since the elements of v_{it} may not fully cancel out through time for each producer, $\hat{\varepsilon}_i$ may contain elements of luck as well as inefficiency. To alleviate this problem, he recommended truncating the distribution of CE_i at its qth and $(1 - q)$th quantiles.

A disadvantage of DFA is the requirement that cost efficiency be time invariant, and this assumption becomes less tenable as T increases. However DFA also has two distinct virtues. First, being based on a sequence of T separate cross-sectional regressions, it allows the structure of production technology to vary flexibly through time (although excessive variation in β' would be difficult to explain). Second, it does not impose a distributional assumption on the u_i; it lets the data reveal the empirical distribution of the $\hat{\varepsilon}_i \cong \hat{u}_i$. Although ε_i is truncated, it need not follow any of the specific distributions we have considered for u_i when discussing the MLE approach.

Using three large ($T = 10$, $I \cong 1,000$) panels of U.S. banks, Berger examined the empirical distributions of $\hat{\varepsilon}_i \cong \hat{u}_i$. Only two of three distributions exhibited the positive skewness one would expect, and all three skewness coefficients were numerically small (0.36, 0.36, −0.21). Histograms of the three distributions appear approximately normal, and Shapiro–Wilks variance ratio test statistics could not reject the normality hypothesis for each distribution.

An important consideration in the DFA approach concerns the length of the panel. If T is "small" the random-noise terms v_{it} may not average zero, and substantial amounts of random noise will appear in the cost inefficiency error component u_i. On the other hand, if T is "large" the time-invariant assumption on u_i is likely to be violated. This suggests that there may exist an optimal value of T on which to base the DFA approach.

DeYoung (1997) has developed a diagnostic test for determining the optimal panel length. The procedure begins by expressing ε_i as $\varepsilon_i(T)$ to indicate that it is based on T time periods and writing it in longhand as

$$\varepsilon_i(T) = \frac{1}{T}[(u_{i1} + \cdots + u_{iT}) + (v_{i1} + \cdots + v_{iT})], \tag{4.4.6}$$

where u_i is now allowed to be time varying and to follow the time path

$$u_{it} = \begin{cases} u_{i1} & \text{for } t \leq S, \\ u_{it-1} + \tau_i \cdot u_{i1} & \text{for } t > S, \end{cases} \tag{4.4.7}$$

where $\tau_i \cdot u_{i1}$ is the annual "drift" in cost inefficiency for the ith producer and $\tau_i \in [-1, +1]$. Substituting equation (4.4.7) into equation (4.4.6) yields

$$\varepsilon_i(T) = u_{i1} + \frac{1}{2T} \cdot (\tau_i \cdot u_{i1}) \cdot \max\{0, |T - S| \cdot (T - S + 1)\} + \frac{1}{T} \sum_t v_{it}. \tag{4.4.8}$$

The first term on the right-hand side of equation (4.4.8) is the initial level of cost inefficiency for the ith producer. The second term is the average annual accumulated drift in cost inefficiency from $t = 1$ to $t = T$. The third term is the mean of the random-noise error component. The general strategy is to select a value of T that is short enough to limit the distortions caused by the temporal drift in u_{it} and long enough to minimize the mean random-noise error component.

For a given value of T, define the cross-sectional mean and variance of $\varepsilon_i(T)$ as

$$\mu(T) = \frac{1}{N} \sum_i \varepsilon_i(T),$$

$$\sigma^2(T) = \frac{1}{N-1} \sum_i [\varepsilon_i(T) - \mu(T)]^2. \tag{4.4.9}$$

Substituting equation (4.4.8) and the expression for $\mu(T)$ into the expression for $\sigma^2(T)$ yields the expression

$$\sigma^2(T) = \frac{1}{N-1}\sum_i\left[\left(u_{i1} - \frac{1}{N}\sum_i u_{i1}\right) + \frac{1}{2T}\max\{0,|T-S|\cdot(T-S+1)\}\right.$$
$$\left.\times\left(\tau_i\cdot u_{i1} - \frac{1}{N}\sum_i\tau_i\cdot u_{i1}\right) + \frac{1}{T}\left(\sum_t v_{it} - \frac{1}{N}\sum_i\sum_t v_{it}\right)\right]^2.$$

$$(4.4.10)$$

Interest centers on how the absolute values of the three terms inside the square brackets change as the value of T increases. The first term (the initial level of cost inefficiency) does not vary with T. The second term (the average annual accumulated drift in cost inefficiency) equals zero from $T = 1$ to $T = S$. For $T > S$ this term increases in absolute value as T increases. The absolute value of the third term (random noise) decreases as T increases. Thus until $T = S$ the magnitude of $\sigma^2(T)$ declines as T increases, and as a result the estimates of cost inefficiency $\varepsilon_i(T)$ will approach the true values u_i. However for $T > S$ the magnitude of $\sigma^2(T)$ either increases, remains constant, or decreases with increases in T, depending on whether the marginal reduction in random noise exceeds, equals, or falls short of the marginal drift in cost inefficiency. The optimal value of T is therefore defined as the first value of T for which $\sigma^2(T)$ stops decreasing. DeYoung conducted a test of the hypothesis that $\sigma^2(T)$ has stopped decreasing by performing a series of F tests of the hypothesis that $\sigma^2(T)/\sigma^2(T+1) = 1$, although he noted that the test is not strictly valid because the numerator and denominator are not independent draws from the same population.

4.5 A GUIDE TO THE LITERATURE

The analytical foundations for the definition and decomposition of cost efficiency were laid by Farrell (1957), and much of the material in this chapter derives ultimately from Farrell's insights. Early research into the estimation of cost functions is summarized by Johnston (1960). Other pioneering research includes that of Nerlove (1963), who followed Shephard (1953) by allowing for homotheticity of the dual production technology and by imposing linear homogeneity in input prices on the Cobb–Douglas cost function he estimated, and Christensen and Greene (1976), who were perhaps the first to estimate a flexible translog cost and input cost share equation system.

The estimation of stochastic cost frontiers began with Schmidt and Lovell (1979, 1980), although a deterministic cost frontier was previously estimated by Førsund and Jansen (1977). Other early studies include those of Greene (1980b) and Stevenson (1980), who introduced two-parameter distributions for the one-sided error component. Progress during the past two decades is surveyed by Schmidt (1985–1986), Bauer (1990b), Greene (1993, 1997), and Cornwell and Schmidt (1996).

New developments and applications appear regularly in the *Journal of Econometrics*, the *Journal of Productivity Analysis*, and a wide variety of field journals. One development worthy of mention concerns the use of flexible functional forms other than translog to model the deterministic kernel of a stochastic cost frontier. The Fourier functional form contains the translog form as a special case, and has been used to model a cost frontier by Berger and Mester (1997), and in several other studies they cite.

5   The Estimation and Decomposition of Profit Efficiency

5.1 INTRODUCTION

In Chapter 4 our efficiency analysis was based on the assumption that producers face exogenously determined input prices and output quantities and attempt to allocate inputs so as to minimize the cost of producing their outputs. Under this assumption inputs, but not outputs, are determined endogenously. While a cost minimization objective is undoubtedly appropriate in some environments, it can be argued that in other environments it is not sufficiently stringent, because for many producers the ultimate objective is to maximize profit. In such an environment the assumption is that producers face exogenously determined input prices and output prices and attempt to allocate inputs and outputs so as to maximize profit. Under this assumption both inputs and outputs are determined endogenously. The main difference between the two frameworks is that when producers attempt to maximize profit, they have to decide not only how much of various inputs to use (which is the case for producers attempting to minimize cost), but also how much of various outputs to produce. In other words, the issue is not just one of finding the cost-minimizing input combination required to produce a given bundle of outputs, but also one of finding the revenue-maximizing output combination as well, and so the number of decision variables increases from N to $M + N$. In this chapter our focus is on efficiency measurement when the objective of producers is to maximize profit.

A natural question to ask in a price-taking, profit-maximizing framework is: Can inefficient producers survive? The answer is: Not for long. In a long-run competitive equilibrium context profit is driven to zero and only efficient producers survive. However in a short-run temporary equilibrium context inefficient producers can survive with some loss, even in a competitive environment, provided that the loss is less than the cost of their fixed inputs. These considerations suggest that if one is interested in estimating profit efficiency in a price-taking environment, then it is appropriate to conduct the exercise within a short-run framework in which some inputs are exogenously determined. Thus the appropriate standard against which to evaluate profit efficiency is the variable profit frontier.

The chapter is organized as follows. In Section 5.2 we consider a situation in which profit-seeking producers produce a single output, and we introduce models based on primal production frontiers in Section 5.2.1 and dual variable profit frontiers in Section 5.2.2. Throughout this section we assume that output price, variable input prices, and quasi-fixed input quantities are exogenously determined. We show how to model technical and allocative inefficiencies, and we derive their impacts on variable profit. We discuss estimation procedures for primal and dual models in both cross-sectional and panel data settings.

In Section 5.3 we relax the single-output assumption and allow profit-seeking producers to produce multiple outputs. These multiple-output models are discussed within a primal distance function framework in Section 5.3.1 and a dual profit frontier framework in Section 5.3.2. We continue to assume that output prices and variable input prices are exogenously determined, and for purely econometric reasons to be explained later we ignore quasi-fixed inputs. We show how to model technical and allocative inefficiencies, and we derive their impacts on profit. We discuss estimation procedures in the context of both cross-sectional and panel data settings.

In Section 5.4 we consider a situation in which producers seek to maximize profit, but they no longer take output prices as exogenously determined. In contrast to the conventional scenarios considered in Sections 5.2 and 5.3, in which prices are assumed to be exogenously determined, perhaps by the forces of competition, in this section we endow producers with some pricing power in their product markets.

The result is an "alternative" profit frontier in which variable input prices and output quantities (rather than output prices) are exogenously determined. Because output prices are no longer taken to be exogenous, the alternative profit frontier incorporates product demand structure as well as technology structure, and so does not provide a dual representation of the structure of production technology. Nonetheless the central problem of modeling and estimating technical and allocative inefficiencies remains unchanged. However since the alternative profit frontier has different regularity conditions than a conventional profit frontier does, estimation procedures are modified. Here, as in Sections 5.2 and 5.3, our discussion of estimation procedures is brief, because only minor modifications to the procedures developed in Chapters 3 and 4 are required.

Section 5.5 contains references to the relevant literature.

5.2 SINGLE-OUTPUT MODELS

In this section we consider a situation in which producers produce a single output. In Section 5.2.1 we use a primal production frontier approach, in which the production frontier and the first-order conditions for variable profit maximization are used to estimate the parameters of the model as well as the magnitudes of technical and allocative inefficiencies and variable profit inefficiency. (Although this material is based on a production frontier, and hence is referred to as a primal approach, it also exploits dual price information, and so it is not really a pure primal approach.) This is followed in Section 5.2.2 with a dual variable profit frontier approach, in which one can either estimate a variable profit frontier using a single-equation method or estimate a system of equations consisting of either the variable profit frontier and the associated variable profit share equations or just the variable profit share equations. The central problem remains one of modeling and estimating technical and allocative inefficiencies and their impact on variable profit.

5.2.1 The Primal Production Frontier Approach

One implicit assumption in the production frontier approach adopted in Chapter 3 is that inputs are exogenous and uncorrelated with technical inefficiency. This assumption seems quite strong, since Mundlak (1961) and others have claimed that more efficient producers tend to produce more output and to use more inputs, given the input prices and the output prices they face. If so, technical inefficiency will be correlated with input use, resulting in inconsistent parameter estimates when a single-equation production frontier model is used. This problem can be alleviated by treating variable inputs as endogenous, which allows correlation between variable inputs and technical inefficiency.

We begin by writing the production frontier as

$$y = f(x, z; \beta) \cdot \exp\{-u\}, \tag{5.2.1}$$

where $y \geq 0$ is scalar output, $x = (x_1, \ldots, x_N) \geq 0$ is a vector of variable inputs, $z = (z_1, \ldots, z_Q) \geq 0$ is a vector of quasi-fixed inputs, $u \geq 0$ represents output-oriented technical inefficiency, and $f(x, z; \beta)$ is the deterministic kernel of a stochastic production frontier. If producers attempt to maximize variable profit (conditional on u), the first-order conditions can be written as

$$f_n(x, z; \beta) \cdot \exp\{-u\} = \frac{w_n}{p} \cdot \exp\{-\xi_n\}, \qquad n = 1, \ldots, N, \tag{5.2.2}$$

where $f_n(x, z; \beta) = \partial f(x, z; \beta)/\partial x_n$, the w_n/p are normalized variable input prices, $w = (w_1, \ldots, w_N) > 0$ is an input price vector, and $p > 0$ is the scalar output price. The ξ_n are interpreted as allocative inefficiencies, nonzero values of which indicate over- or underutilization of a variable input, given normalized prices of the variable inputs and quantities of the quasi-fixed inputs. Such allocative inefficiencies may also arise due to the presence of constraints (other than the production technology) faced by the producer that are not incorporated into the optimization problem. The effect of all of these influences will be captured by the ξ_n, which we call allocative inefficiencies.

The definition of allocative inefficiency in equation (5.2.2) is different from that used in Chapter 4. In Chapter 4 we defined input allocative inefficiencies as departures of marginal rates of substitution (MRS) from the respective input price ratios, whereas in equation (5.2.2) they are defined as departures of variable input marginal products from their normalized prices. The difference is due to the fact that in Chapter 4 we used a cost minimization criterion for which the first-order conditions are expressed by the equality of MRSs with input price ratios. Thus it was natural to define input allocative inefficiencies as departures from this rule. In a variable profit-maximizing framework the first-order conditions are different, but we follow the same principle and define variable input allocative inefficiencies in terms of nonfulfillment of the first-order conditions for variable profit maximization. These two measures are, however, related. The definition used in the cost-minimizing framework is provided by the ratios $\xi_{n1} = \xi_n/\xi_1$ for variable input pairs (x_n, x_1), $n = 2, \ldots, N$.

Cobb–Douglas If the production frontier takes the Cobb–Douglas form, the production frontier in equation (5.2.1) and the first-order conditions for variable profit maximization in equation (5.2.2) can be written in logarithmic form as

$$\ln y = \beta_o + \sum_n \beta_n \ln x_n + \sum_q \gamma_q \ln z_q + v - u, \tag{5.2.3}$$

$$\ln x_n = \beta_o + \ln \beta_n + \sum_k \beta_k \ln x_k + \sum_q \gamma_q \ln z_q - \ln \frac{w_n}{p} - u + \xi_n,$$
$$n = 1, \ldots, N, \tag{5.2.4}$$

where v is the stochastic noise error component associated with the production frontier. In deriving the first-order conditions one has to start with either a deterministic production frontier or a stochastic production frontier evaluated at $v = 0$, or take the median value of output [with the assumption that v is distributed normally with mean 0 as in Kumbhakar (1987)]. The basic conclusion remains unchanged no matter how one treats the stochastic noise component v.

Solving the $(N + 1)$ equations (5.2.3) and (5.2.4) for the optimal values of the $(N + 1)$ endogenous variables gives the following output supply and variable input demand equations:

$$\ln y = \frac{1}{1-r}\beta_o + \frac{1}{1-r}\sum_n \beta_n \left(\ln \beta_n - \ln \frac{w_n}{p} \right)$$
$$+ \frac{1}{1-r}\sum_q \gamma_q \ln z_q + \frac{1}{1-r}\sum_n \beta_n \xi_n - \frac{1}{1-r}u + v, \tag{5.2.5}$$

$$\ln x_k = \frac{1}{1-r}\beta_o + \frac{1}{1-r}\sum_n (\beta_n + (1-r)\delta_{nk})\left(\ln \beta_n - \ln \frac{w_n}{p}\right)$$

$$+ \frac{1}{1-r}\sum_q \gamma_q \ln z_q + \frac{1}{1-r}\sum_n (\beta_n + (1-r)\delta_{nk})\xi_n$$

$$- \frac{1}{1-r}u, \qquad k = 1,\dots, N, \tag{5.2.6}$$

where $r = \Sigma_n\beta_n < 1$ and $\delta_{nk} = 1$ if $n = k$ and $\delta_{nk} = 0$ if $n \neq k$.

It can be seen from equations (5.2.5) and (5.2.6) that variable profit-maximizing output production and variable input use depend on normalized variable input prices and quasi-fixed input quantities. They also depend on the magnitudes of both technical and allocative inefficiencies. In particular, the relatively more technically efficient producers (those with $u \to 0^+$) use more of their variable inputs to produce more output, *ceteris paribus*. This conclusion supports the observation of Mundlak (1961), although it runs counter to the results obtained in Chapter 4. The reason is that input use in a cost mini-mization framework is conditional on exogenous outputs, whereas variable input use in the present variable profit maximization frame-work is unconditional. Moreover the orientation is different. In Chapter 4 technical efficiency was input oriented to maintain consis-tency with the cost minimization orientation, whereas here technical efficiency is output oriented, and relatively more technically efficient producers produce more output with more variable input use.

It is possible to estimate the system of output supply and variable input demand equations (5.2.5) and (5.2.6). However it is easier to estimate an alternative system consisting of the production frontier in equation (5.2.3) and the first-order conditions in equations (5.2.4), because the latter system has a more tractable error structure. Tractability comes at a cost, however, since equations (5.2.4) do not contain a random-noise error component, a structural characteristic we also encountered in Chapter 4. The distributional assumptions on the error components this model does contain are as follows:

(i) $v \sim \text{iid } N(0,\sigma_v^2)$.

(ii) $u \sim \text{iid } N^+(0,\sigma_u^2)$.

(iii) $\xi = (\xi_1,\dots, \xi_N)' \sim \text{iid } N(0,\Sigma)$.

(iv) The elements of ξ are distributed independently of v and u, and v and u are distributed independently of one another.

With these distributional assumptions the log likelihood function for a sample of I producers can be written as

$$\ln L = \text{constant} - \frac{I}{2}\ln \sigma_v^2 - \frac{I}{2}\ln \sigma_u^2 - \frac{I}{2}\ln|\Sigma| + \frac{I}{2}\ln \sigma^2$$
$$- \frac{1}{2}\sum_i a_i + \sum_i \ln \Phi\left(-\frac{\mu_i}{\sigma}\right) + \frac{I}{2}\ln(1-r), \tag{5.2.7}$$

where $a_i = [\Xi_i^2/\sigma_v^2 + (b_i)'\Sigma^{-1}(b_i) - \sigma^2(\Xi_i/\sigma_v^2 + \iota'\Sigma^{-1}b_i)^2]$, $\sigma^2 = [1/\sigma_v^2 + 1/\sigma_u^2 + \iota'\Sigma^{-1}\iota]^{-1}$, $\mu_i = [\sigma^2(\Xi_i/\sigma_v^2 + \iota'\Sigma^{-1}b_i)]$, $\Xi_i = -u_i + v_i$, and $b_i = -\iota u_i + \xi_i$, ι being an $N \times 1$ vector of ones. The final term is the Jacobian of the transformation from $(\xi_i, b_{1i}, \ldots, b_{Ni})$ to $(\ln y_i, \ln x_{1i}, \ldots, \ln x_{Ni})$.

Maximization of this log likelihood function gives consistent and efficient estimates of all technology and inefficiency parameters. Once the parameters have been estimated, the technical inefficiency of each producer can be predicted from either the conditional mean or the conditional mode of u_i given (ξ_i, b_i'). These predictors are

$$E(u_i|\xi_i, b_i') = \mu_i + \sigma\frac{\phi(\mu_i/\sigma)}{\Phi(\mu_i/\sigma)}, \tag{5.2.8}$$

$$M(u_i|\xi_i, b_i') = \begin{cases} \mu_i & \text{if } \mu_i > 0, \\ 0 & \text{otherwise}, \end{cases} \tag{5.2.9}$$

where $\phi(\cdot)$ and $\Phi(\cdot)$ are density and cumulative distribution functions of a standard normal variable. After producer-specific estimates of technical inefficiency have been obtained, producer-specific estimates of the allocative inefficiencies ξ_{ni} can be obtained by subtracting the estimates of either $E(u_i|\xi_i,b_i')$ or $M(u_i|\xi_i,b_i')$ from the residuals of equations (5.2.4). The generalization of this approach to panel data is straightforward, and is discussed in detail in Kumbhakar (1987).

Translog The methodology developed previously for estimating technical and allocative inefficiencies relative to a Cobb–Douglas production frontier can be extended to flexible functional forms. For example, consider a translog production frontier given by

$$\ln y = \beta_o + \sum_n \beta_n \ln x_n + \sum_q \gamma_q \ln z_q + \frac{1}{2}\sum_n \sum_k \beta_{nk} \ln x_n \ln x_k$$

$$+ \frac{1}{2}\sum_q \sum_r \gamma_{qr} \ln z_q \ln z_r + \sum_n \sum_q \delta_{nq} \ln x_n \ln z_q + v - u, \quad (5.2.10)$$

where $\beta_{nk} = \beta_{kn} \; \forall k \neq n$ and $\gamma_{qr} = \gamma_{rq} \; \forall r \neq q$. The first-order conditions for variable profit maximization, evaluated at $v = 0$, can be derived from equations (5.2.2) and (5.2.10) as

$$S_n = \varepsilon_n \cdot \exp\{\xi_n\} = \left[\beta_n + \sum_k \beta_{nk} \ln x_k + \sum_q \delta_{nq} \ln z_q \right] \cdot \exp\{\xi_n\},$$

$$n = 1, \ldots, N,$$

$$(5.2.11)$$

where $S_n = w_n x_n / py$ is the ratio of expenditure on the nth variable input to total revenue, and $\varepsilon_n = \partial \ln f(x; z; \beta)/\partial \ln x_n$ is the elasticity of $f(x, z; \beta)$ with respect to the nth variable input. The random-noise error component in equation (5.2.10) is treated in the same manner as it was in the Cobb–Douglas model. Since y, the x_n, and the S_n are all endogenous, it is necessary to rewrite the share equations (to make the number of endogenous variables equal to the number of equations) as

$$\ln x_n = \ln y_{|v=0} + \ln \frac{w_n}{p} - \ln\left[\beta_n + \sum_k \beta_{nk} \ln x_k + \sum_q \delta_{nq} \ln z_q \right] + \xi_n,$$

$$n = 1, \ldots, N,$$

$$(5.2.12)$$

where the term $\ln y_{|v=0}$ on the left-hand side of equation (5.2.12) is replaced with the deterministic component of its translog expression on the right-hand side of equation (5.2.10). Equations (5.2.10) and (5.2.12) constitute a system of $N + 1$ equations to be estimated. This system collapses to the Cobb–Douglas system given in equations (5.2.3) and (5.2.4) if all second-order parameters are zero. Under the usual assumptions made on the error terms v, u, and ξ, the likelihood function can be derived and consistent estimates of all parameters can be obtained, exactly as in the structurally simpler Cobb–Douglas case. Once the parameters have been estimated the JLMS decomposition technique can be used to obtain producer-specific estimates of technical inefficiency. Producer-specific estimates of the allocative inefficiencies ξ_{ni} can be obtained from the residuals of equation (5.2.12), exactly as in the Cobb–Douglas case. Kumbhakar (1994) provides details.

We conclude this section with an observation concerning the primal approach to the estimation of variable efficiency. We argued in Section 5.1 that if one is interested in estimating profit efficiency in a price-taking environment, it is appropriate to do so within a short-run variable profit-seeking framework. We have done exactly that in this section. However by now it should be clear that specifying a short-run framework in the primal approach raises no new econometric issues. All that happens is that a vector of quasi-fixed inputs is added to the equation system to be estimated; the equations themselves remain unchanged. As with the case of a variable cost frontier in Section 4.2.1.3, the issues raised by quasi-fixed inputs are economic rather than econometric.

5.2.2 The Dual Variable Profit Frontier Approach

Since both types of inefficiency reduce variable profit, it is important to quantify the effect of these inefficiencies on variable profit. To this end we focus directly on the dual variable profit frontier. We begin by deriving some general results, and then we consider Cobb–Douglas and translog functional forms.

We begin by allowing for technical inefficiency only. Corresponding to the production frontier specified in equation (5.2.1) is the dual variable profit frontier

$$v\pi = v\pi(pe^{-u}, w, z;\beta) = v\pi(p, w, z;\beta) \cdot h(p, w, z, u, \beta), \qquad (5.2.13)$$

where $v\pi = py - w^T x = (pe^{-u})(ye^u) - w^T x$. Maximum variable profit in the presence of output-oriented technical inefficiency is

$$v\pi(pe^{-u}, w, z;\beta) = \max_{ye^u, x}\{pe^{-u}ye^u - w^T x : ye^u = f(x, z;\beta)\},$$

and maximum variable profit in the presence of technical efficiency $(u = 0)$ is

$$v\pi(p, w, z;\beta) = \max_{y, x}\{py - w^T x : y = f(x, z;\beta)\}.$$

Consequently $h(p, w, z, u, \beta) = v\pi(pe^{-u}, w, z;\beta)/v\pi(p, w, z;\beta)$ is the ratio of maximum variable profit (allowing for technical inefficiency but assuming allocative efficiency) to maximum variable profit. Thus there is an exact relationship between output-oriented technical inefficiency and variable profit inefficiency, with the functional form of $h(p, w, z, u, \beta)$ depending on the functional form of $v\pi(p, w, z; \beta)$. It is clear that $h(p, w, z, u, \beta) \leq 1$ since $pe^{-u} \leq p \Rightarrow v\pi(pe^{-u}, w, z; \beta) \leq v\pi(p, w, z; \beta)$. It is also clear that the impact of technical inefficiency on variable profit depends on more than just the magnitude of technical inefficiency, since $h(p, w, z, u, \beta)$ depends on (p, w, z) as well as on u. Consequently if one estimates a relationship of the form $\ln v\pi(pe^{-u}, w, z; \beta) = \ln v\pi(p, w, z; \beta) + \alpha u, \alpha \leq 0$, this relationship is misspecified unless the underlying technology satisfies certain restrictions sufficient to cause $\ln h(p, w, z, u, \beta) = \alpha u$.

A result of Lau (1978; 151) can be applied to the present context to show that $f(\lambda x, z; \beta) = \lambda^r \cdot f(x, z; \beta), \lambda > 0 \Leftrightarrow \ln v\pi(pe^{-u}, w, z; \beta) = \ln v\pi(p, w, z; \beta) + \ln h(p, w, z, u, \beta) = \{[(1/(1 - r))\ln p + \ln g(w) + \ln k(z)] - (1/(1 - r))u\}$, where $g(w)$ is homogeneous of degree $[-r/(1 - r)]$. Consequently estimation of the preceding variable profit relationship generates biased and inconsistent parameter estimates unless the underlying technology is homogeneous of degree $0 < r < 1$ in x. The bias and inconsistency arise because $E[h(p, w, z, u, \beta)]$ depends on (p, w, z), which also appear in $v\pi(p, w, z; \beta)$. If technology is homogeneous in x, then $\ln h(p, w, z, u, \beta) = -[1/(1 - r)]u$ is independent of (p, w, z), and so bias and inconsistency do not arise.

The previous results generalize easily to the case in which both technical and allocative inefficiencies are present. If technical inefficiency is output oriented as in equation (5.2.1), and if allocative inefficiencies are modeled as in equation (5.2.2), then the dual variable profit frontier can be expressed as

$$v\pi = v\pi(pe^{-u}, w^s, z; \beta) = v\pi(p, w, z; \beta) \cdot h(p, w, z, u, \beta, \xi), \qquad (5.2.14)$$

where $w^s = (w_1^s, \ldots, w_N^s) = (w_1 \cdot \exp\{-\xi_1\}, \ldots, w_N \cdot \exp\{-\xi_N\})$, $v\pi(pe^{-u}, w^s, z; \beta)$ is maximum variable profit in the presence of both types of inefficiency, $v\pi(p, w, z; \beta)$ is maximum variable profit in the absence of both types of inefficiency, and $h(p, w, z, u, \beta, \xi) = v\pi(pe^{-u}, w^s z; \beta)/v\pi(p, w, z; \beta)$. Since $v\pi(pe^{-u}, w^s, z; \beta) \leq v\pi(p, w, z; \beta)$, $h(p, w, z, u, \beta, \xi) \leq 1$. Thus the variable profit loss due to inefficiency is given by the function $h(p, w, z, u, \beta, \xi)$, whose functional form depends on that of $v\pi(p, w, z; \beta)$.

Unfortunately the function $h(p, w, z, u, \beta, \xi)$ is not generally separable, so that $h(p, w, z, u, \beta, \xi) \neq h_1(p, w, z, u, \beta) \cdot h_2(p, w, z, \beta, \xi)$, and it is not generally possible to decompose profit inefficiency $h(p, w, z, u, \beta, \xi)$ into the product of its technical inefficiency and allocative inefficiency components. However if the production technology is homogeneous of degree r in x, then $\ln v\pi(pe^{-u}, w^s, z; \beta) = \ln v\pi(p, w, z; \beta) + \ln h(p, w, z, u, \beta, \xi) = \ln v\pi(p, w, z; \beta) + \{-(1/(1-r))u + [\ln g(w^s) - \ln g(w)]\}$. Thus under homogeneity $h(p, w, z, u, \beta, \xi) = h_1(p, w, z, u, \beta) \cdot h_2(p, w, z, \beta, \xi)$ with $h_1(p, w, z, u, \beta) = h_1(u)$ and $h_2(p, w, z, \beta, \xi) = h_2(w, \xi)$. Once again ignoring technical inefficiency generates biased and inconsistent parameter estimates unless the underlying technology is homogeneous. Worse still, ignoring allocative inefficiency generates biased and inconsistent parameter estimates even if technology is homogeneous, since $h_2(w, \xi)$ is independent of p and z, but not of w. This adverse impact on parameter estimates also carries over to estimates of supply and demand elasticities and other characteristics of the structure of production technology. This calls into question the assertion of Schmidt (1985–1986; 320) that "[t]he only compelling reason to estimate production frontiers is to measure efficiency." An equally compelling reason is to avoid biased and inconsistent estimates of the structure of production technology, and consequently of efficiency measured relative to that technology.

Cobb–Douglas We start with the homogeneous Cobb–Douglas form for simplicity. To simplify the algebra, we begin with the stochastic production frontier and derive the first-order conditions, conditional on both v and u. Under these conditions $\beta_n(y/x_n) = (w_n/p)\exp\{-\xi_n\} \Rightarrow \ln x_n - \ln y = \ln \beta_n - \ln(w_n / p) + \xi_n, n = 1, \ldots, N$, and a little algebra yields the dual normalized variable profit frontier

$$\ln \frac{v\pi}{p} = \ln\left[\frac{v\pi(p, w, z; \beta)}{p}\right] + \ln v\pi_u + \ln v\pi_\xi + \ln v\pi_v, \qquad (5.2.15)$$

where

$$\ln \frac{v\pi(p, w, z; \beta)}{p} = \frac{1}{1-r}\beta_o + \frac{1}{1-r}\sum_n \beta_n \ln(w_n/p)$$

$$+ \frac{1}{1-r}\sum_q \gamma_q \ln z_q + \ln(1-r) \qquad (5.2.16)$$

is the normalized variable profit frontier in the presence of technical and allocative efficiency, $\ln v\pi_u = -[1/(1-r)]u \leq 0$ represents the impact of technical inefficiency on normalized variable profit, $\ln v\pi_\xi = (E - \ln r) \le 0$ represents the impact of allocative inefficiency on normalized variable profit, where $E = [(1/(1 - r))\Sigma_n\beta_n\xi_n + \ln[1 - \Sigma_n\beta_n\exp\{\xi_n\}]]$, $\ln v\pi_v = [1/(1 - r)]v$ represents the impact of statistical noise on normalized variable profit, and $r = \Sigma_n\beta_n < 1$ measures the degree of homogeneity of $f(x, z; \beta)$ in x.

The normalized variable profit frontier in equation (5.2.15) shows that the overall variable profit inefficiency (the percentage loss of normalized variable profit due to both technical and allocative inefficiencies, $[\ln v\pi_u + \ln v\pi_\xi]$) is independent of output prices, input prices, and quasi-fixed input quantities. Recall that under homogeneity alone, $\ln h_1(p, w, z, u, \beta) = \ln v\pi_u$ is independent of (p, w, z), and $\ln h_2(p, w, z, \beta, \xi) = \ln v\pi_\xi$ is independent of p and z, but not of w. However in the homogeneous Cobb–Douglas case $\ln h_2(p, w, z, \beta, \xi) = \ln v\pi_\xi$ is independent of p, w, and z.

If the normalized variable profit frontier in equation (5.2.15) is rewritten as

$$\ln\frac{v\pi}{p} = \delta_o + \sum_n \delta_n \ln\frac{w_n}{p} + \sum_q \delta_q \ln z_q + v_\pi + u_\pi, \qquad (5.2.17)$$

where δ_o is a constant, $\delta_n = -(1/1 - r)\beta_n \ \forall n$, the $\delta_q = [1/(1 - r)]\gamma_q \ \forall q$, $v_\pi = [1/(1 - r)]v$, and $u_\pi = [\ln \pi_u + \ln \pi_\xi] \le 0$ (which is the overall normalized variable profit inefficiency), then equation (5.2.17) is structurally similar to the stochastic production frontier model in equation (5.2.3). Thus no new tools are required to estimate it. The MLE techniques developed in Chapter 3 are appropriate, and after estimation the JLMS decomposition can be used to generate producer-specific estimates of overall normalized variable profit inefficiency. However if one wants to disentangle the separate effects of technical and allocative inefficiencies, a system approach is required. Kumbhakar (1987) provides the details and we will consider such a system in Chapter 6.

Translog I We begin by allowing for technical inefficiency, but we maintain the assumption of allocative efficiency. If the dual variable profit frontier takes the translog form, then

$$\ln v\pi = \ln v\pi(pe^{-u}, w, z; \beta) = \beta_o + \beta_p \ln(pe^{-u})$$

$$+ \sum_n \beta_n \ln w_n + \sum_q \gamma_q \ln z_q + \frac{1}{2}\beta_{pp}[\ln(pe^{-u})]^2$$

$$+ \frac{1}{2}\sum_n \sum_k \beta_{nk} \ln w_n \ln w_k + \frac{1}{2}\sum_q \sum_r \gamma_{qr} \ln z_q \ln z_r$$

$$+ \sum_n \beta_{pn} \ln(pe^{-u}) \ln w_n + \sum_q \beta_{pq} \ln(pe^{-u}) \ln z_q$$

$$+ \sum_n \sum_q \gamma_{nq} \ln w_n \ln z_q, \tag{5.2.18}$$

where linear homogeneity in (p, w) is imposed by the restrictions $\Sigma_n\beta_n + \beta_p = 1$, $\Sigma_n\beta_{np} + \beta_{pp} = 0$, $\Sigma_k\beta_{nk} + \beta_{np} = 0$ $\forall n$, $\Sigma_n\gamma_{nq} + \beta_{pq} = 0$ $\forall q$. These restrictions can be embedded by writing equation (5.2.18) as a normalized variable profit frontier

$$\ln\frac{v\pi}{p} = \beta_o + \sum_n \beta_n \ln\frac{w_n}{pe^{-u}} + \frac{1}{2}\sum_n \sum_k \beta_{nk} \ln\frac{w_n}{pe^{-u}} \ln\frac{w_k}{pe^{-u}}$$

$$+ \sum_q \gamma_q \ln z_q + \frac{1}{2}\sum_q \sum_r \gamma_{qr} \ln z_q \ln z_r$$

$$+ \sum_n \sum_q \gamma_{nq} \ln\frac{w_n}{pe^{-u}} \ln z_q - u, \tag{5.2.19}$$

which is homogeneous of degree 0 in (pe^{-u}, w). This normalized variable profit frontier can be expressed as

$$\ln\frac{v\pi}{p} = \ln v\pi\left(\frac{w}{p}, z; \beta\right) + \ln h(p, w, z, u, \beta), \tag{5.2.20}$$

where $\ln v\pi(w/p, z; \beta)$ is the translog normalized variable profit frontier in the presence of technical efficiency and

$$\ln h(p, w, z, u, \beta) = -\left[\beta_p + \beta_{pp} \ln p + \sum_n \beta_{pn} \ln w_n + \sum_q \gamma_{pq} \ln z_q\right]u$$

$$+ \frac{1}{2}\beta_{pp}u^2 = -u\left[1 - \sum_n \beta_n - \sum_n \sum_k \beta_{nk} \ln\frac{w_n}{p}\right.$$

$$\left. - \sum_n \sum_q \gamma_{nq} \ln z_q\right] + \frac{1}{2}u^2\sum_n \sum_k \beta_{nk}, \tag{5.2.21}$$

which does not collapse to $\ln h(u)$ unless the underlying technology is homogeneous ($\beta_{pp} = \beta_{pn} = \gamma_{pq} = 0 \; \forall n, q$). Nonetheless, even in the nonhomogeneous translog case, we have an exact relationship between technical inefficiency u and normalized variable profit inefficiency $h(p, w, z, u, \beta)$, and this relationship holds even though the translog form is not self-dual.

Hotelling's lemma may be applied to the variable profit frontier in equation (5.2.18) to generate the actual variable profit share equations

$$-\frac{w_n x_n}{v\pi} = -S_n(pe^{-u}, w; \beta) = \beta_n + \sum_k \beta_{nk} \ln \frac{w_k}{pe^{-u}} + \sum_q \gamma_{nq} \ln z_q,$$
$$n = 1, \ldots, N, \tag{5.2.22}$$

$$\frac{py}{v\pi} = S_p(pe^{-u}, w; \beta) = 1 + \sum_n S_n(pe^{-u}, w; \beta). \tag{5.2.23}$$

Equation (5.2.21) shows that it is impossible to disentangle u from (p, w, z) in the variable profit frontier without sacrificing its flexibility. Consequently estimation is based on the input variable profit share equations, to which we append classical error terms and rewrite as

$$\frac{w_n x_n}{v\pi} = -\left[\beta_n + \sum_k \beta_{nk} \ln \frac{w_k}{p} + \sum_q \gamma_{nq} \ln z_q \right] - \beta_{np} u + \eta_n,$$
$$n = 1, \ldots, N, \tag{5.2.24}$$

where $\Sigma_k \beta_{nk} = -\beta_{np}$. The system of share equations (5.2.24) does not include the intercept term β_o or the parameters γ_q and γ_{qr} associated with the quasi-fixed inputs. Estimation of these parameters is considered beneath equations (5.2.28) and (5.2.29).

In a cross-sectional framework estimation of producer-specific technical inefficiencies requires that u be random. Here we follow standard practice in the stochastic frontier literature by assuming that $u \sim$ iid $N^+(0, \sigma_u^2)$, that $\eta = (\eta_1, \ldots, \eta_N)' \sim$ iid $N(0, \Sigma)$, and that the elements of η are distributed independently of u. The justification for these assumptions is that u is under the control of producers but η is not.

Given a sample of I producers, we need to find the density function of the error vector $[-\beta_{1p}u_i + \eta_{1i}, \ldots, -\beta_{Np}u_i + \eta_{Ni}]'$, $i = 1, \ldots, I$, in equations (5.2.24). Define $\Xi_i = (bu_i + \eta_i)'$, where $b = -(\beta_{1o}, \ldots, \beta_{No})'$. Since both u_i and the η_{ni} are iid across producers, we temporarily delete the producer subscript. The density function of Ξ can be expressed as

$$f(\Xi) = \int_0^\infty f(\Xi, u)du = \int_0^\infty f(\Xi|u)h(u)\,du, \qquad (5.2.25)$$

where $f(\Xi, u)$ is the joint density function of Ξ and u, and $h(u)$ is the density function of u. Using the distributional assumptions on u and η, the density function of Ξ can be expressed as

$$f(\Xi) = \frac{2}{(2\pi)^{(N+1)/2}|\Sigma|^{1/2}\sigma_u} \int_0^\infty \exp\left\{-\frac{1}{2}\left[(\Xi - bu)'\Sigma^{-1}(\Xi - bu) + \frac{u^2}{\sigma_u^2}\right]\right\}du$$

$$= \frac{2\sigma\exp\{-a/2\}}{(2\pi)^{N/2}|\Sigma|^{1/2}\sigma_u}\,\Phi(\Xi'\Sigma^{-1}b\sigma), \qquad (5.2.26)$$

where $\sigma^2 = (1/\sigma_u^2 + b'\Sigma^{-1}b)^{-1}$, $a = \Xi'\Sigma^{-1}\Xi - \sigma^2(\Xi'\Sigma^{-1}b)^2$, and $\Phi(\cdot)$ is the cumulative distribution function of a standard normal variable. Reintroducing producer subscripts, the log likelihood function for a sample of I producers can be expressed as

$$\ln L = \text{constant} - \frac{I}{2}\ln|\Sigma| + I\ln\sigma + \sum_i \Phi\left(\Xi_i'\Sigma^{-1}b\sigma\right)$$

$$- I\ln\sigma_u - \frac{1}{2}\sum_i a_i, \qquad (5.2.27)$$

maximization of which generates consistent estimates of all parameters of the variable profit function that are included in the share equations, as well as of σ_u^2 and the elements of Σ. After obtaining parameter estimates, producer-specific estimates of technical inefficiency can be obtained from the decomposition formula in Kumbhakar (1987), which generalizes the JLMS formula to a simultaneous-equation system. Thus

$$E(u_i|bu_i + \eta_i) = \mu_i + \sigma \frac{\phi(\mu_i/\sigma)}{\Phi(\mu_i/\sigma)}, \tag{5.2.28}$$

$$M(u_i|bu_i + \eta_i) = \begin{cases} \mu_i & \text{if } \mu_i > 0, \\ 0 & \text{otherwise}, \end{cases} \tag{5.2.29}$$

where $\mu_i = \Xi_i' \Sigma^{-1} b \sigma^2$ and $\phi(\cdot)$ is the density function of a standard normal variable.

Once u has been estimated from either the conditional mean or the conditional mode, profit efficiency can be estimated from the expression for $\ln h(p, w, z, u, \beta)$ in the second line of equation (5.2.21), all parameters of which are contained in the input variable profit share equations (5.2.24). Thus in the present formulation it is possible to estimate both technical inefficiency u and the variable profit loss arising from technical inefficiency $h(p, w, z, u, \beta)$.

Estimates of the remaining parameters (β_o, the γ_q, and the γ_{qr}) can be obtained from a second-stage regression conditional on the parameter estimates obtained from the share equations and estimates of u from either equation (5.2.28) or (5.2.29). This second-stage regression uses the following residuals obtained from equation (5.2.19):

$$\ln \frac{v\pi}{p} - \left[\sum_n \beta_n \ln \frac{w_n}{pe^{-u}} - \frac{1}{2} \sum_n \sum_k \beta_{nk} \ln \frac{w_n}{pe^{-u}} \ln \frac{w_k}{pe^{-u}} \right.$$
$$\left. - \sum_n \sum_q \gamma_{nq} \ln \frac{w^n}{pe^{-u}} \ln z_q - u \right],$$

which are regressed using OLS on an intercept, the $(\ln z_q)$, and the $(\ln z_q)$ $(\ln z_r)$. This second-stage regression will give consistent estimates of the remaining parameters in the normalized variable profit frontier given in equation (5.2.19).

If panel data are available, and if one is willing to assume that technical inefficiency is time invariant, then it is possible to estimate all parameters in the model, and u and $h(p, w, z, u, \beta)$ as well, without having to impose strong distributional assumptions. The estimation procedure is simple and straightforward. Imposing the homogeneity restrictions, the normalized variable profit frontier and the associated input variable profit share equations can be written as

$$\ln\frac{\pi_{it}}{p_{it}} = \beta_o + \sum_n \beta_n \ln\frac{w_{nit}}{p_{it}e^{-ui}} + \frac{1}{2}\sum_n\sum_k \beta_{nk} \ln\frac{w_{nit}}{p_{it}e^{-ui}} \ln\frac{w_{kit}}{p_{it}e^{-ui}}$$

$$+ \sum_q \gamma_q \ln z_{qit} + \frac{1}{2}\sum_q\sum_r \gamma_{qr} \ln z_{qit} \ln z_{rit}$$

$$+ \sum_n\sum_q \gamma_{nq} \ln\frac{w_{nit}}{p_{it}e^{-ui}} \ln z_{qit} - u_i + v_{it}, \tag{5.2.30}$$

$$S_{nit} = -\left[\beta_n + \sum_k \beta_{nk} \ln\frac{w_{kit}}{p_{it}e^{-ui}} + \sum_q \gamma_{nq} \ln z_{qit}\right] + \eta_{nit},$$

$$n = 1, \ldots, N, \tag{5.2.31}$$

where v_{it} and the η_{nit} are stochastic noise components, and the u_i are assumed to be producer-specific fixed effects. Under the assumption that v and the η_n have zero means and constant variance–covariance matrix, the system of equations (5.2.30) and (5.2.31) can be estimated using a nonlinear ITSUR procedure. Technical inefficiencies can be estimated relative to the most efficient producer in the sample, as in Schmidt and Sickles (1984). Once the parameters and the u_i have been estimated, profit loss due to technical inefficiency can be estimated for each producer using equation (5.2.21).

It should be noted that technical inefficiency appears in the normalized variable profit frontier both additively as an error component and interactively with the normalized input prices, and so it also appears interactively in the input variable profit share equations. Consequently a specification that includes only producer-specific intercepts in the normalized variable profit frontier to capture the impact of technical inefficiency is misspecified and generates inconsistent parameter estimates.

Translog II We now allow for both technical and allocative inefficiency. Since actual variable profit $v\pi = py - w^T x$, and since $v\pi(pe^{-u}, w^s, z; \beta) = pe^{-u}ye^u - w^{sT}x$, an alternative expression for actual variable profit can be obtained by combining these two expressions to yield

$$v\pi = v\pi(pe^{-u}, w^s, z; \beta) + \sum_n (w_n^s - w_n)x_n$$

$$= v\pi(pe^{-u}, w^s, z; \beta) \cdot \left[1 - \sum_n (\exp\{\xi_n\} - 1)S_n^s\right], \tag{5.2.32}$$

where shadow input prices $w_n^s = w_n \cdot \exp\{-\xi_n\}$ $\forall n$ and shadow input variable profit shares $S_n^s = -\partial \ln v\pi(pe^{-u}, w^s, z; \beta)/\partial \ln w_n^s$ $\forall n$. Observed input variable profit shares can be expressed in terms of shadow input variable profit shares as

$$
\begin{aligned}
S_n &= \frac{w_n x_n(pe^{-u}, w^s, z;\beta)}{v\pi} \\
&= \left[\frac{w_n^s x_n(pe^{-u}, w^s, z;\beta)}{v\pi(pe^{-u}, w^s, z;\beta)}\right]\cdot\left[\frac{v\pi(pe^{-u}, w^s, z;\beta)}{v\pi}\right]\cdot\left[\frac{w_n}{w_n^s}\right] \\
&= \frac{\exp\{\xi_n\}S_n^s}{[1 - \Sigma_k(\exp\{\xi_k\} - 1)S_k^s]}.
\end{aligned}
\tag{5.2.33}
$$

If $v\pi(pe^{-u}, w^s, z; \beta)$ takes the translog functional form, then

$$
\begin{aligned}
\ln v\pi&(pe^{-u}, w^s, z;\beta) \\
&= \beta_o + \beta_p \ln(pe^{-u}) + \sum_n \beta_n \ln w_n^s + \sum_q \gamma_q \ln z_q \\
&\quad + \frac{1}{2}\beta_{pp}[\ln(pe^{-u})]^2 + \frac{1}{2}\sum_n\sum_k \beta_{nk} \ln w_n^s \ln w_k^s \\
&\quad + \frac{1}{2}\sum_q\sum_r \gamma_{qr} \ln z_q \ln z_r + \sum_n \beta_{pn} \ln(pe^{-u})\ln w_n^s \\
&\quad + \sum_q \beta_{pq} \ln(pe^{-u})\ln z_q + \sum_n\sum_q \gamma_{nq}\ln w_n^s \ln z_q,
\end{aligned}
\tag{5.2.34}
$$

and the shadow input variable profit share equations become

$$
\begin{aligned}
S_n^s &= -\frac{\partial \ln v\pi(pe^{-u}, w^s, z;\beta)}{\partial \ln w_n^s} \\
&= -\left(\beta_n + \sum_k \beta_{nk} \ln\frac{w_k^s}{p} + \sum_q \gamma_{nq} \ln z_q - \sum_k \beta_{nk}u\right) \\
&= A_n - \beta_{np}u, \qquad n = 1, \ldots, N,
\end{aligned}
\tag{5.2.35}
$$

where the linear homogeneity restrictions listed beneath equation (5.2.18) have been imposed. Alternatively, if a normalized shadow variable profit function is specified, the homogeneity restrictions are automatically imposed. The normalized version of equation (5.2.34) is

$$\ln v\pi\left(\frac{w^s}{pe^{-u}},z;\beta\right)=\beta_o+\sum_n\beta_n\ln\frac{w_n^s}{pe^{-u}}$$

$$+\frac{1}{2}\sum_n\sum_k\beta_{nk}\ln\frac{w_n^s}{pe^{-u}}\ln\frac{w_k^s}{pe^{-u}}+\sum_q\gamma_q\ln z_q$$

$$+\frac{1}{2}\sum_q\sum_r\gamma_{qr}\ln z_q\ln z_r+\sum_n\sum_q\gamma_{nq}\ln\frac{w_n^s}{pe^{-u}}\ln z_q,$$

$$(5.2.36)$$

and the expression for actual variable profit given in equation (5.2.32) becomes, in normalized form,

$$\ln\frac{v\pi}{p}=\ln v\pi\left(\frac{w^s}{pe^{-u}},z;\beta\right)+\ln\left[1-\sum_n(\exp\{\xi_n\}-1)S_n^s\right]-u.\quad(5.2.37)$$

It is now possible to derive an expression for variable profit inefficiency in the presence of both technical and allocative inefficiency. The generalization of the expression for $\ln h(p,w,z,u,\beta)$ in equation (5.2.21) becomes

$$\ln h(p,w,z,u,\beta,\xi)=\left[\left[1-\sum_n\beta_n-\sum_n\sum_k\beta_{nk}\ln\frac{w_k}{p}+\sum_q\gamma_{pq}\ln z_q\right.\right.$$

$$+\frac{1}{2}\sum_n\sum_k\beta_{nk}(-u)\bigg](-u)\bigg]+\left[\sum_n\beta_n(-\xi_n)\right.$$

$$+\frac{1}{2}\sum_n\sum_k\beta_{nk}(-\xi_n)(-\xi_k)$$

$$+\sum_n\sum_k\beta_{nk}(-\xi_n)\ln\frac{w_k}{p}$$

$$+\ln\left\{1-\sum_n(\exp\{\xi_n\}-1)(A_n)\right\}\right]$$

$$+\left[\ln\left\{1-\sum_n(\exp\{\xi_n\}-1)(-\beta_{np}u)\right\}\right.$$

$$-u\sum_n\sum_k\beta_{nk}(-\xi_n)\bigg]$$

$$=\ln h_1(p,w,z,u,\beta)+\ln h_2(p,w,z,\beta,\xi)$$

$$+\ln h_3(p,w,z,u,\beta,\xi).$$

$$(5.2.38)$$

It is clear that overall variable profit inefficiency $\ln h(p, w, z, u, \beta, \xi)$ cannot be decomposed into a technical inefficiency term $\ln h_1(p, w, z, u, \beta)$ and an allocative inefficiency term $\ln h_2(p, w, z, \beta, \xi)$ unless the interaction term $\ln h_3(p, w, z, u, \beta, \xi) = 0$. This term is zero if the underlying production technology is homogeneous, and even then the separate effects of technical and allocative inefficiencies both depend on (p, w, z).

We now consider how to estimate the translog model in the presence of both technical and allocative inefficiency. We begin by deriving the actual input variable profit share equations, which in the translog case can be expressed in terms of the shadow input variable profit share equations as

$$\frac{S_n \exp\{-\xi_n\}[1 - \Sigma_k(\exp\{\xi_k\} - 1)A_k] - A_n}{\beta_{no} + \exp\{-\xi_n\}S_n \Sigma_k(\exp\{\xi_k\} - 1)\beta_{kp}} = -u, \qquad n = 1, \dots, N.$$

$$(5.2.39)$$

Adding classical error terms η_n to equations (5.2.39) generates a system of N equations with error vector $-(u + \eta)$, ι being an $N \times 1$ column vector of ones. Writing these equations in implicit form, we have

$$q_n\left(S_n, \frac{w}{p}, \xi\right) = -u + \eta_n, \qquad n = 1, \dots, N,$$

$$(5.2.40)$$

or, in vector notation,

$$q\left(S, \frac{w}{p}, \xi\right) = -\iota u + \eta = \Xi.$$

$$(5.2.41)$$

The density function of Ξ is

$$f(\Xi) = \frac{2\sigma \exp\{-a/2\}}{(2\pi)^{N/2}|\Sigma|^{1/2}\sigma_u} \Phi(-\Xi'\Sigma^{-1}\iota\sigma),$$

$$(5.2.42)$$

where $\sigma^2 = (1/\sigma_u^2 + \iota'\Sigma^{-1}\iota)^{-1}$ and $a = \Xi'\Sigma^{-1}\Xi - \sigma^2(\Xi'\Sigma^{-1}\iota)^2$. The log likelihood function is

$$\ln L = \text{constant} - \frac{I}{2}\ln|\Sigma| + I\ln\sigma + \sum_i \ln\Phi(-\Xi_i'\Sigma^{-1}\iota\sigma)$$

$$- I\ln\sigma_u - \frac{1}{2}\sum_i a_i + \sum_i \ln|D_i|,$$

$$(5.2.43)$$

where D_i is the Jacobian of the transformation from $(\Xi_{1i}, \ldots, \Xi_{Ni})$ to $(S_{1i}, \ldots, S_{Ni})$. This log likelihood function can be maximized to obtain estimates of all technology parameters appearing in the share equations, as well as of σ_u^2 and the elements of the Σ matrix. Once the parameters have been estimated, producer-specific estimates of technical efficiency can be obtained from modifications of equations (5.2.28) and (5.2.29). The modifications consist of replacing b with $-\iota$ in the expressions for μ_i and σ^2.

Some of the remaining parameters can be derived by exploiting the homogeneity restrictions. Others can be estimated from a second-stage regression based on the residuals from equation (5.2.36), using the parameter estimates obtained from equation (5.2.43) and estimates of u.

The generalization to panel data follows along lines similar to those discussed for the case in which only technical inefficiency appears. In the presence of both technical and allocative inefficiency the translog normalized variable profit frontier and its associated input variable profit share equations are modified from those appearing in equations (5.2.30) and (5.2.31) to become

$$
\ln \frac{\pi_{it}}{p_{it}} = \beta_o + \sum_n \beta_n \ln \frac{w_{nit}^s}{p_{it}e^{-ui}}
$$

$$
+ \frac{1}{2}\sum_n \sum_k \beta_{nk} \ln \frac{w_{nit}^s}{p_{it}e^{-ui}} \ln \frac{w_{kit}^s}{p_{it}e^{-ui}} + \sum_q \gamma_q \ln z_{qit}
$$

$$
+ \frac{1}{2}\sum_q \sum_r \gamma_{qr} \ln z_{qit} \ln z_{rit}
$$

$$
+ \sum_n \sum_q \gamma_{nq} \ln \frac{w_{nit}}{p_{it}e^{-ui}} \ln z_{qit} + \ln\left[1 - \sum_n (\exp\{\xi_n\} - 1)S_{nit}^s\right]
$$

$$
+ v_{it} - u_i, \tag{5.2.44}
$$

$$
S_{nit} = \frac{S_{nit}^s \exp\{\xi_n\}}{[1 - \Sigma_k(\exp\{\xi_k\} - 1)S_{kit}^s]} + \eta_{nit}, \qquad n = 1, \ldots, N. \tag{5.2.45}
$$

where $w_n^s = w_n \cdot \exp\{-\xi_n\}$ $\forall n$ and the S_n^s are defined in equation (5.2.35). As before, v_{it} and the η_{nit} are stochastic noise error components. The model in equations (5.2.44) and (5.2.45) is structurally similar to the model in equations (5.2.30) and (5.2.31), apart from the allocative inefficiency terms, and estimation proceeds as in the previous case. Details are provided in Kumbhakar (1996b).

We concluded Section 5.2.1 with the observation that incorporating quasi-fixed inputs into a primal approach to the estimation of variable profit efficiency, although theoretically desirable, raises no new econometric issues. The same conclusion applies to a dual approach. Since no new econometric issues are raised in either approach, we ignore quasi-fixed inputs and consider the structurally simpler problem of estimating profit efficiency in the next two sections.

5.3 MULTIPLE-OUTPUT MODELS

In this section we provide a brief overview of the estimation of technical, allocative, and profit inefficiencies when producers produce multiple outputs and seek to maximize profit. We continue to measure technical inefficiency with an output orientation, although the analysis of this and Section 5.2 can be modified to adopt an input orientation. Sections 5.3.1 and 5.3.2 are structured similarly to Sections 5.2.1 and 5.2.2, with the former taking a primal approach and the latter taking a dual approach. There are two differences between this section and Section 5.2. First, here we consider the estimation of profit efficiency rather than of variable profit efficiency. The second difference concerns the modeling and estimation of technical and allocative inefficiencies, and of their impact on profit, in the presence of multiple outputs.

5.3.1 The Primal Distance Function Approach

Let $y = (y_1, \ldots, y_M) \geq 0$ be a vector of M outputs marketed at prices $p = (p_1, \ldots, p_M) > 0$, and let $x = (x_1, \ldots, x_N) \geq 0$ be a vector of N inputs purchased at prices $w = (w_1, \ldots, w_N) > 0$. The structure of production technology is characterized by the output distance function $D_o(x, y; \beta) \leq 1$, where β is a vector of technology parameters to be estimated. Output-oriented technical inefficiency is introduced by writing $D_o(x, y; \beta) = e^{-u} \leq 1 \Leftrightarrow D_o(x, ye^u; \beta) = 1$ for $u \geq 0$, since $ye^u \geq y$ is a technically efficient output vector and $D_o(x, y; \beta)$ is linearly homogeneous in y. If we allow for technical inefficiency but maintain the assumption of allocative efficiency, the producer's profit maximization problem can be written as

$$\max_{y,x}\{p^T y - w^T x : D_o(x, ye^u; \beta) = 1\}, \tag{5.3.1}$$

the first-order conditions for which can be rearranged to yield

$$\frac{w_n}{p_m e^{-u}} = -\frac{\partial D_o(x, ye^u; \beta)/\partial x_n}{\partial D_o(x, ye^u; \beta)/\partial y_m \, e^u}. \tag{5.3.2}$$

Equation (5.3.2), together with the distance function $D_o(x, ye^u; \beta) = 1$ in equation (5.3.1), can in principle be solved for $y_m(pe^{-u}, w; \beta)$ $\forall m$ and $x_n(pe^{-u}, w; \beta)$ $\forall n$. These are the output supply equations and input demand equations that maximize profit in the presence of technical inefficiency and that are to be estimated in order to obtain estimates of technical inefficiency and its impact on profit. Unfortunately "in principle" rarely occurs in practice. We now turn to one case in which it does, and then we consider the options available when it does not.

CET/Cobb–Douglas If the output distance function is separable, it can be written as $D_o(x, ye^u; \beta) = g(ye^u; \beta) - f(x; \beta)$. If, in addition, the functions $g(ye^u; \beta)$ and $f(x; \beta)$ are analytically tractable, an estimable model results. One such specification is the CET/Cobb–Douglas model of Powell and Gruen (1968), in which

$$g(ye^u; \beta) = \left\{ \sum_m \delta_m (y_m e^u)^c \right\}^{1/c} = \left\{ \sum_m \delta_m (y_m)^c \right\}^{1/c} e^u,$$

$$f(x; \beta) = \prod_n x_n^{\beta_n}, \tag{5.3.3}$$

where $c > 1$, $\delta_m > 0$ $\forall m$, $\Sigma_m \delta_m = 1$, $\beta_n > 0$ $\forall n$, and $\Sigma_n \beta_n = r < 1$. The partial elasticity of substitution between each pair of outputs is the constant $c/(1 - c) < 0$.

A lot of tedious algebra generates the profit-maximizing output supply and input demand equations

$$y_m(pe^{-u}, w; \beta) = I(p)^{(cr-1)/c(1-r)} \cdot p_m^{1/(c-1)} \cdot \delta_m^{-1/(c-1)} \prod_n \left(\frac{\alpha_n}{w_n}\right)^{\alpha_n/(1-r)} \cdot e^{-u/1-r},$$

(5.3.4)

$$x_n(pe^{-u}, w; \beta) = I(p)^{(c-1)/c(1-r)} \cdot \prod_k \left(\frac{\alpha_k}{w_k}\right)^{[\alpha_k c + (1-rc)\delta_{nk}]/(1-rc)} \cdot e^{-u/(1-r)},$$

(5.3.5)

where $I(p) = \Sigma_m \delta_m^{-c/(c-1)} p_m^{c/(c-1)}$, and $\delta_{nk} = 1$ if $n = k$ and $\delta_{nk} = 0$ if $n \neq k$. Equations (5.3.4) and (5.3.5) can be used to derive the expression for maximized profit, conditional on the presence of technical inefficiency,

$$\pi = \pi(pe^{-u}, w; \beta) = \sum_m p_m y_m(pe^{-u}, w; \beta) - \sum_n w_n x_n(pe^{-u}, w; \beta)$$

$$= (1-r) \cdot I(p)^{(c-1)/c(1-r)} \cdot \prod_n \left(\frac{\beta_n}{w_n}\right)^{\beta_n(1-r)} \cdot \exp\left\{\frac{-u}{1-r}\right\}$$

$$= \pi(p, w; \beta) \cdot g(u).$$

(5.3.6)

It follows that technical inefficiency reduces profit by $100[1/(1 - r)u]\%$. The fact that $\pi(pe^{-u}, w; \beta) = \pi(p, w; \beta) \cdot g(u)$ follows from the homogeneity of the CET/Cobb–Douglas technology.

Estimation of the system of equations (5.3.4) and (5.3.5) is straightforward. We append classical error terms $\eta_j, j = 1, \ldots, M + N$, to the equations and make the distributional assumptions:

(i) $\eta = (\eta_1, \ldots, \eta_{M+N})' \sim$ iid $N(0, \Sigma)$.

(ii) $u \sim$ iid $N^+(0, \sigma_u^2)$.

(iii) The elements of η are independent of u.

With these assumptions the log likelihood function is similar to that for equations (5.2.24). Defining $\Xi_i = \gamma u_i + \eta_i$, where $\gamma = -\iota 1/(1 - r)$ and ι is an $(M + N) \times 1$ vector of ones, the density function of Ξ_i can be written as

$$f(\Xi_i) = \frac{2\sigma \exp\{-b_i/2\}}{(2\pi)^{(M+N)/2} |\Sigma|^{1/2} \sigma_u} \Phi(\Xi_i' \Sigma^{-1} \gamma \sigma),$$

(5.3.7)

where $\sigma^2 = (1/\sigma_u^2 + \gamma' \Sigma^{-1} \gamma)^{-1}$ and $b_i = \Xi_i' \Sigma^{-1} \Xi_i - \sigma^2 (\Xi_i' \Sigma^{-1} \gamma)^2$. The log likelihood function is

$$\ln L = \text{constant} - \frac{I}{2}\ln|\Sigma| + I\ln\sigma + \sum_i \ln\Phi(\Xi_i'\Sigma^{-1}\gamma\sigma)$$

$$- I\ln\sigma_u - \frac{1}{2}\sum_i b_i. \qquad (5.3.8)$$

Once the parameters have been estimated, estimates of producer-specific technical efficiencies can be obtained from equations (5.2.28) and (5.2.29), in which b is replaced by γ.

With panel data and an assumption of time-invariant technical inefficiencies, the term $[-1/(1-r)]u$ in equations (5.3.4) and (5.3.5) is replaced with $\Sigma_i d_i D_i$, where the D_i are producer dummy variables. The system can be estimated using the nonlinear ITSUR technique, after which technical inefficiencies can be estimated relative to that of the most efficient producer as before.

Translog If $D_o(x, ye^u; \beta)$ takes the translog form, then it follows from Section 3.2.3 that it can be written as

$$-\ln|y| = \beta_o + \sum_n \beta_n \ln x_n + \sum_m \beta_m \ln\frac{y_m}{|y|} + \frac{1}{2}\sum_n\sum_k \beta_{nk}\ln x_n \ln x_k$$

$$+ \frac{1}{2}\sum_m\sum_j \beta_{mj}\ln\frac{y_m}{|y|}\ln\frac{y_j}{|y|} + \sum_n\sum_m \beta_{nm}\ln x_n \ln\frac{y_m}{|y|} + u.$$

$$(5.3.9)$$

It is not possible to derive expressions for the profit-maximizing output supply and input demand equations, and the resulting profit equation, associated with the translog output distance function, so the approach adopted within the CET/Cobb–Douglas framework is infeasible. Even if the separability restrictions $\beta_{nm} = 0 \ \forall n, m$ are imposed on the translog output distance function, derivation of profit-maximizing output supply and input demand equations, and the resulting profit equation, would be infeasible. This leaves two options, both of which suffer from the same problem. The first option is to estimate equation (5.3.9) by itself, after adding a random-noise error component. Although the ALS MLE technique can be applied, after which technical inefficiencies can be predicted using the JLMS decomposition technique, the parameter estimates will be biased and inconsistent because the regressors are not exogenous within a profit maximization framework. The second option is to incorporate additional equations based on the derivative property $\partial D_o(x, y; \beta)/\partial y_m =$

$p_m^s/R^s \; \forall m$, where the p_m^s are output shadow prices and $R^s = \Sigma_m p_m^s y_m$ is shadow revenue. Although this will improve statistical efficiency, it does not address the endogeneity problem. We refer the reader to Atkinson and Primont (1998), who have developed an input-oriented version of such a system, and have proposed the use of instrumental variables estimation techniques to deal with the endogeneity problem.

5.3.2 The Dual Variable Profit Frontier Approach

The material in this section is a modest extension of the material in Section 5.2.2. We begin by revisiting the translog specification, and we continue by examining another flexible functional form.

Translog Allowing for technical inefficiency but maintaining the assumption of allocative efficiency, the translog profit frontier can be written as

$$\ln \pi = \ln \pi(pe^{-u}, w; \beta) = \beta_o + \sum_m \beta_m \ln(p_m e^{-u}) + \sum_n \beta_n \ln w_n$$

$$+ \frac{1}{2} \sum_m \sum_j \beta_{mj} \ln(p_m e^{-u}) \ln(p_j e^{-u}) + \frac{1}{2} \sum_n \sum_k \beta_{nk} \ln w_n \ln w_k$$

$$+ \sum_m \sum_n \beta_{mn} \ln(p_m e^{-u}) \ln w_n. \tag{5.3.10}$$

where the linear homogeneity restrictions are now $\Sigma_m \beta_m + \Sigma_n \beta_n = 1$, $\Sigma_m \beta_{jm} + \Sigma_n \beta_{jn} = 0 \; \forall j$, and $\Sigma_n \beta_{km} + \Sigma_n \beta_{kn} = 0 \; \forall k$. As usual, these restrictions can be imposed by writing the profit frontier in normalized form. The associated output profit share equations and input profit share equations can be derived using Hotelling's lemma and written as

$$R_m = \frac{p_m y_m}{\pi} = \beta_m + \sum_j \beta_{mj} \ln(p_j e^{-u}) + \sum_n \beta_{mn} \ln w_n,$$

$$m = 1, \ldots, M, \tag{5.3.11}$$

$$S_n = \frac{w_n x_n}{\pi} = -\left(\beta_n + \sum_m \beta_{mn} \ln(p_m e^{-u}) + \sum_k \beta_{nk} \ln w_k \right),$$

$$n = 1, \ldots, N. \tag{5.3.12}$$

As in the single-output case it is possible to express the profit function in equation (5.3.10) as $\ln \pi = \ln \pi(p, w; \beta) + \ln \pi_u$, where $\ln \pi_u$ represents the percentage profit loss due to technical inefficiency and is given by

$$\ln \pi_u = -u\left[\sum_m \beta_m + \sum_m \sum_j \beta_{mj} \ln p_j + \sum_m \sum_n \beta_{mn} \ln w_m\right]$$

$$+\frac{u^2}{2}\sum_m \sum_j \beta_{mj}. \tag{5.3.13}$$

Thus even in the multiple-output case there is a closed-form solution for the profit loss due to technical inefficiency. Since $\ln \pi_u$ depends on all prices, omitting technical inefficiency or incorporating its impact in a simple additive form leads to biased and inconsistent parameter estimates.

In the absence of inefficiency, estimation would normally be based on the profit frontier with $(M + N - 1)$ profit share equations added to improve statistical efficiency. However in the present case technical inefficiency interacts with prices in the profit frontier, but not (after a simple rearrangement of terms so as to isolate u) in the profit share equations. Hence we base estimation on just the profit share equations. After appending classical error terms, the rearranged profit share equations can be written as

$$R_m = \beta_m + \sum_j \beta_{mj} \ln p_j + \sum_n \beta_{mn} \ln w_n - \beta_{mo}u + \eta_m, \quad m = 1, \ldots, M,$$

$$\tag{5.3.14}$$

$$S_n = -\left(\beta_n + \sum_m \beta_{mn} \ln p_m + \sum_k \beta_{nk} \ln w_k\right) + \beta_{no}u + \eta_n,$$

$$n = 1, \ldots, N, \tag{5.3.15}$$

where $\beta_{mo} = \Sigma_j \beta_{mj}$ $\forall m$ and $\beta_{no} = \Sigma_m \beta_{mn}$ $\forall n$. A system of $(M + N - 1)$ of these share equations can be estimated, in cross-sectional or panel data contexts, exactly as in the single-output case discussed under Translog I in Section 5.2.2.

The model just discussed can be generalized to allow for allocative inefficiencies, just as the single-output **Translog I** model was generalized to create **Translog II** in Section 5.2.2. All that is required is to replace observed prices (p, w) with shadow prices (p^s, w^s) =

$(p_1, p_2\exp\{-\xi_{21}\}, \dots, p_M\exp\{-\xi_{M1}\}, w_1\exp\{-\zeta_{11}\}, \dots, w_N\exp\{-\zeta_{N1}\})$ and proceed as in **Translog II**. Modeling procedures and estimation strategies are discussed in Kumbhakar (1996a).

Normalized Quadratic An alternative flexible functional form, the normalized quadratic, has also been used to model and estimate profit efficiency in the presence of multiple outputs and both technical and allocative inefficiency. Such a model, due originally to Fuss (1977) and McFadden (1978) and generalized by Diewert and Wales (1987) and Diewert and Ostensoe (1988), has some interesting features. In the formulation of Akhavein, Berger, and Humphrey (1997), the normalized quadratic profit frontier is written as

$$\frac{\pi}{q_1} = \sum_{j>1}(\beta_i - \tau_i)\left(\frac{q_j}{q_1}\right) + \sum_{j>1}\sum_{k>1}\beta_{jk}\left(\frac{1-\xi_j}{2}\right)\xi_k\left(\frac{q_j q_k}{q_1^2}\right) - \tau_1, \qquad (5.3.16)$$

where $q = (p', w')'$ is an $(M + N)$-dimensional vector of netput prices and $q_1 = p_1$. The parameters β_j and $\beta_{jk} = \beta_{kj}$ are technology parameters to be estimated. Hotelling's lemma generates the system of netput equations

$$z_j = \beta_j + \sum_{k>1}\beta_{jk}\xi_k\left(\frac{q_k}{q_1}\right) - \tau_j, \qquad j = 2, \dots, M+N, \qquad (5.3.17)$$

where $z = (y, -x)$ is an $(M + N)$-dimensional netput quantity vector.

Inefficiencies are represented by the τ and ξ terms. Allocative inefficiencies are modeled as usual, by replacing actual price ratios (q_j/q_1) with shadow price ratios $\xi_j(q_j/q_1)$. The profit loss associated with allocative inefficiencies is calculated as

$$\pi(q;\beta,\tau,1) - \pi(q;\beta,\tau,\xi) = \sum_{j>1}\sum_{k>1}\beta_{jk}\left[\frac{1}{2} - \left(\frac{1-\xi_j}{2}\right)\xi_k\right]\left(\frac{q_j q_k}{q_1}\right). \quad (5.3.18)$$

Equation (5.3.18) can itself be decomposed into profit loss attributable to (i) input mix inefficiencies, (ii) output mix inefficiencies, and (iii) input/output mix inefficiencies. Technical inefficiency is modeled through the τ vector, with netput z_j being τ_j units beneath the value that would maximize profit in the face of shadow prices. The profit loss associated with technical inefficiency is calculated as

$$\pi(q;\beta,\tau,\xi) - \pi(q;\beta,0,\xi) = \sum_j \tau_j q_j. \qquad (5.3.19)$$

The generalized quadratic specification differs from the translog specification in a number of ways. First, it is not logarithmic, and so allows for nonpositive values of profit and, in its more popular normalized variable profit form, for nonpositive values of quasi-fixed netputs as well. Second, convexity can be imposed, without reducing flexibility, by constraining the symmetric $(M + N) \times (M + N)$ matrix $\beta = [\beta_{jk}]$ to be positive semidefinite by replacing β with bb', where b is a lower triangular matrix with zero elements in its first column. Third, technical and allocative inefficiencies do not interact, making it possible to calculate the profit loss associated with either one independently of the other. Finally, and unfortunately, technical inefficiency is measured nonradially, as in the Lovell and Sickles (1983) generalized Leontief model, with each of the $M + N$ technical efficiency measures being dependent on the units in which its corresponding netput is measured. Nonetheless, profit loss associated with technical inefficiency is independent of units of measurement.

A subset of $M + N$ independent equations from the system (5.3.16) and (5.3.17) can be estimated, in either a cross-sectional or a panel data context, by adding classical error terms and using nonlinear ITSUR. In a cross-sectional context, and also in a panel data context when the number of producers is large, it is necessary to treat the allocative inefficiency parameters ξ_j as varying across netput ratios but fixed across producers. The composed error terms (involving technical inefficiencies and random noise) can be treated within a conventional fixed-effects framework or, what is essentially the same thing, within a "distribution-free" framework discussed in Section 4.4.2.

5.4 ALTERNATIVE PROFIT FRONTIERS

Underlying the profit frontier $\pi(p, w; \beta)$ [and the variable profit frontier $\pi(p, w, z; \beta)$ as well, z being a vector of quasi-fixed inputs] is the assumption that prices are exogenous and that producers seek to maximize profit (or variable profit) by selecting outputs and inputs under their control. One justification for exogeneity of prices is that producers operate in competitive markets. Suppose, to the contrary, that producers have some degree of monopoly power in their product markets. Under monopoly, the demands would be exploited to determine output prices and quantities jointly, and only input prices would be exogenous. In this context neither a traditional cost frontier (which treats outputs as being exogenous) nor a traditional profit frontier (which treats output prices as being exogenous) would provide an appropriate framework within which to evaluate producer performance.

Recently Humphrey and Pulley (1997) and others have introduced the notion of an "alternative" profit frontier to bridge the gap between a cost frontier and a profit frontier. An alternative profit frontier is defined as

$$\pi^A(y,w;\beta,\delta) = \max_{p,x}\{p^Ty - w^Tx : g(p,y,w;\delta) = 0, \ D_o(x,y;\beta) \le 1\},$$

(5.3.20)

where the endogenous variables are (p,x) and the exogenous variables are (y,w), $D_o(x,y;\beta)$ is the output distance function characterizing the structure of production technology, and $g(p,y,w;\delta)$ represents what Humphrey and Pulley refer to as the producer's "pricing opportunity set," which captures the producer's ability to transform exogenous (y,w) into endogenous product prices p. Thus $\pi^A(y,w;\beta,\delta)$ has the same dependent variable as the standard profit frontier and the same independent variables as the standard cost frontier. However $\pi^A(y,w;\beta,\delta)$ is not dual to $D_o(x,y;\beta)$, because it incorporates both the structure of production technology (incorporated in the parameter vector β) and the structure of the pricing opportunity set (incorporated in the parameter vector δ). Moreover, without specifying the properties satisfied by the function $g(p,y,w;\delta)$, it is not possible to specify the properties satisfied by $\pi^A(y,w;\beta,\delta)$, although it is reasonable to assume that $\pi^A(y,w;\beta,\delta)$ is nondecreasing in the elements of y and nonincreasing in the elements of w.

In the absence of Shephard–Hotelling derivative properties, it is not possible to specify a system of equations on which estimation can be based, as would be the case with standard cost or profit frontiers. Consequently the alternative profit frontier must be estimated as a single-equation model, once a functional form is assigned to $\pi^A(y, w;\beta,\delta)$ and an assumption is made concerning error structure.

One possibility is to assume that $\pi^A(y, w; \beta, \delta)$ takes a translog functional form with composed error structure $(v - u)$, with $v \sim$ iid $N(0, \sigma_v^2)$ and $u \sim$ iid $N^+(0, \sigma_u^2)$, as in the conventional stochastic frontier framework.

5.5 A GUIDE TO THE LITERATURE

The theory underlying profit functions/frontiers and variable profit functions/frontiers goes back to Hotelling (1932). Modern treatments are available in Lau (1972, 1976, 1978), Diewert (1973), and McFadden (1978). The result of Lau (1978) showing the implication of homogeneity of a single-output technology for the structure of the dual variable profit frontier, which is utilized in Section 5.2, also carries over to multiple-output technologies in Section 5.3, in which case homogeneity is replaced with almost homogeneity. Lau also shows the implication of separability of the multiple-output distance function (which he calls a transformation function) for the dual profit frontier.

The use of shadow prices to model allocative inefficiencies within a profit-seeking context is due to Lau and Yotopoulos (1971) and Yotopoulos and Lau (1973), although they assumed a restrictive Cobb–Douglas functional form, as did subsequent research contained in *Food Research Studies* (1979). The generalization to flexible functional forms within a profit-seeking context is apparently due to Atkinson and Halvorsen (1980) (translog, assuming technical efficiency) and Lovell and Sickles (1983) (generalized Leontief, allowing for both technical and allocative inefficiency).

What we have referred to as the primal approach to the estimation of technical, allocative, and profit efficiency has been used by Kumbhakar (1987) (Cobb–Douglas), Kumbhakar, Biswas, and Bailey (1989) (Cobb–Douglas), Kalirajan (1990) (translog), Seale (1990) (Cobb–Douglas), Kalirajan and Obwana (1994a, b) (Cobb–Douglas with random coefficients), and Kumbhakar (1994) (translog).

A detailed treatment of the primal approach in the multiple-output context, with and without separability imposed, is provided by Hasenkamp (1976).

Direct estimation of the dual profit or normalized profit frontier has been used by Hollas and Stansell (1988) (translog), Ali and Flinn

(1989) (translog with random coefficients), Atkinson and Kerkvliet (1989) (translog), Kumbhakar and Bhattacharyya (1992) (translog), Berger, Hancock, and Humphrey (1993) (generalized quadratic), Bhattacharyya and Glover (1993) (generalized quadratic), Ali, Parikh, and Shah (1994) (translog), Kumbhakar (1996b) (translog), Akhavein, Berger, and Humphrey (1997) (generalized quadratic), and Berger and Mester (1997) (Fourier), among many others.

Alternative profit frontiers have been formulated and estimated by Berger, Cummins, and Weiss (1996), Hasan and Hunter (1996), Akhavein, Berger, and Humphrey (1997), Berger and Mester (1997), Humphrey and Pulley (1997), and Lozano Vivas (1997). Each has used a single-equation model, although a variety of functional forms have been specified, and a variety of estimation techniques has been employed. Each has estimated technical inefficiency, and its impact on alternative profit, under an assumption of allocative efficiency.

6 The Shadow Price Approach to the Estimation and Decomposition of Economic Efficiency

6.1 INTRODUCTION

In Chapter 3 technical inefficiency was modeled as an error component within a stochastic frontier framework. In Chapter 4 and parts of Chapter 5 cost inefficiency and profit inefficiency were also modeled as error components within a stochastic frontier framework. Thus the basic strategy in previous chapters has been to construct a composed error stochastic frontier model, and to extract estimates of inefficiency from the parameters describing the structure of the two error components. This procedure is straightforward in single-equation models, in which the sole objective is to *estimate* technical or economic inefficiency. However this procedure is much less straightforward in simultaneous-equation models, in which the dual objectives are to estimate *and decompose* economic inefficiency.

In this chapter we change our strategy. We do not estimate stochastic frontiers. Instead, we model all types of inefficiency parametrically, through the introduction of additional parameters to be estimated, rather than through an error component. The error structure of the estimating equation (or system of equations) is conventional, the same as that employed in the estimation of cost, revenue, or profit *functions* in the nonfrontier literature. Thus the error term is distributed normally in a single-equation model, and the error terms are distributed as multivariate normal in a system of equations model.

216

Technical inefficiency is introduced in two alternative ways. Output-oriented technical inefficiency is introduced by allowing the production function intercept to vary across producers; this generates a cost function in which producers' output vectors are scaled differentially, and a profit function in which producers' output price vectors are scaled differentially. Input-oriented technical inefficiency is introduced by scaling producers' input vectors differentially; this generates a cost function whose intercept varies across producers, and a profit function in which producers' input price vectors are scaled differentially. The input orientation is appropriate in a cost minimization framework, in which the objective of producers is to allocate inputs in such a way as to minimize the cost of producing their chosen output vector. Either orientation is appropriate in a profit maximization framework, in which the objective of producers is to allocate inputs and outputs so as to maximize profit. Allocative inefficiency (an inappropriate input mix, an inappropriate output mix, or an inappropriate scale) is introduced by allowing producers to fail to optimize with respect to observed prices, but by assuming that they do optimize with respect to shadow prices, which are parametrically related to observed prices. The usual approach is to model shadow prices by *scaling* observed prices, although it is also possible to model shadow prices by *translating* observed prices. Hypothesis tests concerning magnitudes and directions of various types of inefficiency, and calculations of the costs of various types of inefficiency, are then based on estimated values of these additional parameters.

Inspiration for the shadow price approach goes back at least to Hopper (1965), who reported the results of his 1954 study of the efficiency of resource allocation and crop mix in Indian agriculture. In his study he estimated the parameters of four-input Cobb–Douglas production functions for each of four crops, and compared the estimated value of each input's marginal product across crops. He found the farmers in his sample to be highly efficient in economizing on their scarce resources. Like Tax (1953) before him, Hopper found subsistence farmers to be "poor but efficient," because the penalty for inefficiency was so great. Although Hopper did not introduce inefficiency parameters explicitly into his analysis, his statistical tests of various allocative efficiency hypotheses amounted to essentially the same thing. The vast shadow price literature that has emerged in recent years, beginning with Lau and Yotopoulos (1971), can be viewed as a formalization and extension of Hopper's ideas.

This chapter is organized as follows. In Section 6.2 we consider cross-sectional models. In a cross-sectional context it is not possible to estimate a technical efficiency parameter for every producer, and so the emphasis is on the estimation of allocative efficiency, there being fewer inputs and outputs to be allocated than producers to allocate them. In Section 6.2.1 we consider models of cost efficiency, and in Section 6.2.2 we consider models of profit efficiency. In each section we consider a wider variety of functional forms than we did in previous chapters. We consider the Cobb–Douglas form for its relative simplicity, and we also consider flexible forms because the shadow price approach to the estimation of allocative efficiency is ideally suited to flexible forms. In Section 6.3 we consider panel data models. The obvious advantage of having panel data is the ability to obtain estimates of more parameters than is possible with cross-sectional data. In this case the additional parameters provide information on variation in technical and allocative efficiency across producers. In Section 6.3.1 we consider models of cost efficiency, and in Section 6.3.2 we consider models of profit efficiency. We concentrate on flexible forms in the panel data models. In Sections 6.2.2 and 6.3.2 we focus on the modeling and estimation of profit efficiency rather than variable profit efficiency, as we did in Section 5.2. It is straightforward to convert our profit efficiency models to variable profit efficiency models, and we leave this exercise to the reader. Section 6.4 concludes with a guide to the relevant literature.

6.2 CROSS-SECTIONAL MODELS

Suppose that cross-sectional data on the quantities of N inputs used to produce a single-output are available for each of I producers. The single-output assumption will be relaxed shortly. Then the production relationship can be expressed as

$$y_i \leq f(x_i; \beta) \cdot \exp\{v_i\}, \tag{6.2.1}$$

where y_i is the scalar output of producer i, $i = 1, \ldots, I$, x_i is a vector of N inputs used by producer i, $f(x_i; \beta)$ is the deterministic kernel of the stochastic production frontier $[f(x_i;\beta)\cdot\exp\{v_i\}]$, β is a vector of technology parameters to be estimated, and v_i is a symmetrically distributed error term with zero mean and constant variance, which captures the effect of random noise on production. The inequality (6.2.1) states that each producer's output cannot exceed maximum possible output, as determined by the stochastic production frontier $[f(x_i;\beta)\cdot\exp\{v_i\}]$.

In the approach adopted in Chapter 3, the inequality (6.2.1) was converted to an equality by introducing an additional error term of the form $\exp\{-u_i\} \leq 1$, with $u_i \geq 0$, which was intended to capture the impact of (output-oriented) technical inefficiency on production. Depending on the assumptions imposed on u_i, estimation was based on LSDV, GLS, or MLE techniques. The strategy adopted in this chapter is to convert the inequality (6.2.1) to an equality in a different way. If we specify technical inefficiency as being output oriented, then the inequality (6.2.1) can be converted to the equality

$$y_i = \phi_i f(x_i;\beta)\cdot\exp\{v_i\}, \tag{6.2.2}$$

where the $0 < \phi_i \leq 1$ are producer-specific scalars that provide output-oriented measures of the technical efficiency of each producer. If we specify technical inefficiency as being input oriented, then the inequality (6.2.1) can be converted to the equality

$$y_i = f(\phi_i x_i;\beta)\cdot\exp\{v_i\}, \tag{6.2.3}$$

where the $0 < \phi_i \leq 1$ are producer-specific scalars that provide input-oriented measures of the technical efficiency of each producer. The difference between these two specifications and the error component specification is that the ϕ_i are producer-specific parameters, whereas $\exp\{-u_i\}$ is a random draw from a probability distribution, and the only parameters in $\exp\{-u_i\}$ are those associated with the probability distribution of u_i.

Specifications (6.2.2) and (6.2.3) are equivalent if, and only if, technology satisfies constant returns to scale, since then, and only then, does $f(\phi_i x_i;\beta) = \phi_i f(x_i;\beta)$. Specification (6.2.2) is preferred if the analysis is based on the estimation of a production function, whereas specification (6.2.3) is preferred if the analysis is based on the estimation of a cost function. Either specification is appropriate if the analysis is based on the estimation of a profit function.

In the multiple-output case the production function in equation (6.2.2) would be replaced with an output distance function, which is dual to a revenue function, for which the output-oriented measure of technical efficiency is appropriate. In this event equation (6.2.2) would become

$$\phi_i^{-1} D_o(x_i, y_i; \beta) = D_o\left(x_i, \frac{y_i}{\phi_i}; \beta\right) = \exp\{v_i\}, \tag{6.2.4}$$

since the output distance function is homogeneous of degree +1 in outputs. In the multiple-output case the production function in equation (6.2.3) would be replaced with an input distance function, which is dual to a cost function, for which the input-oriented measure of technical efficiency is appropriate. In this event equation (6.2.3) would become

$$D_I(y_i, \phi_i x_i; \beta) = \phi_i D_I(y_i, x_i; \beta) = \exp\{-v_i\}, \tag{6.2.5}$$

since the input distance function is homogeneous of degree +1 in inputs.

There is an obvious problem with equations (6.2.2)–(6.2.5): With I cross-sectional observations it is not possible to obtain estimates of the technology parameter vector β, the variance σ_v^2 of the random-noise error term, and I producer-specific technical inefficiency parameters ϕ_i. The most that can be accomplished is to estimate β and σ_v^2, and to estimate ϕ_i for a limited number of groups of producers (say, by type of ownership), and then to test hypotheses concerning the group technical inefficiency parameters. Thus if the objective of the exercise is to obtain producer-specific estimates of technical efficiency, and only cross-sectional data are available, the stochastic frontier approach outlined in Chapter 3 is preferable to the parametric approach developed in this chapter. By modeling technical inefficiency as an error component, as in Chapter 3, it is possible to obtain estimates of technical efficiency for every producer in a cross section, whereas by modeling technical efficiency parametrically, as in this chapter, it is not possible to do so. The approach developed in this chapter does have some advantages in the estimation of allocative efficiency, however, and we now turn to the estimation and decomposition of cost inefficiency.

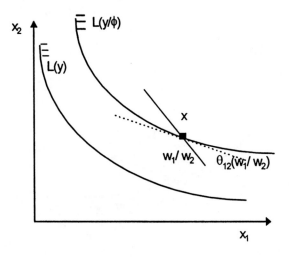

Figure 6.1 The Shadow Price Approach to Estimating Cost Efficiency: Output Orientation

6.2.1 Estimating and Decomposing Cost Inefficiency

In Chapter 4 we saw that estimating cost inefficiency was easy, but decomposing estimated cost inefficiency into its technical and alloca- tive components was not. Decomposition was impossible in a single- equation framework, and while decomposition is theoretically possible in a system of equations framework, it proved to be difficult econometrically. Perhaps the shadow price approach will be more productive.

Suppose that we observe a producer using input vector x, available at input price vector w, to produce scalar output y, with technology characterized by the production function $f(x; \beta)$. The producer is assumed to seek to minimize the cost of producing its chosen rate of output. The problem is illustrated in Figure 6.1, which adopts an output orientation to the measurement of technical efficiency, and in Figure 6.2, which adopts an input orientation to the measurement of technical efficiency. The producer in question is both technically and allocatively inefficient.

In Figure 6.1 an output-oriented measure of the technical efficiency of the producer is provided by $\phi < 1$, since $y/\phi = f(x; \beta)$. The producer is also allocatively inefficient, since the marginal rate of substitution at $x \in \text{Isoq } L(y/\phi; \beta)$ diverges from the input price ratio (w_1/w_2).

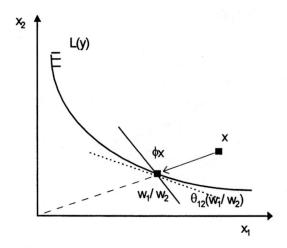

Figure 6.2 The Shadow Price Approach to Estimating Cost Efficiency: Input Orientation

However the producer is allocatively efficient relative to the shadow input price ratio $[\theta_{12}(w_1/w_2)]$, with $\theta_{12} < 1$ because the producer is overutilizing x_1 relative to x_2. Thus, although the producer's input usage is both technically and allocatively inefficient for the observed variables $(y, w_1/w_2)$, it is both technically and allocatively efficient for the shadow variables $[y/\phi, \theta_{12}(w_1/w_2)]$. In this two-input model, the parameters to be estimated are the technology parameters β, the technical inefficency parameter ϕ, and the allocative inefficiency parameter θ_{12}. Once the parameters have been estimated, the next step is to calculate the costs of technical and allocative inefficiency.

In Figure 6.2 an input-oriented measure of the technical efficiency of the producer is provided by $\phi < 1$, since $y = f(\phi x; \beta)$. The producer is also allocatively inefficient, since the marginal rate of substitution at $\phi x \in \mathrm{Isoq}\, L(y; \beta)$ diverges from the input price ratio (w_1/w_2). However the producer is allocatively efficient relative to the shadow input price ratio $[\theta_{12}(w_1/w_2)]$, again with $\theta_{12} < 1$ because the producer is overutilizing x_1 relative to x_2. Thus, although the producer's input usage is both technically and allocatively inefficient for the observed variables $(y, w_1/w_2)$, its contracted input vector ϕx is both technically and allocatively efficient for observed y and the shadow price ratio $[\theta_{12}(w_1/w_2)]$. In this case the parameters to be estimated are $(\beta, \phi, \theta_{12})$.

It should be noted that unless production technology satisfies constant returns to scale, $[\phi, \theta_{12}]$ in the output-oriented framework illustrated in Figure 6.1 will differ from $[\phi, \theta_{12}]$ in the input-oriented framework illustrated in Figure 6.2. This is merely a reflection of the fact, first noted in Chapter 2, that efficiency measures can be sensitive to orientation. Regardless of orientation, however, our strategy becomes one of estimating the additional parameters ϕ and θ_{12}, and then testing the hypotheses, separately or jointly, that $\phi = 1$ and $\theta_{12} = 1$.

The basic idea underlying the output-oriented approach presented in equation (6.2.2) and illustrated in Figure 6.1 can be generalized as follows. The shadow cost function is given by

$$c(y^*, w^*; \beta) = \min_{x}\{w^{*T} x : f(x; \beta) = y^*\}, \tag{6.2.6}$$

where $y^* = y/\phi$ with $0 < \phi \le 1$, and $w^* = (\theta_1 w_1, \ldots, \theta_N w_N)$ with $\theta_n > 0$, $n = 1, \ldots, N$. Since not all N scalars θ_n can be identified, we arbitrarily specify the first input as numeraire and redefine $w^* = [w_1, (\theta_2/\theta_1)w_2, \ldots, (\theta_N/\theta_1)w_N] = (w_1, \theta_{21}w_2, \ldots, \theta_{N1}w_N)$. Since inputs can be under- or overutilized relative to x_1, $\theta_{n1} \gtreqless 1$, $n = 2, \ldots, N$. Application of Shephard's lemma to $c(y^*, w^*; \beta)$ generates the associated shadow input demand equations and shadow input cost share equations

$$x_n(y^*, w^*; \beta) = \frac{\partial c(y^*, w^*; \beta)}{\partial w_n^*}, \qquad n = 1, \ldots, N, \tag{6.2.7}$$

and

$$S_n(y^*, w^*; \beta) = \frac{w_n^* x_n(y^*, w^*; \beta)}{c(y^*, w^*; \beta)}, \qquad n = 1, \ldots, N, \tag{6.2.8}$$

respectively. Although the producer's actual input usage does not minimize cost, it does minimize shadow cost. Consequently the producer's observed input demands coincide with the shadow input demand equations, and so from equations (6.2.7) and (6.2.8) we have

$$x_n = \frac{c(y^*, w^*; \beta) \cdot S_n(y^*, w^*; \beta)}{w_n^*}, \qquad n = 1, \ldots, N. \tag{6.2.9}$$

The producer's observed expenditure and input cost shares are then obtained from equations (6.2.7)–(6.2.9) as

$$E = \sum_n w_n x_n = c(y^*, w^*; \beta) \cdot \sum_n \left[S_n(y^*, w^*; \beta) \cdot (\theta_{n1})^{-1} \right] \qquad (6.2.10)$$

and

$$S_n = \frac{w_n x_n}{E} = \frac{S_n(y^*, w^*; \beta) \cdot (\theta_{n1})^{-1}}{\Sigma_k \left[S_k(y^*, w^*; \beta) \cdot (\theta_{k1})^{-1} \right]}, \qquad n = 1, \ldots, N, \quad (6.2.11)$$

respectively. Equations (6.2.9)–(6.2.11) show that a producer's observed input usage, observed expenditure, and observed input cost shares can be expressed in terms of the corresponding shadow functions. This is important because while (E, y, x_n, w_n, and S_n) are observed, it is the shadow functions that are estimated. All that is required is to assign a functional form to $c(y^*, w^*; \beta)$ and replace y^* and w^* with the observed variables and additional parameters y/ϕ, w_1, and $\theta_{n1} w_n$, $n = 2, \ldots, N$.

The basic idea underlying the input-oriented approach presented in equation (6.2.3) and illustrated in Figure 6.2 can be generalized in a similar manner. In this case the shadow cost function becomes

$$c\left(y, \frac{w^*}{\phi}; \beta \right) = \min_{\phi x} \left\{ \left(\frac{w^*}{\phi} \right)^T (\phi x) : f(\phi x; \beta) = y \right\} = \frac{1}{\phi} c(y, w^*; \beta), \quad (6.2.12)$$

where w^* is defined previously and the second equality is a consequence of the homogeneity of degree +1 of $c(y, w^*; \beta)$ in w^*. Since observed input usage minimizes shadow cost,

$$x_n = \frac{1}{\phi} \frac{c(y, w^*; \beta) \cdot S_n(y, w^*; \beta)}{w_n^*}, \qquad n = 1, \ldots, N, \qquad (6.2.13)$$

$$E = \sum_n w_n x_n = \frac{1}{\phi} c(y, w^*; \beta) \cdot \sum_n \left[S_n(y, w^*; \beta) \cdot (\theta_{n1})^{-1} \right], \qquad (6.2.14)$$

$$S_n = \frac{S_n(y, w^*; \beta) \cdot (\theta_{n1})^{-1}}{\Sigma_k \left[S_k(y, w^*; \beta) \cdot (\theta_{k1})^{-1} \right]}, \qquad n = 1, \ldots, N, \qquad (6.2.15)$$

respectively. Equations (6.2.13)–(6.2.15) show that a producer's observed input usage, observed expenditure, and observed input cost shares can be expressed in terms of the corresponding shadow functions when technical efficiency measurement is input oriented. Since observed output y appears in these equations, all that is required is to assign a functional form to $c(y, w^*; \beta)$ and replace w^* with w_1 and $\theta_{n1} w_n$, $n = 2, \dots, N$.

The only difference between the output-oriented system of equations (6.2.9)–(6.2.11) and the input-oriented system of equations (6.2.13)–(6.2.15) is that the technical inefficiency parameter ϕ appears in simpler form in the latter system, disappearing altogether from the share equations (6.2.15). In a single-output context, if constant returns to scale is assumed, it makes no difference which approach is adopted. In all other contexts the input-oriented approach is simpler. Moreover, in a cost-minimizing framework output(s) is (are) exogenous and inputs are endogenous, making it more appropriate to use the input-oriented measure. (However if the economic orientation were toward revenue maximization rather than cost minimization, the opposite would be true. And in the profit maximization context to be considered in Section 6.2.2, the only determining factor is the relationship between the number of inputs and the number of outputs.)

Both the output-oriented approach given in equations (6.2.6)–(6.2.11) and the input-oriented approach given in equations (6.2.12)–(6.2.15) are based on a shadow input price vector satisfying the normalization $w^* = (w_1, \theta_{21} w_2, \dots, \theta_{N1} w_N)$, with the first input being arbitrarily designated as the numeraire. As a result of this normalization, the expressions for observed expenditure and observed input cost shares given in equations (6.2.10)–(6.2.11) and (6.2.14)–(6.2.15) are highly nonlinear. Nonetheless this normalization has been employed in virtually all empirical studies in which allocative inefficiency has been modeled in a nonparametric fashion. Recently Balk (1997) has proposed, and Balk and van Leeuwen (1997) have estimated, a system based on a different normalization. They require w^* to satisfy $w^{*T} x = w^T x$. As a result of this normalization the expressions for observed expenditure and observed input cost shares simplify considerably, since $\Sigma_k [S_k(y^*, w^*; \beta) \cdot (\theta_{k1})^{-1}] = 1$ in equations (6.2.10)–(6.2.11) and $\Sigma_k [S_k(y, w^*; \beta) \cdot (\theta_{k1})^{-1}] = 1$ in equations (6.2.14)–(6.2.15). However Maietta (1997) has shown that when the cost function is assigned a translog functional form and the normalization $w^{*T}x = w^T x$ is used, neither parameter estimates nor calculated elasticities are invariant to which input cost share equation is deleted. Since no such problem occurs with the normalization $w^* = (w_1, \theta_{21}w_2, \ldots, \theta_{N1}w_N)$, we employ it in the remainder of this chapter.

If cross-sectional data on (y, x) are available, it is possible to estimate equation (6.2.2) to obtain estimates of output-oriented technical efficiency for a limited number of groups of producers. This is not much information, much less than was obtained in Chapter 3, where technical inefficiency was modeled as an error component. However if cross-sectional data on (y, x, w) are available, it is possible to estimate some combination of equations (6.2.9)–(6.2.11) to obtain estimates of output-oriented technical efficiency and input allocative efficiency. However as we noted previously, it is simpler to estimate some combination of equations (6.2.13)–(6.2.15) to obtain estimates of input-oriented technical efficiency and input allocative efficiency. In either case, with cross-sectional data on I producers it is not possible to obtain I estimates of technical efficiency and $(N - 1) \times I$ estimates of input allocative efficiency. It is possible to obtain estimates of a limited number of intergroup technical efficiency differentials, and estimates of $(N - 1)$ systematic allocative efficiencies that vary across input pairs but are the same for all producers. The estimation of such systematic allocative efficiencies is fairly common in the literature. However if I is large relative to N, it is also possible to obtain estimates of a limited number of intergroup allocative efficiency differentials. This is much less common in the literature, and we delay consideration of the estimation of allocative efficiency differentials to Section 6.3.

We now provide three examples of how the shadow price approach to efficiency estimation works. The Cobb–Douglas example has the pedagogical virtue of simplicity, whereas the two subsequent examples share the practical virtue of flexibility, which reduces the likelihood that input allocative inefficiency will be confounded with a misspecification of the underlying functional form. For the time being we suppress producer subscripts and error terms.

Cobb–Douglas If the production function $f(x; \beta)$ takes the Cobb–Douglas form, estimation of input-oriented technical efficiency and systematic input allocative efficiency is relatively straightforward. At least three approaches are available. In the first approach a system of equations consisting of the production function and $(N-1)$ first-order conditions for shadow cost minimization is written in deterministic form as

$$\ln y = [\beta_o + \Delta D] + \sum_n \beta_n \ln x_n \qquad (6.2.16)$$

and

$$\ln x_n - \ln x_1 + \ln w_n - \ln w_1 - \ln\left(\frac{\beta_n}{\beta_1}\right) + \ln \theta_{n1} = 0,$$

$$n = 2, \ldots, N, \qquad (6.2.17)$$

respectively, where D is a dummy variable set to unity if a producer belongs to a particular group and set to zero otherwise. (If more than two groups are specified, more than one dummy variable is required.) Thus the input-oriented technical efficiency of producers in that group relative to that of all other producers is $\exp\{\Delta\} \gtreqless 1$ according as $\Delta \gtreqless 0$, where $\Delta = r \ln \phi$ and $r = \Sigma_n \beta_n$. The $(N-1)$ parameters θ_{n1} measure the divergences of the shadow price ratios $[\theta_{n1}(w_n/w_1)]$ from the observed price ratios (w_n/w_1), and because they are common to all producers they provide estimates of the systematic over- or underutilization in the sample of input x_n relative to the numeraire input x_1.

If a random-error vector is appended to the system of N equations (6.2.16) and (6.2.17), this system can be estimated using MLE under the assumption that the random-error vector is distributed as multivariate normal. An alternative would be to use ITSUR, which does not require the normality assumption. Furthermore the ITSUR estimators, when converged, are equivalent to the ML estimators. The output of the exercise consists of estimates of the technology parameters $(\beta_o, \beta_1, \ldots, \beta_N)$, an estimate of the technical efficiency differential Δ, and estimates of the systematic input allocative inefficiencies θ_{n1}, $n = 2, \ldots, N$. Likelihood ratio tests can be performed to test hypotheses concerning any subset of the parameters $(\Delta, \theta_{21}, \ldots, \theta_{N1})$.

The natural logarithm of total expenditure in the presence of input-oriented technical inefficiency and systematic input allocative inefficiency can be derived from the system of equations (6.2.16) and (6.2.17) as

$$\ln E = \left[B + \frac{1}{r}\ln y + \frac{1}{r}\sum_n \beta_n \ln w_n \right] - \frac{1}{r}(\Delta D) + (A - \ln r), \qquad (6.2.18)$$

where

$$B = \ln r - \frac{\beta_o}{r} - \frac{1}{r}\sum_n \beta_n \ln \beta_n,$$

$$A = \sum_{n>1} \frac{\beta_n}{r}\ln \theta_{n1} + \ln \left[\beta_1 + \sum_{n>1}\frac{\beta_n}{\theta_{n1}} \right].$$

The first term on the right-hand side of equation (6.2.18) is the Cobb–Douglas cost function. The second term is the cost of the technical efficiency differential; this term is zero if, and only if, $\Delta = 0$. The third term is the cost of systematic input allocative inefficiency; this term is nonnegative and attains its minimum value if, and only if, $\theta_{n1} = 1, n = 2, \ldots, N$. Since the third term is a function of the technology and inefficiency parameters, but not of the data, the cost of systematic input allocative inefficiency is also systematic. As we shall see, however, this is a consequence of using the Cobb–Douglas functional form.

A second approach is to solve the system of equations (6.2.16) and (6.2.17) for the system of shadow cost-minimizing input demand equations. These are given in logarithmic form by

$$\ln x_1 = b_o - \frac{1}{r}\Delta D + \ln \beta_1 + \frac{1}{r}\ln y + \frac{1}{r}\sum_n \beta_n \ln \frac{w_n}{w_1}$$

$$+ \frac{1}{r}\sum_{n>1}\beta_n \ln \theta_{n1},$$

$$\ln x_2 = b_o - \frac{1}{r}\Delta D + \ln \beta_2 + \frac{1}{r}\ln y + \frac{1}{r}\sum_n \beta_n \ln \frac{w_n}{w_2}$$

$$+ \frac{1}{r}\sum_{n>1}\beta_n \ln \frac{\theta_{n1}}{\theta_{21}},$$

$$\vdots$$

$$\ln x_N = b_o - \frac{1}{r}\Delta D + \ln \beta_N + \frac{1}{r}\ln y + \frac{1}{r}\sum_n \beta_n \ln \frac{w_n}{w_N}$$

$$+ \frac{1}{r}\sum_{n>1}\beta_n \ln \frac{\theta_{n1}}{\theta_{N1}}, \qquad (6.2.19)$$

where

$$b_o = -\frac{1}{r}\left[\beta_o + \sum_n \beta_n \ln \beta_n\right],$$

$$r = \sum_n \beta_n,$$

$$\Delta = r \ln \phi.$$

The asymmetry of the system of equations (6.2.19) is due to the specification of one input, in this case x_1, as the numeraire. If a random-error vector is appended to the equations in (6.2.19), this system also can be estimated by MLE, under the same distributional assumptions as are maintained in the estimation of the system (6.2.16) and (6.2.17). The system can also be estimated using ITSUR, which does not require a normality assumption on the error vector. The system of equations (6.2.19) generates the same information, and provides the basis for the same hypothesis tests, as does the system (6.2.16) and (6.2.17). The cost implications of the technical efficiency differential and systematic input allocative inefficiency can be inferred from equation (6.2.18).

The third and most straightforward approach is to base the analysis directly on a Cobb–Douglas cost function. The cost function and its associated cost-minimizing input demand equations can be written in deterministic form as

$$c(y,w;\beta) = \gamma_o y^{1/r} \prod_n w_n^{\gamma_n} \tag{6.2.20}$$

and

$$x_1(y,w;\beta) = \gamma_o \gamma_1 y^{1/r} \prod_{n>1}\left(\frac{w_n}{w_1}\right)^{\gamma_n},$$

$$x_2(y,w;\beta) = \gamma_o \gamma_2 y^{1/r} \left(\frac{w_2}{w_1}\right)^{-1} \prod_{n>1}\left(\frac{w_n}{w_1}\right)^{\gamma_n},$$

$$\vdots$$

$$x_N(y,w;\beta) = \gamma_o \gamma_N y^{1/r} \left(\frac{w_N}{w_1}\right)^{-1} \prod_{n>1}\left(\frac{w_n}{w_1}\right)^{\gamma_n}, \tag{6.2.21}$$

respectively, where homogeneity of degree +1 in w of $c(y,w;\beta)$ requires that $\sum_n \gamma_n = 1$, and $r \gtreqless 1$ indicates the degree of homogeneity of the underlying production function. The cost function (6.2.20) is posited as a starting point; it is not derived from the production function (6.2.16) and the first-order conditions (6.2.17). Consequently the parameters in equations (6.2.20) and (6.2.21) are not the same as those appearing in equations (6.2.16)–(6.2.19).

An input-oriented technical efficiency differential can be incorporated into equations (6.2.20) and (6.2.21) by replacing γ_o with $\gamma_o \cdot \exp\{-\Delta D\}$. If, in addition, producers are allocatively efficient with respect to shadow input price ratios $[\theta_{n1}(w_n/w_1)]$, $n > 1$, the input demand equations become, in logarithmic form,

$$\ln x_1 = \ln \gamma_o - \Delta D + \ln \gamma_1 + \frac{1}{r}\ln y + \sum_{n>1} \gamma_n \ln\left[\theta_{n1}\left(\frac{w_n}{w_1}\right)\right],$$

$$\ln x_2 = \ln \gamma_o - \Delta D + \ln \gamma_2 + \frac{1}{r}\ln y$$

$$+ \sum_{n>1} \gamma_n \ln\left[\theta_{n1}\left(\frac{w_n}{w_1}\right)\right] - \ln\left[\theta_{21}\left(\frac{w_2}{w_1}\right)\right], \tag{6.2.22}$$

$$\vdots$$

$$\ln x_N = \ln \gamma_o - \Delta D + \ln \gamma_N + \frac{1}{r}\ln y$$

$$+ \sum_{n>1} \gamma_n \ln\left[\theta_{n1}\left(\frac{w_n}{w_1}\right)\right] - \ln\left[\theta_{N1}\left(\frac{w_N}{w_1}\right)\right],$$

respectively. Total expenditure becomes

$$\ln E = \ln c(y,w;\beta) - \Delta D + \left\{\sum_{n>1} \gamma_n \ln \theta_{n1} + \ln\left[\gamma_1 + \sum_{n>1}\left(\frac{\gamma_n}{\theta_{n1}}\right)\right]\right\}, \tag{6.2.23}$$

where $c(y,w;\beta)$ is defined in equation (6.2.20). Thus the natural logarithm of total expenditure equals the natural logarithm of minimum cost, plus or minus the percentage cost of the technical efficiency differential, plus the percentage cost of systematic input allocative inefficiency. The percentage cost of the technical efficiency differential is given by $-\Delta D$. The percentage cost of systematic input allocative inefficiency is given by the nonnegative term in braces, which attains its minimum value of zero if, and only if, $\theta_{n1} = 1$, $n = 2, \ldots, N$. Once again, in a Cobb–Douglas framework the cost of systematic allocative inefficiency is also systematic. After appending classical error terms to the system of input demand equations (6.2.22), the system can be estimated by ITSUR, with cross-equation parameter restrictions imposed, after which the estimated values of Δ and the θ_{n1} can be inserted into equation (6.2.23) to provide estimates of the technical efficiency cost differential and the cost of systematic input allocative inefficiency.

Generalized Leontief This partially flexible functional form for a cost function was introduced by Diewert (1971), and perhaps first used to model systematic input allocative inefficiency by Toda (1976, 1977). The generalized Leontief minimum cost function can be written as

$$
\begin{aligned}
c(y,w;\beta) &= y \cdot \sum_n \sum_k \beta_{nk} w_n^{1/2} w_k^{1/2} \\
&= y \cdot \left[\sum_n \beta_{nn} w_n + 2 \sum_{k>n} \sum_n \beta_{kn} w_n^{1/2} w_k^{1/2} \right],
\end{aligned}
\tag{6.2.24}
$$

where $\beta_{nk} = \beta_{kn} \geq 0 \; \forall n, k$. $c(y, w; \beta)$ is homogeneous of degree +1 in w, and if at least one $\beta_{nk} > 0$, $c(y, w; \beta)$ is concave in w. An input-oriented technical efficiency differential can be introduced by replacing the input price vector w with $w \cdot \exp\{-\Delta D\}$. Since $c(y, w; \beta)$ is homogeneous of degree +1 in w, this implies that y can be replaced with $y \cdot \exp\{-\Delta D\}$. Note that the underlying technology is assumed to satisfy constant returns to scale, which is why we describe $c(y, w; \beta)$ as being partially flexible.

Application of Shephard's lemma to equation (6.2.24) generates a system of cost-minimizing input demand equations of the form

$$
x_n(y,w;\beta) = y \cdot \exp\{-\Delta D\} \cdot \left[\beta_{nn} + \sum_{k \neq n} \beta_{kn} \left(\frac{w_k}{w_n} \right)^{1/2} \right], \qquad n = 1, \ldots, N.
\tag{6.2.25}
$$

Systematic input allocative inefficiency is introduced by allowing observed input demands to be optimal for shadow price ratios rather than for observed price ratios. The resulting shadow input demand equations can be written as

$$x_n = y \cdot \exp\{-\Delta D\} \cdot \left\{ \beta_{nn} + \sum_{k \neq n} \beta_{kn} \left[\theta_{kn} \left(\frac{w_k}{w_n} \right) \right]^{1/2} \right\}, \quad n = 1, \ldots, N,$$

(6.2.26)

where by symmetry there are $N(N-1)/2$ shadow price parameters $\theta_{kn} > 0, k > n$, to be estimated. Observed expenditure can be expressed as

$$E = \sum_n w_n x_n$$

$$= y \cdot \exp\{-\Delta D\} \cdot \left[\sum_n \beta_{nn} w_n + \sum_{k > n} \sum_n \beta_{kn} (\theta_{kn}^{1/2} + \theta_{kn}^{-1/2}) w_n^{1/2} w_k^{1/2} \right].$$

(6.2.27)

The term $\exp\{-\Delta D\} \gtreqless 1$ according as producers in the reference group ($D = 0$) are more, equally, or less technically efficient than those in the comparison group. If the two groups are equally technically efficient, it should be apparent from equations (6.2.24) and (6.2.27) that $E \geq c(y, w; \beta)$ and that $E = c(y, w; \beta) \Leftrightarrow (\theta_{kn}^{1/2} + \theta_{kn}^{-1/2}) = 2 \Leftrightarrow \theta_{kn} = 1 \ \forall k > n$.

Since E is a linear combination of the x_n, estimation and hypothesis testing is based on the system of shadow input demand equations (6.2.26). After converting the shadow input demand equations to shadow input–output demand equations x_n/y, estimation is conducted by means of iterated SUR, with cross-equation parameter restrictions imposed. Several hypothesis tests are of potential interest. Equal technical efficiency across groups can be tested by testing the hypothesis that $\Delta = 0$. Systematic allocative efficiency can be tested by testing the hypothesis that $\theta_{kn} = 1 \ \forall k > n$. Systematic overutilization of one input relative to another input can be tested by testing the hypothesis that $\theta_{kn} = 1$ against the alternative that $\theta_{kn} < 1$. An example is provided by the Averch–Johnson (1962) overcapitalization hypothesis, in which k designates a rate base input and n designates a nonrate base input. Finally, following Lovell and Sickles (1983), the hypothesis that input allocative inefficiency is consistent across inputs can be tested by testing the hypothesis that $\theta_{nk} = \theta_{nm} \cdot \theta_{mk} \ \forall n > m > k$. After estimation and hypothesis testing, the impact on expenditure of the technical efficiency differential can be calculated from equation (6.2.27) as $\exp\{-\Delta D\}$, and the impact on expenditure of systematic allocative inefficiency can be calculated by comparing predicted expenditure with and without the parametric restrictions $\theta_{kn} = 1 \ \forall k > n$. In sharp contrast to the Cobb–Douglas case, the cost of systematic input allocative inefficiency is producer specific, since it depends on input prices as well as parameters.

Translog I Essentially the same procedure can be used to estimate technical and systematic allocative inefficiency within a translog framework. The advantage of the translog form over the generalized Leontief form lies in the ease with which the translog form can incorporate multiple outputs and model nonhomothetic technologies. The single-output translog cost function and its associated cost-minimizing input cost share equations can be written as

$$
\ln c(y,w;\beta) = \beta_o + \beta_y \ln y + \sum_n \beta_n \ln w_n + \frac{1}{2}\beta_{yy}(\ln y)^2
$$
$$
+ \frac{1}{2}\sum_n \sum_k \beta_{nk}\ln w_n \ln w_k + \sum_n \beta_{yn}\ln y \ln w_n
$$

(6.2.28)

and

$$
S_n(y,w;\beta) = \beta_n + \sum_k \beta_{nk}\ln w_k + \beta_{yn}\ln y, \qquad n=1,\ldots,N, \qquad (6.2.29)
$$

respectively, where symmetry and homogeneity of degree +1 in input prices are imposed through the parameter restrictions $\beta_{nk} = \beta_{kn}$, $k \neq n$, $\Sigma_n\beta_n = 1$, $\Sigma_k\beta_{nk} = 0$, $n = 1,\ldots,N$, and $\Sigma_n\beta_{yn} = 0$. Note that the underlying technology is nonhomothetic unless $\beta_{yn} = 0, n = 1,\ldots,N$, which is a testable parametric restriction.

An output-oriented technical efficiency differential can be introduced by replacing y with $y \cdot \exp\{-\Delta D\}$. In this event output-oriented technical inefficiency does not appear simply in an additive fashion in the expression for total expenditure, as it did in the Cobb–Douglas model given in equation (6.2.23). In the translog model output-oriented technical inefficiency interacts with input prices and output quantity, appearing in $(N + 2)$ terms in the cost equation (6.2.28), and in one term in each of the input cost share equations (6.2.29). However if technical inefficiency is specified as being input oriented, it does appear additively in the expression for total expenditure, modifying the intercept term in the cost equation (6.2.28), and it does not appear at all in the input cost share equations (6.2.29). This illustrates the advantage of using the input-oriented specification in a cost minimization framework, an advantage that multiplies in the multiple-output case.

Using the input-oriented approach to technical efficiency and exploiting equations (6.2.14) and (6.2.15), observed expenditure and observed input cost shares can be expressed in terms of shadow cost and shadow input cost shares as

$$
\ln E = \beta_o - \Delta D + \beta_y \ln y + \frac{1}{2}\beta_{yy}(\ln y)^2 + \sum_n \beta_n \ln(\theta_{n1}w_n)
$$
$$
+ \frac{1}{2}\sum_n\sum_k \beta_{nk}\ln(\theta_{n1}w_n)\ln(\theta_{k1}w_k) + \sum_n \beta_{yn}\ln y\ln(\theta_{n1}w_n)
$$
$$
+ \ln\left\{\sum_n(\theta_{n1})^{-1}\left[\beta_n + \sum_k\beta_{nk}\ln(\theta_{k1}w_k) + \beta_{yn}\ln y\right]\right\} \qquad (6.2.30)
$$

and

$$
S_n = \frac{(\theta_{n1})^{-1}[\beta_n + \Sigma_k\beta_{nk}\ln(\theta_{k1}w_k) + \beta_{yn}\ln y]}{\Sigma_j(\theta_{j1})^{-1}[\beta_j + \Sigma_k\beta_{jk}\ln(\theta_{k1}w_k) + \beta_{yj}\ln y]},
$$
$$
n = 1,\dots, N, \qquad (6.2.31)
$$

respectively. It follows from equations (6.2.28) and (6.2.30) that

$$
\ln E = \ln c(y,w;\beta) - \Delta D + \left\{\sum_n\beta_n\ln\theta_{n1} + \sum_n\sum_k\beta_{nk}\ln w_n\ln\theta_{k1}\right.
$$
$$
\left. + \frac{1}{2}\sum_n\sum_k\beta_{nk}\ln\theta_{n1}\ln\theta_{k1} + \sum_n\beta_{yn}\ln y\ln\theta_{n1}\right\}. \qquad (6.2.32)
$$

Thus the natural logarithm of total expenditure can be expressed as the sum of three components: the translog cost function given in equation (6.2.28), the percentage cost differential due to the input-oriented technical efficiency differential, and the percentage cost of systematic allocative inefficiency. The second term is zero if, and only if, $\Delta = 0$, and the third term is nonnegative and attains its minimum value of zero if, and only if, $\theta_{21} = \cdots = \theta_{N1} = 1$. It is important to note that the percentage cost of systematic allocative inefficiency is not itself systematic in the translog case, since the third term depends on data as well as parameters.

If classical error terms are appended to equations (6.2.30) and (6.2.31), and if one input cost share equation is deleted, the remaining system of N equations can be estimated by ITSUR. After estimation, likelihood ratio tests can be employed to test hypotheses concerning the nature of technical and systematic allocative inefficiency. The effects of the technical efficiency differential and of systematic allocative inefficiency on total expenditure can be calculated from equation (6.2.32).

Generalizing the translog form to accommodate multiple outputs presents no problems, since the impact of input-oriented technical inefficiency appears only in the intercept of the cost function, and the impact of systematic allocative inefficiency modifies only the input prices. All that is required is to increase the number of output-related terms in the cost function and the input cost share equations. Estimation and interpretation of the results are unaffected.

Translog II In the preceding translog framework we created shadow input prices by *scaling* observed prices; we adopted the same approach in the generalized Leontief framework. It is also possible to create shadow input prices by *translating* observed input prices, in either the translog or the generalized Leontief framework. Eakin and Kniesner (1988, 1992), Eakin (1991), and Atkinson and Halvorsen (1992) have done so in a hybrid translog multiple-output cost function framework. A hybrid translog shadow cost function can be written as

$$\ln c^{H}(y,w;\beta,\theta) = \beta_{o} + \sum_{m}\alpha_{m}y_{m} + \sum_{n}\beta_{n}\ln(w_{n}+\theta_{n}) + \frac{1}{2}\sum_{m}\sum_{j}\alpha_{mj}y_{m}y_{j}$$
$$+ \frac{1}{2}\sum_{n}\sum_{k}\beta_{nk}[\ln(w_{n}+\theta_{n})][\ln(w_{k}+\theta_{k})]$$
$$+ \sum_{m}\sum_{n}\gamma_{mn}y_{m}\ln(w_{n}+\theta_{n}), \qquad (6.2.33)$$

where the qualifier "hybrid" refers to the fact that the natural logarithms of output quantities are replaced with the output quantities themselves. This modification of the translog form allows the introduction of nonpositive output quantities, without disturbing the flexibility of the functional form. The parameter vector θ allows shadow input prices to diverge (additively rather than multiplicatively) from observed input prices. The usual parameter restrictions impose linear homogeneity in shadow input prices. Shephard's lemma generates the shadow input cost share equations

$$S_n^H(y,w,\beta,\theta) = \beta_n + \sum_k \beta_{nk} \ln(w_k + \theta_k) + \sum_m \gamma_{mn} y_m ,$$

$$n = 1, \dots, N. \tag{6.2.34}$$

The natural logarithm of observed expenditure, and the observed input cost share equations, can be expressed as

$$\ln E = \ln c^H(y,w;\beta,\theta) + \ln\left[\sum_n \left(\frac{w_n}{w_n + \theta_n}\right)\right.$$

$$\left. \left(\beta_n + \sum_m \gamma_{mn} y_m + \sum_k \beta_{nk} \ln(w_k + \theta_k)\right)\right],$$

$$S_n = \frac{S_n^H(y,w;\beta,\theta)\cdot(w_n/(w_n + \theta_n))}{[\Sigma_j(w_j/(w_j + \theta_j))(\beta_j + \Sigma_m\gamma_{jm} y_m + \Sigma_k\beta_{kj} \ln(w_k + \theta_k))]},$$

$$n = 1, \dots, N, \tag{6.2.35}$$

where the superscript H indicates that the cost function and its associated input cost share equations have the "hybrid" translog functional form. It is clear that $\ln E = \ln c^H(y, w; \beta, \theta)$ and $S_n = s_n^H(y, w; \beta, \theta)$ if $\theta_n = 0$, $n = 1, \dots, N$. It is not so clear, but nonetheless true, that $\ln E > \ln c^H(y, w; \beta, \theta)$ and that $S_n \neq S_n^H(y, w; \beta, \theta)$ otherwise. Once again, however, the percentage cost of systematic input allocative inefficiency is producer specific. Finally, as usual, not all shadow price divergence parameters θ_n are identified, and in this additive formulation the only permissible normalization is to set one element of $\theta = 0$.

After substituting equations (6.2.33) and (6.2.34) into the equation system (6.2.35), deleting one input cost share equation, and adding a multivariate normal error vector to the remaining N equations, estimation via nonlinear SUR can proceed. After estimation, likelihood ratio tests of various hypotheses of interest can be conducted. The hypothesis of overall allocative efficiency is tested by testing the hypothesis that $\theta_n = 0$ $\forall n$. The hypothesis that the mix of inputs n and k is allocatively efficient is tested by testing the hypothesis that $(w_n/w_k) = (w_n + \theta_n)/(w_k + \theta_k)$. Notice that technical inefficiency is not incorporated into the model, although it could be incorporated in a restricted fashion in the same manner as it was in the first translog model.

Translog III In the two preceding translog frameworks (and in the Cobb–Douglas and generalized Leontief frameworks as well) we modeled both technical and systematic input allocative inefficiencies parametrically. As a consequence, it was not possible to obtain separate estimates of a technical inefficiency parameter for all I producers, and we settled for an estimate of a single technical efficiency differential parameter Δ. It is possible, however, to combine the parametric approach to the estimation of systematic input allocative inefficiency with a stochastic approach to the estimation of technical inefficiency. Such a procedure enables us to obtain estimates of systematic input allocative inefficiencies and their producer-specific costs, as before, and also to obtain producer-specific estimates of technical inefficiency and its cost. The procedure works as follows.

Writing equations (6.2.14) and (6.2.15) in translog form, we have

$$\ln E = \beta_o + \beta_y \ln y + \sum_n \beta_n \ln(\theta_{n1} w_n) + \frac{1}{2}\beta_{yy}(\ln y)^2$$

$$+ \frac{1}{2}\sum_n \sum_k \beta_{nk} \ln(\theta_{n1} w_n)\ln(\theta_{k1} w_k) + \sum_n \beta_{yn} \ln y \ln(\theta_{n1} w_n)$$

$$+ \ln\left\{\sum_n (\theta_{n1})^{-1}\left[\beta_n + \sum_k \beta_{nk}\ln(\theta_{k1} w_k) + \beta_{yn}\ln y\right]\right\} - \ln\phi,$$

$$(6.2.36)$$

$$S_n = \frac{(\theta_{n1})^{-1}[\beta_n + \Sigma_k \beta_{nk}\ln(\theta_{k1} w_k) + \beta_{yn}\ln y]}{\Sigma_j(\theta_{j1})^{-1}[\beta_j + \Sigma_k \beta_{jk}\ln(\theta_{k1} w_k) + \beta_{yj}\ln y]}, \qquad n = 1, \ldots, N.$$

$$(6.2.37)$$

After imposing linear homogeneity on equation (6.2.36) (either parametrically or by subtracting $\ln w_1$ from both sides, since $\theta_{11} = 1$) this system can be estimated by MLE. We assume that $-\ln\phi \sim$ iid $N^+(0, \sigma_\phi^2)$. This error component does not represent cost inefficiency as it did in Chapter 4; it represents the cost of input-oriented technical inefficiency only. We add a second error component $v \sim$ iid $N(0, \sigma_v^2)$ to the cost equation and an error vector $v_n \sim$ iid $N(0, \Sigma)$ to $N - 1$ input cost share equations, and we assume that all three error terms are mutually independent and independent of the regressors. The log likelihood function of the system under these distributional assumptions can be expressed as

$$\ln L = \text{constant} - I \ln \sigma + \sum_i \ln \Phi\left(\frac{\varepsilon_i \lambda}{\sigma}\right) - \frac{1}{2\sigma^2} \sum_i \varepsilon_i^2$$

$$- \frac{I}{2}\ln|\Sigma| - \frac{1}{2}\sum_i v_{ni}' \Sigma^{-1} v_{ni}, \qquad (6.2.38)$$

where

$$\varepsilon_i = v_i - \ln \phi_i,$$

$$\sigma^2 = \sigma_v^2 + \sigma_\phi^2,$$

$$\gamma = \frac{\sigma_\phi}{\sigma_v}.$$

Maximization of the preceding log likelihood function generates estimates of all technology parameters and all allocative inefficiency parameters. After estimation, the producer-specific cost of systematic input allocative inefficiency can be determined from the third term on the right-hand side of equation (6.2.32). In addition, the JLMS technique can be used to decompose the cost equation residuals into separate producer-specific estimates of the cost of technical inefficiency and statistical noise. The estimators of $-\ln \phi_i$ are given by

$$E(-\ln \phi_i | \varepsilon_i) = \mu_{*i} + \sigma_* \left[\frac{\phi(-\mu_{*i}/\sigma_*)}{1 - \Phi(-\mu_{*i}/\sigma_*)} \right],$$

$$M(-\ln \phi_i | \varepsilon_i) = \begin{cases} \varepsilon_i(\sigma_\phi^2/\sigma^2) & \text{if } \varepsilon_i \geq 0, \\ 0 & \text{otherwise,} \end{cases}$$

where $\mu_{*i} = \varepsilon_i \sigma_\phi^2/\sigma^2$ and $\sigma_*^2 = \sigma_\phi^2 \sigma_v^2/\sigma^2$.

Since the model is highly nonlinear, the ML estimators might be difficult to obtain, and one could consider a two-step procedure. In the first step $-\ln \phi_i$ is ignored and ITSUR is used to generate consistent estimates of all remaining parameters except for the intercept, which is biased. One can then use standard asymptotic results, available in Gallant (1987; Chapter 5), to test hypotheses concerning the parameters of the cost frontier. In the second step the cost frontier residuals $\varepsilon_i = \beta_o - \ln \phi_i + v_i$ are obtained and distributional assumptions are made on $-\ln \phi_i$ and v_i, such as $-\ln \phi_i \sim$ iid $N^+(0, \sigma_\phi^2)$ and $v_i \sim N(0, \sigma_v^2)$, and $-\ln \phi_i$ and v_i are assumed to be distributed independently. Under these assumptions the log likelihood function can be derived, the maximization of which will generate estimates of β_o, σ_ϕ^2, and σ_v^2 (conditional on the parameter estimates obtained in the first step). Finally, the JLMS procedure can be applied to estimate $-\ln \phi_i$.

6.2.2 Estimating and Decomposing Profit Inefficiency

In this section we adopt the same approach to the estimation and decomposition of profit inefficiency as we did to the estimation and decomposition of cost inefficiency in Section 6.2.1. Failure to maximize profit has a technical inefficiency component, which can be output oriented or input oriented. It also has a systematic allocative inefficiency component, which can involve an inappropriate input mix, an inappropriate output mix (in the case of multiple outputs), and an inappropriate scale. As we saw in Section 2.4.3, the magnitudes, and perhaps even the directions, of the scale and mix components of systematic allocative inefficiency can depend on the orientation of the technical efficiency measure. We begin with a graphical illustration. We then generalize the analysis. We derive a shadow profit function, and we then express observed output quantities, observed input quantities, and observed profit in terms of shadow output prices and shadow input prices. We also derive a normalized shadow profit function, and we express observed output quantities, observed input quantities, and observed normalized profit in terms of shadow output prices and shadow input prices. Finally, we illustrate the analysis using Cobb–Douglas and flexible functional forms. All formulations adopt the multiplicative approach of scaling observed prices to create shadow prices, although each formulation could also adopt the additive approach of translating observed prices to create shadow prices. We leave this exercise to the reader.

Suppose we observe a producer using input vector x to produce scalar output y with production frontier $f(x; \beta)$. The observed output price and the observed input price vector are p and w, respectively, and so observed profit is $\pi = py - w^T x$. The measurement and decomposition of profit efficiency are illustrated in Figure 6.3, which takes an output orientation to the measurement of technical efficiency, and in Figure 6.4, which takes an input orientation to the measurement of technical efficiency. Since in both figures it is assumed that a single

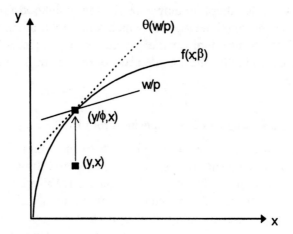

Figure 6.3 The Shadow Price Approach to Estimating Profit Efficiency:
Output Orientation

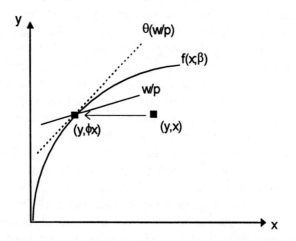

Figure 6.4 The Shadow Price Approach to Estimating Profit Efficiency:
Input Orientation

input is used to produce a single output, the only type of allocative
inefficiency is scale inefficiency.

In Figure 6.3 the producer is technically inefficient, since $y/\phi = f(x;$
$\beta)$, with $0 < \phi \le 1$ providing an output-oriented measure of technical

efficiency. In addition, at the technically efficient projection $(y/\phi, x)$ the producer is operating at an inefficiently small scale, since the marginal product of the input exceeds the observed input–output price ratio. However the producer is scale efficient relative to the larger shadow price ratio $[\theta(w/p)]$, $\theta > 1$.

In Figure 6.4 the producer is also technically inefficient, since $y = f(\phi x; \beta)$, with $0 < \phi \leq 1$ providing an input-oriented measure of technical efficiency. In addition, at the technically efficient projection $(y, \phi x)$ the producer is operating at an inefficiently small scale, since the marginal product of the input exceeds the observed input–output price ratio. However the producer is scale efficient relative to the larger shadow price ratio $[\theta(w/p)]$, $\theta > 1$.

It should be apparent that in general neither parametric efficiency measure in the output-oriented Figure 6.3 has the same value as the corresponding measure in the input-oriented Figure 6.4. It should also be noted that the analysis underlying both figures can be generalized to accommodate multiple inputs and multiple outputs, in which case both input allocative inefficiency and output allocative inefficiency can be modeled parametrically, in the same manner as input allocative inefficiency was modeled in Figures 6.1 and 6.2.

The basic idea underlying the output-oriented approach to the estimation and decomposition of profit inefficiency illustrated in Figure 6.3 can be generalized as follows. In the single-output case a shadow profit function is given by

$$\pi(p^*, w^*; \beta) = \max_x \left\{ p\phi f(x; \beta) - \sum_n \theta_n w_n x_n \right\}, \tag{6.2.39}$$

where $y = \phi f(x; \beta)$, with $0 < \phi \leq 1$ capturing the effect of output-oriented technical inefficiency. Maximization of shadow profit requires $\partial f(x; \beta)/\partial x_n = (\theta_n w_n/\phi p)$, with $\theta_n \gtreqless 1$, $n = 1, \ldots, N$, capturing the effects of systematic input allocative inefficiency. Thus $p^* = \phi p$ and $w_n^* = \theta_n w_n$, $n = 1, \ldots, N$. Unlike the shadow cost function model, in the shadow profit function model it is possible to identify all N input allocative inefficiency parameters θ_n, $n = 1, \ldots, N$; a normalization such as $\theta = [1, \theta_{21}, \ldots, \theta_{N1}]$ is not required.

Hotelling's lemma can be applied to equation (6.2.39) to generate the system of observed output supply and input demand equations

$$y = \frac{\partial \pi(p^*, w^*; \beta)}{\partial p^*}$$

$$= \frac{1}{\phi} \frac{\partial \pi(p^*, w^*; \beta)}{\partial p},$$

$$-x_n = \frac{\partial \pi(p^*, w^*; \beta)}{\partial w_n^*}$$

$$= \frac{1}{\theta_n} \frac{\partial \pi(p^*, w^*; \beta)}{\partial w_n}, \qquad n = 1, \dots, N, \tag{6.2.40}$$

which in turn generate an expression for observed profit

$$\pi = p \frac{\partial \pi(p^*, w^*; \beta)}{\partial p^*} + \sum_n w_n \frac{\partial \pi(p^*, w^*; \beta)}{\partial w_n^*}$$

$$= \frac{p}{\phi} \frac{\partial \pi(p^*, w^*; \beta)}{\partial p} + \sum_n \frac{w_n}{\theta_n} \frac{\partial \pi(p^*, w^*; \beta)}{\partial w_n}. \tag{6.2.41}$$

Estimation can be based either on the $(N+1)$ equations in (6.2.40) or on a system consisting of the profit equation (6.2.41) and N observed profit share equations replacing the $(N + 1)$ observed output supply and input demand equations (6.2.40). All that is required is to impose a functional form on the shadow profit function $\pi(p^*, w^*; \beta)$. However in a shadow profit function framework the linear homogeneity property of $\pi(p^*, w^*; \beta)$ in (p^*, w^*) must be imposed through parametric restrictions. Consequently most empirical analysis has been based on the normalized shadow profit function, following Lau and Yotopoulos (1971). In the single-output case a normalized shadow profit function can be derived from the shadow profit function in equation (6.2.39) as

$$\frac{\pi(p^*, w^*; \beta)}{p} = \phi \cdot \max_x \left\{ f(x; \beta) - \sum_n \left(\frac{\theta_n w_n}{\phi p} \right) x_n \right\}$$

$$= \phi \cdot \pi[(w/p)^*; \beta], \tag{6.2.42}$$

which is homogeneous of degree 0 in (p^*, w^*). The normalized shadow price ratios $(w/p)_n^* = (\theta_n w_n / \phi p)$, $n = 1, \dots, N$, contain both technical and systematic allocative inefficiencies.

Application of Hotelling's lemma to equation (6.2.42) generates the system of observed output supply and input demand equations

$$y = \phi \cdot \pi[(w/p)^*;\beta] - \phi \cdot \sum_n \left(\frac{w}{p}\right)_n^* \frac{\partial \pi[(w/p)^*;\beta]}{\partial (w/p)_n^*}$$

$$= \phi \cdot \pi[(w/p)^*;\beta] - \phi \cdot \sum_n \left(\frac{w}{p}\right)_n \frac{\partial \pi[(w/p)^*;\beta]}{\partial (w/p)_n}$$

$$-x_n = \frac{\partial \pi[(w/p)^*;\beta]}{\partial (w/p)_n^*}$$

$$= \frac{\phi}{\theta_n} \frac{\partial \pi[(w/p)^*;\beta]}{\partial (w/p)_n}, \qquad n = 1, \ldots, N, \tag{6.2.43}$$

which in turn generate an expression for observed normalized profit

$$\frac{\pi}{p} = y - \sum_n \left(\frac{w}{p}\right)_n x_n$$

$$= \phi \cdot \pi[(w/p)^*;\beta] + \phi \cdot \sum_n \frac{1-\theta_n}{\theta_n} \left(\frac{w}{p}\right)_n \frac{\partial \pi[(w/p)^*;\beta]}{\partial (w/p)_n}. \tag{6.2.44}$$

Estimation can also be based either on the system of $(N + 1)$ equations (6.2.43) or on a system consisting of the normalized profit equation (6.2.44) and N observed profit share equations replacing the $(N + 1)$ observed output supply and input demand equations (6.2.43). All that is required is to impose a functional form on the normalized shadow profit function $\pi[(w/p)^*; \beta]$.

The basic idea underlying the input-oriented approach to the estimation and decomposition of profit inefficiency illustrated in Figure 6.4 can be generalized also. In this case the shadow profit function is given by

$$\pi(p, w^\otimes; \beta) = \max_{\phi x} \left\{ pf(\phi x; \beta) - \sum_n \left(\frac{\theta_n w_n}{\phi}\right)(\phi x_n) \right\}, \tag{6.2.45}$$

where $w_n^\otimes = (\theta_n w_n/\phi)$, $n = 1, \ldots, N$. Subsequent derivations follow along lines similar to those developed in equations (6.2.39)–(6.2.44); details are available in Kumbhakar (1996a, c).

We now illustrate the shadow price approach to the estimation and decomposition of profit inefficiency with the Cobb–Douglas functional form, assuming a single output, and with two flexible functional forms, each allowing for multiple outputs.

Cobb–Douglas We follow the strategy of Lau and Yotopoulos (1971, 1979) and Yotopoulos and Lau (1973). Let production technology be characterized by the relationship

$$y = \prod_n x_n^{\beta_n},$$ (6.2.46)

with $\beta_n > 0$, $n = 1, \ldots, N$, and $\Sigma_n \beta_n = r < 1$. The profit function corresponding to this production function is

$$\pi(p, w; \beta) = (1 - r)p^{1/(1-r)} \prod_n \left(\frac{w_n}{\beta_n}\right)^{-\beta_n/(1-r)},$$ (6.2.47)

and the normalized profit function is

$$\frac{\pi(p, w; \beta)}{p} = (1 - r)p^{r/(1-r)} \prod_n \left(\frac{w_n}{\beta_n}\right)^{-\beta_n/(1-r)}.$$ (6.2.48)

Hotelling's lemma can be applied to either equation (6.2.45) or equation (6.2.48) to generate profit-maximizing output supply and input demand equations. They are given by

$$y(p, w, \beta) = p^{r/(1-r)} \prod_n \left(\frac{w_n}{\beta_n}\right)^{-\beta_n/(1-r)},$$

$$x_n(p, w, \beta) = p^{1/(1-r)} \prod_k \left(\frac{w_k}{\beta_k}\right)^{-\beta_k/(1-r)} \left(\frac{w_n}{\beta_n}\right)^{-1}, \quad n = 1, \ldots, N.$$

(6.2.49)

The corresponding profit-maximizing profit share equations are

$$\frac{py(p, w; \beta)}{\pi(p, w; \beta)} = \frac{1}{1 - r},$$

$$\frac{w_n x_n(p, w; \beta)}{\pi(p, w; \beta)} = \left(\frac{\beta_n}{1 - r}\right), \quad n = 1, \ldots, N.$$ (6.2.50)

Now suppose that a producer is technically and allocatively inefficient, and optimizes with respect to shadow price ratios $(\theta_n w_n / \phi p)$, $n = 1, \ldots, N$. Here the θ_ns represent systematic input allocative inefficiency and ϕ represents output-oriented technical inefficiency. Then the producer's observed profit coincides with maximum shadow profit, and so

$$\pi = \pi(p^*, w^*; \beta) = A \cdot \pi(p, w; \beta), \tag{6.2.51}$$

where

$$A = \left[\phi^{1/(1-r)} \cdot (1-r)^{-1} \right] \cdot \left[1 - \sum_n \left(\frac{\beta_n}{\theta_n} \right) \right] \cdot \prod_n \theta_n^{-\beta_n/(1-r)}.$$

Taking the natural logarithm of equation (6.2.51) and using the definition of A shows that the natural logarithm of observed profit is equal to the natural logarithm of maximum profit, plus a term measuring the percentage of maximum profit lost to technical inefficiency, plus a term measuring the percentage of maximum profit lost to systematic input allocative inefficiency. The former loss is nonnegative, and attains its minimum value of zero if, and only if, $\phi = 1$. The latter loss is also nonnegative, and attains its minimum value of zero if, and only if, $\theta_2 = \cdots = \theta_N = 1$ (the normalization $\theta_1 = 1$ is imposed for identification purposes). The same relationship holds between the natural logarithms of observed and maximum normalized profit in equation (6.2.54).

The producer's observed output supply and input demand equations coincide with shadow profit-maximizing output supply and input demand equations, and so

$$y = y(p^*, w^*; \beta) = A_y \cdot y(p, w; \beta),$$
$$x_n = x_n(p^*, w^*; \beta) = A_n \cdot x_n(p, w; \beta), \qquad n = 1, \ldots, N,$$

$$\tag{6.2.52}$$

where

$$A_y = [\phi^{1/(1-r)}] \cdot \left[\prod_n \theta_n^{-\beta_n/(1-r)} \right],$$
$$A_n = [\phi^{1/(1-r)}] \cdot \left[\theta_n^{-1} \prod_k \theta_k^{-\beta_k/(1-r)} \right], \qquad n = 1, \ldots, N.$$

$A_y \gtreqless 1$ and $A_n \gtreqless 1, n = 1, \ldots, N$, depending on the magnitude of technical inefficiency and the directions and magnitudes of systematic input allocative inefficiencies. Thus observed output supply and input demand equations coincide with profit-maximizing output supply and input demand equations if, and only if, $\phi = \theta_2 = \cdots = \theta_N = 1$.

The producer's observed profit shares coincide with shadow profit-maximizing profit shares, and so

$$\frac{py}{\pi} = \frac{py(p^*,w^*;\beta)}{\pi(p^*,w^*;\beta)} = \left[1 - \sum_n \left(\frac{\beta_n}{\theta_n}\right)\right]^{-1},$$

$$\frac{w_n x_n}{\pi} = \frac{w_n x_n(p^*,w^*;\beta)}{\pi(p^*,w^*;\beta)} = \frac{\beta_n}{\theta_n}\left[1 - \sum_k \left(\frac{\beta_k}{\theta_k}\right)\right]^{-1}, \qquad n = 1,\ldots,N.$$

(6.2.53)

These observed profit shares coincide with the profit-maximizing profit shares if, and only if, $\theta_2 = \cdots = \theta_N = 1$. Note that although output-oriented technical inefficiency ϕ appears in the observed output supply and input demand equations (6.2.52), it washes out of the observed profit share equations (6.2.53).

The natural logarithm of observed normalized profit is

$$\ln \frac{\pi}{p} = \ln A^* + \sum_n \beta_n^* \ln \frac{w_n}{p},$$

(6.2.54)

and the corresponding observed normalized input profit share equations are

$$\frac{(w_n/p)x_n}{\pi/p} = \beta_n^{**}, \qquad n = 1,\ldots,N,$$

(6.2.55)

where

$$\ln A^* = (1-r)^{-1} \ln \phi + \ln\left(1 - \sum_n \frac{\beta_n}{\theta_n}\right) - \sum_n \beta_n (1-r)^{-1} \ln \theta_n$$

$$+ \sum_n \beta_n (1-r)^{-1} \ln \beta_n,$$

$$\beta_n^* = -\beta_n(1-r)^{-1}, \qquad n = 1,\ldots,N,$$

$$\beta_n^{**} = \frac{\beta_n/\theta_n}{1 - \sum_k(\beta_k/\theta_k)}, \qquad n = 1,\ldots,N.$$

Empirical analysis is based on the system of $(N+1)$ equations (6.2.54) and (6.2.55), which are estimated jointly using ITSUR. A number of hypothesis tests are available. Two groups of producers are equally efficient with respect to their allocation of inputs ($\theta_n^1 = \theta_n^2$, $n = 1,\ldots,N$) if, and only if, $\beta_n^{**1} = \beta_n^{**2}$, $n = 1,\ldots,N$. Producers are systematically efficient with respect to their allocation of inputs

($\theta_1 = \cdots = \theta_N = 1$) if, and only if, ($\beta_n^* = \beta_n^{**}, n = 1, \ldots, N$). Two groups of producers achieve equal relative profit efficiency if, and only if, ($\ln A^{*1} = \ln A^{*2}$). Finally, two groups of producers achieve equal technical efficiency and equal systematic input allocative efficiency if, and only if, ($\ln A^{*1} = \ln A^{*2}$ and $\beta_n^{**1} = \beta_n^{**2}, n = 1, \ldots, N$). These and other hypothesis tests are described in Lau and Yotopoulos (1971, 1979) and Yotopoulos and Lau (1973).

Generalized Leontief Suppose that the profit function takes the generalized Leontief form, with $M = N = 2$ for ease of exposition. Then, following Lovell and Sickles (1983),

$$
\begin{aligned}
\pi(p, w; \beta) = \ & \beta_{11} p_1 + \beta_{12} p_1^{1/2} p_2^{1/2} + \beta_{13} p_1^{1/2} w_1^{1/2} + \beta_{14} p_1^{1/2} w_2^{1/2} \\
& + \beta_{21} p_2^{1/2} p_1^{1/2} + \beta_{22} p_2 + \beta_{23} p_2^{1/2} w_1^{1/2} + \beta_{24} p_2^{1/2} w_2^{1/2} \\
& + \beta_{31} w_1^{1/2} p_1^{1/2} + \beta_{32} w_1^{1/2} p_2^{1/2} + \beta_{33} w_1 + \beta_{34} w_1^{1/2} w_2^{1/2} \\
& + \beta_{41} w_2^{1/2} p_1^{1/2} + \beta_{42} w_2^{1/2} p_2^{1/2} + \beta_{43} w_2^{1/2} w_1^{1/2} + \beta_{44} w_2 ,
\end{aligned}
$$

$$(6.2.56)$$

where $\beta_{ij} = \beta_{ji} \ \forall j \neq i$. The generalized Leontief profit function is homogeneous of degree $+1$ in (p, w) by construction, and it is convex in (p, w) if $\beta_{ij} \leq 0 \ \forall j \neq i$. Application of Hotelling's lemma to equation (6.2.56) generates the system of profit-maximizing output supply and input demand equations

$$
y_1(p, w, \beta) = \beta_{11} + \beta_{12} \left(\frac{p_1}{p_2} \right)^{-1/2} + \beta_{13} \left(\frac{p_1}{w_1} \right)^{-1/2} + \beta_{14} \left(\frac{p_1}{w_2} \right)^{-1/2} ,
$$

$$
y_2(p, w, \beta) = \beta_{22} + \beta_{21} \left(\frac{p_1}{p_2} \right)^{1/2} + \beta_{23} \left(\frac{p_2}{w_1} \right)^{-1/2} + \beta_{24} \left(\frac{p_2}{w_2} \right)^{-1/2} ,
$$

$$
-x_1(p, w, \beta) = \beta_{33} + \beta_{31} \left(\frac{p_1}{w_1} \right)^{1/2} + \beta_{32} \left(\frac{p_2}{w_1} \right)^{1/2} + \beta_{34} \left(\frac{w_1}{w_2} \right)^{-1/2} ,
$$

$$
-x_2(p, w, \beta) = \beta_{44} + \beta_{41} \left(\frac{p_1}{w_2} \right)^{1/2} + \beta_{42} \left(\frac{p_2}{w_2} \right)^{1/2} + \beta_{43} \left(\frac{w_1}{w_2} \right)^{1/2} .
$$

$$(6.2.57)$$

Technical inefficiency can be introduced into equations (6.2.57) by replacing the four intercepts with ($\beta_{jj} - \phi_j$), $j = 1, \ldots, 4$. However in this event technical inefficiency would be nonneutral and difficult to interpret. Consequently we model only allocative inefficiency, as usual by assuming that a producer optimizes with respect to shadow price ratios. Replacing observed price ratios in equations (6.2.57) with shadow price ratios generates the system of observed output supply and input demand equations

$$y_1 = \beta_{11} + \beta_{12}\left[\theta_{12}\left(\frac{p_1}{p_2}\right)\right]^{-1/2} + \beta_{13}\left[\theta_{13}\left(\frac{p_1}{w_1}\right)\right]^{-1/2} + \beta_{14}\left[\theta_{14}\left(\frac{p_1}{w_2}\right)\right]^{-1/2},$$

$$y_2 = \beta_{22} + \beta_{12}\left[\theta_{12}\left(\frac{p_1}{p_2}\right)\right]^{1/2} + \beta_{23}\left[\theta_{23}\left(\frac{p_2}{w_1}\right)\right]^{-1/2} + \beta_{24}\left[\theta_{24}\left(\frac{p_2}{w_2}\right)\right]^{-1/2},$$

$$-x_1 = \beta_{33} + \beta_{13}\left[\theta_{13}\left(\frac{p_1}{w_1}\right)\right]^{1/2} + \beta_{23}\left[\theta_{23}\left(\frac{p_2}{w_1}\right)\right]^{1/2} + \beta_{34}\left[\theta_{34}\left(\frac{w_1}{w_2}\right)\right]^{-1/2},$$

$$-x_2 = \beta_{44} + \beta_{14}\left[\theta_{14}\left(\frac{p_1}{w_2}\right)\right]^{1/2} + \beta_{24}\left[\theta_{24}\left(\frac{p_2}{w_2}\right)\right]^{1/2} + \beta_{34}\left[\theta_{34}\left(\frac{w_1}{w_2}\right)\right]^{1/2}$$

$$(6.2.58)$$

and the expression for observed profit

$$\pi = \sum_i \beta_{ii} q_i + \sum_i \sum_{j>i} \beta_{ij}\left(\theta_{ij}^{-1/2} + \theta_{ij}^{1/2}\right) q_i^{1/2} q_j^{1/2}, \tag{6.2.59}$$

where $q = (p_1, p_2, w_1, w_2)$.

The system (6.2.58) of observed output supply and input demand equations can be estimated by nonlinear SUR, after which statistical tests of various allocative inefficiency hypotheses can be conducted. The effect of systematic allocative inefficiency on profit is zero if, and only if, all $\theta_{ij} = 1$. If some $\theta_{ij} \neq 1$, the effect of systematic allocative inefficiency (and of each of its components) on profit is producer specific, depending on the prices producers face. The partial effect of systematic output allocative inefficiency on profit is given by the expression

$$\pi(p, w; \beta) - (\pi|\theta_{12} \neq 1) = \beta_{12} p_1^{1/2} p_2^{1/2}\left[2 - \left(\theta_{12}^{-1/2} + \theta_{12}^{1/2}\right)\right], \quad (6.2.60)$$

which is positive unless $\theta_{12} = 1$. If $\theta_{12} \neq 1$, the observed output mix does not maximize profit. The partial effect of systematic input allocative inefficiency on profit is given by the expression

$$\pi(p, w; \beta) - (\pi|\theta_{34} \neq 1) = \beta_{34} w_1^{1/2} w_2^{1/2}\left[2 - \left(\theta_{34}^{-1/2} + \theta_{34}^{1/2}\right)\right], \tag{6.2.61}$$

which is positive unless $\theta_{34} = 1$. If $\theta_{34} \neq 1$ the observed input mix does not maximize profit. The partial effect of systematic scale inefficiency on profit is given by the expression

$$\pi(p, w; \beta) - (\pi|\theta_{13} \neq 1, \ \theta_{14} \neq 1, \ \theta_{23} \neq 1, \ \theta_{24} \neq 1)$$

$$= \sum_i \sum_j \beta_{ij} q_i^{1/2} q_j^{1/2} [2 - (\theta_{ij}^{-1/2} + \theta_{ij}^{1/2})], \tag{6.2.62}$$

where $i = 1, 2$, $j = 3, 4$. This expression is also positive unless $\theta_{13} = \theta_{14} = \theta_{23} = \theta_{24} = 1$. If $(\theta_{13}, \theta_{14}, \theta_{23}, \theta_{24}) \neq (1, 1, 1, 1)$ the observed output–input ratios do not maximize profit.

Producers face four market prices and three independent market price ratios. However we have used six parameters θ_{ij} to model systematic allocative inefficiency. Although the market price ratios can be expected to be consistent, in the sense that any three independent market price ratios can be used to determine the remaining three market price ratios, it is not clear whether the shadow price ratios $[\theta_{ij}(q_i/q_j)]$ can be expected to be consistent also. That is, it is unclear whether or not allocatively inefficient producers can be expected to be consistent in their misperceptions of market price ratios. The preceding analysis, with three independent market price ratios and six independent shadow price ratios, allows for inconsistent systematic allocative inefficiency. Consistent systematic allocative inefficiency can be modeled as a constrained version of the preceding model, by imposing the testable parametric restrictions

$$\theta_{ik} = \theta_{ij} \cdot \theta_{jk}, \qquad i < j < k, \tag{6.2.63}$$

which reduces the number of independent allocative inefficiency parameters from six to three.

Translog The translog profit function was perhaps first used to analyze allocative efficiency by Atkinson and Halvorsen (1980). The translog functional form is particularly well suited to the parametric analysis of technical and systematic allocative inefficiency. We simply apply a translog functional form to a multiple-output generalization of equations (6.2.39)–(6.2.44), in which technical inefficiency is output oriented, or to a similar system of equations built around equation (6.2.45), in which technical inefficiency is input oriented. In both approaches, which are discussed in Kumbhakar (1996a), the first output arbitrarily serves as a numeraire for the measurement of systematic allocative inefficiency. With multiple outputs, systematic allocative inefficiency can exist between output pairs and between input–output pairs, as well as between input pairs. Using an output orientation to the measurement of technical inefficiency, observed normalized profit can be expressed as

$$\frac{\pi}{p_1} = y_1 + \sum_{m>1}\left(\frac{p_m}{p_1}\right)y_m - \sum_n\left(\frac{w_n}{p_1}\right)x_n$$

$$= \phi \cdot \pi[(p,w)^*;\beta] \cdot \left\{1 + \sum_m\left(\frac{1-\kappa_m}{\kappa_m}\right)R_m^* + \sum_n\left(\frac{1-\theta_n}{\theta_n}\right)S_n^*\right\},$$

(6.2.64)

where $\pi[(p,w)^*;\beta]$ is the normalized shadow profit function, $(p,w)^* = [\kappa_m(p_m/p_1),(\theta_n/\phi)(w_n/p_1)]$ is a normalized shadow price vector incorporating both output-oriented technical inefficiency $(0 < \phi \leq 1)$ and systematic allocative inefficiency $(\kappa_m, m = 2,\ldots,M,$ and $\theta_n, n = 1,\ldots,N)$, and

$$R_m^* = \frac{\partial \ln \pi[(p,w)^*;\beta]}{\partial \ln p_m^*}, \qquad m = 2,\ldots,M,$$

$$S_n^* = \frac{\partial \ln \pi[(p,w)^*;\beta]}{\partial \ln w_n^*}, \qquad n = 1,\ldots,N,$$

are output and input shadow profit shares, respectively. Expression (6.2.64) collapses to equation (6.2.44) in the case of a single output.

The relationship between observed normalized profit and shadow normalized profit is given by

$$\ln \frac{\pi}{p_1} = \ln \pi[(p,w)^*;\beta] + \ln H + \ln \phi,$$

(6.2.65)

where

$$H = \left\{1 + \sum_m\left(\frac{1-\kappa_m}{\kappa_m}\right)R_m^* + \sum_n\left(\frac{1-\theta_n}{\theta_n}\right)S_n^*\right\}.$$

The relationship between observed profit shares and shadow profit shares is given by

$$R_m = \frac{p_m y_m}{\pi} = \frac{1}{H}\cdot\frac{1}{\kappa_m}R_m^*, \qquad m = 2,\ldots,M,$$

$$S_n = \frac{w_n x_n}{\pi} = -\frac{1}{H}\cdot\frac{1}{\theta_n}\cdot S_n^*, \qquad n = 1,\ldots,N.$$

(6.2.66)

All that is required now is to assign a translog functional form to the normalized shadow profit function $\pi[(p,w)^*;\beta]$ and exploit equations (6.2.64)–(6.2.66), which establish the relationships between observed normalized profit and shadow normalized profit and between observed profit shares and shadow profit shares. A translog normalized shadow profit function can be written as

$$\ln \pi[(p,w)^*;\beta]$$

$$= \beta_o + \sum_m \beta_m \ln p_m^* + \sum_n \gamma_n \ln w_n^* + \frac{1}{2} \sum_j \sum_m \beta_{jm} \ln p_j^* \ln p_m^*$$

$$+ \frac{1}{2} \sum_k \sum_n \gamma_{kn} \ln w_k^* \ln w_n^* + \sum_m \sum_n \delta_{mn} \ln p_m^* \ln w_n^*,$$

$$(6.2.67)$$

and the associated shadow profit shares can be written as

$$R_m^* = \beta_m + \sum_j \beta_{jm} \ln p_j^* + \sum_n \delta_{mn} \ln w_n^*, \qquad m = 1, \ldots, M,$$

$$S_n^* = \gamma_n + \sum_k \gamma_{kn} \ln w_k^* + \sum_m \delta_{mn} \ln p_m^*, \qquad n = 1, \ldots, N, \qquad (6.2.68)$$

The system of equations to be estimated consists of

$$\ln \frac{\pi}{p_1} = \ln \pi[(p,w)^*;\beta] + \ln H + \ln \phi,$$

$$R_m = \frac{R_m^*}{H \cdot \kappa_m}, \qquad m = 2, \ldots, M,$$

$$S_n = \frac{-S_n^*}{H \cdot \theta_n}, \qquad n = 1, \ldots, N, \qquad (6.2.69)$$

where $\ln \pi[(p,w)^*;\beta]$ is defined in equation (6.2.67) and H is defined beneath equation (6.2.65) after substitution of R_m^* and S_n^* from equations (6.2.68).

It is clear, but misleading, from equation (6.2.69) that technical inefficiency enters the expression for observed normalized profit additively. However it also appears in the $\ln H$ term through the w^* terms in its R_m^* and S_n^* components, and it also appears in the $\ln \pi[(p,w)^*;\beta]$ term through the w^* terms. Consequently the effect of technical inefficiency on profit is not additive as it was in the translog cost minimization framework (with input-oriented technical inefficiency). In fact, profit loss due to technical inefficiency depends on prices, regardless of the orientation of the technical efficiency measurement. Consequently technical inefficiency also enters each of the $M + N - 1$ profit share equations, through the R_m^* and S_n^* components of the $\ln H$ term. One implication of the complicated form in which technical inefficiency appears in the system of equations (6.2.69) is that its omission will lead to biased and inconsistent estimates of all parameters in the model. Thus estimates of the systematic allocative inefficiency parameters, and of the profit loss due to systematic allocative inefficiency, will be biased and inconsistent. So too will estimates of the structure of the underlying technology, such as substitution and scale elasticities.

It is possible to illustrate this point by rewriting equation (6.2.69) as

$$\ln \frac{\pi}{p_1} = \ln \pi^o + \ln H_o + \ln H_{\phi\theta}, \qquad (6.2.70)$$

where

$$\ln \pi^o = \beta_o + \sum_m \beta_m \ln \frac{\kappa_m p_m}{p_1} + \sum_n \gamma_n \ln \frac{\theta_n w_n}{p_1}$$

$$+ \frac{1}{2} \sum_j \sum_m \beta_{jm} \ln \frac{\kappa_j p_j}{p_1} \ln \frac{\kappa_m p_m}{p_1}$$

$$+ \frac{1}{2} \sum_k \sum_n \gamma_{kn} \ln \frac{\theta_k w_k}{p_1} \ln \frac{\theta_n w_n}{p_1}$$

$$+ \sum_m \sum_n \beta_{mn} \ln \frac{\kappa_m p_m}{p_1} \ln \frac{\theta_n w_n}{p_1},$$

$$\ln H_o = \ln \left\{ \sum_m \left[(\kappa_m)^{-1} - 1 \right] \left[\beta_m + \sum_j \beta_{jm} \ln \frac{\kappa_j p_j}{p_1} + \sum_n \delta_{mn} \ln \frac{\theta_n w_n}{p_1} \right] \right.$$

$$\left. + \sum_n \left[(\theta_n)^{-1} - 1 \right] \left[\gamma_n + \sum_k \alpha_{kn} \ln \frac{\theta_k w_k}{p_1} + \sum_m \delta_{mn} \ln \frac{\kappa_m p_m}{p_1} \right] \right\},$$

$$\ln H_{\phi\theta} = \ln \phi - \ln \phi \cdot \left\{ \sum_n \gamma_n + \sum_n \sum_k \gamma_{kn} \ln \frac{\theta_n w_n}{p_1} \right.$$

$$\left. + \sum_m \sum_n \delta_{mn} \ln \frac{\kappa_m p_m}{p_1} - \frac{1}{2} \ln \phi \cdot \sum_k \sum_n \gamma_{kn} \right\} + \ln \left\{ 1 - \left(\frac{\psi}{H_o} \right) \ln \phi \right\},$$

$$\psi = \sum_m \left[((\kappa_m)^{-1} - 1) \sum_n \delta_{mn} \right] + \sum_n \left[((\theta_n)^{-1} - 1) \sum_k \gamma_{kn} \right].$$

The first two terms on the right-hand side of equation (6.2.70) define observed normalized profit in the presence of systematic allocative inefficiency, but in the absence of technical inefficiency.

The third term represents the profit loss due to technical inefficiency, and so the expression for $\ln H_{\phi\theta}$ provides an exact relationship between the magnitude of technical inefficiency and the profit loss it causes. This term is zero if, and only if, $\phi = 1$. Thus neglecting technical inefficiency is equivalent to omitting $\ln H_{\phi\theta}$ from equation (6.2.70). Since $\ln H_{\phi\theta}$ includes all input and output prices, its omission leads to biased and inconsistent parameter estimates.

We conclude that it is not generally possible to decompose profit loss into a component reflecting the cost of systematic allocative inefficiency and a component reflecting the cost of technical inefficiency, since the term $\ln H_{\phi\theta}$ includes both ϕ and θ. This is to be expected in light of Proposition 2.5. However it is easy to see that the term $\ln H_{\phi\theta}$ is independent of θ, and represents a pure technical inefficiency effect, if $\Sigma_n \delta_{mn} = \Sigma_k \gamma_{kn} = 0$. This is a testable restriction, and it corresponds to the condition that the underlying technology be almost homogeneous of degrees +1 and $0 < \Sigma_n \gamma_n < 1$; see Lau (1972) and Hasenkamp (1976).

After $[(\kappa_m p_m/p_1), (\theta_n/\phi)(w_n/p_1)]$ are substituted for $(p, w)^*$, and a multivariate normal error vector is added to the system of equations (6.2.69), the system can be estimated by nonlinear ITSUR. However due to the complicated way in which technical inefficiency enters into the normalized profit function, it is preferable to base estimation on just the $M + N - 1$ profit share equations; the only parameter not estimated in this approach is the normalized profit function intercept. Estimation of the profit share equations proceeds as follows. First, rewrite $R_m^* = R_m^o - \delta_{om} \cdot (\ln \phi)$ and $S_n^* = S_n^o - \gamma_{on} \cdot (\ln \phi)$, where $\delta_{om} = \Sigma_n \delta_{nm}$ and $\gamma_{on} = \Sigma_k \gamma_{kn}$, and

$$R_m^o = \beta_m + \sum_j \beta_{jm} \ln\left[\kappa_j\left(\frac{p_j}{p_1}\right)\right] + \sum_n \delta_{mn} \ln\left[\theta_n\left(\frac{w_n}{p_1}\right)\right],$$

$$S_n^o = \gamma_n + \sum_k \gamma_{kn} \ln\left[\theta_k\left(\frac{w_k}{p_1}\right)\right] + \sum_m \delta_{mn} \ln\left[\kappa_m\left(\frac{p_m}{p_1}\right)\right].$$

The observed profit share equations can now be rewritten as

$$R_m = \frac{R_m^*}{H \cdot \kappa_m} \Leftrightarrow \frac{\kappa_m \cdot R_m \cdot H_o - R_m^o}{\delta_{om} - \kappa_m \cdot \Psi \cdot R_m} = -\ln \phi,$$

$$S_n = -\frac{S_n^*}{H \cdot \theta_n} \Leftrightarrow -\frac{\theta_n \cdot S_n \cdot H_o - S_n^o}{\gamma_{on} + \theta_n \cdot \Psi \cdot S_n} = -\ln \phi, \tag{6.2.71}$$

where H_o and ψ are defined beneath equation (6.2.70). If we assume that $-\ln\phi$ is distributed as multivariate $N^+(0,\sigma_\phi^2)$, and if we add a random error vector v distributed as multivariate $N(0,\sigma_v^2)$, the system of $M + N - 1$ equations in (6.2.71) is simply a multiple-equation system of equations analogous to the composed error stochastic production frontier model first encountered in Chapter 3. This system of equations can be estimated by MLE to obtain estimates of all technology parameters and all allocative inefficiency parameters, after which the Kumbhakar (1987) generalization of the JLMS decomposition technique can be employed to obtain estimates of technical inefficiency, which can be inserted into the expression for $\ln H_{\phi\theta}$ to obtain producer-specific estimates of the percentage profit loss due to technical inefficiency. Details of the estimation procedure are available in Kumbhakar (1996a).

6.3 PANEL DATA MODELS

In this section we assume that we have panel data on the prices and the quantities of N inputs used and M outputs produced by each of I producers over T time periods. Producers are allowed to be technically and allocatively inefficient. In Section 6.3.1 we show how to estimate and decompose cost inefficiency in a panel data context, and in Section 6.3.2 we show how to estimate and decompose profit inefficiency in a panel data context. Since the estimation and decomposition of cost inefficiency proceeds independently of the allocative efficiency of producers in output markets, we maintain the single-output assumption in Section 6.3.1, for simplicity and without loss of generality. However the estimation and decomposition of profit inefficiency does involve output allocative inefficiency, and so in Section 6.3.2 we assume that producers produce and market multiple outputs.

In a cross-sectional context information concerning inefficiency is limited. In a strictly parametric framework (e.g., **Translog I** and **II**) it is possible to obtain estimates of technical efficiency differentials among a small number of groups of producers, and it is also possible to obtain estimates of systematic allocative efficiency parameters, which vary across pairs of variables but which are invariant across producers, although the cost of systematic allocative inefficiency is

data dependent and so does vary across producers. In a partly parametric, partly stochastic framework (**Translog III**) it is possible to
obtain producer-specific estimates of both technical efficiency and the
cost of systematic allocative efficiency, although the former estimates
are not consistent. In a panel data context both limitations can be
relaxed. It is possible to obtain consistent estimates of producer-
specific technical efficiency, using either fixed- or random-effects procedures or MLE. It is also possible to obtain consistent estimates of
allocative efficiency parameters, which vary across pairs of variables
and either across producers (if T is large relative to I) or through time
(if I is large relative to T). This is another illustration of the value of
having access to panel data.

6.3.1 Estimating and Decomposing Cost Inefficiency

In this section we extend the analysis of Section 6.2.1 to the panel
data context. We begin by showing how the basic framework given
by equations (6.2.12)–(6.2.15) is generalized when panel data are
available. Although a variety of functional forms can be applied
to this generalization, we concentrate on the translog form and
leave the application to other forms to the reader. We begin by
following a procedure originally suggested by Atkinson and Cornwell
(1994a).

Adopting an input orientation to the measurement of technical
efficiency, a shadow cost function can be written as

$$c\left(y_{it}, \frac{w_{it}^*}{\phi_i}; \beta\right) = \min_{\phi_i x_{it}}\left\{\left(\frac{w_{it}^*}{\phi_i}\right)^T (\phi_i x_{it}): f(\phi_i x_{it}; \beta) = y_{it}\right\}$$

$$= \frac{1}{\phi_i} c\left(y_{it}, w_{it}^*; \beta\right), \tag{6.3.1}$$

where $i = 1, \ldots, I$ indexes producers and $t = 1, \ldots, T$ indexes time
periods. The parameters $0 < \phi_i \leq 1$, $i = 1, \ldots, I$, provide producer-
specific but time-invariant measures of input-oriented technical
efficiency. The shadow input prices are defined as $w_{it}^* = [w_{1it}, \theta_{21i}w_{2it},$
$\ldots, \theta_{N1i}w_{Nit}]$, $i = 1, \ldots, I$, $t = 1, \ldots, T$. Thus allocative inefficiency is
no longer systematic, as it was in a cross-sectional framework; it is
now producer specific as well as specific to pairs of inputs, although

it remains time invariant. In addition to the technology parameter vector β, there are I technical efficiency parameters and $(N-1) \times I$ allocative efficiency parameters to be estimated.

The corresponding shadow input demand equations and shadow input cost share equations are given by

$$x_{nit}\left(y_{it}, w_{it}^{*}; \beta\right) = \frac{1}{\phi_i} \cdot \frac{\partial c\left(y_{it}, w_{it}^{*}; \beta\right)}{\partial w_{nit}^{*}}, \qquad n = 1, \ldots, N, \qquad (6.3.2)$$

and

$$\begin{aligned}
S_{nit}\left(y_{it}, w_{it}^{*}; \beta\right) &= \frac{w_{nit}^{*} x_{nit}\left(y_{it}, w_{it}^{*}; \beta\right)}{(1/\phi_i)c\left(y_{it}, w_{it}^{*}; \beta\right)} \\
&= \frac{w_{nit}^{*}\left[\partial c\left(y_{it}, w_{it}^{*}; \beta\right)/\partial w_{nit}^{*}\right]}{c\left(y_{it}, w_{it}^{*}; \beta\right)}, \qquad n = 1, \ldots, N,
\end{aligned}$$

$$(6.3.3)$$

respectively. Note that the technical efficiency parameters appear in the shadow input demand equations, but they do not appear in the shadow input cost share equations.

Since observed input usage minimizes shadow cost, observed input demand equations can be written as

$$\begin{aligned}
x_{nit} &= \frac{1}{\phi_i} \cdot \frac{\partial c\left(y_{it}, w_{it}^{*}; \beta\right)}{\partial w_{nit}^{*}} \\
&= \frac{1}{\phi_i} \cdot \frac{c\left(y_{it}, w_{it}^{*}; \beta\right) \cdot S_{nit}\left(y_{it}, w_{it}^{*}; \beta\right)}{w_{nit}^{*}}, \qquad n = 1, \ldots, N. \quad (6.3.4)
\end{aligned}$$

Observed total expenditure becomes

$$E_{it} = \sum_{n} w_{nit} x_{nit} = \frac{1}{\phi_i} \cdot c\left(y_{it}, w_{it}^{*}; \beta\right) \cdot \sum_{n}\left[S_{nit}\left(y_{it}, w_{it}^{*}; \beta\right) \cdot (\theta_{n1i})^{-1}\right], \quad (6.3.5)$$

and observed input cost share equations become

$$S_{nit} = \frac{w_{nit} x_{nit}}{E_{it}} = \frac{S_{nit}\left(y_{it}, w_{it}^*; \beta\right) \cdot \left(\theta_{n1i}\right)^{-1}}{\sum_k \left[S_{kit}\left(y_{it}, w_{it}^*; \beta\right) \cdot \left(\theta_{k1i}\right)^{-1}\right]}, \qquad n = 1, \ldots, N. \quad (6.3.6)$$

If the shadow cost function $c(y_{it}, w_{it}^*/\phi_i; \beta)$ takes on a translog form, it can be written as

$$\ln c\left(y_{it}, \frac{w_{it}^*}{\phi_i}; \beta\right) = \beta_o + \beta_y \ln y_{it} + \sum_n \beta_n \ln w_{nit}^*$$

$$+ \frac{1}{2}\beta_{yy}(\ln y_{it})^2 + \frac{1}{2}\sum_k \sum_n \beta_{kn}\left(\ln w_{kit}^*\right)\left(\ln w_{nit}^*\right)$$

$$+ \sum_n \beta_{ny}\left(\ln w_{nit}^*\right)(\ln y_{it}) + \ln\frac{1}{\phi_i}, \qquad (6.3.7)$$

and the corresponding shadow input cost share equations can be written as

$$S_{nit}\left(y_{it}, w_{it}^*; \beta\right) = \beta_n + \sum_k \beta_{kn} \ln w_{kit}^* + \beta_{ny} \ln y_{it},$$

$$n = 1, \ldots, N. \qquad (6.3.8)$$

From equations (6.3.5), (6.3.7), and (6.3.8), observed expenditure is

$$\ln E_{it} = \beta_o + \beta_y \ln y_{it} + \sum_n \beta_n \ln w_{nit}^* + \frac{1}{2}\beta_{yy}(\ln y_{it})^2$$

$$+ \frac{1}{2}\sum_k \sum_n \beta_{kn}\left(\ln w_{kit}^*\right)\left(\ln w_{nit}^*\right) + \sum_n \beta_{ny}\left(\ln w_{nit}^*\right)(\ln y_{it})$$

$$+ \ln\left\{\sum_n (\theta_{n1i})^{-1}\left[\beta_n + \sum_k \beta_{kn}\left(\ln w_{kit}^*\right) + \beta_{ny} \ln y_{it}\right]\right\} + \ln\frac{1}{\phi_i},$$

$$(6.3.9)$$

and observed input cost shares are

$$S_{nit} = \frac{(\theta_{n1i})^{-1}\left[\beta_n + \Sigma_k \beta_{kn} \ln w_{kit}^* + \beta_{ny} \ln y_{it}\right]}{\Sigma_j (\theta_{j1i})^{-1}\left[\beta_j + \Sigma_k \beta_{kj} \ln w_{kit}^* + \beta_{jy} \ln y_{it}\right]}, \qquad n = 1, \ldots, N. \quad (6.3.10)$$

Estimation of the system consisting of equations (6.3.9) and (6.3.10) can be accomplished in three alternative ways, depending on the assumptions one is willing to make. Atkinson and Cornwell used a random-effects approach, which allows the effects [the $\ln(1/\phi_i)$] to be random without imposing a distributional assumption on them, and which allows for the inclusion of time-invariant regressors. After deleting one input cost share equation and adding a multivariate normal error vector to the remaining N equations, all parameters in the model can be estimated by iterative feasible GLS. Not all ϕ_i are identified, and so one producer is called technically efficient, just as in the random-effects approach outlined in Section 3.3.1. It is also possible to follow a fixed-effects approach based on LSDV, which imposes no distributional assumption on the effects, and which allows the effects to be correlated with the regressors. At the cost of considerable degrees of freedom, it is also possible to allow technical efficiency to be time varying by adapting the Cornwell, Schmidt, and Sickles (1990) approach discussed in Section 3.3.2. Finally, if one is willing to make distributional and independence assumptions, it is possible to estimate the system using MLE techniques. After estimation, the JLMS decomposition technique can be used to obtain estimates of the $\ln(1/\phi_i)$ for each producer, although these estimates are not consistent. In all three approaches the output of the exercise includes estimates of the technology parameter vector β, estimates of the technical efficiency parameter ϕ_i (or perhaps ϕ_{it}) for each producer, and estimates of the allocative inefficiency parameters θ_{n1i}, $n = 2, \ldots, N$, for each producer. Potential cost savings resulting from eliminating either technical or allocative inefficiency can be estimated by comparing fitted expenditure with and without the appropriate parameter restrictions imposed.

6.3.2 Estimating and Decomposing Profit Inefficiency

Any of the three functional forms for a normalized profit function – Cobb–Douglas in the single-output case, generalized Leontief or translog in the multiple-output case – studied in Section 6.2.2 can be adapted to the panel data context. Here we consider only the translog form, for its complete flexibility. The analysis follows the translog analysis of Section 6.2.2, with the addition of time subscripts where appropriate. The estimating equations consist of intertemporal versions of equations (6.2.69), which we write as

$$\ln\left(\frac{\pi}{p_1}\right)_{it} = \ln \pi\left[(p,w)_{it}^*;\beta\right] + \ln H_{it} + \ln \phi_i,$$

$$R_{mit} = \frac{R_{mit}^*}{H_{it}\cdot\kappa_{mi}}, \qquad m = 2,\dots,M,$$

$$S_{nit} = \frac{-S_{nit}^*}{H_{it}\cdot\theta_{ni}}, \qquad n = 1,\dots,N, \qquad\qquad (6.3.11)$$

where all variables and parameters are defined, apart from time subscripts, in Section 6.2.2. Like the translog cost system considered in Section 6.3.1, this system can be estimated in three ways. Since the techniques require so little modification, we refer the reader to Kumbhakar (1996a, b) for details.

6.4 A GUIDE TO THE LITERATURE

In this chapter we have studied a parametric shadow price approach to the estimation of technical and allocative efficiency, and we have used an inflexible Cobb–Douglas functional form and flexible generalized Leontief and translog functional forms to conduct our analyses. An excellent collection of papers based on the Cobb–Douglas form appears in *Food Research Studies* (1979), and Kumbhakar (1996a, b, c) provides detailed discussions of modeling and estimation procedures for the translog form.

Other papers employing these techniques to estimate cost efficiency in a cross-sectional context include Atkinson and Halvorsen (1984, 1986) (translog) and Bhattacharyya, Parker, and Raffiee (1994) (translog). Studies employing these techniques to estimate profit efficiency in a cross-sectional context include Sidhu (1974) (Cobb–Douglas), Trosper (1978) (Cobb–Douglas), Hollas and Stansell (1988) (translog), Atkinson and Kerkvliet (1989) (translog), Kumbhakar and Bhattacharyya (1992) (translog), and Ali, Parikh, and Shah (1994) (translog).

Atkinson and Cornwell (1993, 1994b) (translog), Balk and van Leeuwen (1997) (translog), and Maietta (1997) (translog) have used these techniques to estimate cost efficiency in a panel data context, and Sickles, Good, and Johnson (1986) (generalized Leontief) and

Kumbhakar (1996b) (translog) have used these techniques to estimate profit efficiency in a panel data context. Finally Atkinson and Cornwell (1998a) (translog) have used these techniques to estimate cost efficiency in a panel data context in which our equations (6.3.9) and (6.3.10) are augmented with an additional equation allowing output price to diverge from shadow marginal cost.

7 Incorporating Exogenous Influences on Efficiency

7.1 INTRODUCTION

The analysis of productive efficiency has, or at least should have, two components. The first is the estimation of a stochastic production (or cost or profit or other) frontier that serves as a benchmark against which to estimate the technical (or cost or profit or other) efficiency of producers. Thus the objective of the first component is to estimate the efficiency with which producers allocate their inputs and their output(s), under some maintained hypothesis concerning behavioral objectives. This first component is by now reasonably well developed, and has been the subject of our investigation in Chapters 3–6.

The second component is equally important, although much less frequently explored. It concerns the incorporation of exogenous variables, which are neither inputs to the production process nor outputs of it, but which nonetheless exert an influence on producer performance. The objective of the second component is to associate variation in producer performance with variation in the exogenous variables characterizing the environment in which production occurs. Examples include the degree of competitive pressure, input and output quality indicators, network characteristics, ownership form, various managerial characteristics, and the like. We have been deliberately vague about the specific role of the exogenous variables in explaining producer "performance." They may influence the structure of the technology by which conventional inputs are converted to

261

output(s), or they may influence the efficiency with which inputs are converted to output(s).

Exogenous variables have been incorporated into efficiency measurement models in a variety of ways, some more appropriate than others. In this brief chapter we discuss some of the more useful approaches to the incorporation of exogenous influences on efficiency.

The chapter is organized as follows. In Sections 7.2 and 7.3 we discuss the incorporation of exogenous influences within the framework of the estimation of *technical* efficiency, and so we are building on models developed in Chapter 3. The analysis would be essentially unchanged if we were to shift the framework to the estimation of cost efficiency, as in Chapters 4 and 6, or to the estimation of profit efficiency, as in Chapters 5 and 6. In these two sections we confine our treatment of exogenous influences to a cross-sectional context, although it is straightforward to extend the treatment to a panel data context. In Section 7.2 we discuss three early approaches to the incorporation of exogenous influences, and we note the drawbacks of each approach. In Section 7.3 we discuss a series of more recent approaches to the incorporation of exogenous influences, and we note the advantages and disadvantages of each. Section 7.4 provides a brief guide to the slim literature.

7.2 EARLY APPROACHES TO THE INCORPORATION OF EXOGENOUS INFLUENCES

Let $x = (x_1, \ldots, x_N) \geq 0$ be an input vector used to produce scalar output $y \geq 0$, and let $z = (z_1, \ldots, z_Q)$ be a vector of exogenous variables that influence the structure of the production process by which inputs x are converted to output y. The elements of z capture features of the environment in which production takes place, and they are generally considered to be conditioning variables beyond the control of those who manage the production process. If z influences the production process itself, as is the case with network characteristics in transportation studies, it is entirely appropriate to include z along with x in a stochastic production frontier, which we write as

$$\ln y_i = \ln f(x_i, z_i; \beta) + v_i - u_i, \qquad i = 1, \ldots, I, \qquad (7.2.1)$$

where i indexes producers, $\ln f(x_i, z_i; \beta)$ is the deterministic kernel of the stochastic production frontier $[\ln f(x_i, z_i; \beta) + v_i]$, $v_i \sim$ iid $N(0, \sigma_v^2)$ captures the effect of random noise on the production process, $u_i \geq 0$ captures the effect of technical inefficiency, and the parameter vector β to be estimated now includes both technology parameters and environmental parameters. In this formulation z_i is assumed to influence y_i directly, by influencing the structure of the production frontier relative to which the efficiency of producers is estimated. In this sense z_i is incorporated essentially as we incorporated a vector of quasi-fixed inputs in a short-run cost frontier in Section 4.2.1.3.

Equation (7.2.1) has exactly the same structure as a conventional stochastic production frontier model discussed in Section 3.2, and all the estimation techniques proposed there carry over to this expanded formulation. However if a maximum likelihood approach is followed, say with $u_i \sim$ iid $N^+(\mu, \sigma_u^2)$, it is assumed that the elements of z_i, as well as the elements of x_i, are uncorrelated with each disturbance component v_i and u_i. The exogenous variables influence performance not by influencing efficiency, with which they are assumed to be uncorrelated, but by influencing the structure of the production frontier bounding the relationship between x_i and y_i. Thus what is accomplished by this formulation is a more accurate characterization of production possibilities than would be provided by a formulation that excluded z_i from $f(x_i, z_i; \beta)$, and consequently more accurate estimates of producer efficiencies. However variation in efficiency is left unexplained by this formulation.

A second early approach to the incorporation of exogenous influences has sought to associate variation in *estimated* efficiency with variation in exogenous variables. In this approach the exogenous variables play a very different role in the analysis. The second approach consists of two stages. In the first stage a stochastic frontier such as equation (7.2.1) is estimated (excluding the exogenous variables), typically by MLE under the usual distributional and independence assumptions, and the regression residuals are decomposed using the JLMS technique. The estimated efficiencies are then regressed against the exogenous variables in a second-stage regression of general form

$$E(u_i | v_i - u_i) = g(z_i; \gamma) + \varepsilon_i, \qquad (7.2.2)$$

where $\varepsilon_i \sim$ iid $N(0, \sigma_\varepsilon^2)$ and γ is a parameter vector to be estimated. Of course $M(u_i|v_i - u_i)$ can be substituted for $E(u_i|v_i - u_i)$, as can $E(\exp\{-u_i\}|v_i - u_i)$. Since the dependent variable in any of its formulations is bounded by zero and one, OLS is inappropriate and either the dependent variable must be transformed prior to estimation or a limited dependent variable estimation technique such as Tobit must be employed.

In this two-stage formulation it is assumed that z_i influences y_i indirectly, through its effect on estimated efficiency. Exogenous variables do not influence the structure of the production frontier, but they do influence the efficiency with which producers approach the production frontier. Thus variation in estimated efficiency is explained, which was the whole point of the exercise. In sharp contrast to the first approach, however, it is hoped that the elements of z_i are correlated with u_i, or at least with $E(u_i|v_i - u_i)$, since no explanation is achieved if they are not.

Unfortunately there are serious econometric problems with this two-stage formulation. First, it must be assumed that the elements of z_i are uncorrelated with the elements of x_i. If they are correlated, then ML estimates of $(\beta, \sigma_v^2, \sigma_u^2)$ are biased due to the omission of the relevant variables z_i in the first-stage stochastic frontier model. Consequently the estimated efficiencies being explained in the second-stage regression are biased estimates of the true efficiencies, because they have been estimated relative to a biased representation of the production frontier. In these circumstances it is not clear that even a "successful" second-stage regression contributes anything to our understanding of the determinants of efficiency variation.

Second, it is assumed in the first stage that the inefficiencies are identically distributed, but this assumption is contradicted in the second-stage regression in which predicted efficiencies are assumed to have a functional relationship with z_i. Stated somewhat differently, in the first stage it is assumed that $E(u_i)$ is a constant $[= (2/\pi)^{1/2}\sigma_u$ in the half normal case], but in the second stage $E(u_i|v_i - u_i)$ is assumed to vary with z_i. This has led one observer to refer to the two-stage approach as "schizophrenic."

A third early approach, developed by Deprins and Simar (1989a, b) and summarized and extended by Deprins (1989), attempted to overcome the drawbacks of the first two formulations. They expressed the production frontier relationship as

$$\ln y_i = \ln f(x_i; \beta) - u_i, \tag{7.2.3}$$

$$E(u_i|z_i) = \exp\{\gamma' z_i\}, \tag{7.2.4}$$

where β and γ are technology and environment parameter vectors to be estimated, $u_i \geq 0$ represents technical inefficiency, and $\exp\{\gamma' z_i\}$ expresses the systematic part of the relationship between technical inefficiency and the exogenous variables. The exponentiation operator in equation (7.2.4) ensures that $E(u_i|z_i) > 0$. Combining equations (7.2.3) and (7.2.4) and adding a random-noise error term yields the single-stage production frontier model

$$\ln y_i = \ln f(x_i; \beta) - \exp\{\gamma' z_i\} + \varepsilon_i, \tag{7.2.5}$$

where ε_i is assumed to have zero mean and constant variance, and the requirement that $u_i \geq 0$ requires that $\varepsilon_i \leq \exp\{\gamma' z_i\}$. Note that ε_i is not identically distributed since its support depends on z_i; this observation turns out to be important later. The frontier model given in equation (7.2.5) is nonlinear in the parameters, and can be estimated by nonlinear least squares by minimizing $\varepsilon_i' \varepsilon_i$, or more efficiently by MLE if a suitable one-sided distribution for $u_i = \exp\{\gamma' z_i\} - \varepsilon_i$ is specified. Details of both techniques are available in Deprins (1989), who provides log likelihood functions for four different one-sided distributions for u_i (gamma, Weibull, log-normal, and log-logistic).

After estimation the performance of each producer is evaluated by forming the expression

$$\exp\{\varepsilon_i\} = \frac{y_i}{f(x_i; \beta)} \cdot \exp\{\exp\{\gamma' z_i\}\}, \qquad i = 1, \dots, I. \tag{7.2.6}$$

The first term on the right-hand side of equation (7.2.6) provides an estimate of technical efficiency; this term is bounded above by unity since $u_i \geq 0 \Rightarrow y_i \leq f(x_i; \beta)$. The second term is an adjustment term, which provides an estimate of the contribution of the exogenous variables to the performance of each producer; this term is bounded below by unity. Relatively large values of the adjustment term correspond to relatively unfavorable operating environments, and generate relatively large upward adjustments to raw efficiency scores in recognition of the fact that they were achieved under relatively adverse operating conditions.

The third approach is an improvement on the first approach, since it actually achieves an explanation of efficiency, and provides an adjustment to raw efficiency scores, which reflects the nature of the operating environments in which they were achieved. It is also an improvement on the second approach, since the omitted variables and independence problems are avoided by incorporating the exogenous variables in a single frontier estimation stage. The major difficulty with the third approach is that it is based on a deterministic frontier model given in equation (7.2.3), which contains no symmetric error component to capture the effects of random noise on the production process. In light of our attitude toward deterministic frontiers, we consider it desirable to generalize the third approach by embedding it within a stochastic frontier framework. The approaches discussed in Section 7.3 accomplish this objective in various ways and with varying degrees of success.

A final point, apparently first made by Deprins and Simar, is worth repeating. Elements of z_i may belong in the frontier along with the conventional inputs x_i, or they may belong in the one-sided error component. Some studies have even incorporated a time trend in both locations, the argument being that in the frontier the passage of time captures technical change, whereas in the error component it captures time-varying efficiency. In most cases, however, it is not obvious whether an exogenous variable is a characteristic of production technology or a determinant of productive efficiency. This is frequently a judgment call. However if an exogenous variable is judged to be a determinant of efficiency, it should be incorporated in an econometrically defensible manner.

7.3 RECENT APPROACHES TO THE INCORPORATION OF EXOGENOUS INFLUENCES

Kumbhakar, Ghosh, and McGuckin (1991) specify a stochastic production frontier model as

$$\ln y_i = \ln f(x_i; \beta) + v_i - u_i, \tag{7.3.1}$$

$$u_i = \gamma' z_i + \varepsilon_i, \tag{7.3.2}$$

where, in contrast to the Deprins and Simar formulation, random noise in the production process is introduced through the error component $v_i \sim$ iid $N(0, \sigma_v^2)$ in equation (7.3.1). The second error component, which captures the effects of technical inefficiency, has a systematic component $\gamma' z_i$ associated with the exogenous variables and a random component ε_i.

Inserting equation (7.3.2) into equation (7.3.1) yields the single-stage production frontier model

$$\ln y_i = \ln f(x_i; \beta) + v_i - (\gamma' z_i + \varepsilon_i). \tag{7.3.3}$$

The requirement that $u_i \geq 0$ requires that $\varepsilon_i \geq -\gamma' z_i$, which does not require $\gamma' z_i \geq 0$. However it is necessary to impose distributional assumptions on v_i and ε_i, and to impose the restriction $\varepsilon_i \geq -\gamma' z_i$, in order to derive the likelihood function.

A simpler approach, followed by Kumbhakar, Ghosh, and McGuckin, is to use the specification in equation (7.3.1), impose distributional assumptions on v_i and u_i, and ignore ε_i. If $u_i \sim N^+(\gamma' z_i, \sigma_u^2)$, the one-sided error component representing technical inefficiency has truncated normal structure, with variable mode depending on z_i, and it is still not necessary that $\gamma' z_i$ be positive. Moreover if $z_{1i} = 1$ and $\gamma_2 = \cdots = \gamma_Q = 0$, this model collapses to Stevenson's (1980) truncated normal stochastic frontier model with constant mode γ_1, which in turn collapses to the ALS half normal stochastic frontier model with zero mode if $\gamma_1 = 0$. Each of these restrictions is testable.

If it is assumed that $v_i \sim$ iid $N(0, \sigma_v^2)$ and $u_i \sim N^+(\gamma' z_i, \sigma_u^2)$, and that v_i and u_i are distributed independently, the parameters in equation (7.3.1) can be estimated by MLE. The log likelihood function is a straightforward generalization of that of the truncated normal model appearing in Chapter 3, with constant mode μ being replaced with variable mode $\mu_i = \gamma' z_i$, and so we have

$$\ln L = \text{constant} - \frac{1}{2} \ln(\sigma_v^2 + \sigma_u^2) - \sum_i \ln \Phi\left(\frac{\gamma' z_i}{\sigma_u}\right)$$
$$+ \sum_i \ln \Phi\left(\frac{\mu_i^*}{\sigma^*}\right) - \frac{1}{2} \sum_i \frac{(e_i + \gamma' z_i)^2}{\sigma_v^2 + \sigma_u^2}, \tag{7.3.4}$$

where

$$\mu_i^* = \frac{\sigma_v^2 \gamma' z_i - \sigma_u^2 e_i}{\sigma_v^2 + \sigma_u^2},$$

$$\sigma^{*2} = \frac{\sigma_v^2 \sigma_u^2}{\sigma_v^2 + \sigma_u^2},$$

and the $e_i = \ln y_i - \ln f(x_i; \beta)$ are the residuals obtained from estimating equation (7.3.1). This log likelihood function collapses to the one given in equation (3.2.48) when μ_i is a constant, and it collapses further to the one given in equation (3.2.26) when $\mu_i = 0$.

The log likelihood function can be maximized to obtain ML estimates of $(\beta, \gamma, \sigma_v^2, \sigma_u^2)$. These estimates can be used to obtain producer-specific estimates of technical inefficiency, using the JLMS decomposition. These estimates are either

$$E(u_i|e_i) = \mu_i^* + \sigma^* * \frac{\phi(\mu_i^*/\sigma^*)}{\Phi(\mu_i^*/\sigma^*)} \tag{7.3.5}$$

or

$$M(u_i|e_i) = \begin{cases} \mu_i^* & \text{if } \mu_i^* \geq 0, \\ 0 & \text{otherwise.} \end{cases} \tag{7.3.6}$$

Once technical efficiency has been estimated, the effect of each environmental variable on technical inefficiency can be calculated from either $[\partial E(u_i|e_i)/\partial z_{ik}]$ or $[\partial M(u_i|e_i)/\partial z_{ik}]$.

Reifschneider and Stevenson (1991) formulated a hybrid model that combines features of the Deprins and Simar model with features of the Kumbhakar, Ghosh, and McGuckin model. Their model consists of the production relationship given in equation (7.3.1) and the technical inefficiency relationship

$$u_i = g(z_i; \gamma) + \varepsilon_i, \tag{7.3.7}$$

where the effects of random noise are captured by the error component $v_i \sim$ iid $N(0, \sigma_v^2)$ (in keeping with Kumbhakar, Ghosh, and McGuckin). The requirement that $u_i = [g(z_i; \gamma) + \varepsilon_i] \geq 0$ is ensured by specifying a functional form for the systematic component of inefficiency satisfying $g(z_i; \gamma) \geq 0$ (in keeping with Deprins and Simar), and also by assuming that the random component of inefficiency $\varepsilon_i \sim$ iid $N^+(0, \sigma_\varepsilon^2)$. Substituting equation (7.3.7) into equation (7.3.1) yields

$$\ln y_i = \ln f(x_i; \beta) - g(z_i; \gamma) + v_i - \varepsilon_i, \tag{7.3.8}$$

which is structurally indistinguishable from the basic composed error stochastic frontier model discussed in Chapter 3, and so no modification to the standard MLE procedure is required. The assignment of a one-sided distribution to ε_i simplifies estimation of the model by eliminating the statistical problems with the additive formulation of Kumbhakar, Ghosh, and McGuckin. Simplification comes at a cost, however, since the two conditions $g(z_i; \gamma) \geq 0$ and $\varepsilon_i \sim$ iid $N^+(0, \sigma_\varepsilon^2)$ are sufficient, but not necessary, for $u_i \geq 0$. The statistical motivation for imposing $\varepsilon_i \geq 0$ in equation (7.3.7) is clear: It simplifies estimation. However this restriction has an interesting economic implication. If $\varepsilon_i \geq 0$, then $u_i \geq g(z_i; \gamma)$, and inefficiency is at least as great as minimum possible inefficiency achievable in an environment characterized by the exogenous variables z_i. Thus the function $g(z_i; \gamma)$ in equation (7.3.7) can be interpreted as a deterministic minimum inefficiency frontier. Whereas the Deprins and Simar formulation has a deterministic production frontier and a stochastic inefficiency relationship, the Reifschneider and Stevenson formulation has a stochastic production frontier and a deterministic inefficiency relationship.

Huang and Liu (1994) specified a model very similar to the two preceding models, but with two wrinkles. Their model consists of equations (7.3.1) and (7.3.7), which when combined yield equation (7.3.8), which we rewrite as

$$\ln y_i = \ln f(x_i; \beta) + v_i - [g(z_i; \gamma) + \varepsilon_i], \tag{7.3.9}$$

which is identical to equation (7.3.3) with $\gamma' z_i$ replaced by $g(z_i; \gamma)$. The requirement that $u_i = [g(z_i; \gamma) + \varepsilon_i] \geq 0$ is met by truncating ε_i from below such that $\varepsilon_i \geq -g(z_i; \gamma)$, and by assigning a distribution to ε_i such as $\varepsilon_i \sim N(0, \sigma_\varepsilon^2)$. Thus instead of truncating a normal distribution with variable mode from below at zero (as in Kumbhakar, Ghosh, and McGuckin), Huang and Liu truncate a normal distribution with zero mode from below at a variable truncation point $[-g(z_i; \gamma)]$. This allows $\varepsilon_i \leq 0$, but enforces $u_i \geq 0$. Estimation is by MLE with only minor modifications to the analysis in Chapter 3. The log likelihood function for this model is a straightforward generalization of the log likelihood function for the truncated normal model given in equation (3.2.48), replacing the parameter μ with the function $-g(z_i; \gamma)$.

The essential novelty of this model is that the function $g(z_i; \gamma)$ is allowed to include interactions between elements of z_i and elements of x_i. Thus Huang and Liu expand the function $g(z_i; \gamma)$ to the function

$$g(z_i, x_i; \gamma) = \sum_q \gamma_q z_{qi} + \sum_q \sum_n \gamma_{qn} z_{qi} \ln x_{ni}, \qquad (7.3.10)$$

from which it follows that the expected value of a producer's technical efficiency can be expressed as

$$E\left[\frac{y_i}{f(x_i; \beta) + v_i}\right] = \exp\left\{\sigma_\varepsilon\left(\rho + \frac{1}{2}\sigma_\varepsilon\right)\right\}\frac{1 - \Phi(\sigma_\varepsilon + \rho)}{1 - \Phi(\rho)}, \qquad (7.3.11)$$

where

$$\rho = \sigma_\varepsilon^{-1} \cdot \left[\sum_q \gamma_q z_{qi} + \sum_q \sum_n \gamma_{qn} z_{qi} \ln x_{ni}\right].$$

The expression for $E[y_i/f(x_i; \beta) + v_i]$ is a straightforward generalization of the expression for $TE_i = E(\exp\{-u_i\}|\varepsilon_i)$ given in equation (3.2.52), although the interpretation of ε_i is different. It follows from equation (7.3.11) that

$$\frac{\partial E[y_i/f(x_i; \beta) + v_i]}{\partial z_{qi}} = E\left[\frac{y_i}{f(x_i; \beta) + v_i}\right] \cdot \psi \cdot \left[\gamma_q + \sum_n \gamma_{qn} \ln x_{ni}\right],$$

$$(7.3.12)$$

where

$$\psi = \sigma_\varepsilon^{-1}\left[\sigma_\varepsilon + \frac{\phi(\rho)}{1 - \Phi(\rho)} - \frac{\phi(\sigma_\varepsilon + \rho)}{1 - \Phi(\sigma_\varepsilon + \rho)}\right].$$

Equation (7.3.12) shows that when the exogenous variables are interacted with the inputs, they can have nonneutral effects on technical efficiency. This sets the Huang and Liu model apart from all other stochastic frontier models we have encountered, each of which assumes that technical inefficiency is neutral with respect to its impact on input usage. Of course neutrality of the impact of a single exogenous variable z_{qi} can be tested by testing the hypothesis that

$\gamma_{qn} = 0 \; \forall n$, and simultaneous neutrality of all exogenous variables can be tested by testing the hypothesis that $\gamma_{qn} = 0 \; \forall q, n$.

Battese and Coelli (1995) have formulated a model that is essentially the same as that of Huang and Liu, with two exceptions: (i) Their model is formulated within a panel data context, and (ii) they do not include inputs in their specification of $g(z_i; \gamma)$. Their model consists of equations (7.3.1) and (7.3.2), with the nonnegativity requirement $u_i = (\gamma' z_i + \varepsilon_i) \geq 0$ being modeled as $\varepsilon_i \sim N(0, \sigma_\varepsilon^2)$, with the distribution of ε_i being bounded below by the variable truncation point $-\gamma' z_i$. Battese and Coelli note that this distributional assumption on ε_i is consistent with the distributional assumption on u_i that $u_i \sim N^+(\gamma' z_i, \sigma_u^2)$. This formulation differs from that of Reifschneider and Stevenson in that ε_i is assumed to be independently but not identically distributed. In addition, the mode $\gamma' z_i$ of the normal distribution being truncated at zero is not required to be nonnegative for every producer, so that $\varepsilon_i \leq 0$ is possible in a relatively unfavorable environment (i.e., if $\gamma' z_i > 0$).

The technical efficiency of the ith producer is given by

$$TE_i = \exp\{-u_i\} = \exp\{-\gamma' z_i - \varepsilon_i\}, \tag{7.3.13}$$

a predictor for which is provided by

$$E[\exp\{-u_i\}|(v_i - u_i)] = \left[\exp\left\{-\mu_{*i} + \frac{1}{2}\sigma_*^2\right\}\right] \cdot \left[\frac{\Phi[(\mu_{*i}/\sigma_*) - \sigma_*]}{\Phi(\mu_{*i}/\sigma_*)}\right], \tag{7.3.14}$$

where

$$\mu_{*i} = \frac{\sigma_v^2(\gamma' z_i) - \sigma_u^2(\varepsilon_i)}{\sigma_v^2 + \sigma_u^2},$$

$$\sigma_*^2 = \frac{\sigma_v^2 \sigma_u^2}{\sigma_v^2 + \sigma_u^2}.$$

A truncated normal distribution is a two-parameter distribution, with one parameter characterizing placement and the other characterizing spread. The logic underlying some of the previous models has been to relax the constant-mode property of the truncated normal distribution, by allowing the mode to be a function of the exogenous variables. This allows inefficiency, which depends on the mode of the truncated normal distribution, to depend on exogenous variables. It is also possible to relax the constant-variance property of the truncated normal distribution (or of the single-parameter half normal distribution), by allowing the variance to be a function of the exogenous variables. This also allows inefficiency, which also depends on the variance of the truncated (or half) normal distribution, to depend on exogenous variables.

Reifschneider and Stevenson proposed, but did not implement, such a formulation of the model. In this formulation $\ln y_i = \ln f(x_i; \beta) + v_i - u_i$, with $v_i \sim$ iid $N(0, \sigma_v^2)$ as always, but with $u_i \sim N^+(0, \sigma_{ui}^2)$. They suggested the specification $\sigma_{ui}^2 = \sigma_{uo}^2 + g(z_i; \gamma)$, with $g(z_i; \gamma) \geq 0$ [although $g(z_i; \gamma) \geq -\sigma_{uo}^2$ would suffice]. Mester (1993) and Yuengert (1993) implemented very simple versions of this suggestion, in which z_i is a set of dummy variables assigning producers to different ownership forms or to different size categories, respectively. The log likelihood function for the Mester model is the following straightforward generalization of equation (3.2.26):

$$
\begin{aligned}
\ln L = \text{constant} + \sum_i \Bigg\{ &(1 - D_i) \left[-\ln \sigma_1 + \ln \Phi\left(\frac{-\varepsilon_{1i}\lambda_1}{\sigma_1} \right) - \left(\frac{1}{2\sigma_1^2} \right) \varepsilon_{1i}^2 \right] \\
&+ (D_i) \left[-\ln \sigma_2 + \ln \Phi\left(\frac{-\varepsilon_{2i}\lambda_2}{\sigma_2} \right) - \left(\frac{1}{2\sigma_2^2} \right) \varepsilon_{2i}^2 \right] \Bigg\},
\end{aligned}
\tag{7.3.15}
$$

where $D_i = 1$ if a producer belongs to category 1 and $D_i = 0$ otherwise, and ε_i, λ, and σ are interpreted as usual, apart from their subscripts denoting the two categories of producer whose inefficiency error components are allowed to have different variances. After estimation, estimates of the efficiencies of each producer in each category can be obtained by way of straightforward extensions of equations (3.2.28)–(3.2.31). Of course this procedure generalizes to more than two categories, and the hypothesis of equal variances (and equal category mean efficiencies) is testable.

It should be apparent that a stochastic frontier model in which the one-sided error component is distributed as $u_i \sim N^+(0, \sigma_{ui}^2)$ conforms exactly to one type of heteroskedasticity discussed in Section 3.4. There we showed that unmodeled heteroskedasticity in u_i leads to biased estimates of all parameters in the model, and hence to biased estimates of the efficiencies of individual producers. Consequently formulating a stochastic frontier model with $u_i \sim N^+(0, \sigma_{ui}^2)$ offers the possibility of solving two problems at once: correcting for one source of heteroskedasticity and incorporating exogenous influences on efficiency.

Since it is not possible to estimate I separate variance parameters σ_{ui}^2 in a single cross section, we modeled heteroskedasticity as $\sigma_{ui}^2 = g_2(z_i; \delta_2)$, derived the log likelihood function, and discussed alternative specifications for the function $g_2(z_i; \delta_2)$. That discussion is obviously directly relevant to the present problem of incorporating exogenous influences on inefficiency, since the function $g_2(z_i; \delta_2)$ serves both purposes.

We now consider a model developed independently by Simar, Lovell, and Vanden Eeckaut (1994) and Caudill, Ford, and Gropper (1995). It is based on the conventional stochastic frontier model given in equation (7.3.1), with $v_i \sim$ iid $N(0, \sigma_v^2)$, $u_i \geq 0$, and v_i and u_i independently distributed. We assume that inefficiency u_i is associated with a vector of exogenous variables z_i by means of

$$u_i = \exp\{\gamma' z_i\} \cdot \eta_i, \qquad (7.3.16)$$

with the η_i being iid with $\eta_i \geq 0$, $E(\eta_i) = 1$, and $V(\eta_i) = \sigma_\eta^2$. Under these assumptions $u_i \geq 0$ with $E(u_i) = \exp\{\gamma' z_i\} > 0$ and $V(u_i) = \exp\{2\gamma' z_i\} \cdot \sigma_\eta^2 > 0$. Thus the variance of u_i is producer specific, although the coefficient of variation of u_i, $C(u_i) = \sigma_\eta$, is independent of i. To see how an element of z_i influences efficiency, recall from equation (3.4.6) that

$$M(u_i|\varepsilon_i) = \begin{cases} -\varepsilon_i \left[\dfrac{1}{1 + \sigma_v^2 / \sigma_{u_i}^2} \right] & \text{if } \varepsilon_i \leq 0, \\ 0 & \text{otherwise,} \end{cases} \qquad (7.3.17)$$

where $\varepsilon_i = v_i - u_i$. It follows from $V(u_i) = \exp\{2\gamma' z_i\} \cdot \sigma_\eta^2$ that $\partial M(u_i|\varepsilon_i)/\partial z_{qi} = \Lambda \gamma_q$, where $\Lambda > 0$. Thus positive (negative) values of γ_q lead to upward (downward) adjustments to estimated inefficiencies. The intuition is the same as in the deterministic model of Deprins and Simar: Efficiency scores achieved in a relatively favorable environment are adjusted downward, whereas those achieved in a relatively difficult environment are adjusted upward.

We now consider how to estimate the model. Inserting equation (7.3.16) into equation (7.3.1) yields

$$\ln y_i = \ln f(x_i; \beta) - \exp\{\gamma' z_i\} \cdot \eta_i + v_i$$
$$= \ln f(x_i; \beta) - \exp\{\gamma' z_i\} + \varepsilon_i, \qquad (7.3.18)$$

where

$$\varepsilon_i = \ln y_i - E(\ln y_i)$$
$$= v_i - \exp\{\gamma' z_i\} \cdot (\eta_i - 1).$$

The ε_is are independently but not identically distributed, with

$$E(\varepsilon_i) = 0,$$
$$E(\varepsilon_i^2) = \sigma_\varepsilon^2 = \sigma_v^2 + \exp\{2\gamma' z_i\} \cdot \sigma_\eta^2,$$
$$E(\varepsilon_i^3) = -\exp\{3\gamma' z_i\} \cdot E\big[(\eta_i - 1)^3\big].$$

Equation (7.3.18) is the stochastic frontier model to be estimated. It is based on equation (7.3.16), in which inefficiency $u_i = \exp\{\gamma' z_i\} \cdot \eta_i$ is a "scale" transformation of some underlying process η_i. This is a more convenient transformation than a "location" transformation of the form $u_i = \exp\{\gamma' z_i\} + \eta_i$ first used by Deprins and Simar in a deterministic setting, and later used by other authors cited previously in a stochastic setting. This is because with the location transformation the requirement that $u_i \geq 0$ requires that $\eta_i \geq -\exp\{\gamma' z_i\}$, which implies that the η_i are not iid. In addition, Caudill, Ford, and Gropper stress the computational advantages of the scale transformation, noting that it is easily constrained to yield the homoskedastic case in which the exogenous variables have no influence on efficiency.

The parameters in equation (7.3.18) can be estimated by nonlinear least squares (NLLS), by means of

$$(\hat{\beta}, \hat{\gamma}) = \arg\min \sum_i [\ln y_i - \ln f(x_i; \beta) + \exp\{\gamma' z_i\}]^2. \qquad (7.3.19)$$

The resulting parameter estimates are consistent, but not efficient since $E(\varepsilon_i^2) = \sigma_\varepsilon^2$ is not independent of i, as shown beneath equation (7.3.18). Alternatively it is possible to use nonlinear weighted least squares (NLWLS) to obtain

$$(\hat{\beta}, \hat{\gamma}) = \arg\min \sum_i \left[\frac{\ln y_i - \ln f(x_i; \beta) + \exp\{\gamma' z_i\}}{\sigma_\varepsilon}\right]^2. \qquad (7.3.20)$$

However since σ_ε is unknown, it is necessary to construct a feasible NLWLS estimator. This requires that a one-sided distribution be specified for η so that the unknown σ_ε^2 can be estimated from an estimate of σ_η^2. If we assume that $\eta \sim N^+(\mu, \sigma^2)$, then

$$f(\eta) = \frac{1}{\sqrt{2\pi}\sigma} \cdot \left[\Phi\left(\frac{\mu}{\sigma}\right)\right]^{-1} \cdot \exp\left\{-\frac{1}{2}\left(\frac{\eta - \mu}{\sigma}\right)^2\right\},$$

$$E(\eta) = 1 = \mu + c\sigma \Rightarrow c = \frac{\phi(\mu/\sigma)}{\Phi(\mu/\sigma)},$$

$$V(\eta) = \sigma^2 + \mu - 1 = \sigma^2 - c\sigma,$$

$$E\left[(\eta - E(\eta))^3\right] = -c\sigma^3 + c^2\sigma^2 + c\sigma, \tag{7.3.21}$$

and it follows that

$$E(\varepsilon_i) = 0,$$
$$E(\varepsilon_i^2) = \sigma_v^2 + \exp\{2\gamma' z_i\}\cdot(\sigma^2 - c\sigma),$$
$$E(\varepsilon_i^3) = -\exp\{3\gamma' z_i\}\cdot(-c\sigma^3 + c^2\sigma^2 + c\sigma). \tag{7.3.22}$$

Using the NLLS results, the two equations

$$\frac{1}{I}\sum_i \left[\frac{\varepsilon_i}{\exp\{\gamma' z_i\}}\right]^3 = (-c\sigma^3 + c^2\sigma^2 + c\sigma),$$

$$\mu + c\sigma = 1 \tag{7.3.23}$$

provide estimates of μ and σ, which yield an estimate of c. Together these yield an estimate of σ_v^2 by means of

$$\hat{\sigma}_v^2 = \frac{1}{I}\sum_i [\hat{\varepsilon}_i^2 - \exp\{2\hat{\gamma}' z_i\}\cdot(\hat{\sigma}^2 - c\hat{\sigma})]. \tag{7.3.24}$$

This provides all the information required to estimate σ_ε, which is used in NLWLS in equation (7.3.20).

The procedure simplifies considerably if we assume that $\eta \sim N^+(0, \sigma^2)$. In this case $\mu = 0 \Rightarrow c = (2/\pi)^{1/2} \Rightarrow \sigma = (\pi/2)^{1/2} \Rightarrow \sigma_\eta^2 = (\pi/2) - 1$. Hence

$$E(\varepsilon_i^2) = \sigma_v^2 + \exp\{2\gamma' z_i\}\cdot\left(\frac{\pi}{2} - 1\right),$$

$$\sigma_v^2 = \frac{1}{I}\sum_i \left[\varepsilon_i^2 - \exp\{2\gamma' z_i\}\cdot\left(\frac{\pi}{2} - 1\right)\right], \tag{7.3.25}$$

which provides all the information required to estimate σ_ε, which is used in NLWLS.

Thus when $\eta \sim N^+(\mu, \sigma^2)$ with the restriction $\mu + c\sigma = 1$ it follows that $u_i \sim N^+(\mu_i, \sigma_i^2)$, with $\mu_i = \mu \cdot \exp\{\gamma' z_i\}$ and $\sigma_i = \sigma \cdot \exp\{\gamma' z_i\}$, subject to the same restriction that $\mu + c\sigma = 1$. This generalizes Stevenson's (1980) truncated normal model. When $\eta \sim N^+(0, \sigma^2)$ we have $u_i \sim N^+(0, \sigma_i^2)$, with $\sigma_i = (\pi/2)^{1/2} \cdot \exp\{\gamma' z_i\}$, which generalizes the ALS half normal model.

However if one is going to go to the trouble of specifying a distribution for η, more efficient estimators can be obtained by using MLE techniques. Caudill, Ford, and Gropper derive the likelihood function for the case in which η is exponentially distributed, and Simar, Lovell, and Vanden Eeckaut derive likelihood functions for the gamma and truncated normal distributions, as well as for their exponential and half normal special cases. In light of numerical optimization problems encountered by Greene (1990) and Ritter and Simar (1997a, b) in the gamma case, we consider only the truncated normal distribution for η.

In the truncated normal case, $\ln f(\varepsilon_i)$ can be derived from Stevenson (1980), with (μ, σ) being replaced with $(\mu \cdot \exp\{\gamma' z_i\}, \sigma \cdot \exp\{\gamma' z_i\})$ and with the constraint $\mu + c\sigma = 1$. In this case

$$
\ln f(\varepsilon_i) = -\ln \Phi\left(\frac{\mu}{\sigma}\right) - \frac{1}{2}\ln(\sigma_v^2 + \sigma^2 \cdot \exp\{2\gamma' z_i\})
$$

$$
+ \ln \phi\left[\frac{\ln y_i - \ln f(x_i; \beta) + \mu \cdot \exp\{\gamma' z_i\}^{\frac{1}{2}}}{\sigma_v^2 + \sigma^2 \cdot \exp\{2\gamma' z_i\}}\right]
$$

$$
+ \ln \Phi\left[\sigma_v^2 + \sigma^2 \cdot \exp\{2\gamma' z_i\}\right]^{-\frac{1}{2}}
$$

$$
\times\left[\frac{\sigma_v}{\mu\sigma \cdot \exp\{\gamma' z_i\}} - \frac{\sigma \cdot \exp\{\gamma' z_i\}}{\sigma_v}(\ln y_i - \ln f(x_i; \beta))\right],
$$

$$
(7.3.26)
$$

and so

$$
(\hat{\beta}, \hat{\gamma}, \hat{\mu}, \hat{\sigma}, \hat{\sigma}_v) = \arg\max \sum_i \ln f(\varepsilon_i),
$$

$$
\text{s.t.} \quad \mu + \frac{\phi(\mu/\sigma)}{\Phi(\mu/\sigma)} \cdot \sigma = 1.
$$

$$
(7.3.27)
$$

In the half normal case the problem is easy to solve since $\mu = 0$ and $\sigma = (\pi/2)^{1/2}$, but in the truncated normal case the optimization problem is difficult to solve due to the nonlinear constraint. However this difficulty can be overcome when the expression $\exp\{\gamma'z_i\}$ has a constant term, so that $\gamma' = (\gamma_o, \gamma_1')$ and $z_i' = (1, z_{1i}')$. Consequently $u_i = \exp\{\gamma'z_i\} \cdot \eta_i = \exp\{\gamma_1'z_{1i}\} \cdot \eta_{oi}$, where now $E(\eta_{oi}) = \exp\{\gamma_o\}$ and $V(\eta_{oi}) = \exp\{2\gamma_o\} \cdot \sigma^2$. In this case μ becomes $\mu_i = \mu_o \cdot \exp\{\gamma_1'z_{1i}\}$ where $\mu_o = \mu \cdot \exp\{\gamma_o\}$, and σ becomes $\sigma_i = \sigma_o \cdot \exp\{\gamma_1'z_{1i}\}$ where $\sigma_o = \sigma \cdot \exp\{\gamma_o\}$. With this reparameterization μ_o and σ_o are unconstrained, since $E(\eta_{oi}) = \mu_o + c\sigma_o = \exp\{\gamma_o\}$ and γ_o is free. The density of the error term ε_i in the stochastic frontier model given by equation (7.3.18) can now be expressed as

$$\ln f(\varepsilon_i) = -\ln\Phi\left(\frac{\mu_o}{\sigma_o}\right) - \frac{1}{2}\ln\left(\sigma_v^2 + \sigma_o^2 \cdot \exp\{2\gamma_1'z_{1i}\}\right)$$

$$+\ln\phi\left[\frac{y_i - \ln f(x_i;\beta) + \mu_o \exp\{\gamma_1'z_{1i}\}}{\left(\sigma_v^2 + \sigma_o^2 \exp\{2\gamma_1'z_{1i}\}\right)^{1/2}}\right]$$

$$+\ln\Phi\left[\left(\sigma_v^2 + \sigma_o^2 \exp\{2\gamma_1'z_{1i}\}\right)^{-1/2} \cdot \left(\frac{\sigma_v\mu_o}{\sigma_o \exp\{\gamma_1'z_{1i}\}}\right.\right.$$

$$\left.\left.-\frac{\sigma_o \exp\{\gamma_1'z_{1i}\}}{\sigma_v}(y_i - \ln f(x_i;\beta))\right)\right]. \tag{7.3.28}$$

Maximizing the log likelihood function $\ln L = \Sigma_i \ln f(\varepsilon_i)$ with respect to the parameters generates estimates of $(\beta, \gamma_1, \mu_o, \sigma_o, \sigma_v)$. An estimate of γ_o is then obtained from the expression $\gamma_o = \ln\{\mu_o + \sigma_o \cdot [\phi(\mu_o/\sigma_o)/\Phi(\mu_o/\sigma_o)]\}$. With these estimates in hand, producer-specific estimates of efficiency can be obtained from obvious modifications of equations (3.2.50)–(3.2.52).

7.4 A GUIDE TO THE LITERATURE

This chapter is based on Simar, Lovell, and Vanden Eeckaut (1994).

Many authors have followed one of the first two early approaches discussed in Section 7.2, some appropriately enough when exogenous variables are hypothesized to influence the production process itself rather than the efficiency with which the production process is operated. Two early examples in the efficiency measurement literature are Pitt and Lee (1981) and Sickles, Good, and Johnson (1986), and more recent examples are provided by Bauer and Hancock (1993), Berger, Hancock, and Humphrey (1993), and Berger and Mester (1997). Among those who have adopted the second two-stage approach to explanation is Mester (1993, 1997), who used a logistic regression in the second stage. We are unaware of studies which have used the deterministic frontier approach of Deprins and Simar (1989a, b), although their work has obviously influenced our own work.

Relatively few studies have followed the various recent approaches, which are appropriate when exogenous variables are hypothesized to influence the efficiency with which the production process is operated. The Battese and Coelli model has been used by Audibert (1997), and has been compared with the Huang and Liu model by Battese and Broca (1997). Bhattacharyya, Kumbhakar, and Bhattacharyya (1995) have estimated a stochastic translog variable cost frontier model with both mean and variance of $u \geq 0$ being firm and time specific. This allows for the incorporation of both determinants of inefficiency and heteroskedasticity.

8 The Estimation of Efficiency Change and Productivity Change

8.1 INTRODUCTION

Productivity change occurs when an index of outputs changes at a different rate than an index of inputs does. Two questions immediately arise. First, how can productivity change be measured? Second, what are the sources of measured productivity change? Diewert (1992) has answered the first question. Productivity change can be calculated using index number techniques to construct a superlative Fisher (1922) or Törnqvist (1936) productivity index. Both indexes require quantity and price information, as well as assumptions concerning the structure of technology and the behavior of producers, but neither requires the estimation of anything. Productivity change can also be calculated using nonparametric techniques, or estimated using econometric techniques, to construct what has come to be known as a Malmquist (1953) productivity index. These latter techniques do not require price information or technological and behavioral assumptions, but they do require calculation or estimation of a representation of production technology. Thus information on the structure of the technology that generates the quantity data can serve as a substitute for price data and assumptions.

A disadvantage of index number techniques is that they do not provide an answer to the second question, whereas nonparametric techniques and econometric techniques do. Although nonparametric techniques and econometric techniques are capable of providing answers to both questions, only the econometric approach is capable

279

of doing so in a stochastic environment. In this chapter we show how to use econometric techniques to estimate the magnitude of productivity change, and then to decompose estimated productivity change into its various sources.

Early econometric studies of productivity change used a primal approach, based on the assumption of a single output and the estimation of a production function. More recently, with the development of duality theory, the majority of econometric studies of productivity change have used a dual approach, which allows for multiple outputs and which can be based on the estimation of either a cost function or a profit function. The estimation and decomposition of productivity change is by now well developed within a cost function framework, although it is much less well developed within a profit function framework.

Until very recently econometric models of productivity change ignored the contribution of efficiency change to productivity change; hence the word *function* in place of the word *frontier* in the preceding paragraph. Productivity change was initially allocated exclusively to shifts in production technology (the magnitude of neutral technical change); eventually roles were also assigned to the biases of technical change and the structure of the technology (scale economies). However if inefficiency exists, then efficiency change provides an independent contribution to productivity change. If efficiency change is omitted from the analysis, its omission leads to an overstatement of the unexplained residual, which Abramovitz (1956) aptly referred to as a "measure of our ignorance about the causes of economic growth," and also to an erroneous allocation of productivity change to its included sources. Accordingly, it is desirable to incorporate the possibility of efficiency change, both technical and allocative, into econometric models of productivity change. This is our objective in this chapter.

We begin by using a production frontier approach to obtain estimates of productivity change, and to decompose estimated productivity change into a technical change component, a returns to scale component, and a component associated with change in technical efficiency. We continue by doing essentially the same thing using a cost frontier approach, although we also include a component attributable to change in input allocative efficiency. Finally we use a profit frontier approach, and we demonstrate that the profit frontier approach gives essentially the same productivity change decomposition as the production frontier approach does, provided that the first-order conditions for profit maximization are used in the production frontier approach. A considerable advantage of the two dual approaches is that the productivity change decomposition can be conducted within a multiple-output framework.

We follow the format of preceding chapters and break down our discussion of the contribution of efficiency change to productivity change into three sections. In Section 8.2 we develop the primal (production frontier) approach to the estimation and decomposition of productivity change in the presence of technical inefficiency. The material in this section builds on the material developed in Chapter 3. In Sections 8.3 and 8.4 we develop a pair of dual (cost frontier and profit frontier) approaches to the estimation and decomposition of productivity change in the presence of both technical and allocative inefficiency. The material in these sections builds on the material developed in Chapters 4–6. Since the primary issue is one of productivity change, we assume throughout this chapter that panel data are available. Section 8.5 concludes with a guide to the relevant literature.

8.2 THE PRIMAL (PRODUCTION FRONTIER) APPROACH

In this section we develop a quantity-based approach to the estimation and decomposition of productivity change. We associate productivity change with either four or three components, depending on whether or not price information is also available. In Section 8.2.1 we develop an analytical framework in which productivity change is defined and the two decompositions are derived analytically. In the likely event that price information is unavailable, productivity change is decomposed into technical change, technical efficiency change, and the contribution of returns to scale. In Section 8.2.2 we discuss estimation of a composed error translog production frontier, in which the technical inefficiency error component is allowed to be time varying. We also show how the parameter estimates can be used to obtain estimates of the three components of productivity change.

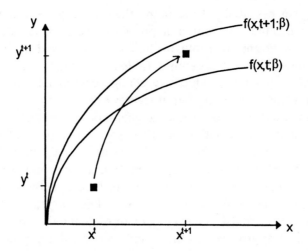

Figure 8.1 The Primal Approach to the Estimation and Decomposition of Productivity Change

The general structure of the primal approach is illustrated in Figure 8.1, in which a single input is used to produce a single output, and a producer expands from (x^t, y^t) to (x^{t+1}, y^{t+1}). Production technology is characterized by decreasing returns to scale, and technical progress has occurred between periods t and $t + 1$, since $f(x, t + 1; \beta) > f(x, t; \beta)$. Assuming away noise for the moment, it is clear that production is technically inefficient in both periods, since $y^t < f(x^t, t; \beta)$ and $y^{t+1} < f(x^{t+1}, t + 1; \beta)$, and that technical efficiency has improved from period t to period $t + 1$, since $[y^t/f(x^t, t; \beta)] < [y^{t+1}/f(x^{t+1}, t + 1; \beta)]$. It is also clear that productivity growth has occurred, since $(y^{t+1}/x^{t+1}) > (y^t/x^t)$. The initial econometric problem is to attribute output growth to input growth and productivity growth. The estimated rate of productivity growth must then be decomposed into contributions associated with returns to scale, technical change, and change in technical efficiency.

8.2.1 The Analytical Framework

We start with the deterministic production frontier

$$y = f(x, t; \beta) \cdot \exp\{-u\}, \tag{8.2.1}$$

where y is the scalar output of a producer, $f(x, t; \beta)$ is the deterministic kernel of a stochastic production frontier with technology parameter vector β to be estimated, $x = (x_1, \ldots, x_N) \geq 0$ is an input vector, t is a time trend serving as a proxy for technical change, and $u \geq 0$ represents output-oriented technical inefficiency. Technical change is not restricted to be neutral with respect to the inputs; neutrality requires that $f(x, t; \beta) = A(t) \cdot g(x; \beta)$.

A primal measure of the rate of technical change is provided by

$$TA = \frac{\partial \ln f(x, t; \beta)}{\partial t}. \tag{8.2.2}$$

$TA \gtreqless 0$ according as technical change shifts the production frontier up, leaves it unchanged, or shifts it down. A primal measure of the rate of change in technical efficiency is given by

$$TEA = -\frac{\partial u}{\partial t}. \tag{8.2.3}$$

$TEA \gtreqless 0$ according as technical inefficiency declines, remains unchanged, or increases through time. TEA can be interpreted as the rate at which a producer moves toward or away from the production frontier, which itself may be shifting through time.

In the scalar output case a conventional Divisia index of productivity change is defined as the difference between the rate of change of output and the rate of change of an input quantity index, and so

$$\begin{aligned} T\dot{F}P &= \dot{y} - \dot{X} \\ &= \dot{y} - \sum_n S_n \dot{x}_n, \end{aligned} \tag{8.2.4}$$

where a dot over a variable indicates its rate of change [e.g., $\dot{y} = (1/y)(dy/dt) = d \ln y/dt$], $S_n = w_n x_n / E$ is the observed expenditure share of input x_n, $E = \sum_n w_n x_n$ is total expenditure, and $w = (w_1, \ldots, w_N) > 0$ is an input price vector. Totally differentiating equation (8.2.1) and inserting the resulting expression for $\dot{y}$ into equation (8.2.4) yields

$$\begin{aligned} T\dot{F}P &= TA + \sum_n (\varepsilon_n - S_n) \dot{x}_n + TEA \\ &= TA + (\varepsilon - 1) \cdot \sum_n \left(\frac{\varepsilon_n}{\varepsilon}\right) \dot{x}_n + \sum_n \left[\left(\frac{\varepsilon_n}{\varepsilon}\right) - S_n\right] \dot{x}_n + TEA, \end{aligned} \tag{8.2.5}$$

where $\varepsilon_n = \varepsilon_n(x, t; \beta) = x_n f_n(x, t; \beta)/f(x, t; \beta)$, $n = 1, \ldots, N$, are elasticities of output with respect to each of the inputs. The scale elasticity

$\varepsilon = \varepsilon(x, t; \beta) = \Sigma_n \varepsilon_n(x, t; \beta) \gtreqqless 1$ provides a primal measure of returns to scale characterizing the production frontier. The relationship in equation (8.2.5) decomposes productivity change into a technical change component $[T\Delta]$, a scale component $[(\varepsilon - 1) \cdot \Sigma_n(\varepsilon_n/\varepsilon)\dot{x}_n]$, a technical efficiency change component $[TE\Delta]$, and an allocative inefficiency component $[\Sigma_n[(\varepsilon_n/\varepsilon) - S_n]\dot{x}_n]$. This decomposition of productivity change is very similar to the decomposition obtained by Bauer (1990a; 289).

Interpretation of three components is straightforward. If either production technology or technical efficiency is time invariant, then it makes no contribution to productivity change. The contribution of scale economies depends on technology and data. Under constant returns to scale input growth or contraction makes no contribution to productivity change. Nonconstant returns to scale makes a positive contribution to productivity change if the scale elasticity $\varepsilon(x, t; \beta)$ > 1 and input use expands $[\Sigma_n(\varepsilon_n/\varepsilon)\dot{x}_n > 0]$, or if the scale elasticity $\varepsilon(x, t; \beta) < 1$ and input use contracts $[\Sigma_n(\varepsilon_n/\varepsilon)\dot{x}_n < 0]$.

Interpretation of the allocative inefficiency component is a bit more involved. This component clearly captures the impact of deviations of inputs' normalized output elasticities from their expenditure shares or, somewhat less clearly, of input prices from the value of their marginal products $[w_n \gtreqqless pf_n(x, t; \beta) \cdot \exp\{-u\}, n = 1, \ldots, N]$, where p is the price at which y is sold. The allocative inefficiency component can represent either input allocative inefficiency $[f_n(x, t; \beta)/f_k(x, t; \beta) \neq w_n/w_k]$ or scale inefficiency $[f_n(x, t; \beta)/f_k(x, t; \beta) = w_n/w_k$ but $w_n \neq pf_n(x, t; \beta) \cdot \exp\{-u\}]$ or a combination of the two. If producers are allocatively efficient, then $f_n(x, t; \beta) = (w_n/p) \cdot \exp\{u\}$, $n = 1, \ldots, N$, the allocative inefficiency component vanishes, and the scale component becomes $(\varepsilon - 1) \cdot \Sigma_n S_n \dot{x}_n$.

If price information is unavailable the allocative inefficiency component cannot be calculated empirically, whether or not allocative inefficiency exists. In this case it is implicitly assumed that $S_n = (\varepsilon_n/\varepsilon)$ $\forall n$, and the decomposition in equation (8.2.5) simplifies to

$$T\dot{F}P = T\Delta + (\varepsilon - 1) \cdot \sum_n \left(\frac{\varepsilon_n}{\varepsilon} \right) \dot{x}_n + TE\Delta, \qquad (8.2.6)$$

which contains only quantity information. If technical efficiency is time invariant, then the third component on the right-hand side of equation (8.2.6) drops out, and the decomposition collapses to that of Denny, Fuss, and Waverman (1981; 193), in which productivity change is composed of technical change and a scale economies effect. If technical efficiency is time invariant and constant returns to scale prevail, the second and third components on the right-hand side of equation (8.2.6) both drop out, and productivity change consists solely of technical change. Thus only in the presence of time-invariant technical efficiency, persistent allocative efficiency, and constant returns to scale is it possible to associate productivity change with technical change, as was customary in early econometric studies of productivity change.

8.2.2 Estimation and Decomposition

The components of productivity change derived in Section 8.2.1 can be estimated within a stochastic production frontier framework. We assume that we have panel data on I producers through T time periods, and that the time-varying production frontier can be expressed in translog form as

$$\ln y_{it} = \beta_o + \sum_n \beta_n \ln x_{nit} + \beta_t t + \frac{1}{2} \sum_n \sum_k \beta_{nk} \ln x_{nit} \ln x_{kit}$$

$$+ \frac{1}{2} \beta_{tt} t^2 + \sum_n \beta_{nt} \ln x_{nit} t + v_{it} - u_{it}, \tag{8.2.7}$$

where $v_{it} \sim$ iid $N(0, \sigma_v^2)$ is the random-noise error component and $u_{it} \geq 0$ is the technical inefficiency error component. Technical change is neutral with respect to inputs if, and only if, $\beta_{nt} = 0 \ \forall n$, and absent if, and only if, $\beta_t = \beta_{tt} = \beta_{nt} = 0 \ \forall n$. Since we assume that we do not have input price information, the productivity change decomposition we wish to implement is that appearing in equation (8.2.6).

Equation (8.2.7) is structurally similar to the panel data models considered in Section 3.3, and all of the estimation techniques considered there are applicable in this context. The only difference here is the appearance of t as a regressor intended to capture the effects of technical change. The principal econometric problem is to disentangle the two roles played by t: as a proxy for technical change in the deterministic kernel of the stochastic production frontier and as an indicator of technical efficiency change in the second error component.

In Chapter 3 we discussed several time-varying specifications for the technical inefficiency error component. These are: (i) $u_{it} = u_i \cdot \gamma(t)$, where $\gamma(t)$ is a parametric function of time and u_i is a nonnegative random variable [Kumbhakar (1990) and Battese and Coelli (1992)]; (ii) $u_{it} = u_i \cdot \gamma_t$, where the γ_t are time effects represented by time dummies and the u_i can be either fixed or random producer-specific effects [Lee and Schmidt (1993)]; and (iii) $u_{it} = \Omega_{1i} + \Omega_{2i}t + \Omega_{3i}t^2$, where the Ωs are producer-specific parameters [Cornwell, Schmidt, and Sickles (1990)].

In specification (i) the separate time effects can be disentangled by positing a nonlinear specification for $\gamma(t)$. We consider this model, with distributional assumptions $v_{it} \sim$ iid $N(0, \sigma_v^2)$ and $u_{it} = u_i \cdot \exp\{-\gamma(t - T)\}$ with $u_i \sim$ iid $N^+(\mu, \sigma_u^2)$. Based on these assumptions, one can derive the probability density function of the composite error term $v_{it} - u_{it}$, and hence the log likelihood function for the model in equation (8.2.7). Once maximum likelihood estimates of the parameters in (8.2.7) are obtained, one can use the best linear unbiased predictor of technical efficiency. Formulation and estimation of this model, although without time as a regressor, was considered in Section 3.3.2, and additional details are available in Battese and Coelli (1992).

Since our interest centers on the estimation of productivity change and its sources given in equation (8.2.6), we need to obtain estimates of $T\Delta$, $TE\Delta$, ε_n $\forall n$, and ε. These can be derived from the parameter estimates obtained from equation (8.2.7) by means of

$$\hat{T}\Delta = \hat{\beta}_t + \hat{\beta}_{tt}t + \sum_n \hat{\beta}_{nt} \ln x_{nit},$$

$$\hat{TE}\Delta = \hat{u}_i \cdot \hat{\gamma} \cdot \exp\{-\hat{\gamma}(t - T)\},$$

$$\hat{\varepsilon}_n = \hat{\beta}_n + \sum_k \hat{\beta}_{nk} \ln x_{kit} + \hat{\beta}_{nt}t, \qquad n = 1, \dots, N,$$

$$\hat{\varepsilon} = \sum_n \left(\hat{\beta}_n + \sum_k \hat{\beta}_{nk} \ln x_{kit} + \hat{\beta}_{nt}t \right).$$

Once these components are estimated, the productivity change index in equation (8.2.6) can be estimated and decomposed for each producer. Notice that all three components of equation (8.2.6) are time and producer specific unless certain parametric restrictions are satisfied. $T\Delta$ varies across producers unless it is neutral with respect to inputs ($\beta_{nt} = 0$ $\forall n$), and $T\Delta$ varies through time unless $\beta_{tt} = \beta_{nt} = 0$ $\forall n$. $TE\Delta$ varies across producers through its u_i component, and

$TE\Delta$ varies through time, with the same trend for each producer, unless $\gamma = 0$. Finally $[(\varepsilon - 1)\cdot\Sigma_n(\varepsilon_n/\varepsilon)\dot{x}_{nit}]$ varies across producers and through time unless technology takes the linearly homogeneous Cobb–Douglas form ($\Sigma_n\beta_n = 1$ and $\beta_{nk} = \beta_{nt} = 0$ $\forall n, k$) or unless $\dot{x}_{nit} = 0$ $\forall n, i, t$. Each of these parametric restrictions is testable.

8.3 A DUAL (COST FRONTIER) APPROACH

In this section we use quantity and price information to estimate and decompose productivity change. This dual approach is based on a cost frontier. In Section 8.3.1 we develop a pair of analytical frameworks in which dual productivity change is expressed in terms of technical change, technical efficiency change, and the contribution of scale economies, as in the primal approach given in equation (8.2.6). However the dual approach also enables us to derive a component that captures the effect of change in input allocative inefficiency. The two analytical frameworks differ in that one models the *costs* of technical and input allocative inefficiency as error components in a stochastic cost frontier, whereas the other models the *magnitudes* of technical and input allocative inefficiency by treating them as additional parameters to be estimated. The two frameworks generate identical technical change and scale components, but they generate different technical efficiency change and input allocative efficiency change components. In Section 8.3.2 we consider estimation and decomposition of productivity change using the second framework and a translog stochastic cost frontier. Sections 8.3.1 and 8.3.2 are consistent with Sections 8.2.1 and 8.2.2 in the sense that both assume that a single output is produced. Section 8.3.3 exploits the ability of a cost frontier to easily accommodate multiple outputs, and develops a decomposition of productivity change in a multiple-output context. This section is brief, because our emphasis is on introducing efficiency change into a productivity change decomposition rather than on expanding the dimensionality of output space.

The general structure of the dual cost frontier approach is illustrated in Figure 8.2, in which N inputs are used to produce a single output, and a producer expands from (y^t, E^t) to (y^{t+1}, E^{t+1}). Production technology is characterized by decreasing returns to scale, and

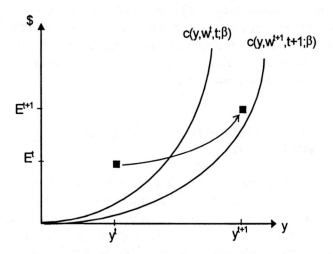

Figure 8.2 The Dual Approach to the Estimation and Decomposition of Productivity Change

technical progress has occurred between periods t and $t + 1$, since $c(y, w^{t+1}, t + 1; \beta) < c(y, w^t, t; \beta)$ and since we assume that $w^{t+1} \geq w^t$. Assuming away noise for the moment, it is clear that production is cost inefficient in both periods, since $E^t > c(y^t, w^t, t; \beta)$ and $E^{t+1} > c(y^{t+1}, w^{t+1}, t + 1; \beta)$, and that cost efficiency has improved from period t to period $t + 1$, since $[E^{t+1}/c(y^{t+1}, w^{t+1}, t + 1; \beta)] < [E^t/c(y^t, w^t, t; \beta)]$. It is also clear that productivity growth has occurred, since $(E^{t+1}/y^{t+1}) < (E^t/y^t)$. The initial econometric problem is to attribute expenditure growth to output growth and productivity growth. The estimated rate of productivity growth must then be decomposed into contributions associated with returns to scale, technical change, and change in cost efficiency, which itself may be due to change in technical and/or input allocative efficiency.

8.3.1 The Analytical Framework

A dual cost minimization framework is widely used in the productivity literature to estimate and decompose productivity change. Although it is possible to use a primal framework and invoke the first-order conditions for cost minimization to derive an expression for productivity change, we prefer to use a dual framework. The main

reason for using a dual framework is that it is useful from an estimation point of view. We begin with a completely general formulation, which is not parameterized and which has been used as the basis
for empirical research when the contribution of efficiency change to
productivity change is ignored. We then continue with a preferred
parameterized formulation on which estimation can be based in the
presence of efficiency change.

Consider the deterministic cost frontier

$$\ln E = \ln c(y,w,t;\beta) + u_T + u_A, \tag{8.3.1}$$

where $E = w^T x$ is total expenditure, $x = (x_1, \ldots, x_N) \geq 0$ is an input
vector, $w = (w_1, \ldots, w_N) > 0$ is an input price vector, $y \geq 0$ is scalar
output, t is a time trend that serves as a proxy for technical change,
$c(y,w,t;\beta)$ is the deterministic kernel of a stochastic cost frontier with
technology parameter vector β to be estimated, $u_T \geq 0$ is the cost
of technical inefficiency, and $u_A \geq 0$ is the cost of input allocative
inefficiency. Totally differentiating equation (8.3.1), solving for $\dot{y}$, and
substituting the expression for $\dot{y}$ into equation (8.2.4) yields an initial
expression for dual productivity change

$$T\dot{F}P = [1 - \varepsilon(y,w,t;\beta)]\dot{y} - \dot{c}(y,w,t;\beta) - \sum_n S_n(y,w,t;\beta)\dot{w}_n$$

$$- \sum_n \left(\frac{w_n x_n}{E}\right)\dot{x}_n + \dot{E} - \frac{\partial u_T}{\partial t} - \frac{\partial u_A}{\partial t}, \tag{8.3.2}$$

where the cost elasticity $\varepsilon(y,w,t;\beta) = \partial \ln c(y,w,t;\beta)/\partial \ln y = [\varepsilon(x,t;
\beta)]^{-1}$ provides a dual measure of returns to scale and the $S_n(y,w,t;\beta)$
$= \partial \ln c(y,w,t;\beta)/\partial \ln w_n, n = 1, \ldots, N$, are efficient input cost shares.
Next, noting that $\dot{E} - \Sigma_n(w_n x_n/E)\dot{x}_n = \Sigma_n(w_n x_n/E)\dot{w}_n$ and substituting
this equality into equation (8.3.2) yields the final expression for dual
productivity change

$$T\dot{F}P = [1 - \varepsilon(y,w,t;\beta)]\dot{y} - \dot{c}(y,w,t;\beta)$$

$$+ \sum_n [S_n - S_n(y,w,t;\beta)]\dot{w}_n - \frac{\partial u_T}{\partial t} - \frac{\partial u_A}{\partial t}, \tag{8.3.3}$$

where the $S_n = w_n x_n/E, n = 1, \ldots, N$, are actual input cost shares.

Equation (8.3.3) provides a decomposition of dual productivity
change that is identical to that obtained by Bauer (1990a; 291).
The first component is a scale effect, which makes no contribution to

productivity change if either $\varepsilon(y, w, t; \beta) = 1$ or $\dot{y} = 0$. However output growth in the presence of scale economies $[\varepsilon(y, w, t; \beta) < 1]$ contributes to productivity growth, as does output contraction in the presence of diseconomies of scale $[\varepsilon(y, w, t; \beta) > 1]$. Conversely output growth in the presence of diseconomies of scale retards productivity growth, as does output contraction in the presence of scale economies. The second component is a technical change effect that shifts the cost frontier down if technical change is progress or up if technical change is regress. The third component captures the impact of deviations of actual input cost shares from efficient input cost shares. This component is zero if the input mix is allocatively efficient, since then $S_n = S_n(y, w, t; \beta) \; \forall n$. However this term is also zero in the presence of input allocative inefficiency if all input prices change at the same rate because $\Sigma_n[S_n - S_n(y, w, t; \beta)] = 0$. The final two components capture the separate contributions to productivity change of changes in the costs of technical and input allocative inefficiency.

The dual productivity change decomposition given in equation (8.3.3) parallels the two primal productivity change decompositions given in equations (8.2.6) and (8.2.5), although not exactly. Both primal and dual decompositions contain components measuring the contributions of technical change and scale economies to productivity change. However the dual technical change component in equation (8.3.3) is not identical to the primal technical change component in equations (8.2.6) and (8.2.5) unless constant returns to scale prevail. Ohta (1974) has shown that

$$-\dot{c}(y, w, t; \beta) = \varepsilon(y, w, t; \beta) \cdot T\Delta, \tag{8.3.4}$$

so that $[-\dot{c}(y, w, t; \beta)] \gtreqless T\Delta$ according as $\varepsilon(y, w, t; \beta) = [\varepsilon(x, t; \beta)]^{-1} \gtreqless 1$. The dual scale component in equation (8.3.3) is related to the primal scale component in equations (8.2.5) and (8.2.6) by way of

$$[1 - \varepsilon(y, w, t; \beta)]\dot{y} = (\varepsilon - 1) \cdot \sum_n \left(\frac{\varepsilon_n}{\varepsilon}\right)\dot{x}_n + [1 - \varepsilon^{-1}] \cdot T\Delta. \tag{8.3.5}$$

Thus the two scale components are equal under constant returns to scale, in which case both are zero, or in the absence of technical change. In addition, the primal and dual technical efficiency change components differ, the former measuring the contribution of changes in the magnitude of output-oriented technical inefficiency and the latter measuring the contribution of changes in the cost of technical inefficiency whose orientation is as yet unspecified. Finally the primal formulation in equation (8.2.5) contains one allocative efficiency change component, and the simpler primal formulation in equation (8.2.6) contains no allocative efficiency change component, whereas the dual formulation in equation (8.3.3) contains a pair of allocative efficiency change components.

The problem with Bauer's dual productivity change decomposition given in equation (8.3.3) lies with the two error components u_T and u_A. We saw in Chapter 4 how difficult it is to estimate the costs of technical and input allocative inefficiencies as error components within a flexible cost frontier model. In the present context this leaves us with two options. The first is to simplify equation (8.3.1) by replacing the two error components u_T and u_A with a single error component u_{T+A} representing the cost of both types of inefficiency. This leads to the replacement of the two terms $-\partial u_T/\partial t$ and $-\partial u_A/\partial t$ in equations (8.3.2) and (8.3.3) with the single term $-\partial u_{T+A}/\partial t$ representing change in the cost of both types of inefficiency. The second option is to base our decomposition of productivity change on a parametric model along the lines developed in Chapter 6. Since it is difficult enough to interpret, much less to estimate, the dual technical and allocative efficiency change components within a composed error framework, we follow the second option by developing a partially parameterized dual formulation in which the contributions of changes in technical and input allocative efficiency are relatively easy to interpret and estimate.

Consider the cost minimization problem

$$\min_{x}\{w^T x: y = f(x \cdot \exp\{-\tau\}, t; \beta)\}, \tag{8.3.6}$$

where $f(x, t; \beta)$ is the production frontier and $\exp\{-\tau\}$ represents input-oriented technical inefficiency with $\tau \geq 0$. In addition to allowing for technical inefficiency, we also allow for input allocative inefficiency by expressing the first-order conditions for equation (8.3.6) as

$$\frac{f_n(x \cdot \exp\{-\tau\}, t; \beta)}{f_1(x \cdot \exp\{-\tau\}, t; \beta)} = \frac{w_n}{w_1} \cdot \exp\{-\xi_n\}, \qquad n = 2, \ldots, N. \tag{8.3.7}$$

This formulation allows the technically efficient input vector $x \cdot \exp\{-\tau\}$ to be allocatively inefficient relative to the observed input price vector w. A producer is allocatively efficient relative to w if, and only if, $\xi_n = 0$, $n = 2, \ldots, N$. The technically efficient input vector $x \cdot \exp\{-\tau\}$ is, however, allocatively efficient relative to the shadow input price vector $[w_1, w_2 \cdot \exp\{-\xi_2\}, \ldots, w_N \cdot \exp\{-\xi_N\}]$.

Defining the shadow input price vector as $w^s = [w_1, w_2 \cdot \exp\{-\xi_2\}, \ldots, w_N \cdot \exp\{-\xi_N\}]$ and the corresponding shadow cost frontier (which does not incorporate technical inefficiency) as $c^s(y, w^s, t; \beta) = \Sigma_n w_n^s x_n$, and substituting w^s into the optimization problem (8.3.6), generates the shadow cost frontier (which does incorporate technical inefficiency)

$$c(y, w^s, t; \beta) = \sum_n w_n^s x_n \cdot \exp\{-\tau\} = \exp\{-\tau\} \cdot c^s(y, w^s, t; \beta). \qquad (8.3.8)$$

A lot of tedious algebra leads to the following expression for actual expenditure $E = w^T x$:

$$\begin{aligned}
\ln E &= \ln c^s(y, w^s, t; \beta) + \ln G(y, w^s, t; \beta) \\
&= \ln c(y, w^s, t; \beta) + \ln G(y, w^s, t; \beta) + \tau, \qquad (8.3.9)
\end{aligned}$$

where

$$G(y, w^s, t; \beta) = \sum_n S_n^s \cdot \exp\{\xi_n\},$$

$$\begin{aligned}
S_n^s &= \frac{w_n^s x_n}{c^s(y, w^s, t; \beta)} \\
&= \frac{\partial \ln c^s(y, w^s, t; \beta)}{\partial \ln w_n^s} \\
&= \frac{\partial \ln c(y, w^s, t; \beta)}{\partial \ln w_n^s}.
\end{aligned}$$

Totally differentiating equation (8.3.9) and the equality $E = w^T x$, and setting the two expressions equal, gives an initial decomposition of dual productivity change

$$\begin{aligned}
T\dot{F}P &= [1 - \varepsilon^s(y, w^s, t; \beta)]\dot{y} - \dot{c}^s(y, w^s, t; \beta) \\
&\quad + \sum_n (S_n \dot{w}_n - S_n^s \dot{w}_n^s) - \frac{\partial \ln G(y, w^s, t; \beta)}{\partial t} - \frac{\partial \tau}{\partial t}, \qquad (8.3.10)
\end{aligned}$$

where $\varepsilon^s(y, w^s, t; \beta) = \partial \ln c^s(y, w^s, t; \beta)/\partial \ln y$. This expression can be rewritten in terms of the cost frontier $c(y, w, t; \beta)$ [which is dual to the original production frontier $f(x, t; \beta)$], on which both technical and allocative efficiency hold, as

$$T\dot{F}P = [1 - \varepsilon(y, w, t; \beta)]\dot{y} - \dot{c}(y, w, t; \beta) - \frac{\partial \tau}{\partial t} + \rho(y, w, t; \beta), \qquad (8.3.11)$$

where the cost elasticity $\varepsilon(y, w, t; \beta) = \partial \ln c(y, w, t; \beta)/\partial \ln y$ measures returns to scale on the cost frontier $c(y, w, t; \beta)$, $[-\dot{c}(y, w, t; \beta)]$ measures technical change on the cost frontier $c(y, w, t; \beta)$, $[-\partial \tau/\partial t]$ measures technical efficiency change, and

$$\begin{aligned}\rho(y, w, t; \beta) &= [\dot{c}(y, w, t; \beta) - \dot{c}^s(y, w^s, t; \beta)] \\ &+ [\varepsilon(y, w, t; \beta) - \varepsilon^s(y, w^s, t; \beta)]\dot{y} \\ &+ \sum_n (S_n \dot{w}_n - S_n^s \dot{w}_n^s) - \frac{d}{dt}\left[\ln\left\{\sum_n S_n^s \left(\frac{w_n}{w_n^s}\right)\right\}\right]\end{aligned}$$

measures the contribution of change in input allocative inefficiency to productivity change. The term $\rho(y, w, t; \beta) = 0$ if the input mix is allocatively efficient, in which case $w_n^s = w_n \Leftrightarrow \xi_n = 0, n = 2, \ldots, N$. However $\rho(y, w, t; \beta) = 0$ is also possible in the presence of input allocative inefficiency. The first term in $\rho(y, w, t; \beta)$ is zero if technical change is the same when measured on $c(y, w, t; \beta)$ as when measured on $c^s(y; w^s, t; \beta)$. The second term is zero if scale economies are the same on $c(y, w, t; \beta)$ and $c^s(y, w^s, t; \beta)$. The third term is zero if $\dot{w}_n = \dot{w}_n^s = \dot{w}_k = \dot{w}_k^s \; \forall n, k$. The final term is zero if the (w_n/w_n^s) are independent of time. Each of these cases, and all of them collectively, is consistent with the presence of input allocative inefficiency.

The dual productivity change decomposition given in equation (8.3.11) is similar to the decomposition given in equation (8.3.3). They contain identical scale and technical change components. However the technical efficiency change component in equation (8.3.11) measures the contribution of change in the *magnitude* of technical inefficiency, whereas that in equation (8.3.3) measures the contribution of change in the *cost* of technical inefficiency. Finally, the two remaining components $[\rho(y, w, t; \beta)$ in equation (8.3.11) and $\{\Sigma_n[S_n - S_n(y, w, t; \beta)]\dot{w}_n - \partial u_A/\partial t\}$ in equation (8.3.3)] provide different characterizations of the contribution of change in allocative efficiency. The allocative efficiency component in equation (8.3.11) measures the contribution of changes in the *magnitudes* of allocative inefficiency represented by the parameter vector ξ, whereas the allocative efficiency component in equation (8.3.3) measures the contribution of changes in the *cost* of allocative inefficiency. Finally, if persistent technical and allocative efficiency hold, then the final two components in equation (8.3.11) disappear, and our dual productivity change decomposition collapses to that of Denny, Fuss, and Waverman (1981; 195).

8.3.2 Estimation and Decomposition

It is possible to base estimation and decomposition of dual productivity change on equations (8.3.1)–(8.3.3). All that is required is to follow the estimation strategy outlined in Section 4.3.2, preferably with a flexible specification for the cost frontier and with t added as a regressor to serve as a proxy for technical change. After estimation, estimated values of the technology parameters and the parameters of the technical and allocative inefficiency distributions can be used to implement the productivity change decomposition in equation (8.3.3). However, as we mentioned in Chapter 4, and repeated beneath equation (8.3.5), estimation of the model is complicated by its error structure.

Here we consider estimation and decomposition of dual productivity change based on equations (8.3.6)–(8.3.11). We begin by assigning a translog functional form to the shadow cost frontier $c^s(y, w^s, t; \beta)$, which we write as

$$
\ln c^s (y_{it}, w^s_{it}, t; \beta) = \beta_o + \beta_y \ln y_{it} + \sum_n \beta_n \ln w^s_{nit} + \beta_t t
$$

$$
+ \frac{1}{2} \beta_{yy} [\ln y_{it}]^2 + \frac{1}{2} \sum_n \sum_k \beta_{nk} [\ln w^s_{nit}][\ln w^s_{kit}]
$$

$$
+ \frac{1}{2} \beta_{tt} t^2 + \sum_n \beta_{yn} [\ln y_{it}][\ln w^s_{nit}]
$$

$$
+ \beta_{yt} [\ln y_{it}] t + \sum_n \beta_{nt} [\ln w^s_{nit}] t. \tag{8.3.12}
$$

The corresponding shadow input cost share equations are

$$
S^s_{nit} (y_{it}, w^s_{it}, t; \beta) = \beta_n + \sum_k \beta_{nk} \ln w^s_{kit} + \beta_{yn} \ln y_{it} + \beta_{nt} t,
$$

$$
n = 1, \ldots, N. \tag{8.3.13}
$$

Using equation (8.3.9) and the expressions beneath it, actual expenditure and the actual input cost share equations can be expressed as

$$\ln E_{it} = \ln c^s(y_{it}, w^s_{it}, t; \beta)$$

$$+ \ln\left[\sum_n S^s_{nit}(y_{it}, w^s_{it}, t; \beta) \cdot \exp\{\xi_{nit}\}\right] + \tau_{it} + v_{it},$$

$$(8.3.14)$$

$$S_{nit} = \frac{S^*_{nit}(y_{it}, w^s_{it}, t; \beta) \cdot \exp\{\xi_{nit}\}}{\Sigma_k S^*_{kit}(y_{it}, w^s_{it}, t; \beta) \cdot \exp\{\xi_{kit}\}} + \eta_{nit}, \qquad n = 1, \ldots, N,$$

$$(8.3.15)$$

where τ_{it} is the magnitude (and the cost) of input-oriented technical inefficiency, and v_{it} and the η_{nit} are classical random-error terms.

The estimation strategy depends on the nature of the assumptions made on τ_{it} and the ξ_{nit}. If both τ_{it} and the ξ_{nit} are assumed to be random, and distributional assumptions are made on them, it is not possible to derive the likelihood function for the system of N equations consisting of equation (8.3.14) and $N - 1$ of the equations (8.3.15). Therefore, to keep the estimation problem tractable, we assume that the allocative inefficiencies (the ξ_{nit}) are fixed parameters that are constant across producers and through time (and so become ξ_n). Although it is somewhat restrictive, the discussion beneath equation (8.3.11) demonstrates that this assumption does not imply that productivity growth is independent of the ξ_n. We also make the Battese and Coelli (1992) distributional assumption that $\tau_{it} = \tau_i \cdot \exp\{-\gamma(t - T)\}$, where $\tau_i \sim$ iid $N^+(\mu, \sigma^2_\tau)$, and we also assume that $v_{it} \sim$ iid $N(0, \sigma^2_v)$, $\eta_{it} \sim N(0, \Sigma_\eta)$, with v distributed independently of τ and η, and τ distributed independently of η. With this specification the likelihood function for the preceding system of equations can easily be derived.

Due to the highly nonlinear nature of equations (8.3.14) and (8.3.15), obtaining maximum likelihood estimators is apt to be computationally difficult. However if the estimators can be obtained, estimates of τ_{it} can be calculated from the residuals of equation (8.3.14) using the JLMS procedure. Under this specification for τ_{it} the contribution of technical efficiency change to productivity change is given by $[-\partial\tau_{it}/\partial t] = \gamma \cdot \tau_{it}$. The remaining components of productivity change identified in equation (8.3.11) can be obtained directly from the estimated parameters in the expenditure equation (8.3.14).

Estimation can be simplified somewhat by using the following two-step procedure. In the first step the input cost share equations are estimated using ITSUR (which does not require distributional assumptions on η). The estimates of S^s_n and ξ_n can be used to obtain an estimate of $[\Sigma_n S_{nit}^s(y_{it}, w_{it}^s, t; \beta) \cdot \exp\{\xi_n\}]$. In the second step maximum likelihood techniques are used to estimate the transformed expenditure equation

$$\ln E_{it} - \ln\left[\sum_n S_{nit}^s(y_{it}, w_{it}^s, t; \beta) \cdot \exp\{\xi_n\}\right] = \ln c^s(y_{it}, w_{it}^s, t; \beta) + \tau_{it} + v_{it}. \quad (8.3.16)$$

Since $\ln c^s(y_{it}, w_{it}^s, t; \beta)$ depends on the ξ_n via the w_{nit}^s, further simplification in estimation can be achieved by treating w_{nit}^s as the price of x_{nit} calculated using the relationship $w_{nit}^s = w_{nit} \cdot \exp\{\xi_n\}$, and not estimating the ξ_n again in the second step. Under this scenario, estimation of the transformed expenditure equation in the second step is not different from estimating technical inefficiency in the Battese and Coelli (1992) model.

8.3.3 An Extension to Multiple Outputs

The analysis, estimation, and decomposition of dual productivity change in Sections 8.3.1 and 8.3.2 is based on the assumption that only a single output is produced. In this section we extend the analysis to the multiple-output case. Our exposition is brief, because the analytical and econometric extensions are straightforward and, more importantly, because our interest centers on the introduction of efficiency change into a decomposition of productivity change, and the extension to multiple outputs is of secondary interest.

The key difference between the decomposition of productivity change in the multiple-output case and in the single-output case lies in the definition of productivity change. When there are M outputs $y = (y_1, \ldots, y_M) \geq 0$, the Divisia index of productivity change given in equation (8.2.4) becomes

$$\begin{aligned} T\dot{F}P &= \dot{Y} - \dot{X} \\ &= \sum_m R_m \dot{y}_m - \sum_n S_n \dot{x}_n, \end{aligned} \quad (8.3.17)$$

where $R_m = p_m y_m/R$ is the observed revenue share of output y_m, p_m is the price of output y_m, and $R = \Sigma_m p_m y_m$ is total revenue. If the scalar output y in the deterministic cost frontier given in equation (8.3.1) is replaced by the output vector $y = (y_1, \ldots, y_M)$, then the analysis of Section 8.3.1 can be adapted to the multiple-output case.

Adapting the error components analysis in equations (8.3.1)–(8.3.3) to the multiple-output case leads to the following expression for productivity change:

$$T\dot{F}P = [1 - \varepsilon(y,w,t;\beta)]\dot{Y}^c - \dot{c}(y,w,t;\beta) + \sum_n [S_n - S_n(y,w,t;\beta)]\dot{w}_n$$

$$+ (\dot{Y} - \dot{Y}^c) - \frac{\partial u_T}{\partial t} - \frac{\partial u_A}{\partial t}, \qquad (8.3.18)$$

where

$$\dot{Y}^c = \sum_m \left[\frac{\varepsilon_m(y,w,t;\beta)}{\varepsilon(y,w,t;\beta)} \right] \dot{y}_m$$

provides a measure of aggregate output growth using efficient cost elasticity weights in place of revenue share weights, the $\varepsilon_m(y,w,t;\beta)$ $= \partial \ln c(y,w,t;\beta)/\partial \ln y_m$ are elasticities of minimum cost with respect to y_m, $m = 1, \ldots, M$, and $\varepsilon(y,w,t;\beta) = \Sigma_m \varepsilon_m(y,w,t;\beta)$ is the dual multiproduct measure of scale economies.

Expression (8.3.18) appears in Bauer (1990a; 292) and, in simplified form, in Denny, Fuss, and Waverman (1981; 197). It decomposes productivity change into a scale effect, a technical change effect, an input allocative efficiency effect, and a pair of efficiency cost effects, as in the single-output version given in equation (8.3.3). The effect $(\dot{Y} - \dot{Y}^c)$ is new, and captures the impact on productivity change of departures from marginal cost pricing, or of departures from equiproportionate markups over marginal cost pricing, since $(\dot{Y} - \dot{Y}^c) = 0$ if $p_m = \theta \partial c(y, w,t;\beta)/\partial y_m$, $m = 1, \ldots, M$. This term does not appear in equation (8.3.3), apparently because there is no question of appropriate output weights in the single-output case, despite the fact that $p \neq \partial c(y,w,t;\beta)/\partial y$ remains possible in the single-output case.

In principle productivity change can be estimated and decomposed in the multiple-output composed error framework; Bauer (1990a) did so under several restrictive assumptions. However, as we indicated previously, the complicated error structure makes the model exceedingly difficult to estimate, regardless of the number of outputs, and so we now consider a multiproduct model in which technical and input allocative inefficiency are modeled parametrically rather than through error components. This approach extends the analysis and estimation in equations (8.3.6)–(8.3.16) to the multiple-output case.

Equation (8.3.11) provides a decomposition of dual productivity change in the single-output case. The extension to multiple outputs is given by

$$TFP = [1 - \varepsilon(y,w,t;\beta)]\dot{Y}^c - \dot{c}(y,w,t;\beta) - \frac{\partial \tau}{\partial t} + \rho(y,w,t;\beta), \qquad (8.3.19)$$

where

$$\rho(y,w,t;\beta) = [\dot{c}(y,w,t;\beta) - \dot{c}^s(y,w^s,t;\beta)]$$
$$+ \{[\varepsilon(y,w,t;\beta)]\dot{Y}^c - [\varepsilon^s(y,w^s,t;\beta)]\dot{Y}^{cs}\}$$
$$+ (\dot{Y} - \dot{Y}^c) + \sum_n [S_n \dot{w}_n - S_n^s \dot{w}_n^s] - \frac{d}{dt}\left[\ln\left\{\sum_n S_n^s\left(\frac{w_n}{w_n^s}\right)\right\}\right]$$

and $\dot{Y}^{cs} = \Sigma_m[\varepsilon_m^s(y,w^s,t;\beta)/\varepsilon^s(y,w^s,t;\beta)]\dot{y}_m$ provides a measure of aggregate output growth using shadow input prices to construct cost elasticity weights. All other terms are as defined before.

Equation (8.3.19) decomposes dual productivity change into a scale term, a technical change term, a technical efficiency change term, and an input allocative efficiency change term, exactly as equation (8.3.11) does in the single-output case. The technical change and technical efficiency change terms are unchanged from their single-output versions. The scale term is a straightforward generalization of the single-output scale term. The input allocative efficiency change term $\rho(y,w,t;\beta)$ is a multiple-output generalization of the single-output expression introduced beneath equation (8.3.11), with one exception. The component $(\dot{Y} - \dot{Y}^c)$ is new, and captures disproportionate departures from marginal cost pricing. Thus, as in the single-output case, the effect of input allocative inefficiency on productivity change has several components: (i) a technical change component, which is zero if technical change is the same on $c(y,w,t;\beta)$ and $c^s(y, w^s,t;\beta)$; (ii) a scale component, which is zero if returns to scale are the same on $c(y,w,t;\beta)$ and $c^s(y,w^s,t;\beta)$; (iii) a disproportionate departures from marginal cost pricing term; and (iv) a miscellaneous term, which is zero if actual and shadow input cost shares are the same and the (w_n/w_n^s) are constant for all $n = 1, \ldots, N$.

Estimation and decomposition in the multiple-output case proceed exactly as in the single-output case discussed in Section 8.3.2. All that is required is to replace the scalar output y_{it} with a vector of outputs y_{mit}, $m = 1, \ldots, M$, in the translog cost frontier system given in equations (8.3.12)–(8.3.16).

8.4 A DUAL (PROFIT FRONTIER) APPROACH

A dual profit-maximizing framework is not widely used to analyze, estimate, and decompose productivity change, although it is possible to do so. Two approaches are available. It is possible to use a primal framework and invoke the first-order conditions for profit maximization to derive an expression for productivity change. Alternatively, it is possible to use a dual framework to begin with. In this section we follow the latter approach. The analytical framework we develop in Section 8.4.1 is structurally similar to the analytical framework we developed in Section 8.3.1 for use in a cost-minimizing environment. The estimation and decomposition procedures we develop in Section 8.4.2 are also similar to the empirical procedures we developed in Section 8.3.2 for use in a cost-minimizing environment. Finally, the extension to multiple outputs in Section 8.4.3 is also similar to the extension we developed in Section 8.3.3.

8.4.1 The Analytical Framework

A conventional profit frontier $\pi(p, w, t; \beta)$ is defined as the solution to the constrained maximization problem

$$\pi(p,w,t;\beta) = \max_{y,x}\{py - w^T x: y = f(x,t;\beta)\}, \tag{8.4.1}$$

where $f(x, t; \beta)$ is the deterministic kernel of a stochastic production frontier, $y \geq 0$ is scalar output with price $p > 0$, $x = (x_1, \ldots, x_N) \geq 0$ is an input quantity vector with price vector $w = (w_1, \ldots, w_N) > 0$, and β is a vector of technology parameters to be estimated. Technical inefficiency can be introduced in either input-oriented or output-oriented form; in output-oriented form it is introduced by scaling output y to technically efficient output $y \cdot \exp\{u\}$ with $u \geq 0$. Input allocative inefficiency can be introduced by replacing input prices with shadow input prices $w^s = [w_1, w_2 \cdot \exp\{-\xi_2\}, \ldots, w_N \cdot \exp\{-\xi_N\}]$. The corresponding shadow profit frontier is

$$\pi^s(p^s, w^s, t;\beta) = \max_{y,x}\{p^s y \cdot \exp\{u\} - w^{sT} x: y \cdot \exp\{u\} = f(x,t;\beta)\}, \tag{8.4.2}$$

where $p^s = p \cdot \exp\{-u\}$ is the shadow price of technically efficient output $y \cdot \exp\{u\}$.

From the expression for $\pi^s(p^s, w^s, t; \beta)$ it follows that the rate of change of shadow profit can be written as

$$\dot{\pi}^s = \left(\frac{\partial \ln \pi^s}{\partial \ln p^s}\right)\dot{p}^s + \sum_n \left(\frac{\partial \ln \pi^s}{\partial \ln w_n^s}\right)\dot{w}_n^s + \frac{\partial \ln \pi^s}{\partial t}$$

$$= \frac{1}{\pi^s}\left\{py\dot{p}^s - c^s\sum_n S_n^s\dot{w}_n^s\right\} + \frac{\partial \ln \pi^s}{\partial t}, \tag{8.4.3}$$

since $\partial \pi^s/\partial p = y$ and $\partial \pi^s/\partial w_n^s = -x_n, n = 1, \ldots, N$, by Hotelling's lemma. Since shadow profit can also be expressed as $\pi^s = py - \Sigma_n w_n^s x_n$, we have

$$\dot{\pi}^s = \frac{py}{\pi^s}\{\dot{y} + \dot{p}\} - \frac{c^s}{\pi^s}\sum_n \{S_n^s\dot{x}_n + S_n^s\dot{w}_n^s\}. \tag{8.4.4}$$

Setting equations (8.4.3) and (8.4.4) equal yields, after some algebraic manipulations,

$$\pi^s\left(\frac{\partial \ln \pi^s}{\partial t}\right) = py\left(\dot{y} - \sum_n S_n\dot{x}_n\right) + py\sum_n S_n\dot{x}_n$$

$$- c^s\sum_n S_n^s\dot{x}_n + py\left(\frac{\partial u}{\partial t}\right)$$

$$= py(T\dot{F}P) - py(\varepsilon^s - 1)\sum_n S_n^s\dot{x}_n$$

$$- py\sum_n (S_n^s - S_n)\dot{x}_n + py\left(\frac{\partial u}{\partial t}\right), \tag{8.4.5}$$

where $\varepsilon^s = \Sigma_n(\partial \ln y/\partial \ln x_n)$ evaluated using the first-order conditions for profit maximization, so that $\varepsilon^s = \Sigma_n w_n^s x_n/py = c^s/py$. Alternatively, $\varepsilon^s = [1 - (\partial \ln \pi^s/\partial \ln p^s)^{-1}]$. Solving equation (8.4.5) for the measure of productivity change yields

$$T\dot{F}P = \frac{\pi^s}{py}\frac{\partial \ln \pi^s}{\partial t} + (\varepsilon^s - 1)\sum_n S_n^s\dot{x}_n + \sum_n (S_n^s - S_n)\dot{x}_n - \frac{\partial u}{\partial t}. \tag{8.4.6}$$

Equation (8.4.6) provides a decomposition of dual productivity change into four components. Applying the envelope theorem to equation (8.4.2) yields $\partial \pi^s/\partial t = p^s \cdot [\partial f(x, t; \beta)/\partial t]$, which in turn implies that $(\pi^s/py)(\partial \ln \pi^s/\partial t) = [f(x, t; \beta)]^{-1} \cdot [\partial f(x, t; \beta)/\partial t]$. Thus the first component on the right-hand side of equation (8.4.6) is equivalent to $T\Delta$ in equations (8.2.5) and (8.2.6). Similarly ε^s and the S_n^s are the same as ε and the S_n in equations (8.2.5) and (8.2.6) when the first-order conditions for profit maximization are imposed. Consequently the second component on the right-hand side of equation (8.4.6) provides a dual measure of the contribution of scale economies to productivity change. Also when $\xi_n = 0 \; \forall n$, $S_n^s = S_n$ and the third component on the right-hand side of equation (8.4.6) disappears. Finally the fourth component on the right-hand side of equation (8.4.6) is a dual measure of the contribution of output-oriented technical efficiency change to productivity change, and corresponds to $TE\Delta$ in equations (8.2.5) and (8.2.6).

There is, however, one important difference between the decomposition in equation (8.2.5) and that in equation (8.4.6). In deriving equation (8.2.5) we used quantity data only, and we did not impose any optimization conditions explicitly, whereas in equation (8.4.6) we used both quantity and price data, and we imposed a profit maximization condition in the allocation of the input and output quantities. It is these optimization conditions that enable us to show that the primal and dual productivity change decompositions are identical. In the absence of these conditions, the two decompositions can differ, as they did in the cost-oriented analysis in Section 8.3.

Each of the terms appearing on the right-hand side of equation (8.4.6) can be expressed in terms of the shadow profit function and its derivatives, and so estimation of the shadow profit function enables one to estimate and decompose dual productivity growth. The requisite terms and their expressions are as follows:

$$py = \pi^s \left(\frac{\partial \ln \pi^s}{\partial \ln p^s} \right),$$

$$(\varepsilon^s - 1) = -\left(\frac{\partial \ln \pi^s}{\partial \ln p^s} \right)^{-1},$$

$$S_n^s = \frac{\partial \ln \pi^s / \partial \ln w_n^s}{\Sigma_k (\partial \ln \pi^s / \partial \ln w_k^s)}, \qquad n = 1, \ldots, N,$$

$$S_n = \frac{(\partial \ln \pi^s / \partial \ln w_n^s)(w_n / w_n^s)}{\Sigma_k [\partial \ln \pi^s / \partial \ln w_k^s)(w_k / w_k^s)]}, \qquad n = 1, \ldots, N,$$

$$\dot{x}_n = \frac{\partial^2 \ln \pi^s}{\partial \ln w_n^s \partial t} \left[\frac{\partial \ln \pi^s}{\partial \ln w_n^s} \right]^{-1} + \frac{\partial \ln \pi^s}{\partial t} - \frac{\partial \ln w_n^s}{\partial t}, \qquad n = 1, \ldots, N.$$

The productivity growth decomposition given in equation (8.4.6) can also be expressed in terms of the profit frontier $\pi(p, w, t; \beta)$. In this decomposition we define returns to scale and technical change on the profit frontier and rewrite equation (8.4.6) as

$$T\dot{F}P = \frac{\pi}{py}\frac{\partial \ln \pi}{\partial t} + (\varepsilon - 1)\sum_n S_n \dot{x}_n - \frac{\partial u}{\partial t} + \rho(p,w,t,\xi,u), \qquad (8.4.7)$$

where

$$\rho(p,w,t,\xi,u) = \frac{\pi^s}{py}\frac{\partial \ln \pi^s}{\partial t} - \left[\frac{\partial \ln \pi}{\partial \ln p}\right]^{-1}\frac{\partial \ln \pi}{\partial t} + (\varepsilon^s - 1)\sum_n S_n^s \dot{x}_n$$
$$- (\varepsilon - 1)\sum_n S_n \dot{x}_n + \sum_n (S_n^s - S_n)\dot{x}_n.$$

In this formulation dual productivity change is decomposed into a technical change component, a scale component, and an efficiency change component, each defined relative to the profit frontier $\pi(p, w, t; \beta)$, and a miscellaneous term. The miscellaneous term is zero if technical change is the same along $\pi(p, w, t; \beta)$ and $\pi^s(p^s, w^s, t; \beta)$, if returns to scale are the same along $\pi(p, w, t; \beta)$ and $\pi^s(p^s, w^s, t; \beta)$, and if shadow input cost shares coincide with actual input cost shares. Expressions for ε and the S_n can be obtained from the expressions for ε^s and the S_n^s given previously, by substituting π for π^s, w_n for w_n^s, and p for p^s. Note that ρ depends on output-oriented technical inefficiency u, and so $\rho \neq 0$ even in the absence of input allocative inefficiency.

8.4.2 Estimation and Decomposition

In this section we consider estimation of the productivity change components that are derived from the shadow profit function $\pi^s(p^s, w^s, t; \beta)$. A single-output and multiple-input production technology is assumed. Our starting point is the relationship between actual profit $\pi = py - w^T x$ and shadow profit $\pi^s(p^s, w^s, t; \beta)$ in the presence of both technical and allocative inefficiencies. From the relationships developed in Chapters 5 and 6 we have

$$\ln \pi = \ln \pi^s + \ln\left[SR^s - \sum_n SC_n^s \cdot \exp\{\xi_n\}\right], \qquad (8.4.8)$$

where

$$\ln \pi^s = \beta_o + \beta_p \ln p^s + \sum_n \beta_n \ln w_n^s + \beta_t t + \frac{1}{2}\beta_{pp}(\ln p^s)^2$$
$$+ \frac{1}{2}\sum_n\sum_k \beta_{nk} \ln w_n^s \ln w_k^s + \frac{1}{2}\beta_{tt}t^2 + \sum_n \beta_{pn} \ln p^s \ln w_n^s$$
$$+ \beta_{pt} \ln p^s t + \sum_n \beta_{nt} \ln w_n^s t, \qquad (8.4.9)$$

$$SR^s = \beta_p + \beta_{pp} \ln p^s + \sum_n \beta_{pn} \ln w_n^s + \beta_{pt} t, \tag{8.4.10}$$

$$-SC_n^s = \beta_n + \sum_k \beta_{nk} \ln w_k^s + \beta_{pn} \ln p^s + \beta_{nt} t, \qquad n = 1, \ldots, N, \tag{8.4.11}$$

and $SR^s = p^s y/\pi^s = \partial \ln \pi^s / \partial \ln p^s$ and $SC_n^s = w_n^s x_n / \pi^s = -\partial \ln \pi^s / \partial \ln w_n^s$, $n = 1, \ldots, N$, are shadow profit shares. The shadow profit function $\pi^s(p^s, w^s, t; \beta)$ is homogeneous of degree +1 in (p^s, w^s), which together with symmetry imposes the parameter restrictions $\beta_p + \Sigma_n \beta_n = 1$, $\beta_{pp} + \Sigma_n \beta_{pn} = 0$, $\beta_{pn} + \Sigma_k \beta_{nk} = 0 \; \forall n$, $\beta_{pt} + \Sigma_n \beta_{nt} = 0$, $\beta_{nk} = \beta_{kn} \; \forall n \neq k$. The actual profit share equations are

$$SR = \frac{py}{\pi} = \frac{SR^s}{SR^s - \Sigma_k SC_k^s \cdot \exp\{\xi_k\}}, \tag{8.4.12}$$

$$SC_n = \frac{w_n x_n}{\pi} = \frac{SC_n^s \cdot \exp\{\xi_n\}}{SR^s - \Sigma_k SC_k^s \cdot \exp\{\xi_k\}}, \qquad n = 1, \ldots, N. \tag{8.4.13}$$

The problem is to estimate the system of equations (8.4.12) and (8.4.13). However even if we assume that the allocative inefficiencies are fixed parameters invariant through time and across producers, this system cannot be estimated in the same way as the corresponding cost system can be estimated. The reason for this is that the profit share equations are affected by the presence of technical inefficiency via the output shadow price p^s. That is, SR^s and the SC_n^s depend on u, and since u is random it is virtually impossible to derive the distribution of the error vector (or simplify the variance–covariance matrix) in the system of equations (8.4.12) and (8.4.13).

Here we suggest three methods of estimation, although none of these methods is entirely satisfactory. The first approach uses a very restrictive specification of production technology, which simplifies matters considerably at an equally considerable sacrifice of flexibility. The second and third approaches retain flexibility, but they are difficult to estimate.

We begin by assuming a Cobb–Douglas functional form, in which case the deterministic production frontier is

$$\ln y = b_o + \sum_n b_n \ln x_n + b_t t - u, \tag{8.4.14}$$

and the corresponding shadow profit frontier is

$$\ln \pi^s = \beta_o + \beta_p \ln p^s + \sum_n \beta_n \ln w_n^s + \beta_t t, \tag{8.4.15}$$

where $\beta_p = 1 - \Sigma_n \beta_n$, $\beta_n = -b_n/(1 - \Sigma_n b_n)$, $n = 1, \ldots, N$, and $\Sigma_n b_n < 1$. In this simplified model the input profit share equations become

$$SC_n = \frac{\beta_n \cdot \exp\{\xi_n\}}{(1 - \Sigma_k \beta_k) + \Sigma_k \beta_k \cdot \exp\{\xi_k\}}, \qquad n = 1, \ldots, N, \tag{8.4.16}$$

and the output profit share equation is $SR = 1 - \Sigma_n SC_n$.

It is clear from equations (8.4.16) that even though we have restricted ourselves to the Cobb–Douglas case, the allocative errors ξ_n do not appear linearly in the actual profit share equations. What this means is that if one considers the ξ_n as random variables, estimation of the actual profit share equations in (8.4.16) will still be difficult. This problem can, however, be avoided if one uses the production frontier and the first-order conditions for profit maximization, and considers the system of equations

$$\ln y - b_o - \sum_n b_n \ln x_n - b_t t = v - u,$$

$$\ln x_n - \sum_k b_k \ln x_k - b_t t - \ln p + \ln w_n - \ln b_n - \ln b_o = \xi_n - u,$$

$$n = 1, \ldots, N. \tag{8.4.17}$$

In this specification $v \sim$ iid $N(0, \sigma_v^2)$ is a random-noise error component and $u \geq 0$ represents output-oriented technical inefficiency. If distributional assumptions are imposed on u and the ξ_n, this system can be estimated following procedures outlined in Kumbhakar (1987, 1990). Once the parameters are estimated [including u from the generalization of the JLMS procedure given in Kumbhakar (1987)], all of the productivity change components given at the end of Section 8.4.1 can be derived.

Next we return to the original system of profit share equations given in equations (8.4.12) and (8.4.13), which are based on a flexible translog specification. It is important to note that even if u (embedded in p^s) and the ξ_n are time invariant, productivity change is nonetheless not independent of technical or allocative inefficiencies. This is because π^s, ε^s, and the S_n^s all depend on u and the ξ_n. However if the allocative inefficiencies ξ_n are modeled as fixed parameters, invariant across producers and through time, and if the technical inefficiencies u are modeled as time-invariant parameters, then it is possible to estimate the system (8.4.12) and (8.4.13) using a nonlinear ITSUR approach. However if the number of producers is large, estimation is still likely to be a problem.

The final approach to estimation we consider is based on an approach we introduced in Chapter 6. We begin by rewriting the shadow profit share equations (8.4.10) and (8.4.11) as $SR^s = SR^o - u\beta_{pp}$ and $-SC_n^s = -SC_n^o - u\beta_{pn}$, $n = 1, \ldots, N$, where

$$SR^o = \beta_p + \beta_{pp} \ln p + \sum_n \beta_{pn} \ln w_n^s + \beta_{pt}t,$$

$$-SC_n^o = \beta_n + \sum_k \beta_{nk} \ln w_k^s + \beta_{pn} \ln p + \beta_{nt}t, \qquad n = 1, \ldots, N.$$

Then the denominators in equations (8.4.12) and (8.4.13) become

$$SR^s - \sum_k SC_k^s \cdot \exp\{\xi_k\} = SR^o - \sum_k SC_k^o \cdot \exp\{\xi_k\} - uA_o$$

$$= D_o - uA_o,$$

where $A_o = \beta_{pp} + \Sigma_k \beta_{pk} \cdot \exp\{\xi_k\}$. Using these results, the actual profit share equations can be rewritten as

$$\frac{D_o SR - SR^o}{A_o SR - \beta_{pp}} = u,$$

$$\frac{D_o SC_n - SC_n^o}{A_o SC_n + \beta_{pn}} = u, \qquad n = 1, \ldots, N. \qquad (8.4.18)$$

Next we eliminate u from these actual profit share equations by subtracting each input profit share equation from the output profit share equation to obtain

$$\frac{D_o SR - SR^o}{A_o SR - \beta_{pp}} - \frac{D_o SC_n - SC_n^o}{A_o SC_n + \beta_{pn}} = \eta_n, \qquad n = 1, \ldots, N, \qquad (8.4.19)$$

where the η_n are classical error terms. There is no loss of information in using N of $N + 1$ profit share equations, since only N share equations are independent. Assuming that the ξ_n are producer- and time-invariant fixed parameters, and that the error vector η has zero mean and constant variance–covariance matrix, the system of equations (8.4.19) can be estimated using the nonlinear ITSUR procedure. As can be seen from the expressions for SR^o and the SC_n^o, the system in (8.4.19) is highly nonlinear. The only comfort is that the parameters are estimated without making any distributional assumptions. Technical inefficiency u is not estimated from the system in (8.4.19). It can, however, be estimated from (8.4.18), from the mean of the left-hand sides of the $N + 1$ profit share equations using the estimated parameters from equations (8.4.19). Since some of the parameters in π^s do not appear in the profit share equations, and are therefore not estimated, we need another step to estimate the remaining parameters. This step involves use of the shadow profit function in (8.4.9), after substituting the parameters already estimated, to obtain a regression equation of the form $Z = \beta_o + \beta_t t + (1/2)\beta_{tt}t^2$, where $Z = \ln \pi^s - \ln[SR^s - \Sigma_n SC_n^s \cdot \exp\{\xi_n\}]$ – all terms on the right-hand side of (8.4.9) except the intercept and the terms involving t and t^2.

8.4.3 An Extension to Multiple Outputs

As in Section 8.3.3 we define productivity change in the multiple-output case as $T\dot{F}P = \dot{Y} - \dot{X} = \Sigma_m R_m \dot{y}_m - \Sigma_n S_n \dot{x}_n$. Again we work with a profit function $\pi(p, w, t; \beta)$ and a shadow profit function $\pi^s(p^s, w^s, t; \beta)$, where now $p = (p_1, \ldots, p_M)$ and $p^s = p \cdot \exp\{-u\}$. Totally differentiating the shadow profit function yields

$$\dot{\pi}^s = \sum_m \left(\frac{\partial \ln \pi^s}{\partial \ln p_m^s}\right)\dot{p}_m^s + \sum_n \left(\frac{\partial \ln \pi^s}{\partial \ln w_n^s}\right)\dot{w}_n^s + \frac{\partial \ln \pi^s}{\partial t}$$

$$= \frac{1}{\pi^s}\left\{R\sum_m R_m \dot{p}_m^s - C^s \sum_n S_n^s \dot{w}_n^s\right\} + \frac{\partial \ln \pi^s}{\partial t}, \qquad (8.4.20)$$

where $R = \Sigma_m p_m y_m$ and $R_m = p_m y_m / R$, $m = 1, \ldots, M$. Since shadow profit can also be expressed as $\pi^s = \Sigma_m p_m y_m - \Sigma_n w_n^s x_n$, we obtain

$$\dot{\pi}^s = \frac{R}{\pi^s}\left\{\sum_m R_m \dot{y}_m + \sum_m R_m \dot{p}_m\right\} - \frac{C^s}{\pi^s}\sum_n \{S_n \dot{x}_n + S_n \dot{w}_n^s\}. \qquad (8.4.21)$$

Equating equations (8.4.20) and (8.4.21) yields

$$\pi^s\left(\frac{\partial \ln \pi^s}{\partial t}\right) = R\left(\sum_m R_m \dot{y}_m - \sum_n S_n \dot{x}_n\right)$$

$$+ R\sum_n S_n \dot{x}_n - C^s \sum_n S_n \dot{x}_n + \frac{R \partial u}{\partial t}$$

$$= R(T\dot{F}P) - R(\varepsilon^s - 1)\sum_n S_n^s \dot{x}_n$$

$$- R\sum_n \{S_n^s - S_n\}\dot{x}_n + \frac{R \partial u}{\partial t}, \qquad (8.4.22)$$

from which we obtain the following expression for dual productivity change:

$$T\dot{F}P = \frac{\pi^s}{R}\frac{\partial \ln \pi^s}{\partial t} + (\varepsilon^s - 1)\sum_n S_n^s \dot{x}_n + \sum_n \{S_n^s - S_n\}\dot{x}_n - \frac{\partial u}{\partial t},$$

(8.4.23)

which is identical to the single-output productivity change decomposition given in equation (8.4.6), apart from the replacement of py with $R = \Sigma_m p_m y_m$. The interpretation of this decomposition, and of its relationship to the primal decomposition in equations (8.2.5) and (8.2.6), is essentially unchanged.

One feature of equation (8.4.23) warrants mention, because it has no counterpart in the single-output case. The first component on the right-hand side of equation (8.4.23) can be rewritten as

$$\frac{\pi^s}{R}\frac{\partial \ln \pi^s}{\partial t} = \frac{1}{R}\frac{\partial \pi^s}{\partial t}$$

$$= \frac{1}{R}\sum_m p_m\left(\frac{\partial y_m}{\partial t}\right)$$

$$= \sum_m R_m\left(\frac{\partial \ln y_m}{\partial t}\right).$$

(8.4.24)

Thus the technical change component of productivity change in equation (8.4.23) can also be interpreted as a revenue share weighted average of output-specific rates of technical change. Equation (8.4.24) is thus a dual multiple-output version of the primal technical change component $T\Delta$ appearing in equation (8.2.2).

Estimation is difficult in the single-output case, as we mentioned in Section 8.4.2. The problems there involved nonlinearities rather than the number of inputs and outputs, so adding additional outputs to the model causes no serious additional complications. Nonetheless, it does not make estimation any easier.

8.5 A GUIDE TO THE LITERATURE

A good introduction to index number approaches to productivity change measurement is provided by Balk (1998). More detailed surveys are provided by Diewert (1981a, b, 1987, 1992); these four papers, and others as well, are collected in Diewert and Nakamura (1993).

The primal approach to the econometric estimation of productivity change originated with Solow (1957), who assumed constant returns to scale and technical efficiency, and associated productivity change with technical change. The fact that Solow found such a large residual [which he called productivity growth and Abramovitz (1956) called "a measure of our ignorance"] in the United States during the first half of the twentieth century led to the development of growth accounting. The objective of growth accounting was to eliminate various errors of aggregation and measurement, in an effort to minimize the unexplained residual and to arrive at a more accurate measure of productivity change. Influential work of Denison and Jorgenson and Griliches is contained in a special issue of the *Survey of Current Business* (1972).

The next development in the econometric estimation of productivity change resulted from the application of duality theory to the problem. Ohta (1974) derived the relationships between primal and dual cost measures of scale economies and technical change. Caves, Christensen, and Swanson (1980), Denny, Fuss, and Waverman (1981), and Nadiri and Schankerman (1981) used flexible cost functions to estimate and decompose dual productivity change. These last two papers, and several other productivity studies exploiting duality theory, appear in an excellent conference volume edited by Cowing and Stevenson (1981). A closely related body of literature concerns the measurement, estimation, and decomposition of productivity change in the presence of what Berndt and Fuss (1986) call "temporary equilibrium," due perhaps to the presence of quasi-fixed inputs. Early contributions to this literature include Caves, Christensen, and Swanson (1981), Hulten (1986), Morrison (1985, 1986), and Schankerman and Nadiri (1986), and a comprehensive survey is provided by Morrison (1993).

The introduction of efficiency change as a source of productivity change was pioneered by Nishimizu and Page (1982), who used a deterministic translog production frontier to decompose productivity change in Yugoslavia into technical change and technical efficiency change. Much later Bauer (1990a) merged the work cited in the previous paragraph with that of Nishimizu and Page to derive detailed primal and dual (cost) decompositions of productivity change. Much of the material in Sections 8.2 and 8.3 is based on Bauer's work. Despite the fact that Bauer's work is nearly a decade old, little subsequent effort has been devoted to the introduction of efficiency change into econometric models of productivity change. Surveys of the literature, both econometric and noneconometric, are provided by Grosskopf (1993) and Lovell (1996). More recently interest in an econometric approach to the construction of Malmquist-type productivity indexes has grown rapidly. Noteworthy examples include Atkinson and Cornwell (1998b), who contrast frontier and nonfrontier approaches; Atkinson and Primont (1998), who use shadow cost and distance functions; Coelli (1997), who uses a stochastic production frontier approach; and Fuentes, Grifell-Tatjé, and Perelman (1997), who use stochastic distance functions.

References

Abramovitz, M. (1956) "Resource and Output Trends in the United States since 1870," *American Economic Review* 46:2 (May), 5–23.

Afriat, S. N. (1972) "Efficiency Estimation of Production Functions," *International Economic Review* 13:3 (October), 568–98.

Ahmad, M., and B. E. Bravo-Ureta (1996) "Technical Efficiency Measures for Dairy Farms Using Panel Data: A Comparison of Alternative Model Specifications," *Journal of Productivity Analysis* 7:4 (October), 399–415.

Ahn, S. C., Y. H. Lee, and P. Schmidt (1994) "GMM Estimation of a Panel Data Regression Model with Time-Varying Individual Effects," Working Paper, Department of Economics, Michigan State University, East Lansing, MI.

Aigner, D. J., T. Amemiya, and D. J. Poirier (1976) "On the Estimation of Production Frontiers: Maximum Likelihood Estimation of the Parameters of a Discontinuous Density Function," *International Economic Review* 17:2 (June), 377–96.

Aigner, D. J., and S. F. Chu (1968) "On Estimating the Industry Production Function," *American Economic Review* 58:4 (September), 826–39.

Aigner, D. J., C. A. K. Lovell, and P. Schmidt (1977) "Formulation and Estimation of Stochastic Frontier Production Function Models," *Journal of Econometrics* 6:1 (July), 21–37.

Aigner, D. J., and P. Schmidt, eds. (1980) "Specification and Estimation of Frontier Production, Profit and Cost Functions," *Journal of Econometrics* 13:1 (May).

Akhavein, J. D., A. N. Berger, and D. B. Humphrey (1997) "The Effects of Megamergers on Efficiency and Prices: Evidence from a Bank Profit Function," *Review of Industrial Organization* 12, 95–139.

Alchian, A. (1965) "Some Economics of Property Rights," *Il Politico* 30:4 (December), 816–29.

Alchian, A., and R. Kessel (1962) "Competition, Monopoly, and the Pursuit of Money," in *Aspects of Labor Economics*. Princeton, NJ: Princeton University Press for the National Bureau of Economic Research.

311

Ali, F., A. Parikh, and M. K. Shah (1994) "Measurement of Profit Efficiency Using Behavioural and Stochastic Frontier Approaches," *Applied Economics* 26, 181–88.

Ali, M., and J. C. Flinn (1989) "Profit Efficiency among Basmati Rice Producers in Pakistan Punjab," *American Journal of Agricultural Economics* 71:2 (May), 303–10.

Arrow, K. J., H. B. Chenery, B. S. Minhas, and R. M. Solow (1961) "Capital-Labor Substitution and Economic Efficiency," *Review of Economics and Statistics* 63:3 (August), 225–50.

Atkinson, S. E., and C. Cornwell (1993) "Measuring Technical Efficiency with Panel Data: A Dual Approach," *Journal of Econometrics* 59, 257–62.

Atkinson, S. E., and C. Cornwell (1994a) "Parametric Estimation of Technical and Allocative Inefficiency with Panel Data," *International Economic Review* 35:1 (February), 231–44.

Atkinson, S. E., and C. Cornwell (1994b) "Estimation of Output and Input Technical Efficiency Using a Flexible Functional Form and Panel Data," *International Economic Review* 35:1 (February), 245–55.

Atkinson, S. E., and C. Cornwell (1998a) "Profit versus Cost Frontier Estimation of Price and Technical Inefficiency: A Parametric Approach with Panel Data," *Southern Economic Journal* 64:3 (January), 753–64.

Atkinson, S. E., and C. Cornwell (1998b) "Estimating Radial Measures of Productivity Growth: Frontier vs. Non-Frontier Approaches," *Journal of Productivity Analysis* 10:1 (July), 35–46.

Atkinson, S. E., R. Färe, and D. Primont (1998) "Stochastic Estimation of Firm Inefficiency Using Distance Functions," Working Paper, Department of Economics, University of Georgia, Athens, GA.

Atkinson, S. E., and R. Halvorsen (1980) "A Test of Relative and Absolute Price Efficiency in Regulated Utilities," *Review of Economics and Statistics* 62:1 (February), 81–88.

Atkinson, S. E., and R. Halvorsen (1984) "Parametric Efficiency Tests, Economies of Scale, and Input Demand in U.S. Electric Power Generation," *International Economic Review* 25:3 (October), 647–62.

Atkinson, S. E., and R. Halvorsen (1986) "The Relative Efficiency of Public and Private Firms in a Regulated Environment: The Case of U.S. Electric Utilities," *Journal of Public Economics* 29, 281–94.

Atkinson, S. E., and R. Halvorsen (1992) "Estimating a Non-Minimum Cost Function for Hospitals: Comment," *Southern Economic Journal* 58:4 (April), 1114–17.

Atkinson, S. E., and J. Kerkvliet (1989) "Dual Measures of Monopoly and Monopsony Power: An Application to Regulated Electric Utilities," *Review of Economics and Statistics* 71, 250–57.

Atkinson, S. E., and D. Primont (1998) "Stochastic Estimation of Firm Technology, Inefficiency and Productivity Growth Using Shadow Cost and Distance Functions," Working Paper, Department of Economics, University of Georgia, Athens, GA.

Audibert, M. (1997) "Technical Inefficiency Effects among Paddy Farmers in the Villages of the 'Office du Niger,' Mali, West Africa," *Journal of Productivity Analysis* 8:4 (November), 379–94.

Averch, H., and L. L. Johnson (1962) "Behavior of the Firm under Regulatory Constraint," *American Economic Review* 52:5 (December), 1052–69.

Balk, B. (1997) "The Decomposition of Cost Efficiency and the Canonical Form of Cost Function and Cost Share Equations," *Economics Letters* 55, 45–51.

Balk, B. (1998) *Industrial Price, Quantity, and Productivity Indexes: The Micro-Economic Theory and an Application.* Boston: Kluwer Academic Publishers.

Balk, B. M., and G. van Leeuwen (1997) "Parametric Estimation of Technical and Allocative Efficiencies and Productivity Changes: A Case Study," Research Paper No. 9728, Division Research and Development, Department of Statistical Methods, Statistics Netherlands, Voorburg, The Netherlands.

Baltagi, B. H., and J. M. Griffin (1988) "A General Index of Technical Change," *Journal of Political Economy* 96:1 (February), 20–41.

Barten, A. P. (1969) "Maximum Likelihood Estimation of a Complete System of Demand Equations," *European Economic Review* 1 (Fall), 7–73.

Battese, G. E. (1992) "Frontier Production Functions and Technical Efficiency: A Survey of Empirical Applications in Agricultural Economics," *Agricultural Economics* 7, 185–208.

Battese, G. E., and S. S. Broca (1997) "Functional Forms of Stochastic Frontier Production Functions and Models for Technical Inefficiency Effects: A Comparative Study for Wheat Farmers in Pakistan," *Journal of Productivity Analysis* 8:4 (November), 395–414.

Battese, G. E., and T. J. Coelli (1988) "Prediction of Firm-Level Technical Efficiencies with a Generalized Frontier Production Function and Panel Data," *Journal of Econometrics* 38, 387–99.

Battese, G. E., and T. J. Coelli (1992) "Frontier Production Functions, Technical Efficiency and Panel Data: With Application to Paddy Farmers in India," *Journal of Productivity Analysis* 3:1/2 (June), 153–69.

Battese, G. E., and T. J. Coelli (1995) "A Model for Technical Inefficiency Effects in a Stochastic Frontier Production Function for Panel Data," *Empirical Economics* 20, 325–32.

Battese, G. E., and T. J. Coelli, eds. (1997) "Efficiency and Productivity Measurement," *Journal of Productivity Analysis* 8:4 (November).

Battese, G. E., and G. S. Corra (1977) "Estimation of a Production Frontier Model: With Application to the Pastoral Zone off Eastern Australia," *Australian Journal of Agricultural Economics* 21:3, 169–79.

Bauer, P. W. (1985) "An Analysis of Multiproduct Technology and Efficiency Using the Joint Cost Function and Panel Data: An Application to the U.S. Airline Industry," Unpublished Doctoral Dissertation, University of North Carolina, Chapel Hill, NC.

Bauer, P. W. (1990a) "Decomposing TFP Growth in the Presence of Cost Inefficiency, Nonconstant Returns to Scale, and Technological Progress," *Journal of Productivity Analysis* 1:4 (June), 287–99.

Bauer, P. W. (1990b) "Recent Developments in the Econometric Estimation of Frontiers," *Journal of Econometrics* 46:1/2 (October/November), 39–56.

Bauer, P. W., A. N. Berger, and D. B. Humphrey (1993) "Efficiency and Productivity Growth in U.S. Banking," in H. O. Fried, C. A. K. Lovell, and S. S. Schmidt, eds., *The Measurement of Productive Efficiency*. New York: Oxford University Press.

Bauer, P. W., and D. Hancock (1993) "The Efficiency of the Federal Reserve in Providing Check Processing Services," *Journal of Banking and Finance* 17:2/3 (April), 287–311.

Beckers, D. E., and C. J. Hammond (1987) "A Tractable Likelihood Function for the Normal-Gamma Stochastic Frontier Model," *Economics Letters* 24, 33–38.

Bera, A. K., and N. C. Mallick (1998) "Information Matrix Tests for the Composite Error Frontier Model," Working Paper, Department of Economics, University of Illinois, Champaign, IL.

Bera, A. K., and S. C. Sharma (1996) "Estimating Production Uncertainty in Stochastic Frontier Production Frontier Models," Working Paper, Department of Economics, University of Illinois, Champaign, IL.

Berger, A. N. (1993) "'Distribution-Free' Estimates of Efficiency in the U.S. Banking Industry and Tests of the Standard Distributional Assumptions," *Journal of Productivity Analysis* 4:3 (September), 261–92.

Berger, A. N., P. L. Brockett, W. W. Cooper, and J. T. Pastor, eds. (1997) "New Approaches for Analyzing and Evaluating the Performance of Financial Institutions," *European Journal of Operational Research* 98:2 (April 16).

Berger, A. N., D. Cummins, and M. Weiss (1996) "The Coexistence of Multiple Distribution Systems for Financial Services: The Case of Property Liability Insurance," Working Paper, Wharton Financial Institutions Center, University of Pennsylvania, Philadelphia, PA.

Berger, A. N., D. Hancock, and D. B. Humphrey (1993) "Bank Efficiency Derived from the Profit Function," *Journal of Banking and Finance* 17:2/3 (April), 317–47.

Berger, A. N., and D. B. Humphrey (1991) "The Dominance of Inefficiencies Over Scale and Product Mix Economies in Banking," *Journal of Monetary Economics* 28, 117–48.

Berger, A. N., and D. B. Humphrey (1992) "Measurement and Efficiency Issues in Commercial Banking," in Z. Griliches, ed., *Output Measurement in the Service Sectors*. National Bureau of Economic Research Studies in Income and Wealth, Volume 56. Chicago: University of Chicago Press.

Berger, A. N., and L. J. Mester (1997) "Inside the Black Box: What Explains Differences in the Efficiencies of Financial Institutions?" *Journal of Banking and Finance* 21:7 (July), 895–947.

Berndt, E. R., and L. R. Christensen (1973) "The Translog Function and the Substitution of Equipment, Structures, and Labor in U.S. Manufacturing 1929–1968," *Journal of Econometrics* 1:1 (March), 81–114.

Berndt, E. R., and M. A. Fuss (1986) "Productivity Measurement with Adjustments for Variations in Capacity Utilization and Other Forms of Temporary Equilibrium," *Journal of Econometrics* 33:1/2 (October/November), 7–29.

Bhattacharyya, A., and T. F. Glover (1993) "Profit Inefficiency of Indian Farms: A System Approach," *Journal of Productivity Analysis* 4:4 (November), 391–406.

Bhattacharyya, A., S. C. Kumbhakar, and A. Bhattacharyya (1995) "Ownership Structure and Cost Efficiency: A Study of Publicly Owned Passenger–Bus Transportation Companies in India," *Journal of Productivity Analysis* 6:1 (April), 47–62.

Bhattacharyya, A., E. Parker, and K. Raffiee (1994) "An Examination of the Effect of Ownership on the Relative Efficiency of Public and Private Water Utilities," *Land Economics* 70:2 (May), 197–209.

Boles, J. N. (1966) "Efficiency Squared – Efficient Computation of Efficiency Indexes," *Proceedings of the Thirty Ninth Annual Meeting of the Western Farm Economics Association*, 137–42.

Bressler, R. G. (1966) "The Measurement of Productive Efficiency," *Proceedings of the Thirty Ninth Annual Meeting of the Western Farm Economics Association*, 129–36.

Caudill, S. B., and J. M. Ford (1993) "Biases in Frontier Estimation Due to Heteroskedasticity," *Economics Letters* 41, 17–20.

Caudill, S. B., J. M. Ford, and D. M. Gropper (1995) "Frontier Estimation and Firm-Specific Inefficiency Measures in the Presence of Heteroskedasticity," *Journal of Business and Economic Statistics* 13:1 (January), 105–11.

Caves, D. W., L. R. Christensen, and J. A. Swanson (1980) "Productivity in U.S. Railroads, 1951–1974," *Bell Journal of Economics* 11:1 (Spring), 166–81.

Caves, D. W., L. R. Christensen, and J. A. Swanson (1981) "Productivity Growth, Scale Economies, and Capacity Utilization in U.S. Railroads, 1955–74," *American Economic Review* 71:5 (December), 994–1002.

Charnes, A., W. W. Cooper, and E. Rhodes (1978) "Measuring the Efficiency of Decision-Making Units," *European Journal of Operational Research* 2:6, 429–44.

Christensen, L. R., and W. H. Greene (1976) "Economies of Scale in U.S. Electric Power Generation," *Journal of Political Economy* 84:4, 655–76.

Christensen, L. R., D. W. Jorgenson, and L. J. Lau (1971) "Conjugate Duality and the Transcendental Logarithmic Production Function," *Econometrica* 39, 255–56.

Christensen, L. R., D. W. Jorgenson, and L. J. Lau (1973) "Transcendental Logarithmic Production Frontiers," *Review of Economics and Statistics* 55:1 (February), 28–45.

Cobb, C., and P. H. Douglas (1928) "A Theory of Production," *American Economic Review* Supplement, 18, 139–65.

Coelli, T. (1995) "Estimators and Hypothesis Tests for a Stochastic Frontier Function: A Monte Carlo Analysis," *Journal of Productivity Analysis* 6:4, 247–68.

Coelli, T. (1997) "Total Factor Productivity Growth in Australian Coal-Fired Electricity Generation: A Malmquist Index Approach," Working Paper,

Department of Econometrics, University of New England, Armidale, Australia.

Coelli, T., and S. Perelman (1996) "Efficiency Measurement, Multiple-Output Technologies and Distance Functions: With Application to European Railways," Working Paper, CREPP, Université de Liège, Liège, Belgium.

Coelli, T., D. S. Prasada Rao, and G. E. Battese (1998) *An Introduction to Efficiency and Productivity Analysis*. Boston: Kluwer Academic Publishers.

Cornes, R. (1992) *Duality and Modern Economics*. Cambridge: Cambridge University Press.

Cornwell, C., and P. Schmidt (1996) "Production Frontiers and Efficiency Measurement," in L. Mátyás and P. Sevestre, eds., *The Econometrics of Panel Data: A Handbook of the Theory with Applications*. Second Revised Edition. Boston: Kluwer Academic Publishers.

Cornwell, C., P. Schmidt, and R. C. Sickles (1990) "Production Frontiers with Cross-Sectional and Time-Series Variation in Efficiency Levels," *Journal of Econometrics* 46:1/2 (October/November), 185–200.

Cowing, T. G., and R. E. Stevenson, eds. (1981) *Productivity Measurement in Regulated Industries*. New York: Academic Press.

"Culture of Thrift," *The Economist*, July 12, 1997, 67.

de Alessi, L. (1974) "An Economic Analysis of Government Ownership and Regulation: Theory and the Evidence from the Electric Power Industry," *Public Choice* 19:1, 1–42.

de Alessi, L. (1983) "Property Rights, Transaction Costs, and X-Efficiency: An Essay in Economic Theory," *American Economic Review* 73:1 (March), 64–81.

Debreu, G. (1951) "The Coefficient of Resource Utilization," *Econometrica* 19:3 (July), 273–92.

Debreu, G. (1959) *Theory of Value*. New York: Wiley.

Denny, M., M. Fuss, and L. Waverman (1981) "The Measurement and Interpretation of Total Factor Productivity in Regulated Industries, with an Application to Canadian Telecommunications," in T. G. Cowing and R. E. Stevenson, eds., *Productivity Measurement in Regulated Industries*. New York: Academic Press.

Deprins, D. (1989) *Estimation de Frontières de Production et Mésures de l'Efficacité Technique*. Louvain-la-Neuve, Belgium: CIACO.

Deprins, D., and L. Simar (1989a) "Estimation de Frontières Déterministes avec Facteurs Exogènes d'Inefficacité," *Annales d'Economie et de Statistique* 14, 117–50.

Deprins, D., and L. Simar (1989b) "Estimating Technical Inefficiencies with Corrections for Environmental Conditions with an Application to Railway Companies," *Annals of Public and Cooperative Economics* 60:1 (January/March), 81–102.

DeYoung, R. (1997) "A Diagnostic Test for the Distribution-Free Estimator: An Example Using U.S. Commercial Bank Data," *European Journal of Operational Research* 98:2 (April 16), 243–49.

Diewert, W. E. (1971) "An Application of the Shephard Duality Theorem: A

Generalized Leontief Production Function," *Journal of Political Economy* 79:3 (May/June), 481–507.

Diewert, W. E. (1973) "Functional Forms for Profit and Transformation Functions," *Journal of Economic Theory* 6:3 (June), 284–316.

Diewert, W. E. (1974) "Functional Forms for Revenue and Factor Requirements Functions," *International Economic Review* 15:1 (February), 119–30.

Diewert, W. E. (1981a) "The Theory of Total Factor Productivity Measurement in Regulated Industries," in T. G. Cowing and R. E. Stevenson, eds., *Productivity Measurement in Regulated Industries*. New York: Academic Press.

Diewert, W. E. (1981b) "The Economic Theory of Index Numbers: A Survey," in A. Deaton, ed., *Essays in the Theory and Measurement of Consumer Behaviour in Honour of Sir Richard Stone*. Cambridge: Cambridge University Press.

Diewert, W. E. (1982) "Duality Approaches to Microeconomic Theory," in K. J. Arrow and M. D. Intriligator, eds., *Handbook of Mathematical Economics, Volume II*. Amsterdam: North-Holland.

Diewert, W. E. (1987) "Index Numbers," in J. Eatwell, M. Milgate, and P. Newman, eds., *The New Palgrave: A Dictionary of Economics*, Volume 2. New York: Macmillan.

Diewert, W. E. (1992) "The Measurement of Productivity," *Bulletin of Economic Research* 44:3, 163–98.

Diewert, W. E., and A. O. Nakamura, eds. (1993) *Essays in Index Number Theory, Volume 1*. Amsterdam: North-Holland.

Diewert, W. E., and L. Ostensoe (1988) "Flexible Functional Forms for Profit Functions and Global Curvature Conditions," in W. A. Barnett, E. R. Berndt, and H. White, eds., *Dynamic Econometric Modeling*. Cambridge: Cambridge University Press.

Diewert, W. E., and T. J. Wales (1987) "Flexible Functional Forms and Global Curvature Conditions," *Econometrica* 55:1 (January), 43–68.

Domar, E. D. (1966) "The Soviet Collective Farm as a Producer Cooperative," *American Economic Review* 56:4 (September), 734–57.

Eakin, B. K. (1991) "Allocative Inefficiency in the Production of Hospital Services," *Southern Economic Journal* 58:1 (July), 240–48.

Eakin, B. K., and T. J. Kniesner (1988) "Estimating a Non-Minimum Cost Function for Hospitals," *Southern Economic Journal* 54:3 (January), 583–97.

Eakin, B. K., and T. J. Kniesner (1992) "Estimating a Non-Minimum Cost Function for Hospitals: Reply," *Southern Economic Journal* 58:4 (April), 1118–21.

Färe, R. (1988) *Fundamentals of Production Theory*. New York: Springer-Verlag.

Färe, R., and S. Grosskopf (1994) *Cost and Revenue Constrained Production*. Bilkent University Lecture Series. Berlin: Springer-Verlag.

Färe, R., S. Grosskopf, and C. A. K. Lovell (1985) *The Measurement of Efficiency of Production*. Boston: Kluwer-Nijhoff.

Färe, R., S. Grosskopf, and C. A. K. Lovell (1988) "An Indirect Efficiency Approach to the Evaluation of Producer Performance," *Journal of Public Economics* 37:1 (October), 71–89.

Färe, R., S. Grosskopf, and C. A. K. Lovell (1992) "Indirect Productivity Measurement," *Journal of Productivity Analysis* 2:4 (February), 283–98.

Färe, R., S. Grosskopf, and C. A. K. Lovell (1994) *Production Frontiers.* Cambridge: Cambridge University Press.

Färe, R., and D. Primont (1995) *Multi-Output Production and Duality: Theory and Applications.* Boston: Kluwer Academic Publishers.

Färe, R., and D. Primont (1996) "The Opportunity Cost of Duality," *Journal of Productivity Analysis* 7:2/3 (July), 213–24.

Farrell, M. J. (1957) "The Measurement of Productive Efficiency," *Journal of the Royal Statistical Society,* Series A, General, 120, Part 3, 253–81.

Ferrier, G. D., and C. A. K. Lovell (1990) "Measuring Cost Efficiency in Banking: Econometric and Linear Programming Evidence," *Journal of Econometrics* 46:1/2 (October/November), 229–45.

Fisher, I. (1922) *The Making of Index Numbers.* Boston: Houghton Mifflin.

Food Research Studies (1979) 17:1.

Førsund, F. R., and E. S. Jansen (1977) "On Estimating Average and Best Practice Homothetic Production Functions via Cost Functions," *International Economic Review* 18:2 (June), 463–76.

Førsund, F. R., C. A. K. Lovell, and P. Schmidt (1980) "A Survey of Frontier Production Functions and of Their Relationship to Efficiency Measurement," *Journal of Econometrics* 13:1 (May), 5–25.

Fried, H. O., C. A. K. Lovell, and S. S. Schmidt, eds. (1993) *The Measurement of Productive Efficiency: Techniques and Applications.* New York: Oxford University Press.

Fuentes, H., E. Grifell-Tatjé, and S. Perelman (1997) "A Parametric Stochastic Distance Function Approach for Malmquist Index Estimation: The Case of Spanish Insurance Companies," Working Paper, CREPP, Université de Liège, Liège, Belgium.

Fuss, M. A. (1977) "Dynamic Factor Demand Systems with Explicit Costs of Adjustment," in E. R. Berndt, M. A. Fuss, and L. Waverman, eds., *Dynamic Models of the Industrial Demand for Energy.* Palo Alto, CA: Electric Power Research Institute.

Gallant, A. R. (1987) *Nonlinear Statistical Models.* New York: Wiley.

Gathon, H.-J., and S. Perelman (1992) "Measuring Technical Efficiency in European Railways: A Panel Data Approach," *Journal of Productivity Analysis* 3:1/2 (June), 135–51.

Gong, B.-H., and R. C. Sickles (1989) "Finite Sample Evidence on the Performance of Stochastic Frontier Models Using Panel Data," *Journal of Productivity Analysis* 1:3 (December), 229–61.

Gorman, W. M. (1968) "Measuring the Quantities of Fixed Factors," in J. N. Wolfe, ed., *Value, Capital and Growth: Essays in Honour of Sir John Hicks.* Chicago: Aldine Publishing Co.

Greene, W. H. (1980a) "Maximum Likelihood Estimation of Econometric Frontier Functions," *Journal of Econometrics* 13:1 (May), 27–56.

Greene, W. H. (1980b) "On the Estimation of a Flexible Frontier Production Model," *Journal of Econometrics* 13:1 (May), 101–15.

Greene, W. H. (1990) "A Gamma-Distributed Stochastic Frontier Model," *Journal of Econometrics* 46:1/2 (October/November), 141–64.

Greene, W. H. (1993) "The Econometric Approach to Efficiency Analysis," in H. O. Fried, C. A. K. Lovell, and S. S. Schmidt, eds., *The Measurement of Productive Efficiency: Techniques and Applications.* New York: Oxford University Press.

Greene, W. H. (1997) "Frontier Production Functions," in M. H. Pesaran and P. Schmidt, eds., *Handbook of Applied Econometrics, Volume II: Micro-economics.* Oxford: Blackwell Publishers, Ltd.

Griliches, Z. (1996) "The Discovery of the Residual: A Historical Note," *Journal of Economic Literature* 34:3 (September), 1324–30.

Grosskopf, S. (1993) "Efficiency and Productivity," in H. O. Fried, C. A. K. Lovell, and S. S. Schmidt, eds., *The Measurement of Productive Efficiency: Techniques and Applications.* New York: Oxford University Press.

Gulledge, T. R., and C. A. K. Lovell, eds. (1992) "International Applications of Productivity and Efficiency Analysis," *Journal of Productivity Analysis* 3:1/2 (June).

Hansmann, H. (1988) "Ownership of the Firm," *Journal of Law, Economics and Organization,* 4:2 (Fall), 267–304.

Harris, C. M. (1992) "Technical Efficiency in Australia: Phase I," in R. E. Caves, ed., *Industrial Efficiency in Six Nations.* Cambridge, MA: MIT Press.

Hasan, I., and W. C. Hunter (1996) "Efficiency of Japanese Multinational Banks in the US," *Research in Finance 14* (A. H. Chan, ed.), Greenwich, CT: JAI Press, 157–73.

Hasenkamp, G. (1976) *Specification and Estimation of Multiple-Output Production Functions.* New York: Springer-Verlag.

Hausman, J. A. (1978) "Specification Tests in Econometrics," *Econometrica* 46:6 (November), 1251–71.

Hausman, J. A., and W. E. Taylor (1981) "Panel Data and Unobservable Individual Effects," *Econometrica* 49:6 (November), 1377–98.

Heshmati, A., and S. C. Kumbhakar (1994) "Farm Heterogeneity and Technical Efficiency: Some Results from Swedish Dairy Farms," *Journal of Productivity Analysis* 5:1 (April), 45–61.

Hetemaki, L. (1996) *Essays on the Impact of Pollution Control on a Firm: A Distance Function Approach.* Research Papers 609, Finnish Forest Research Institute, Helsinki, Finland.

Hicks. J. R. (1935) "The Theory of Monopoly: A Survey," *Econometrica* 3:1 (January), 1–20.

Hjalmarsson, L., S. C. Kumbhakar, and A. Heshmati (1996) "DEA, DFA and SFA: A Comparison," *Journal of Productivity Analysis* 7:2/3 (July), 303–27.

Hoch, I. (1955) "Estimation of Production Function Parameters and Testing for Efficiency," *Econometrica* 23:3 (July), 325–26.

Hoch, I. (1962) "Estimation of Production Function Parameters Combining Time-Series and Cross-Section Data," *Econometrica* 30:1 (January), 34–53.

Hollas, D. R., and S. R. Stansell (1988) "An Examination of the Effects of Ownership Form and Price Efficiency: Proprietary, Cooperative and Municipal Electric Utilities," *Southern Economic Journal* 55:2 (October), 336–50.

Holmstrom, B. R., and J. Tirole (1989) "The Theory of the Firm," in R. Schmalensee and R. D. Willig, eds., *Handbook of Industrial Organization, Volume 1*. Amsterdam: Elsevier Science Publishers.

Hopper, W. D. (1965) "Allocation Efficiency in a Traditional Indian Agriculture," *Journal of Farm Economics* 47:3 (August), 611–24.

Horrace, W. C., and P. Schmidt (1995) "Multiple Comparisons with the Best, with Applications to the Efficiency Measurement Problem," Working Paper, Department of Economics, Michigan State University, East Lansing, MI.

Horrace, W. C., and P. Schmidt (1996) "Confidence Statements for Efficiency Estimates from Stochastic Frontier Models," *Journal of Productivity Analysis* 7:2/3 (July), 257–82.

Hotelling, H. (1932) "Edgeworth's Taxation Paradox and the Nature of Demand and Supply Functions," *Journal of Political Economy* 40, 577–616.

Huang, C. J., and J.-T. Liu (1994) "Estimation of a Non-Neutral Stochastic Frontier Production Function," *Journal of Productivity Analysis* 5:2 (June), 171–80.

Hulten, C. R. (1986) "Productivity Change, Capacity Utilization, and the Sources of Efficiency Growth," *Journal of Econometrics* 33:1/2 (October/November), 31–50.

Humphrey, D. B., and L. B. Pulley (1997) "Banks' Responses to Deregulation: Profits, Technology and Efficiency," *Journal of Money, Credit and Banking* 29, 73–93.

Johnston, J. (1960) *Statistical Cost Analysis*. New York: McGraw-Hill.

Jondrow, J., C. A. K. Lovell, I. S. Materov, and P. Schmidt (1982) "On the Estimation of Technical Inefficiency in the Stochastic Frontier Production Function Model," *Journal of Econometrics* 19:2/3 (August), 233–38.

Kahana, N. (1989) "The Duality Approach in the Case of Labour-Managed Firms," *Oxford Economic Papers* 41:3 (July), 567–72.

Kalirajan, K. P. (1990) "On Measuring Economic Efficiency," *Journal of Applied Econometrics* 5, 75–85.

Kalirajan, K. P., and M. B. Obwana (1994a) "Frontier Production Function: The Stochastic Coefficients Approach," *Oxford Bulletin of Economics and Statistics* 56:1, 87–96.

Kalirajan, K. P., and M. B. Obwana (1994b) "A Measurement of Firm- and Input-Specific Technical and Allocative Efficiencies," *Applied Economics* 26, 393–98.

Klein, L. R. (1947) "The Use of Cross-Section Data in Econometrics with Application to a Study of Production of Railroad Services in the United States," mimeograph. New York: National Bureau of Economic Research.

Kmenta, J., and R. F. Gilbert (1968) "Small Sample Properties of Alternative Estimators of Seemingly Unrelated Regressions," *Journal of the American Statistical Association* 63 (December), 1180–1200.

Koopmans, T. C. (1951) "An Analysis of Production as an Efficient Combination of Activities," in T. C. Koopmans, ed., *Activity Analysis of Production and*

Allocation, Cowles Commission for Research in Economics, Monograph No. 13. New York: Wiley.

Kopp, R. J., and W. E. Diewert (1982) "The Decomposition of Frontier Cost Function Deviations into Measures of Technical and Allocative Efficiency," *Journal of Econometrics* 19:2/3 (August), 319–31.

Kumbhakar, S. C. (1987) "The Specification of Technical and Allocative Inefficiency in Stochastic Production and Profit Frontiers," *Journal of Econometrics* 34, 335–48.

Kumbhakar, S. C. (1990) "Production Frontiers, Panel Data, and Time-Varying Technical Inefficiency," *Journal of Econometrics* 46:1/2 (October/November), 201–12.

Kumbhakar, S. C. (1991) "The Measurement and Decomposition of Cost-Efficiency: The Translog Cost System," *Oxford Economic Papers* 43, 667–83.

Kumbhakar, S. C. (1994) "Efficiency Estimation in a Profit Maximizing Model Using Flexible Production Function," *Agricultural Economics* 10, 143–52.

Kumbhakar, S. C. (1996a) "Efficiency Measurement with Multiple Outputs and Multiple Inputs," *Journal of Productivity Analysis* 7:2/3 (July), 225–56.

Kumbhakar, S. C. (1996b) "A Parametric Approach to Efficiency Measurement Using a Flexible Profit Function," *Southern Economic Journal* 63:2 (October), 473–87.

Kumbhakar, S. C. (1996c) "Production Efficiency and Profit Functions: Some Results and Their Implications," Working Paper, Department of Economics, University of Texas, Austin, TX.

Kumbhakar, S. C. (1996d) "Estimation of Cost Efficiency with Heteroskedasticity: An Application to Electricity Utilities," *The Statistician* 45:3, 319–35.

Kumbhakar, S. C. (1997) "Modeling Allocative Inefficiency in a Translog Cost Function and Cost Share Equations: An Exact Relationship," *Journal of Econometrics* 76:1/2 (January/February), 351–56.

Kumbhakar, S. C., and A. Bhattacharyya (1992) "Price Distortions and Resource-Use Efficiency in Indian Agriculture: A Restricted Profit Function Approach," *Review of Economics and Statistics* 74:2 (May), 231–39.

Kumbhakar, S. C., B. Biswas, and D. Bailey (1989) "A Study of Economic Efficiency of Utah Dairy Farmers: A System Approach," *Review of Economics and Statistics* 71:4 (November), 595–604.

Kumbhakar, S. C., S. Ghosh, and J. T. McGuckin (1991) "A Generalized Production Frontier Approach for Estimating Determinants of Inefficiency in US Dairy Farms," *Journal of Business and Economic Statistics* 9:3 (July), 279–86.

Kumbhakar, S. C., and A. Heshmati (1995) "Efficiency Measurement in Swedish Dairy Farms: An Application of Rotating Panel Data, 1976–1988," *American Journal of Agricultural Economics* 77, 660–74.

Kumbhakar, S. C., and L. Hjalmarsson (1993) "Technical Efficiency and Technical Progress in Swedish Dairy Farms," in H. O. Fried, C. A. K. Lovell, and S. S. Schmidt, eds., *The Measurement of Productive Efficiency: Techniques and Applications*. New York: Oxford University Press.

Kumbhakar, S. C., and M. Löthgren (1998) "A Monte Carlo Analysis of Technical Inefficiency Predictors," Working Paper, Department of Economics, University of Texas, Austin, TX.

Lau, L. J. (1972) "Profit Functions of Technologies with Multiple Inputs and Outputs," *Review of Economics and Statistics* 54:3 (August), 281–89.

Lau, L. J. (1976) "A Characterization of the Normalized Restricted Profit Function," *Journal of Economic Theory* 12:1 (February), 131–63.

Lau, L. J. (1978) "Applications of Profit Functions," in M. Fuss and D. McFadden, eds., *Production Economics: A Dual Approach to Theory and Applications, Volume 1*. Amsterdam: North-Holland.

Lau, L. J., and P. A. Yotopoulos (1971) "A Test for Relative Efficiency and Application to Indian Agriculture," *American Economic Review* 61:1 (March), 94–109.

Lau, L. J., and P. A. Yotopoulos (1979) "The Methodological Framework," *Food Research Studies* 17:1, 11–22.

Lee, L.-F. (1983) "A Test for Distributional Assumptions for the Stochastic Frontier Functions," *Journal of Econometrics* 22:3 (August), 245–67.

Lee, L.-F., and W. G. Tyler (1978) "The Stochastic Frontier Production Function and Average Efficiency," *Journal of Econometrics* 7:3 (June), 385–89.

Lee, Y. H., and P. Schmidt (1993) "A Production Frontier Model with Flexible Temporal Variation in Technical Inefficiency," in H. O. Fried, C. A. K. Lovell, and S. S. Schmidt, eds., *The Measurement of Productive Efficiency: Techniques and Applications*. New York: Oxford University Press.

Leibenstein, H. (1966) "Allocative Efficiency vs. 'X-Efficiency'," *American Economic Review* 56:3 (June), 392–415.

Leibenstein, H. (1975) "Aspects of the X-Efficiency Theory of the Firm," *Bell Journal of Economics* 6:2 (Autumn), 580–606.

Leibenstein, H. (1976) *Beyond Economic Man*. Cambridge, MA: Harvard University Press.

Leibenstein, H. (1978) "X-Inefficiency Exists – Reply to an Xorcist," *American Economic Review* 68:1 (March), 203–11.

Leibenstein, H. (1987) *Inside the Firm*. Cambridge, MA: Harvard University Press.

Lewin, A. Y., and C. A. K. Lovell, eds. (1990) "Frontier Analysis: Parametric and Nonparametric Approaches," *Journal of Econometrics* 46:1/2 (October/November).

Lewin, A. Y., and C. A. K. Lovell, eds. (1995) "Productivity Analysis: Parametric and Non-Parametric Applications," *European Journal of Operational Research* 80:3 (February 2).

Lindsay, C. M. (1976) "A Theory of Government Enterprise," *Journal of Political Economy* 84:5 (October), 1061–77.

Lovell, C. A. K. (1996) "Applying Efficiency Measurement Techniques to the Measurement of Productivity Change," *Journal of Productivity Analysis* 7:2/3 (July), 329–40.

Lovell, C. A. K., and R. C. Sickles (1983) "Testing Efficiency Hypotheses in Joint Production: A Parametric Approach," *Review of Economics and Statistics* 65:1 (February), 51–58.

Lozano Vivas, A. (1997) "Profit Efficiency for Spanish Savings Banks," *European Journal of Operational Research* 98:2 (April 16), 381–94.

Maietta, O. W. (1997) "A Measurement of Technical and Allocative Efficiency with a Panel Data of Italian Dairy Farms: The Effect of the Normalisation of the Shadow Price Vector," Working Paper, CSREAM, via Università 96, Portici (NA), Italy.

Malmquist, S. (1953) "Index Numbers and Indifference Surfaces," *Trabajos de Estadistica* 4, 209–42.

Materov, I. S. (1981) "On Full Identification of the Stochastic Production Frontier Model," *Ekonomika i Matematicheskie Metody* 17, 784–88 (in Russian).

McFadden, D. (1978) "Cost, Revenue and Profit Functions," in M. Fuss and D. McFadden, eds., *Production Economics: A Dual Approach to Theory and Applications, Volume 1*. Amsterdam: North-Holland.

Meeusen, W., and J. van den Broeck (1977) "Efficiency Estimation from Cobb–Douglas Production Functions with Composed Error," *International Economic Review* 18:2 (June), 435–44.

Melfi, C. A. (1984) "Estimation and Decomposition of Productive Efficiency in a Panel Data Model: An Application to Electric Utilities," Unpublished Ph.D. Dissertation, University of North Carolina, Chapel Hill, NC.

Mensah, Y. M. (1994) "A Simplification of the Kopp–Diewert Method of Decomposing Cost Efficiency and Some Implications," *Journal of Econometrics* 60, 133–44.

Mester, L. J. (1993) "Efficiency in the Savings and Loan Industry," *Journal of Banking and Finance* 17:2/3 (April), 267–86.

Mester, L. J. (1997) "Measuring Efficiency at US Banks: Accounting for Heterogeneity Is Important," *European Journal of Operational Research* 98:2 (April 16), 230–42.

Morrison, C. J. (1985) "Primal and Dual Measures of Economic Capacity Utilization: An Application to Productivity Measurement in the U.S. Automobile Industry," *Journal of Business and Economic Statistics* 3:4 (October), 312–24.

Morrison, C. J. (1986) "Productivity Measurement with Nonstatic Expectations and Varying Capacity Utilization: An Integrated Approach," *Journal of Econometrics* 33:1/2 (October/November), 51–74.

Morrison, C. J. (1993) *A Microeconomic Approach to the Measurement of Economic Performance*. New York: Springer-Verlag.

Morrison, C. J., and W. E. Johnston (1997) "Efficiency in New Zealand Sheep and Beef Farming: Pre- and Post-Reform," Working Paper, Department of Agricultural and Resource Economics, University of California, Davis, CA.

Mundlak, Y. (1961) "Empirical Production Function Free of Management Bias," *Journal of Farm Economics* 43:1 (February), 44–56.

Nadiri, M. I., and M. A. Schankerman (1981) "The Structure of Production, Technological Change, and the Rate of Growth of Total Factor Productivity in the U.S. Bell System," in T. G. Cowing and R. E. Stevenson, eds., *Productivity Measurement in Regulated Industries*. New York: Academic Press.

Neary, H. M. (1988) "The Comparative Statics of the Ward–Domar LMF: A Profit Function Approach," *Journal of Comparative Economics* (June).

Nerlove, M. (1963) "Returns to Scale in Electricity Supply," in C. Christ, et al., eds., *Measurement in Economics: Studies in Mathematical Economics and Econometrics in Memory of Yehuda Grunfeld*. Stanford, CA: Stanford University Press.

Nishimizu, M., and J. M. Page Jr. (1982) "Total Factor Productivity Growth, Technological Progress and Technical Efficiency Change: Dimensions of Productivity Change in Yugoslavia, 1965–78," *The Economic Journal* 92:368 (December), 920–36.

Niskanen, W. A. Jr. (1971) *Bureaucracy and Representative Government*. Chicago: Aldine Press.

Ohta, M. (1974) "A Note on the Duality between Production and Cost Functions: Rate of Return to Scale and Rate of Technical Progress," *Economic Studies Quarterly* 25:3 (December), 63–65.

Olesen, O. B., N. C. Petersen, and C. A. K. Lovell, eds. (1996) "Efficiency and Frontier Analysis: Proceedings of a Research Workshop on State-of-the-Art and Future Research in Efficiency Analysis," *Journal of Productivity Analysis* 7:2/3 (July).

Olson, J. A., P. Schmidt, and D. M. Waldman (1980) "A Monte Carlo Study of Estimators of Stochastic Frontier Production Functions," *Journal of Econometrics* 13:1 (May), 67–82.

Osiewalski, J., and M. F. J. Steel (1998) "Numerical Tools for the Bayesian Analysis of Stochastic Frontier Models," *Journal of Productivity Analysis* 10:1 (July), 103–17.

Park, B. U., R. C. Sickles, and L. Simar (1998) "Stochastic Panel Frontiers: A Semiparametric Approach," *Journal of Econometrics* 84:2 (June), 273–301.

Park, B. U., and L. Simar (1994) "Efficient Semiparametric Estimation in a Stochastic Frontier Model," *Journal of the American Statistical Association* 89:427 (September), 929–36.

Pitt, M., and L. F. Lee (1981) "The Measurement and Sources of Technical Inefficiency in the Indonesian Weaving Industry," *Journal of Development Economics* 9, 43–64.

Powell, A. A., and F. H. G. Gruen (1968) "The Constant Elasticity of Substitution and Linear Supply System," *International Economic Review* 9, 315–28.

Reifschneider, D., and R. Stevenson (1991) "Systematic Departures from the Frontier: A Framework for the Analysis of Firm Inefficiency," *International Economic Review* 32:3 (August), 715–23.

Reinhard, S., and G. Thijssen (1997) "Sustainable Efficiency of Dutch Dairy Farms: A Parametric Distance Function Approach," Working Paper, Agricultural Economics Research Institute, The Hague, The Netherlands.

Richmond, J. (1974) "Estimating the Efficiency of Production," *International Economic Review* 15:2 (June), 515–21.

Ritter, C., and L. Simar (1997a) "Pitfalls of Normal-Gamma Stochastic Frontier Models," *Journal of Productivity Analysis* 8:2 (May), 167–82.

Ritter, C., and L. Simar (1997b) "Another Look at the American Electrical Utility Data," Working Paper, CORE and Institut de Statistique, Université Catholique de Louvain, Louvain-la-Neuve, Belgium.

Russell, R. R. (1998) "Distance Functions in Consumer and Producer Theory," in R. Färe, P. Roos, and R. R. Russell, eds., *Index Number Theory: Essays in Honor of Sten Malmquist*. Boston: Kluwer Academic Publishers.

Schankerman, M., and M. I. Nadiri (1986) "A Test of Static Equilibrium Models and Rates of Return to Quasi-Fixed Factors, with an Application to the Bell System," *Journal of Econometrics* 33:1/2 (October/November), 97–118.

Schmidt, P. (1976) "On the Statistical Estimation of Parametric Frontier Production Functions," *Review of Economics and Statistics* 58:2 (May), 238–39.

Schmidt, P. (1984) "An Error Structure for Systems of Translog Cost and Share Equations," Working Paper No. 8309, Department of Economics, Michigan State University, East Lansing, MI.

Schmidt, P. (1985–1986) "Frontier Production Functions," *Econometric Reviews* 4:2, 289–328.

Schmidt, P., and T.-F. Lin (1984) "Simple Tests of Alternative Specifications in Stochastic Frontier Models," *Journal of Econometrics* 24:3 (March), 349–61.

Schmidt, P., and C. A. K. Lovell (1979) "Estimating Technical and Allocative Inefficiency Relative to Stochastic Production and Cost Frontiers," *Journal of Econometrics* 9, 343–66.

Schmidt, P., and C. A. K. Lovell (1980) "Estimating Stochastic Production and Cost Frontiers when Technical and Allocative Inefficiency Are Correlated," *Journal of Econometrics* 13:1 (May), 83–100.

Schmidt, P., and R. C. Sickles (1984) "Production Frontiers and Panel Data," *Journal of Business and Economic Statistics* 2:4 (October), 367–74.

Seale, J. L., Jr. (1990) "Estimating Stochastic Frontier Systems with Unbalanced Panel Data: The Case of Floor Tile Manufactories in Egypt," *Journal of Applied Econometrics* 5, 59–74.

Seitz, W. D. (1966) "Efficiency Measures for Steam-Electric Generating Plants," *Proceedings of the Thirty Ninth Annual Meeting of the Western Farm Economics Association*, 143–51.

Seitz, W. D. (1971) "Productive Efficiency in the Steam-Electric Generating Industry," *Journal of Political Economy* 79:4 (July/August), 878–86.

Shephard, R. W. (1953) *Cost and Production Functions*. Princeton: Princeton University Press.

Shephard, R. W. (1970) *The Theory of Cost and Production Functions*. Princeton: Princeton University Press.

Shephard, R. W. (1974) *Indirect Production Functions*. Mathematical Systems in Economics, No. 10. Meisenheim Am Glan: Verlag Anton Hain.

Sickles, R. C., D. Good, and R. L. Johnson (1986) "Allocative Distortions and the Regulatory Transition of the U.S. Airline Industry," *Journal of Econometrics* 33, 143–63.

Sidhu, S. S. (1974) "Relative Efficiency in Wheat Production in the Indian Punjab," *American Economic Review* 64:4 (September), 742–51.

Simar, L., C. A. K. Lovell, and P. Vanden Eeckaut (1994) "Stochastic Frontiers Incorporating Exogenous Influences on Efficiency," Discussion Paper No. 9403, Institut de Statistique, Université Catholique de Louvain, Louvain-la-Neuve, Belgium.

Simioni, M., ed. (1994) "Efficacité et Productivité dans l'Agriculture," *Cahiers d'Economie et Sociologie Rurales* 31:2.

Simon, H. (1955) "A Behavioral Model of Rational Choice," *Quarterly Journal of Economics* 69:1 (February), 99–118.

Simon, H. (1957) *Models of Man.* New York: Wiley.

Sitorus, B. L. (1966) "Productive Efficiency and Redundant Factors of Production in Traditional Agriculture of Underdeveloped Countries," *Proceedings of the Thirty Ninth Annual Meeting of the Western Farm Economics Association,* 153–58.

Solow, R. M. (1957) "Technical Change and the Aggregate Production Function," *Review of Economics and Statistics* 39:3 (August), 312–20.

Stevenson, R. E. (1980) "Likelihood Functions for Generalized Stochastic Frontier Estimation," *Journal of Econometrics* 13:1 (May), 57–66.

Stigler, G. J. (1976) "The Xistence of X-Efficiency," *American Economic Review* 66:1 (March), 213–16.

Survey of Current Business (1972) "The Measurement of Productivity," 52:5, Part II, (May).

Tax, S. (1953) *Penny Capitalism.* Chicago: University of Chicago Press.

Timmer, C. P. (1971) "Using a Probabilistic Frontier Production Function to Measure Technical Efficiency," *Journal of Political Economy* 79:4 (July/August), 776–94.

Toda, Y. (1976) "Estimation of a Cost Function when the Cost Is Not Minimum: The Case of Soviet Manufacturing Industries, 1958–1971," *Review of Economics and Statistics* 58:3 (August), 259–68.

Toda, Y. (1977) "Substitutability and Price Distortion in the Demand for Factors of Production: An Empirical Estimation," *Applied Economics* 9, 203–17.

Törnqvist, L. (1936) "The Bank of Finland's Consumption Price Index," *Bank of Finland Monthly Bulletin* 10, 1–8.

Trosper, R. L. (1978) "American Indian Relative Ranching Efficiency," *American Economic Review* 68:4 (September), 503–16.

Tulkens, H., ed. (1998), "Selected Papers from the Fourth European Workshop on Efficiency and Productivity Analysis," *Journal of Productivity Analysis* 10:1 (July).

van den Broeck, J., G. Koop, J. Osiewalski, and M. F. J. Steel (1994) "Stochastic Frontier Models: A Bayesian Perspective," *Journal of Econometrics* 61, 273–303.

Ward, B. (1958) "The Firm in Illyria: Market Syndicalism," *American Economic Review* 48:4 (September), 566–89.

White, H. (1982) "Maximum Likelihood Estimation of Misspecified Models," *Econometrica* 50, 1–25.

Williamson, O. E. (1964) *The Economics of Discretionary Behavior: Managerial Objectives in a Theory of the Firm.* Englewood Cliffs, NJ: Prentice-Hall.

Winsten, C. B. (1957) "Discussion on Mr. Farrell's Paper," *Journal of the Royal Statistical Society* Series A, General, 120, Part 3, 282–84.

Yotopoulos, P. A., and L. J. Lau (1973) "A Test for Relative Economic Efficiency: Some Further Results," *American Economic Review* 63:1 (March), 214–23.

Yuengert, A. W. (1993) "The Measurement of Efficiency in Life Insurance: Estimates of a Mixed Normal-Gamma Error Model," *Journal of Banking and Finance* 17:2/3 (April), 483–96.

Zieschang, K. D. (1983) "A Note on the Decomposition of Cost Efficiency into Technical and Allocative Components," *Journal of Econometrics* 23:3 (December), 401–5.

Author Index

329

Subject Index